Women of All Nations

A Record of Their Characteristics, Habits, Manners, Customs and Influence

A CHINESE LADY.
DRAWN BY NORMAN H. HARDY.

FRONTISPIECE --1

Women of All Nations

A Record of Their Characteristics, Habits, Manners, Customs and Influence

IN TWO VOLUMES

Edited by

T ATHOL JOYCE

N W THOMAS

Fellows of the Royal Anthropological Institute

With 647 black and white and 24 colour illustrations

VOL. 1

GYAN

GYAN PUBLISHING HOUSE

NEW DELHI

Women of All Nations
*(Women's studies, Sociology, Authropology,
Culture History)*

ISBN : 81-212-0002-4 (Set)

ISBN : 81-212-0157-8 (Vol-I)

Published in 1997 in India by
Gyan Publishing House
5, Ansari Road,
New Delhi-110 002

Printed at Goyal Offset Printers Delhi

CONTENTS

LIST OF COLOUR-PLATES

FROM DRAWINGS BY NORMAN H. HARDY

FIJIAN BASKETWORK:
One girl is making a mat, the other a fish-basket.

Photograph by J. W. Waters

WOMEN OF ALL NATIONS

INTRODUCTION

BANGALA WOMAN WITH BASKET.
Note the scars down the centre of the forehead.

The Position of Women.

SINCE man rose above the lowest grade of savagery, if not ever since the world began, woman has been the theme of poets, the model of artists and of sculptors, and the despair of the male sex generally. Biologists may tell us that the female is physically at a lower stage than her mate; misogynists and pessimists like Schopenhauer may assure us that she is mentally the inferior of the stronger sex; and, going to the opposite extreme, believers in woman's rights may sacrilegiously, if unwittingly, pull woman down from the pedestal on which she has been placed by modern, no less than by mediæval, chivalry. But the sound judgment of the average man will reject the paradoxes of the man of science, and by a simple process of natural selection eliminate from the character of future generations of the fair sex what is unpleasing in the advanced woman of the present day; he will not suffer woman to fall below the level of the woman that is or has been.

The Ascent of Woman.

Taking a broad view of history, we may say that in one aspect it is the story of how woman has ceased to be the slave of man, as she is among the peoples on the lowest planes of culture, and has become his help-meet. To trace the course of this development here is impossible; but in the sequel the reader will find in the description of woman, as she is at the present day among the peoples of the world, ample materials for a reconstruction of the story of the advance of woman from the lowest grade to the place she occupies among us to-day. But while this is true from one standpoint, we must not overlook the fact that the women who stand on a pedestal are only a fraction of the grown-up females of the world. Go to the victim of the sweater in the East End of London; go to the chain-makers of Cradley Heath, and the other white slaves of England, and the impression of woman's portion which is gained by the contemplation of the lot of the leisured classes and the cultured part of the population in general will be well-nigh effaced. If, at the present day, woman at her highest is far above anything which the uncivilised world can show, woman at her lowest is not so happy as her savage sister. If the latter suffers, she has her happy moments; but it is difficult to imagine how any human being can be happy whose whole life is one incessant struggle against starvation without a single gleam of light to relieve the gloom. And there are lower depths still to which woman may fall or be dragged; savagery untouched by the white man's influence rarely or never shows such pictures of disease and vice as prevail among the lowest stratum of our population. If, therefore, woman has risen, she has also fallen; and who shall say that the result on the whole is for better or for worse?

To give a connected survey of the points which the following pages will suggest would lead us far beyond the scope of this introduction, which can only glance at some of the salient features of woman's life.

The Question of Beauty.

The pages which follow will contain many photographs from all parts of the world. They will, in many cases, be selected because they are typical of the people whom they represent; in other cases they may be as little typical of the mass as the photograph of the most beautiful woman in England would be of the average of her sisters who toil for their daily bread.

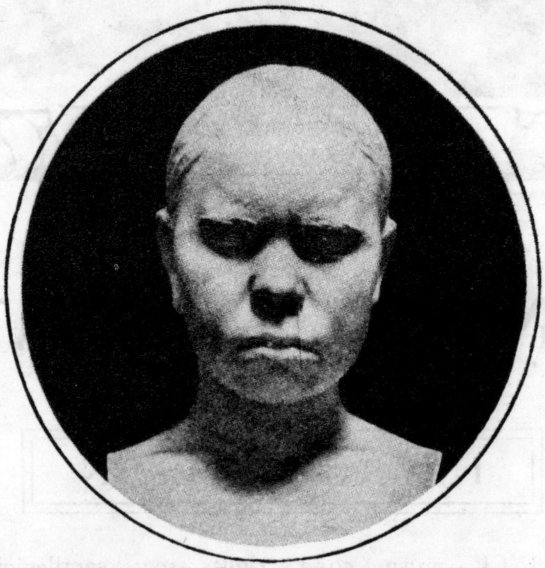

WOMAN OF THE GOULBURN TRIBE, VICTORIA, AUSTRALIA.

Photographed from a plaster cast to show the different effect produced by an alteration in colour.

It is a curious and interesting problem how far the judgment of the European, as regards beauty in woman, falls into line with that of the people whose type of beauty is in question. For it by no means follows that our idea of beauty is universally accepted. Quite apart from differences of colour, the set of the eyes, the arrangement of the hair, the presence or absence of deformation by ornaments or simple scars, and a thousand other elements count for much in European and non-European eyes.

Colour.

European taste looks chiefly at beauty of form and feature, and, other things being equal, colour, be it black, brown or red, does not obscure the perception of it; but savage races, especially when they come in contact with European women for the first time, often complain that their sickly hue is not to their liking, and commiserate them; *das ewig Weibliche* apparently ceases to be attractive, if it is too far from the type to which man is accustomed. The Christy Minstrel of the streets shows us how far the European face is transfigured by the addition of colour, and the illustration on p. 2 shows what is the effect of the opposite process. Probably few people would recognise in the face shown the lineaments of an aboriginal Australian; and, though the abnormal smoothness of the hair, which is in real life left to grow as it pleases, contributes to the result, it is the change of tint which chiefly renders identification difficult. The illustration is from a plaster cast in the South Kensington Museum, which was moulded on the living face.

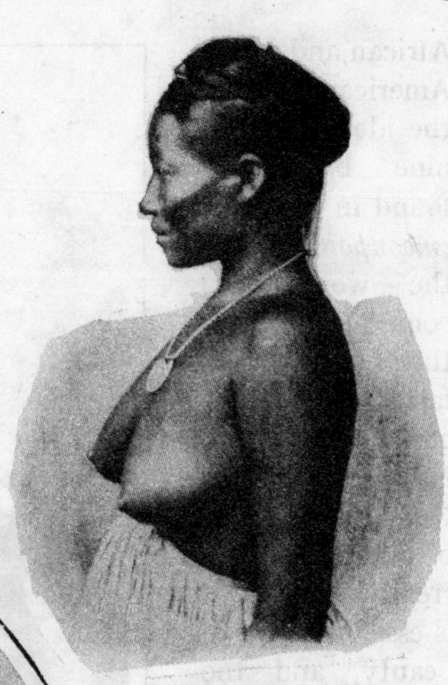

Photograph by Dr. Th. Koch.

DESANA WOMAN.

Feminine Adornments.

"A woman without ornament is like a field without water," runs the Eastern proverb, and, in spite of the fact that the Maoris of New Zealand urge that, "though a woman be ever so plain, men will still run after her," the female sex throughout the world is never averse to add to its personal charms by adventitious aids.

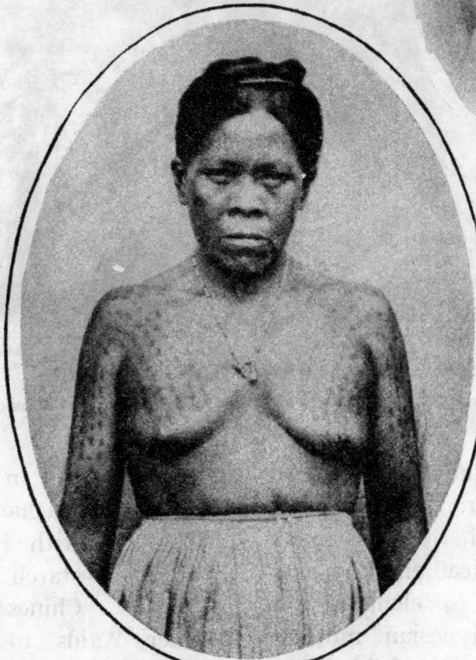

Photograph by Dr. Th. Koch.

UANANA WOMAN.

At the same time it must not be thought that among savages are to be found the choicest and most elaborate *toilettes*, at least as far as the ladies are concerned. Within certain limits it is true to say that the lower we descend in the scale of civilisation, the more nearly the human race is found to approximate to the brute creation, in the fact that it is the sterner sex which is the more brilliantly ornamented. Under the conditions of latter day civilisation, of course, the position is reversed, and the varieties of feminine adornment quite eclipse the sombre garb of mere man—the uniforms of the "Services," the coats of huntsmen and golfers, and the ties and waistcoats of undergraduates, forming rare exceptions. The most primitive form of ornament consists in the attempt to alter the form of the body in order that it may approximate to some ideal of beauty; and, as ideals vary from tribe to tribe, and from people to people, this attempt is made in diverse ways.

Photograph by Dr. Th. Koch.

TARIANA WOMAN.

Women from the Rio Caiary, Uanpes, South America: Showing face and body painting, the most primitive form of ornamentation.

To take a few examples: in Persia, among some of the Turkish and Moorish peoples, and certain

African and South American tribes, the ideal of feminine beauty is found in excessive *embonpoint*, and the women in consequence suit their diet to the fashion. Among certain of the inhabitants of the North-West Coast of America, a retreating forehead is essential to true beauty, and the heads of infants are deformed by means of a special appliance fixed to the cradle, so that they may acquire the requisite slope from nose-tip to crown. In some localities in South America tight bandages are worn below the knee in order to produce a swollen calf, and many tribes in Africa employ artificial means to elongate the breasts. Polynesian mothers mould the noses of their children to prevent them from growing prominent; the Tahitians frequently said to the missionary Williams, "What a pity it is that English mothers pull the children's noses so much and make them so frightfully long!" In China the feet of the women are so compressed as to be practically useless, but, though this sacrifice to fashion must be exceedingly irksome, it is not in reality fraught with such serious consequences as the waist-compression practised by their "civilised" sisters in modern Europe. The fundamental object of such aids to beauty was naïvely admitted by a Chinese girl, on whom a lady missionary was trying to impress the folly of foot-bandaging: "Me squeezy foot; you squeezy waist; all same what for, get husband."

Ideals of Beauty Compared.

Photograph by Spooner.

MAORI WOMAN, NEW ZEALAND.

Showing the peculiar form of tattoo on the chin found among this people.

Painting the body as a form of ornament is another primitive aid to beauty, and is correspondingly widespread, especially in America, that is to say, savage America. Frequently in Africa and Australia it is a sign of mourning. The commonest colours are red, yellow, white and black obtained from various kinds of ochre, powdered wood, lime and charcoal. The familiar rice-powder is found in Java; in Tibet many devotees of fashion adorn their cheeks with a fascinating mosaic of starch and seeds, while the Chinese use the starch only. Further "aids to beauty" are the lac applied to the teeth of the women of the south-east of the Asiatic continent, and the henna employed by Oriental ladies to colour their nails and hair. The woad of our ancient Britannic ancestresses must not be forgotten, and it must be confessed that the cheeks, lips and hair of many of our European belles are not always innocent of "improvement": in fact, the "divinely fair" owes her complexion to the chemist as often as the "divinely tall" her stature to the boot-maker.

"Paint and Powder."

A more permanent form of coloration is found in the tattooing practised by many of the fairer races, among whom may be mentioned the Maori, whose women ornament the chin in this fashion; the Ainu, by whom a coquettish

Photograph: Geiser, Algiers.

ALGERIAN WOMAN: Tattooed by the method usual among comparatively fair-skinned people.

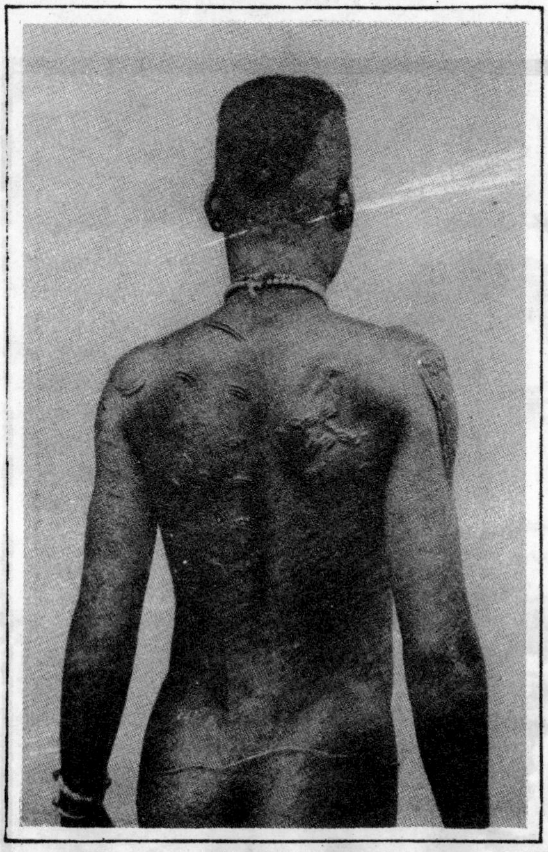

SANGO WOMAN, CONGO FREE STATE.
Showing the raised scars with which dark-skinned peoples often ornament their bodies.

little moustache tattooed on the upper lip is considered essential for women of fashion; the Algerians (*see* p. 5) and the Chukchi of North-east Siberia. Among the duskier peoples, in whose case this form of ornament would not be very apparent, incisions are made in the skin, the healing of which is retarded so that prominent scars result, which form intricate patterns on the parts of the body so ornamented. This custom is widespread in Africa, especially among the Congo tribes, as shown on this and the opposite page, and is also found among the Australians (*see* p. 8) and Melanesians. The filing or chipping of the teeth is a common form of "ornament" throughout Africa (*see* p. 9).

Fashions in Tattooing.

When we come to speak of the multitudinous objects worn on and around the body and limbs, their variety at first seems to baffle all description; but a short consideration elicits the fact that there are very few which have not their counterpart in the highest European circles. There is not, after all, a very great difference between a necklace of diamonds and one of teeth, each in its appropriate surroundings. The live birds carried in the ears of New Zealanders have their parallel in the fireflies worn by Central American beauties, and the live tortoises attached to the girdles of fashionable Parisiennes. It will be sufficient to say that savage belles enhance their charms by all the armoury of "jewellery" known to their European sisters. There are, however, a few forms of ornament which the latter have outgrown, and these are perhaps worthy of a few moments' consideration.

Objects of Adornment.

One of the little Pygmy ladies who lately visited London had her upper lip pierced in three places, and often wore small brass rings through the punctures. Exaggerated forms of this species of ornament are found among some tribes of British Central Africa, where the women wear large plugs of wood or ivory in the upper lip, distending the latter to an extent which, to European eyes, is hideous in the extreme (*see* p. 8). Similar large lip-plugs, but in this case worn in the lower lip, embellish the features of certain tribes in North-west and South America, while smaller ones are found among the Eskimo. The last named, as well as some South Americans, wear discs of this kind in the cheeks.

Lip and Nose Ornaments.

The nose, again, is frequently the support of an ornament of some sort. In New Guinea, Australia, and parts of Africa and the Malay States, slender bars of wood or bone are worn through a hole in the septum (*see* p. 10), while the nose-ring and nose-stud are common in India, and the former among the Tartars.

A HAIDA WOMAN OF QUEEN CHARLOTTE ISLAND (NORTH-WEST AMERICA).
Shewing Lip-Plug.
DRAWN BY NORMAN H. HARDY.

Facing on page 6

Heavy metal collars, such as is illustrated on this page, often weighing as much as thirty pounds or more, are frequently worn by belles of the Congo, while in East Africa thick iron wire is often coiled round arms and legs until the greater part of the limbs are covered (*see* p. 11); heavy coiled collars are also so worn. Nor are these latter confined to Africa. The women of a certain hill-tribe in Burma wear long neck ornaments of this nature, which tend to lengthen the neck to an abnormal extent (*see* p. 12).

Collars.

But, of all the parts of the body, the ear is perhaps the most suitable for the attachment of jewellery, and consequently there are few tribes which do not make use of it in this way. Besides rings, which are almost universal, the tribes of South-east Asia, Borneo (*see* p. 13), East Africa (*see* pp. 16 and 17) and elsewhere, insert large and heavy plugs in the lobes, which are often so distended that they reach the shoulders. The upper part of the ear is also pierced in many parts of Africa, and ornamented with rings or sticks of wood. The turn of that irresponsible wheel, fashion, has again brought the ear-ring into prominence in England, and so prevented the disappearance among a civilised people of one of the last relics of a very barbarous form of decoration. In fact, it may not be so pleasing to those who pride themselves on belonging to a civilised nation, to realise how slight is the essential difference between the customs of the despised savage and of the British aristocracy in the matter of ornament. Not only all the world over are women, in this respect, in the words of Kipling, "as like as a row of pins," but a tyrannical fashion has decreed that, for the daughters of Eve, the French proverb, "*il faut souffrir pour être belle,*" shall have a very real meaning.

"Ear-Rings."

Another use of personal ornament must not be omitted, viz., that of indicating a certain status For instance, the crown, or some analogous form of decoration, as an emblem of royalty is too widespread to need comment. But the crown is not only a sign of temporal power; in many countries it is worn as a token of supremacy over the masculine heart, and as such it is the mark of a bride—a custom especially familiar in Norway.

Significant Ornaments.

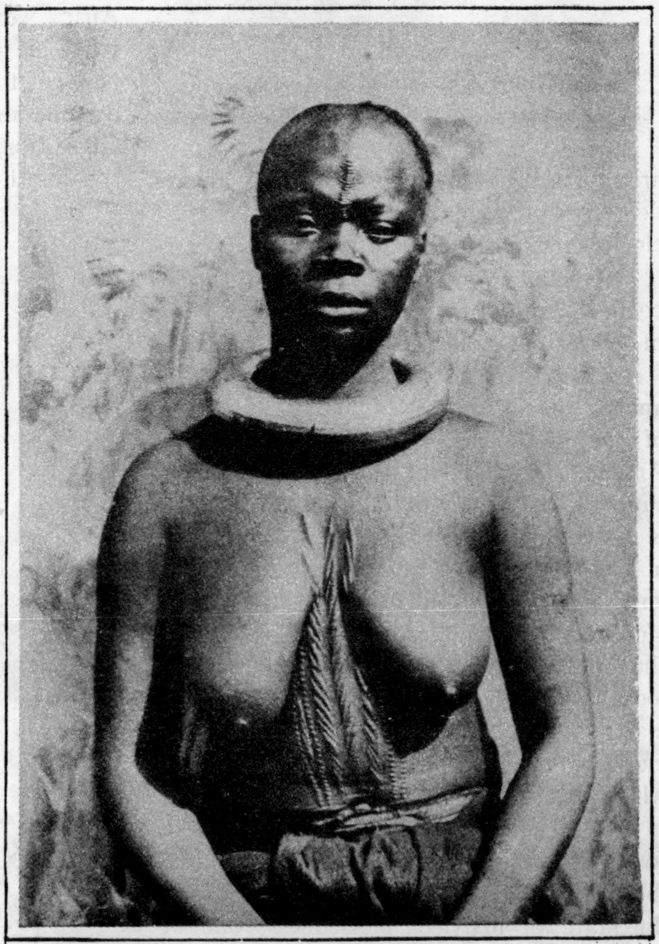

WANGATA WOMAN, CONGO FREE STATE.

With heavy brass collar: these collars often weigh 30 lbs. or more. The ornamental scars on face and body should be noticed.

In accordance with the idea that ornament is a sign of personal importance we find that among the tribes where women

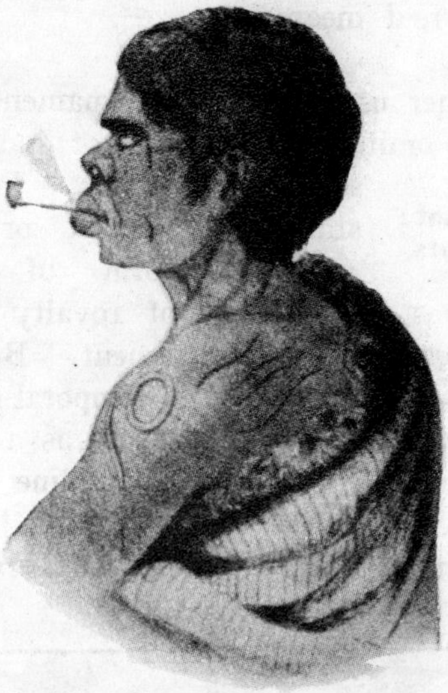

NATIVE WOMAN OF S.-E. AUSTRALIA.
Showing ornamental scars. From a sketch by Blandowski.

are of little account, they are nearly always deprived by fashion of all save the most elementary form of adornment.

But many forms of ornament are closely connected with matrimony. The tattooing of a girl usually corresponds with the "coming out" so familiar with us, and, among the aborigines of Malay, the filing of the teeth has a similar signification. Among the Hopi of Arizona a *coiffure* supposed to represent the squash-blossom is a sign of virginity (*see* p. 20), while the matron signifies her married estate by two long tresses representing the squash-fruit. More closely resembling our own custom is that prevailing in Fiji, where the hanging locks which distinguish the unmarried maiden (*see* p. 21) are cut off upon her marriage. The Kikuyu girl of British East Africa wears an ornament corresponding to our engagement-ring, and there are also countless forms of adornment which, like the plain gold circlet of Europe, betoken the state of married blessedness, one of the most peculiar of which is the "tail" attached to the back of the girdle of Nilotic negresses (*see* p. 22).

Clothes and Conventions.

From ornament we pass imperceptibly to the question of clothing, and indeed there is no real difference, in so far as the former has evolved out of the latter. We may even go further, and say that it is not an innate feeling of modesty which has produced clothing, but clothing which is responsible for the feeling of modesty in man. We have only to look at a few of the non-European races to see how entirely conventional this feeling is, and how it differs in various parts of the globe. The first care of a Mahometan woman surprised at her bath is to conceal her face; the Chinese lady would feel excessive shame at the uncovering of her foot; the Sumatran at the exposure of her knee; and a woman of a certain tribe in Africa would be terribly upset if the small twig at the back of her girdle should happen to fall off. Some Asiatics think it unseemly for a woman to show her finger-tips, and in America a woman of the North-west could not bear to be seen

By permission of D. Fülleborn and Messrs. Dietrich Reimer.

YAO WOMAN, EAST AFRICA.
Showing the ivory stud worn in the upper lip by women of this tribe.

without her lip-plug, while a Carib beauty would far rather appear in public without her girdle than *minus* her paint.

Another instance of the conventionality of modesty is seen in certain aspects of Japanese life and ideas as compared with our own. Among this people the two sexes in some places still take their baths in common without finding the process at all awkward, yet the representation of the nude in Japanese art is rare, and even considered improper. With us, of course, the reverse is the case; in few places in England is mixed bathing, even in full costume, allowed, yet the nude in art, thanks to classical traditions, is common and, generally, passes unchallenged.

Photograph by Sir H. H. Johnston

NATIVES OF THE UPPER CONGO.
Showing ornamental scars and filed teeth.

Climatic Influence on Clothing.

A German savant has propounded an ingenious and attractive theory, according to which he divides clothing into two types, tropical and arctic. The first of these is based on the waist-cloth or girdle, which varies between the string of beads (*see* p. 15) and the cloak as its two extremes; the second is composed of jacket and trousers, and serves as much for the protection of the body as for its adornment.

The two types will be seen to shade into one another as we pass from the equator to the poles, until, among the Eskimo, the ladies are found wearing the bifurcated nether garments which, with us, are usually associated with the male sex The difference of clothing of the two sexes in Europe is interesting; it may be explained by the fact that while the occupations of the man take him out of doors, the woman is usually relegated to the house, and so has not found the necessity of discarding the old "tropical" garb. Further, may it not be regarded as a significant fact that the "emancipation" of woman, so important a social item in the last half century, has been accompanied by the occasional adoption of "rational" costume for certain out-door occupations such as cycling?

It is noticeable that in countries where much outdoor work is performed by the female members of the household the latter are often found to have adopted the garment which is usually considered typical of the sterner sex; this is common as near home as Champéry in Switzerland (*see* p. 29). The amount of clothing worn by a people, however, is not absolutely conditioned by climate, as can be seen by comparing the very full costume of the Arabs with the almost complete nakedness of the inhabitants of the extremity of South America, where practically arctic conditions prevail.

But the clothing of the women of the world will be amply illustrated in the subsequent pages. Here we need only recall the original purpose of clothes and ornament—to make the wearer beautiful in the eyes of the other sex, and especially of the suitor.

As is known to every grown-up person, not to speak of many who are only growing up, courtship is a serious matter, and while it lasts it appears to be a very engrossing occupation. The beginning of courtship can be traced in the tender unconscious premonitions of childhood, no less than in the unmistakable love motive of a large class of games, which are sometimes reminiscences of old and long forgotten marriage customs, sometimes a sort of preliminary canter over the course. All the world over where games are found at all (in some countries, India for example, they have few or no games, but make up for it by marrying earlier), children play at being husbands and wives. In Australia the little black Queenslander builds his hut and sits in its shade with his "gin," till a rival disturbs his marital felicity by suddenly abducting the girl and carrying her off into the bush in the most approved Australian style; of course the original owner disputes possession with the abductor and a

Love and Courtship.

Photograph by B. Cerruti, Esq.

SAKAI GIRLS, MALAY STATES.

The central figure is wearing the nose-pin which is a common ornament among primitive peoples.

Photograph by Sir H. H. Johnston.

MASAI GIRL, EAST AFRICA PROTECTORATE.

Having her ornaments of iron wire adjusted.

battle royal ensues; or the couple may disappear into the bush.

When love-making passes from the unconscious stage of childhood to the conscious —painfully conscious—stage of youth, the main note in both sexes is what may be called self-exhibition. The hair is Nature's covering for the head; man has found it necessary to add the hat, but in the civilised world the hat and, still more conspicuously, the hair have long outgrown their original purpose, at any rate so far as the softer sex is concerned. But although woman instinctively seeks for an opportunity of display in the presence of the opposite sex, her efforts are veiled under a show of modesty which tells her that in the alternate seeking and fleeing, which we see in the female of many species of birds, lie her strength and much of her attraction to the male.

Misogynists like Schopenhauer, and ascetics like Tolstoi, have set out in uncompromising terms the real meaning of the female fashions in dress. Women, it is true, protest indignantly against the implication that their intention is to ensnare the male animal; but the *décolleté* gown tells the whole story. A woman seldom displays her charms for the benefit of her own sex; when she sets herself to outshine her rivals in an exclusively feminine environment she is like the miser who begins by saving money for a purpose, and ends by hoarding it for its own sake. Woman begins by decking herself out to catch the eye of man, and ends by arraying herself in all her glory when man is absent. She is accustomed to gratify her feelings by triumphing over hated rivals with the aid of decorative arts, and the desire for triumph remains when the cause of the desire, the love motive, cannot be gratified. How early this feature appears—it seems to be almost innate in the female mind—is apparent from the intense importance which a three-year-old child will attach to her hair, from the interest which she will take in the hair of her companions, and from the enhanced value attached to a doll with real hair.

Feminine Charms.

But it would be unfair to suggest that the male underrates the importance of physical charms in love matters. On the contrary, there is no surer sign of budding manhood than the intense effort to make the best of every outward advantage. If the dress of the European male gives little opportunity for display he makes the most of his small resources. In our own age the essential element of this display has ceased, in deference to a more stringent code of morals, to manifest itself in striking forms like those of the male garments of the fifteenth century, which find their parallels in savage decorations. In the lower stages of culture additions to Nature's garb may be adopted either for warmth or decorative purposes. Modesty is not one of the motives which sway the savage; in fact, much of his costume at a mixed dance is solely for the purpose of enhancing his charms. His girdle decorations were originally, and still are, intended for purposes which we cannot connect with our ideas of clothing; and some of the strange fashions of the fifteenth century may fairly be put in the same category, as a brief study of the fashion plates of the period shows.

Man's Effort to Attract.

Photograph by Watts & Skeen, Rangoon.

SHAN WOMAN, BURMA.

Showing ear ornaments.

This is not the only means of self-exhibition. The male sex is everywhere given to displaying martial prowess, strength, or courage before females. It is this suggestion of martial prowess, no less than the uniform, which makes the soldier such an enviable possession; perhaps the policeman and the volunteer may profit by this same feeling.

Much of primitive dancing is an exhibition of one sex before the other, and though the civilised world has practically abolished this kind of dance in favour of more direct methods of stimulation, it has developed all sorts of games to take the place of this saltatory display.

With the progress of civilisation the opportunities for display have become greater. Primitive man does not invite his neighbours, much less their wives, to dinner; in fact, a man's own wife in early stages of society usually gets no more of the meal she sets before him than the bones he throws over his shoulder. "*Nous avons changé tout cela*"—but the sigh of relief that rises from the masculine heart when the ladies retire after dinner testifies to the strain put upon him by his habits of self-exhibition.

Leap-year traditions apart, wooing is with us, as with other white nations, and many of the lower races, a matter for the male. But it would be a great mistake to imagine that there are no countries where the bashful bachelor does not have to wait to be wooed. In the Torres Straits Islands it would be the height of bad form for a young man to make the first advances; at most he may scent himself, and so declare his willingness to be won. But even after the preliminary steps, which consist of the exchange of bracelets, all is not plain sailing; the young man must still hang back. If the admiring damsel sends him food he gives it to his relations, for "perhaps woman he gammon" as they say in their "pidgin" English. Even when they meet, the girl must make the running; she sends a message to her young man to meet her in the bush.

Where the Woman Woos

Photograph by Watts & Skeen, Rangoon.

PADAUNG WOMAN, BURMA.

Showing neck ornaments of wire.

Breaking the embarrassing silence the

youth considerately asks, "You like me proper?"

"Yes," says the girl, "I like you proper with my heart inside. Eye along my heart see you. You my man."

This is satisfactory, but the well-brought-up young man needs more declarations of affection before he gives himself away.

"How you like me?" he inquires.

"I like your fine leg, you got fine body, your skin good, I like you altogether."

This probably overcomes all difficulties, and following up her advantage the lady presses her young man to name the day. When matters have got as far as this, it is no longer incumbent upon him to wait to be pressed, so the man replies "To-morrow, if you like," and they go home and tell their relations, who promptly celebrate the occasion by a general mêlée.

Photograph by R Shelford, Esq.

TANJONG GIRL, BORNEO.—**Showing ear-lobes distorted by heavy ornaments.**

The coming of the missionary has changed much of this; but even now the proposal often comes from the girl, and the tender missive, singular to relate, does not always take the form of a letter—stationery being scarce on the islands. A school slate has been pressed into the service of Cupid by an impatient maid, and if the messenger is not marvellously discreet there must be a certain publicity about the love affair.

Among some of the rude tribes of India the woman's courtship is a far less agreeable experience. If the man of her choice does not respond, she takes a jar of rice beer, and sits down in the man's house. The women of the family know what the rice beer means, and if they don't want the marriage to "come off," they are allowed to use any means short of personal violence to eject the fair wooer from their doors. They may put pepper on the fire, drench her with water, or load her with opprobrious epithets, but to gain the man of her choice the lady has only to hold out some two or three hours, and the bridegroom is hers.

In the bazaar marriage of the Santals we have an instance of a similar practice on the part of the man.

Marriage by Mark.

If the girl of his heart is shy and stand-offish, he dips his fingers into red paint or earth and waits his opportunity to slip unobserved to her side, and make a mark on her brow. If he is prudent he loses no time in making his escape, for her male relatives will otherwise give him a thrashing; but the marriage is valid, and the girl can only escape by getting a divorce in due form.

African princesses apart, whose wooings and weddings will be described in the chapter on Africa, the Torres Straits Islanders show us woman's rights at the apex of their development.

Various Methods of Wooing.

At the other end of the scale are the nearest neighbours of the islanders—the Australians, whose bold wooers make sure of their lady-loves by first knocking them on the head with a club and then carrying them off. Between these two extremes, as the sequel will show, there are all varieties of courtship.

If the Torres Straits method is typical, the maxim "Feed the brute," well known to the civilised world as the recipe for post-matrimonial happiness, seems to be likewise a method of securing a lover. In this connection it may be noted that the dinner party and the dance—of which the supper is one of the most important features—are not unknown among ourselves. More conspicuous among methods of wooing are music and poetry. At the present day they do not enjoy very great popularity, at any rate in England; for though breach of promise cases provide us with examples of poetry, the verses are rather evidence of the lover's affection than desperate assaults upon the citadel of a maiden's heart; and the serenade has no longer a place in the armoury of the modern lover.

Music and Lovers.

Among savage tribes the strains of music and the allurements of poetry are so strong that bachelors are positively prohibited from pouring forth their souls in this way, at any rate to an audience, on the ground that such things are demoralising. The too susceptible heart of the Chukma maiden is liable to be carried by storm, and in the interests of morality the young man is forbidden to sing within the village. In the jungle, however, the regulation does not appear to prevail, hence the great popularity of picnics among this people.

With ourselves music is on the whole divorced from love-making, but this has not always been the case in the long history of man's development. Whether the lover in barbarous and semi-civilised races has seized the opportunity offered him by the greater development of musical skill, or whether, as seems probable, the use of music in winning the heart of the fair has done much to raise the standard and the executive skill in music, is a problem on which the man of science has yet to make up his mind. It is a curious and suggestive fact that we can trace among birds a similar tendency. Some species pair, it is said, for life; others are polygamous, not to say promiscuous, in their love affairs; and it is remarkable that the monogamous males entertain their mates with graceful and harmonious utterances—there is even a well marked type of song—while the voices of the polygamous species are vehement rather than beautiful, at any rate from our point of view, but what the hen bird thinks about it is another matter.

Kissing Customs.

For the European the word courtship calls up a complex set of ideas, and one of the factors in it is kissing. A kiss has been defined as the approach of two pairs of curved surfaces as far as the point of contact; but this hardly seems to do justice to the operation in question, at any rate when the performers are young and of different sexes. The kiss seems to have originated in Babylonia or the Eastern Mediterranean. At the outset it was by no means specifically sexual; in fact it may well have been a salutation exchanged, not between intimates but between those of unequal rank. Even at the present day the kiss is far from being universally known. Europeans have no doubt introduced it into some lands, where the fair maidens were disposed at first to suspect their white adorers of cannibalistic designs.

Leaving the imported kiss out of the question it may be said that salutations with the lips are found in Europe and West Asia, Africa, and part of America; but it by no means follows that these correspond to what we call kissing. The Red Indian lays his lips softly on the cheek of the salutee, and no sound is heard nor motion made, and the Jew did not kiss on the lips. In fact the kiss proper, the kiss given to, and received from, a beloved woman is an exclusively European possession, and on it we may found our claim to be called civilised. Ignorance of the kiss is a mark of barbarism or savagery, for no people that had once possessed the kiss could possibly forget it.

Everyone has heard of nose-rubbing—a custom found from Lapland to Greenland, and from further India to Easter Island. The name is an unfortunate one, for the contact is not the essential element; the nose-kiss as it might be called is fundamentally a smelling of the recipient. In reality therefore it comes very near the kiss on the cheek.

JA-LUO FISHERWOMEN AND THEIR BASKETS.

Photograph by Sir H. H. Johnston.

Women of the Ja-Luo, a Nilotic tribe dwelling around Kavirondo Bay, Uganda Protectorate, who take their part in the fishing operations conducted on the lake. They are here shown with their large conical fishing baskets, into which the fish are driven. They are one of the least clad people in the world.

Courtship Dangers.

Courtship is not unattended with dangers; in fact some races, wise in their generation, manage all these things by proxy. Woman likes to feel herself the bone—or flesh—of contention; and it is with the utmost satisfaction that a would-be bride sees two champions do battle for her hand, whether they be blacks in the wilds of Australia, mediæval knights, or hooligans of the twentieth century.

By permission of A. C. Hollis, Esq.

KIKUYU GIRL.

Showing ear ornaments, consisting of large wooden cylinders in the lobe of the ear, and wooden rods in the upper part.

Instinct rather than reason led the early girl to give herself to the all-comers' champion; and as a strong arm and a skilful hand were in those days the essentials for successful housekeeping, it may be said that her instinct was a sound one. In our own day the views of the fair sex are very different; money is more attractive than muscle; but this does not make courtship less dangerous, it only exposes the suitor to one kind of risk instead of another. The specifically English institution of the breach of promise case is an illustration of the instinct in the modern girl.

Courtship had other dangers in days gone by; the musician who wooed the susceptible heart with the guitar was ill-provided when his rival appeared to make matters lively by a hand to hand encounter; but these dangers are things of the past. Between the Scylla of the sleepy householder, ready to pour the vials of his wrath—not to mention less innocuous vessels—on the disturber of his midnight rest, and the Charybdis of the constable, the suitor is reduced to silence, and can only pour out his soul in silence.

But all these dangers of courtship, due to the existence of rivals, pale before the supreme risk—that courtship may end in marriage. Among civilised nations a man may escape, but in the lower stages of culture bachelordom is practically unknown. To be a bachelor argues some infirmity, and the infirm probably find an early grave, not infrequently in the stomachs of their comrades.

It must not, however, be imagined that the savage is more rash than civilised man. It must be remembered that the duties of a husband in a state of nature are comparatively simple; money is probably unknown, and the wife cannot beg for a "duck of a hat," for she does not wear one. Education is not expensive, the mother looks after the girls, the father after the boys, and there are no extras; house rent is unknown, the tax-collector does not call, pipes do not burst with the frost, and the cook does not give notice on the eve of a big dinner. It is true that in some parts of the world a married man may be called upon to defend his title to his wife against any one who happens to take a fancy to her. But, after all, it is better to deal with these matters by an appeal to arms, than to carry on warfare by the more indirect weapons of dress-makers' bills and diamonds. A broken head may heal itself, but not the adverse balance at the banker's. In fact the savage may congratulate himself on being better placed than the civilised husband; for the victory of the former depends on his biceps, while the latter has to reckon with the caprices of the fair sex, as well as with the bank balance of his foe.

When the savage makes up his mind to get married, the first thing he does is to select a suitable mate, if custom does

Photograph by Rev. A. N. Wood.

WASAGARA GIRL, EAST AFRICA PROTECTORATE.

Showing ear plugs. Front view.

not require him to leave that to be settled by his relatives. Having got thus far, he has to decide how he will secure possession of her. The two main methods in vogue are (1) buying, and (2) stealing; but if he has a sister handy, it is often convenient to barter her, instead of paying for his bride in cattle, or other valuables. Where the second method is in use formalities are disregarded; at most, the aid of a few stout-hearted and active friends is secured. But the peaceful form of procuring a bride is attended with greater pomp and circumstance. Negotiations may begin at a very early stage, for, improvident as the savage usually is, he takes time by the forelock when it is a question of securing a wife. In order to make quite sure, he applies to be betrothed soon after a girl is born, if not before. He naturally has to wait some years, for thirteen is about the earliest age at which he can take his bride from her mother, and meantime, in Australia at any rate, he consoles himself with an older woman; for there age is no disqualification for a woman—she is never too old to marry. A Hegelian philosopher of our own day has suggested that love at first sight is due to the fact that the parties were friends, or lovers, in a previous incarnation; it is gratifying to record that he has been anticipated by the Australians, who say that the young man who marries an old woman must have loved her when he was on earth before, but was then unable to marry her because he died.

Methods of Securing a Wife.

The Marrying Age.

If a wife is sometimes unduly young according to Western ideas, so, too, is the husband in some parts of the world. The religious duties imposed upon the son in some areas of India have brought it to pass that marriage is contracted by the males at the age of seven or eight; the woman

Photograph by Rev. A. N. Wood.

WASAGARA GIRL.

Showing ear plugs. Back view.

may be older than her nominal husband by ten years or more and becomes his unofficial step-mother, but the legal fiction of the infant marriage provides the step-son with an heir who will in turn furnish him with a wife, and so *ad infinitum.* This curious arrangement is, it need hardly be than speaking ill of her in proverbs; old women are sacrificed to their god Gualitshu, and the favourite victim is the mother-in-law of the *pater familias*, who has to provide the sacrifice. But this custom is an exception, as a rule the mother-in-law is simply avoided. In South Africa the Amakosa, and other tribes, also prohibit the son-in-law from pronouncing any words in which the most important syllable of the name of his mother-in-law figures. In Australia a man must avoid not only his actual mother-in-law but also all the women who *might* have been his mothers-in-law. The observance of this custom, which would make it difficult to use the streets in England, is simplified by the camping

Photograph by M. Geiser, Algiers.

ALGERIAN GIRL.

Wearing ornaments both in the upper and lower ear.

Photograph by Watts & Skeen, Rangoon.

TAMIL WOMAN.

With ears loaded with rings and wearing a nose-stud.

said, far from common; in fact in many savage tribes father-in-law and daughter-in-law, mother-in-law and son-in-law, are strictly prohibited from speaking to one another, and may even be compelled to avoid seeing one another; where conversation is permitted it must be carried on at a distance or in low tones, or is hedged about with other restrictions, so that the mother-in-law question cannot be described as acute among the lower races.

The Mother-in-law.

The mother-in-law is far and wide the butt of the jester; "*Schwiegermutter-Tigermutter*," says a pregnant German proverb. The Ranqueler Indians of Argentina go further arrangements of the blacks, and by the fact that perhaps only one-eighth of the women of a tribe are possible mothers-in-law.

Marriage Ceremonies Compared.

To characterise the marriage ceremonies of the world, and discover in them a central feature such as has been shown to exist in courtship is impossible. It must not be imagined that a marriage ceremony exists in every case. Marriage among Australian aboriginals, for example, consists in fetching the bride home from her parents, or in knocking her on the head and carrying her off. In the former instance there is a rite of betrothal or something which marks the girl as appropriated to a certain man ; but of marriage ceremony there is hardly a trace in all the continent, unless we include under that head the ritual which was customary in the Dieri tribe when a man or woman, already married, obtained a few additional spouses.

Where a marriage ceremony exists it very often takes the form of marking with blood. At the present day there are many Indian ceremonies which seem to bear this interpretation ; and perhaps it was in use in Europe at one time. At any rate there is a Norwegian story about a youth who was curious about the Huldren, or wood-women. These faery creatures are said to live during the winter in the huts occupied by human beings in summer, and the youth in question made his way to one and hid under a tub. Unluckily the Huldren smelled human flesh, like the giant of our youthful days, and when a maiden pointed at him the youth scratched her finger and drew blood. Thereupon the whole party surrounded him and insisted that he must now marry the girl, because he had marked her with blood. There was more than one objection to this course, an important item being that the fair maiden had a tail ; but there was nothing else for it, and fortunately when the bride was baptised, her tail fell off like a tadpole's, and they lived happily ever after.

Another widely spread custom is that known to the Romans as *Confarreatio*, the eating of the round sacrificial cake by the bride and bridegroom. This, too, is a Hindu marriage rite, and the remarkable part of it is that the pair eat together at the wedding for the first and last time in

Photograph by J. Brocherel, Aosta, Italy.

HAIR-DRESSING IN AFRICA.

their lives ; for one of the strange ritual prohibitions which are often called " tabus " forbids them to take their meals with one another thereafter. This custom of eating together to symbolise the union in marriage must have been widely spread in Europe, too, if we may judge by the strange survivals at the present day. In one part of France custom decrees that the newly-married couple shall partake of a dish of which the ingredients are a cock and a cat ; and in many parts of Germany it was the custom for bride and bridegroom to partake of the

Photograph by C. C. Pierce.

UNMARRIED HOPI GIRL, ARIZONA.

With hair dressed to imitate the squash-blossom, the sign of virginity.

Not the least curious among marriage ceremonies are those in which a human being is wedded to an inanimate object. In India it is held to be unlucky to marry a third wife, and the husband who does so is expected to leave his wife desolate after no long period. The Brahmans therefore evade the difficulty by marrying him first to an arca plant, and then to the woman, who counts as his fourth wife. The plant is decorated with cloth and a piece of string and all the ceremonies performed as for a regular marriage, and then the plant is cut down.

In the same way among peoples whose customs direct that the eldest brother of a family must marry first, it is the practice for the eldest brother, who for any reason is prevented from marrying a woman, to go through this ceremony with a plantain, and thus set his brothers free to marry.

"*Brauthahn*" either on their wedding day or on the following morning.

In not a few cases we find that some trial of strength is at once the condition of obtaining a wife, and the marriage ceremony itself. In the Malay Peninsula some of the wild tribes make the bride and bridegroom race round a mound, and if he does not succeed in catching her, he has to wait till another day — perhaps kiss-in-the-ring is a childish imitation of this rite, as so many children's games are. We find traces of similar customs in Europe again, though here it is the suitors who run and not the bride. Pausanias tells us that Odysseus won his wife Penelope by conquering in a race at Sparta, and a Libyan king Antæus is said to have put his daughter Barce at the end of a race-course as a prize for the man who should first touch her hand.

Photograph by C. C. Pierce.

HOPI MATRON, ARIZONA.

With hair dressed to imitate the squash-fruit, the emblem of fertility.

Photograph by J. W. Waters.

FIJIAN GIRL.

The locks of hair falling on her right shoulder show that she is unmarried. When she weds they will be cut.

Widows and Widowhood.

From marriage we naturally come to speak of widows. The advice of Weller, Senior, to beware of widows, has been largely taken—in advance — by savages. For them a widow, especially one in the early stages of mourning, is a very dangerous person. It is not that her charms are so very overpowering—her husband's relatives see to that; and she has often to smear her face with a filthy compound, or, *horribile dictu*, to carry her deceased husband's mouldering remains on her back. Authorities are not agreed as to why the widow is so dangerous: some think that the ghost of the dead man is supposed to hang round her somehow; others think that our savage brethren look on death as something contagious which can be communicated by the corpse, or anyone who has had to do with a corpse, to another entirely healthy person.

However this may be, the widow has a very unhappy time of it, even if her satisfaction at her husband's death be unalloyed. But in other parts of the world people are, or were, less merciful: the dead man needs an attendant in the future life, and the most suitable person to serve him is his widow; so in India and Africa the unfortunate woman was compelled to sacrifice herself, or was sacrificed *nolens volens*, so that her lord and master might be recognised as a man of worth in the land of souls.

For the benefit of advocates of women's rights, it may be mentioned that mere man has not had it all his own way in the matter of suttee. In West Africa a widower had to dance attendance in the same way on his deceased wife, when she was of higher rank than himself. The mere man is also liable to the same mourner's disabilities and tabus as woman, so that really in this respect the sexes are on something like an equality.

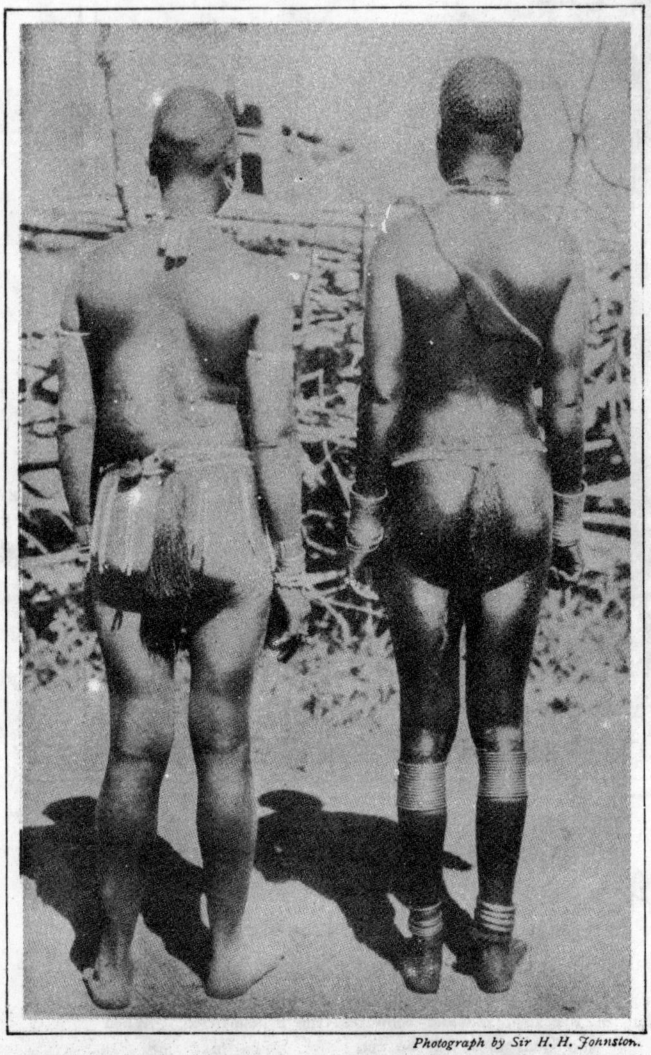

Photograph by Sir H. H. Johnston.

KAVIRONDO WOMEN, UGANDA PROTECTORATE.
Showing the "tail" worn as a sign of marriage.

Woman's Sphere in Tribe and Nation.

But the social and intellectual side of woman must not be neglected; ever since the beginning of time woman's influence for good or ill has been a very real force in the family, tribe, state or empire. Though the sphere of women, from the earliest and most primitive days, when the care of the camp fire and the preparation of the food was relegated to her, has been nominally confined to the home, yet, in reality, it has always transcended this limit, and even amongst the savage peoples, where her position is little above that of a domestic animal, she has proved at least a very potent cause of war. Helen of Troy was by no means the first or last woman to involve whole tribes in disaster. Taken at her lowest value, woman has always been something for which to fight, and since a fight always discovers what is best or worst in man, the sphere of woman's influence, if it has any limits at all, has a far wider extent than appears on the surface.

"They talk about a woman's sphere,
As though it had a limit;
There's not a place in earth or heaven,
There's not a task to mankind given
There's not a blessing or a woe,
There's not a whisper yes or no,
There's not a life or death or birth
That has a featherweight of worth,
Without a woman in it."

But even in the limited circle of the primitive home the part assigned to her was all-important. The care of the fire which has been mentioned seems a small thing in these days of lucifer matches; but the extinction of the camp fire in the days of the stone-age hunter—in the days when the production of fire, even by the rubbing together of two sticks, was probably unknown—might well have spelt very severe hardship, if not death, to the family.

It has been said that among some tribes women are regarded as little better than domestic animals, but this does not necessarily mean that their lot is a very bad one. In Africa, it is true, agriculture is almost entirely the work of the women, but individually they are not compelled to work nearly so hard as some of the peasant women in Europe, nor is their position much lower than in certain Oriental countries of far higher civilisation. It is in the most primitive nomadic tribes where food is scanty and the supply uncertain that the lot of woman is hardest—as, for instance, among the Australian aborigines; and there she is quite as much the victim of circumstance as of sheer masculine selfishness. As she is, in most cases, a non-combatant, her comfort must be sacrificed to the efficiency of the fighting and hunting element, on which the very existence of the tribe depends.

The question of the relative proportion of men and women in a tribe also has a considerable influence on the status of

By permission of A. C. Hollis, Esq.

KAVIRONDO WOMAN.
Showing the decorated goat-skin worn by matrons.

women. Where the number of women is greater than that of the men we find that polygamy is the custom, and women being plentiful are considered of less value. Where women are few, as a general rule, monogamy or even polyandry prevails, the latter being the name of the custom in accordance with which a woman marries two or more men, usually brothers. This custom is found in parts of India and Tibet, and naturally under such circumstances the influence of women in society is great. Europe, with the exception of Turkey, stands outside the question of the balance of the sexes, for the reason that monogamy has become a doctrine of the Christian religion.

Woman's Work.

To return to the work of woman; agriculture almost all over the world falls within her province, though the heavy labour of clearing the ground is usually left to the stronger sex. The making of pots, basketry, and woven materials is also part of her duty, especially in America; though in Africa and elsewhere tribes are often found among whom these are essentially the tasks of men. In parts of British Central Africa, for instance, the husband makes his wife's clothes, and bad workmanship in this respect has been urged as an excuse for a divorce.

In hut-building, too, woman usually takes her part, though here also the heavier work is done by the men; and when the dwelling attains to the dignity of a solidly built house, as in New Zealand and on the North-west coast of America, she has very little share in the construction.

Certain occupations, such as the tending of cattle, hunting, the working of metal, heavier forms of wood-working, and canoe-building, seem universally excused her among less civilised tribes, though the first of these duties, at any rate in Europe, has often been allotted her.

Woman in War.

As to war, woman has already been mentioned as a very fruitful cause of strife; but she has in all ages played a part, though usually a minor one, in military operations, more especially in the defence of towns, as witness the many stories of female heroism in the accounts of sieges which have come down to us from the Middle Ages. Of the many warriors who have met their deaths at the hands of feminine foes, the names of Holofernes, Sisera, and Pyrrhus will occur at once to everyone.

Stories of tribes of warrior women, such as the Amazons, have been common since the days of Homer; but the only instance of women as professional fighters, except in isolated individual cases, occurs in Dahomey. Here, since the early eighteenth century a regular corps of celibate women has existed, divided into two wings and a bodyguard for the king. At first composed of criminals, they were later selected from the whole of the population, and came to be quite as formidable in fight as their brothers in arms.

Less creditable to the gentler sex is the share they have had almost everywhere in the killing of wounded, and the torture and slaughter of prisoners, especially in North America and New Zealand.

Where Women are of Importance.

A few words have already been said in general on the subject of the status and influence of women in different parts of the world, but this subject well deserves more detailed consideration. Among some peoples—in particular the Caribs of South America, several tribes in the Northern part of the continent, the Sumatrans, and certain African tribes—a man on marrying leaves his own village and takes up his abode in the village or house of his father-in-law. In this way the daughters of a family play an important part, in-so-far as they are the means of securing fresh supporters for the tribe or village. Indeed, in Africa a man will often be found fighting on the side of his wife's village against his own. Somewhat analogous in Europe is the occasional adoption by a man of his wife's name if she happens to be an heiress.

Of still more frequent occurrence than the above, among primitive peoples, is woman in her *rôle* of transmitter of property and rank. In many places, especially in Africa, inheritance runs in the female line, so that a man inherits the property of his maternal uncle, not of his father. Chieftainship, too, follows the same lines. Among some tribes of the North-west coast of America, a man marrying the daughter of a chief, or influential individual, receives with her certain rank and privileges not strictly regarded as his own, but to be held in trust for their children, the heirs of his own personal property being the sons of his sister.

Photograph by B. W. Caney, Durban

PREPARING FOR THE WEDDING.

Kaffir beer-carriers *en route* to a marriage feast, S. Africa.

Ancient Egypt seems to afford a striking example of this system. Here the sovereign was regarded as an actual god, but his divinity was transmitted rather to his daughter than to his son, and, through her, to her husband. Hence usurpers, or founders of new dynasties, frequently established their position as sovereigns, and acquired the divinity inseparable from that position, by marriage with the daughter of the last king. This idea seems to have been the origin of the practice that the king's son should marry his sister, the effect being to secure his succession to the throne. Where such a custom prevailed it was natural that the women of the princely house should be regarded with the utmost deference.

The Position of Woman.

It has been said that though many of the uncivilised races regard women as little better than domestic animals, yet they do not, after all, hold her of less account than many peoples at a far more advanced state of culture. In fact it may be said that the position of woman in countries where the harem system prevails is less enviable than among savage races. Among the latter woman at least enjoys a reasonable amount of personal freedom, and the inferiority of her position relative to man is less keenly felt in proportion as her intelligence is of a lower order.

It is in countries such as Turkey that she claims our greatest sympathy. Here, in the harems of the upper classes, are found women quite as intelligent and well educated as those of Western Europe—in fact, often more so. Many of them have had English governesses, speak two or three languages, are well versed in the literature of other countries as well as their own, and perhaps—most bitter of all—are perfectly well acquainted with the freedom of life enjoyed by their Western sisters. They are on quite a different footing from the women of the savage world, in-so-far as they are capable of realising the inferiority of their position, a subject to which the savage woman in all probability never gives a thought.

Yet even the harem system, repressive as it is, cannot prevent woman's influence from making itself felt even in the most important matters of state, and many an Eastern potentate has owed his power to the tact, diplomacy and intrigue of his mother. The superior status of women of the upper and middle classes in Western Europe is due to a number of causes, one of which may well be the high esteem in which women were held by the ancient Germans, as described by Tacitus; to this succeeded the chivalrous ideal of womanhood evolved in the Middle Ages. Though at this period the treatment of woman in the concrete often left much to be desired, yet the reverence for her in the abstract is reflected in most of the old romances.

But her influence was not active; it is true that many a young knight found the thought of his lady-love a mighty stimulus to splendid deeds; for her he fought, and to win her smile dared many a desperate encounter. The result was that woman became relegated to a pedestal, and on that pedestal she was content to remain until comparatively lately. In these recent days she has found her quarters there somewhat cramped, with the result that she has made great efforts to come down, and meet man on his own ground in many walks of life. At the same time the pedestal has never been quite discarded; woman keeps it handy as a refuge whither she may fly, if at any time in the life-struggle she feels that the superior strength of man is placing her at a disadvantage, and on which she may take her stand secure in her position as a member of the Privileged Sex.

Colonisation and the Position of Woman.

Besides the spread of education the rise of colonisation has no doubt contributed largely to the emancipation of woman. The married colonist in the hard fight of taming a wild country has found that his wife could prove a most efficient partner in his work. Close association, under severe conditions, has bred a respect for woman in the concrete which could never have been evolved from mere idealisation in the abstract. In the colonies woman has been given the opportunities, lacking in the mother-country, to show that she is worthy of a place in the outside world to which the Early Victorian girl at home would never have dreamed of aspiring. The return of colonial families to England, ease of travelling, and our close relations with America, have wrought a marvellous revolution in Western Europe; and herein lies a paradox. Though woman in primitive tribes is so often regarded as a creature on a plane quite below man, yet the reversion of civilised man to the primitive conditions inseparable from life in a young colony has been a potent cause of her emancipation. Civilisation alone is not enough to raise woman's status; the ancient Greeks were in many respects a people of very high culture, yet among them women as a general rule occupied a very subordinate position indeed.

Photograph by J. Geiser, Algiers.

ALGERIAN WOMAN.

Showing outdoor costume.

Woman and the State.

As regards the active participation of women in the affairs of state, such participation may be primary or secondary. The secondary influence—the influence that every woman worthy of her sex exercises over the males with whom she is in close relation—may be disregarded here; but it may be mentioned that the spirit of Mrs. Caudle would seem to be absolutely ubiquitous. That worthy and justly celebrated lady is in fact peculiar to no age and to no race; she is cosmopolitan and omnipresent. And Mr. Caudle will continue to vote just as Mrs. Caudle tells him to the end of time.

But woman has occasionally, though rarely, a more direct influence upon politics than this; in certain parts of the world, for instance among the Maoris, the women were allowed a voice in the tribal councils; and it is a coincidence that in New Zealand of to-day female suffrage is an accomplished fact. Even in our country the lady orator is a frequent feature of election meetings, and the word suffragette, though French in form, has a meaning for most Englishmen, however poor their linguistic powers.

But it is strange to find that the conditions which that magic word conjures up to the imagination existed in the days of the early colonisation of Africa by the Portuguese, the continent which, for the average man, shows woman on her lowest level compared with the sterner sex. In the "countries of Sofala" in South-east Africa, the following custom prevailed, according to Purchas, quoting from a sixteenth century chronicler. Here, when the chief died—to give the quaint form of the original—"Hee whom the decessed had named his Successor, goeth to the King's House where the King's Women abide in expectation, and by their consent hee enters the house . . . Sometimes there are many Competitors, and then

Hee succeeds whom the women admit to the King's House; for none may enter by Law without their leave, nor can bee King without peaceable entrance; forcible entrie forfeiting his Right and Title. By bribes, therefore, and other wayes they seeke to make the Women on their side." What good, they have been very good, when they have been bad, they have been horrid."

Women sovereigns have been known from the earliest times; the legend of Semiramis, variously chronicled as the Queen of Babylon and Assyria, is at

Photograph by C. C. Pierce.

WOMAN AS THE WEARER OF TROUSERS.

A Chinese Girl.

more could the most ardent and optimistic suffragette desire?

From woman as an elector to woman as the ruler is a natural transition, and this is a subject to which it is impossible to do justice in the narrow limits of this chapter. Though women in a position of paramount authority are rare, yet such as have attained it have usually acquired celebrity owing to their excellence or the reverse; in fact, as the rhyme has it, "when they have been

any rate evidence that female rule was not unknown at a remote period; in Egypt, where there is reason to suppose that the divine essence of kingship was transmitted in the female line, Queen Hatshepsut not only did much to raise the country from the decadence into which it had fallen, but also actively encouraged foreign exploration, if her sculptured records are to be trusted. This lady, moreover, though

Women as Rulers.

living in an age long past, certainly belonged to the class of woman called "new"; in so far as she was wont to spell her name with a masculine termination and was depicted in reliefs in masculine garb. In our own country periods of the most notable progress have coincided with feminine rule; the remarkable growth of sea-power and the magnificent activity under Elizabeth, the architectural and military triumphs under Anne, and the extraordinary scientific progress and colonial expansion under the wise rule of Victoria the Good, form some of the brightest pages in the history of our islands.

A striking example of remarkable political influence exerted by a woman is afforded by the recent history of China. The personality of the Dowager Empress has made itself felt not only throughout the whole of that vast empire, but has also had a not inconsiderable effect in the Western world. Japan, too, has experienced the benefits of female autocracy, as the legends of the

Photograph by J. Brocherel, Aosta, Italy.

WOMAN AS THE WEARER OF TROUSERS: WOMEN OF CHAMPÉRY, SWITZERLAND.

Empress Jingo bear ample witness; and Cleopatra of Egypt, Catherine of Russia, and Isabella of Spain are names familiar to everyone.

Even among savage tribes women of the highest rank, though rarely attaining to a position of sole authority, often exercise a considerable amount of direct executive power. A chief who is the ruler of a number of scattered villages will often entrust the administration of each to one of his wives, whom he settles on the spot. Equally, if not more extensive, was the influence exerted by the Dowager Queen of Uganda, who had a separate little court of her own.

Women and Religion.

The relation of women to religion and superstition generally, including magic, still remains to be considered; and in this connection woman may be regarded in two aspects, as the victim of religion and superstition, and as its minister. First then as the victim. It is noticeable that nearly all religions enforce the inferiority of women as compared with men, and, speaking generally, as the scale of civilisation is descended the insistence on this point becomes more peremptory. In fact so many superstitious practices, among primitive peoples, seem to have been invented solely with the purpose of keeping the woman in a proper state of subjection, that one is almost tempted to believe that the fair sex is by nature unruly. Ceremonies at which no woman may present herself are common, and in the rites are employed certain paraphernalia which if seen by a woman, even accidentally, would cause her instant death. Thus in Australia the instrument known as a "bull-roarer" is carefully hidden from the female ken, and the noise it makes attributed to a supernatural being; so, too, in different parts of Africa there is the frequent phenomenon of the masked dancer supposed to represent a spirit, on whose appearance the women hasten to hide themselves. Any woman who gave the slightest intimation that she had penetrated the fraud would infallibly be killed.

A more unfair instance of religious terrorism relates to food. Throughout the savage world we very frequently find that certain foods are forbidden to women, under the threat of incurring the most terrible supernatural punishments. It would be charitable to suppose that such prohibitions arose from the fact that a woman had once died in some way inexplicable to the native mind, or had met with a severe accident, after partaking of some particular dish; but when it is noticed that the prohibited foods are invariably the chief delicacies, a suspicion as to how far the ordinance was inspired by masculine greed may not unnaturally arise. More pleasing, because they emphasise the closeness of the tie between husband and wife, are the restrictions sometimes laid upon the latter when the former is away on a warlike expedition, or hunting in the forest. For instance, a Dyak woman, when her husband is away on a head-hunt, must wear a sword, refrain from sleep during the day, and sit up as late as possible, lest her lord might be forgetful of his weapons or be caught napping by his foes. Similar practices are found all over the world, especially in Africa and South America. Attention may also be called to the religious sanction, which in our country subordinates the female sex to the male, and which is expressed in the bride's promise to honour and obey her husband.

Other-World Legends and Woman.

Many non-European peoples can give a long account of the perils to which the soul is exposed on its way to the other world, and of the joys, or the reverse, which it may expect when it gets there. As a rule, however, women do not figure very largely in these recitals. The important people in the next world among the Polynesians are precisely those who have been important in this, viz., warriors and chiefs. The kings of Dahomey and other West African potentates were so sure that they would enjoy the same rank in the next life, and so sure that a number of wives were necessary to keep up their dignity, that it was the proper thing to kill most or all of the widows at, or soon after, the funeral of a king. Other peoples, more merciful, have made up their minds that woman has no soul, and consequently they see no object in killing her when her husband dies. The Hindus were not of their number; for the horrid rite of suttee, or widow burning, has only been abolished in India within living memory.

A question, an answer to which will be found in the Bible, has also occurred to non-Christian peoples; the lot of the widow in the future world has given rise to many searchings of heart. In India the Santals have decided that she will belong to the first husband. As a wife is purchased among them it is accordingly the custom for a man who marries a widow to get her at half the price paid by the first husband, as when she joins the latter in the next world she will become his property again, and the second husband will have no claim on her.

The question of the old maid and her future lot has troubled primitive peoples but little, for the simple reason that she is unknown among them. Europeans are less merciful; it is the belief of some that old maids are condemned to take the form of peewits, and thus expiate for all eternity the spinsterhood which, if the truth were told, was probably not precisely their own choice. Another belief condemns them to make ropes of sand for ever, or, like Tregeagle, to bail out a quantity of water with a vessel that will not hold a drop. By the side of these penalties the punishment of women in Fiji who are not tattooed sounds comparatively mild; according to the pagan belief they were condemned to be dismembered in the future life, and to serve as food for the gods.

Even in the matter of a future life, however, man has not had it all his own way. On the Guinea coast a princess was allowed to choose as her husband any specially good-looking man; if she or her eldest son died before him he was put to death, for he was her slave both in this life and in the world to come. All things considered, the absence of good looks may have its advantages, even though it does involve marrying a less important personage than a princess.

Magic and Witchcraft.

With the subject of religion is closely interwoven that of magic. We are not here concerned with the distinction between them, and it is sufficient to characterise very briefly the position of women with regard to magic, and the main cause which has put her in that position. It is difficult to say what proportion of the average European man's (and woman's) time is taken up with love affairs or dreams. In the well-conducted individual they come to an end with marriage, and where intrigue and jealousy still prevail no one resorts to magic to heal his wounds. But, from the lowest depths of savagery up to the decay of the universal belief in witchcraft in the seventeenth century, love charms and love potions played a great part; and they are very far from unknown in the folklore of to-day.

In Europe of the present time it is almost always the old woman who is accused of magical practices. The predominance of women seems to date back at any rate to the tenth or eleventh century, and the magical character of old women is even earlier; but it is not easy to say exactly how it came about. One important factor in bringing women to the fore was certainly their greater activity in the weaving of love spells, and the use of love potions; and side by side with this, the use of poison as a means of revenge. All the world over we find a belief that women are especially skilled in certain kinds of magic, and it is to the love element that this must be attributed. Man can remove a rival or, if need be, bid for the heart of beauty by bolder methods. Woman has had to summon poison and magic to supplement the effect of her own charms.

In her second capacity as a maker of magic, or a minister of religion, woman has always played a most important part from the earliest times. Hebrew tradition credits Lilith, the first wife of Adam, with great magical powers; and to take an instance from contemporary literature, does not Kipling relate how the First Woman "sat up combing her hair. She took the bone of the shoulder of mutton—the big flat blade bone—and she looked at the wonderful marks on it, and she threw more wood on the fire, and she made a magic. She made the First Singing Magic in the world." And as it was at first so it is now, it is among women chiefly that are found the small superstitions as to what is lucky and unlucky, small observances and customs in daily life, which are in reality survivals of beliefs universally current in primeval times. This is due to the greater conservatism of woman compared with man, and this conservatism is in itself due to the nature of her occupations. The principal work of woman has always been in the home, and its character has altered far less under civilisation than the habits and occupations of her consort. Far less affected by changing conditions, she has preserved inherited traditions to a much greater degree. Beliefs change with the advance of time, and all beliefs are the heritage of a past age, consequently there is always a section of the population who are in advance of the beliefs generally current, and whom the latter fail to satisfy. Women, the greater conservatives and less affected, as remarked above, by changing conditions, are rarely numbered among this section, and are therefore, as a whole, usually found to be more devout than men.

But her *rôle* is often more important than this; she not unfrequently obtains as it were official recognition of her powers, and the witch-doctress or sorceress is a familiar figure in Asia, Africa and America. Often her magic is connected with the healing art, and under this aspect her most recent representative is the "wise woman" who is not quite extinct in England of the present day. More important still does her position become when her services are dedicated to some particular power, and she becomes a priestess. In this guise she appears in West Africa, North America, and Asia.

In countries where a more or less advanced stage of civilisation is found, the status and influence of the priestess is proportionately higher; nothing for instance could have exceeded the veneration with which the Vestal Virgins were regarded in Ancient Rome. Often, too, the priestess becomes the mouthpiece of the power she serves, as in the case of the priestess at Delphi and the Sibyl at Rome, of whom the prototypes are found also in the savage world.

The Origin of Woman.

In regard to the origin of woman, biologists have been known to maintain that she was not invented but simply "growed," and they proceed to trace her back to an amœba, and show how she was gradually evolved.

Originally, as the reader knows, living beings were sexless, and it was not until after many thousands of years of effort that a better way of managing things was discovered. In this period a cell set to work and grew, and when it had grown too big it split in two and then there was a great debate as to which was the baby and which was the mother; only they didn't talk then, and had never heard of babies; at any rate nobody knew which was the elder and which was the younger. Another curious result of these arrangements was that nobody ever died, though after a time he or she was entitled to ask whether he was himself or not, when so many fragments of him or herself, in bulk much greater than the original, were swimming about in the primeval sea.

To cut a long story short, the cell became a colony of cells, and the colony of cells became woman (and sometimes man), and now biologists, as is the wont of learned men, trace back the different qualities of man and woman to the remote period when nature agreed that division of labour was a good thing, and decided that there should be male and female, the former's duty being mainly connected with nutrition, the latter's with reproduction. Unfortunately for the

OLD STYLE ZULU WEDDING CEREMONY.

Photographs by B. W. Casey, Durban.

These pictures show in a very striking manner the changes which civilisation is introducing into the life of natives of South Africa. Each represents a Zulu native wedding. The first shows the women and girls dancing with the bride in the centre, the latter holding a knife to signify that she is severing her connection with her unmarried life; the second gives a view of the ceremony as conducted on European lines.

biologists the mental qualities of men and women happen to be precisely opposite to what an unbiassed observer would expect to result from the katabolic male element, and the anabolic female element; but that does not prevent the man of science from weaving a very pretty story, for which the curious may look in works on evolution.

From the fact that the original male cell was lively, while the original female cell was the reverse, the biologist deduces that man ought to be more variable than woman, more adventurous and inventive, should have a greater variety of ideas, greater powers of concentration, abstraction and generalisation, while woman's task is rather to conserve the species as she finds it, to make the best use of past conquests, and to apply old ideas; she has continuity, patience and stability. All of which would be very impressive if it were a prophecy from the known to the unknown; as it happens to be a prophecy from the unknown to the known, it is less convincing, especially as some of the statements are, if not untrue, at least unproved.

The Psychological Differences of Sex.

If the average man is asked to say how woman differs from man from the psychological point of view, he is probably nonplussed; he knows that man is stronger, but he has little information beyond that. Experiment shows that woman is man's inferior not only in strength but also in rapidity of movement, resistance to fatigue, and, though to a much smaller extent, in precision of movement. How far these facts hold good outside America is, however, another matter; the experiments were tried on American college students.

Experimental psychologists are accustomed to ascertain by trial the "threshold" for a given sense; that is to say, at what point we just perceive a noise, a smell, and so on, without being able to qualify it in any way. It is a curious thing that man is quicker at perceiving a light, woman at perceiving tastes, smells, colours, and simple sensations of touch; as regards musical notes men and women seem to perceive both high and low notes of the same pitch with equal ease. Although woman is so far ahead in detecting the first signs of a sensation, she does not have it all her own way; for man is ahead of her in discrimination. Woman holds her own as regards the pitch of a musical note and as regards colours, except shades of grey, but man is her master when it is a matter of distinguishing differences of weight, taste, etc., or of estimating by the aid of sight. In the matter of temperature, odours, and simple pressure, the two sexes seem to be equally gifted.

As regards the purely intellectual qualities the experiments show that man is perhaps superior in ingenuity, and that the social consciousness is more developed in him; while woman is better at feats of memory, and has a stronger religious consciousness.

The faculty of inventiveness is sometimes denied to women—by members of the other sex, be it understood, and in the absence of suffragettes. But it is quite possible that the human race owes far more to woman than it knows. Everywhere in primitive society we find woman charged with the task of collecting the vegetable food, and though mere man sometimes, even among the very primitive blacks of Australia, plays an important part in the harvesting of grass seed and other desirable dainties, the view has been seriously put forward that it is to woman we owe our cereals and our cultivated plants in general.

Dropping the biological standpoint there is a very close connection between the social, economic, and intellectual status of women generally

The question of genius cannot be approached here; genius is the peculiar attribute of no sex, country or age, and, whenever it occurs, is something abnormal; it is rather the distinguishing characteristics of the sex as a whole that will be treated. That the intelligence of woman is inferior to that of man ought not to be advanced as a serious proposition by anyone in these days. Even among savages where women rank considerably below men they frequently show even superior intelligence. The fact is that the male and female intelligences differ in kind rather than in quantity, and that difference is due in main to the difference in occupation. Woman has always since the beginning of time been occupied with details, and her life has always been regulated more by routine than that of man.

The girl has always received from her elders the precise rules—often emphasised by superstition—according to which this or that household task should be performed, and her mind has become trained to an observance of exact detail. Now it is quite true that her primitive consort is also a slave to routine, but at the same time in war, hunting and other forms of competition, where the observance of exact routine is absolutely impossible, he has been forced to learn that the interpretation of a rule must depend very much on circumstances. Consequently the masculine mind has become more trained to the search for first principles, leaving the practical application of them to the inspiration of the moment.

But it is just the faculty of patient application to detail which renders the work of women of such importance to modern science, and surely it is not for nothing that Science is usually personified by a female figure?

Photograph by O. Kurkdjian.

JAVANESE DANCING GIRLS.

By courtesy of Mr. J. J. Lister.

TONGAN GIRLS FISHING WITH NETS ON THE REEF.

POLYNESIA

By A. HINGSTON, M.A.

I

Geographical Position—Physical Type—Beauty: Its Attainment and Preservation—Personal Decoration—Physical Deformations—Tattooing—Dress—Tapa and Its Manufacture—Samoan Mat-Clothing—Ornaments—Birth and Childhood—Infanticide—Pampered Childhood.

A LINE drawn in a north-westerly direction from New Zealand, across the Pacific through Fiji to Hawaii, roughly cuts off Polynesia (πολύς = many, νῆσος = island) on the east from Micronesia and Melanesia on the west; it includes island clusters studding areas perhaps 1,000 miles in diameter, and lonely islets hundreds of leagues from any neighbour; some are lofty and volcanic, but the majority are low coral atolls; on some the inhabitants form a dense population, and on others the barren and waterless conditions are incapable of supporting life.

The most important of the island groups stretch eastwards from Fiji, just north of the Tropic of Capricorn. These are Tonga, or the Friendly Isles; Samoa, or the Navigator group; Hervey or Cook Isles; Society Isles, including Tahiti; and the innumerable islets of the Paumotu or Low Archipelago, seldom rising more than three feet above the sea. To the north of the Paumotu, and nearing the equator, are the Marquesas, and far away across the equator and lying south of the Tropic of Cancer are the Hawaiian Islands, called by Captain Cook the Sandwich Isles.

All these groups of islands are inhabited by one race, the Polynesian, and all their languages belong to the same family, the Oceanic or Malayo-Polynesian.*

Physical Type.

The men are usually tall, with strong, well-made limbs and an erect graceful carriage. The head-form is more or less broad, the hair black or dark brown, straight or wavy, and luxuriant. The skin colour is a warm yellow or brownish tint; the nose is

* Austronesian of P. W. Schmidt.

straight and prominent; the cheek-bones are fairly salient, but the superciliary arches little marked. Travellers and residents alike have pronounced the Polynesians to be one of the finest races of the world, and many do not hesitate to describe the women as perfect types of feminine beauty.

Poets have sung of their charms, of their grace and beauty, of their child-like simplicity, and have told of their eyes, shining like lustrous stars beneath the deep fringed lids; of their skin of the tenderest olive, the olive that has a shade of gold in it, like a honeycomb that has entangled a sunbeam, and is therewith transfigured; of heads turbaned with glossy ropes of hair casting a twilight shade over brows of purest olive; of full ripe lips, parting in a smile, disclosing teeth that are in themselves a smile.

And Byron has immortalised the

> "Gentle savage of the wild
> In growth a woman tho' in years a child;
> The infant of an infant world, as pure;
> From nature—lovely, warm and premature,
> With eyes that were a language and a spell—
> A form like Aphrodite's in her shell."

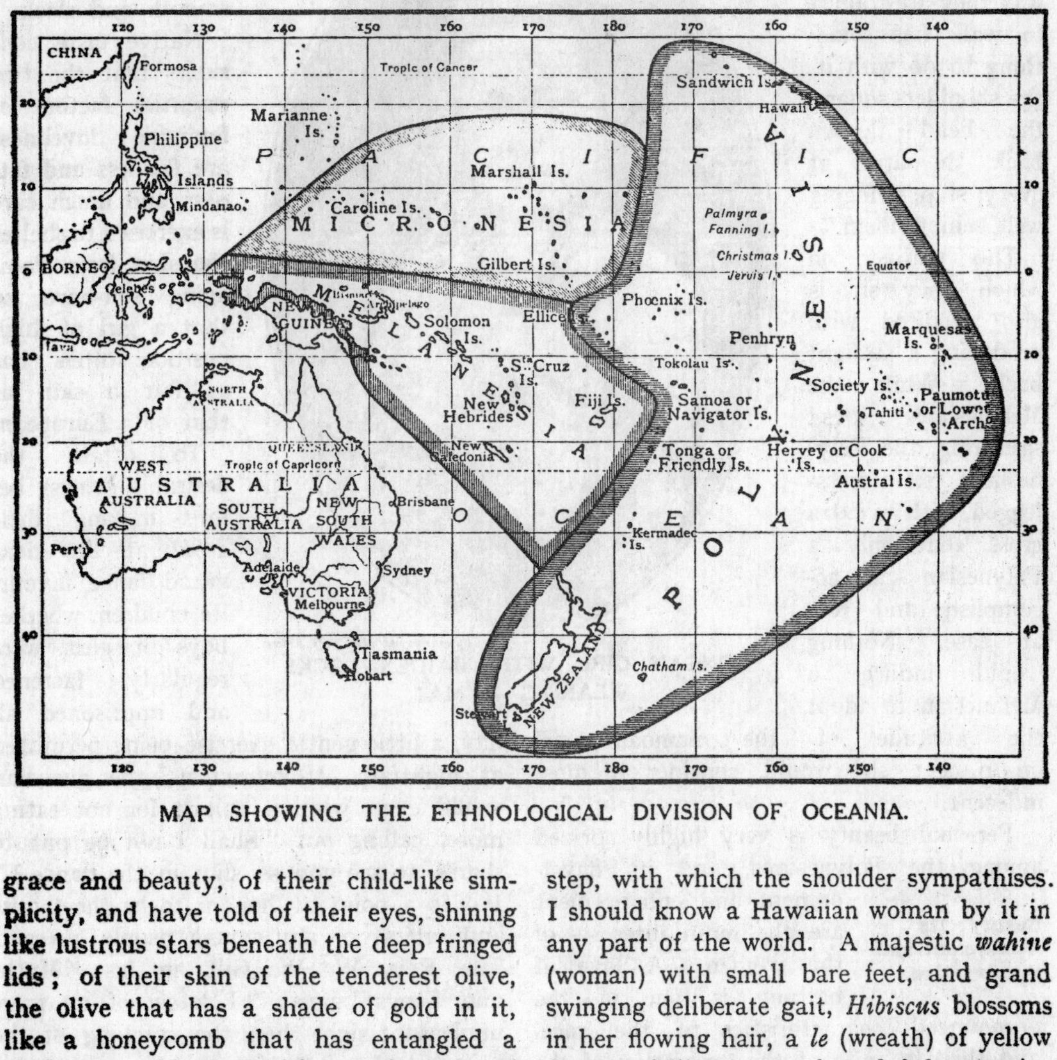

MAP SHOWING THE ETHNOLOGICAL DIVISION OF OCEANIA.

The walk of the Polynesian has often attracted attention. Mrs. Bishop (Isabella Bird) thus describes the Hawaiian gait: "The women have a most peculiar walk, with a swinging motion from the hips at each step, with which the shoulder sympathises. I should know a Hawaiian woman by it in any part of the world. A majestic *wahine* (woman) with small bare feet, and grand swinging deliberate gait, *Hibiscus* blossoms in her flowing hair, a *le* (wreath) of yellow flowers falling over her *holuku* (native garment), marching through the streets has a tragic grandeur of appearance, which makes the diminutive fair-skinned *haole* (foreigner) trotting along hesitatingly in high-heeled shoes look grotesque by comparison."

Another traveller, describing the Tongan

women, speaks of their "perfect busts, and figures that seem to tread on air. The women carry themselves even better than the men—and it is remarkable that the old women do not become hags, but the figure remains perfectly slim and upright, and very elegant. The way they are trained to walk has something to do with it, the shoulders square, the head thrown back, the arms at every step swinging well behind them."

The manner in which they sit is also credited with producing a straight back. While the Melanesians rest squatting, the Polynesians sit cross-legged, with an extra cross that only a Polynesian can accomplish and rest at ease. Nothing would induce a Melanesian to adopt the attitude of the Samoan girl on p. 43; she would consider it most indecent.

By courtesy of Mr. J. J. Lister.

TONGAN GIRL WITH MAIDEN LOCKS WEARING A MAT.

Beauty: Its Attainment and Preservation.

Personal beauty is very highly prized among the Polynesians, and its development and enhancement are the main interests of the women. A love of bathing is one of the pronounced characteristics of the race, and this, in spite of the proximity of the sea, is always performed in fresh water. Even if the women have spent nearly all day in the sea—fishing, wading, shell-fish collecting, etc.—they will invariably bathe in fresh water on their way homeward. Sometimes a red earth, which lathers slightly in the water, is used as soap, or the juice of fresh green oranges answers the same purpose. These frequent bathings, together with the subsequent oiling with fragrant oil, and shampooings, make the skin peculiarly soft and supple, with a sheen like that of rich satin. It is noticeable that in Fiji, where the skin is not rubbed with oil, it is much less smooth and sleek.

Native taste considers that the two essential factors of feminine loveliness are fairness and fatness, and much care is exercised to shelter the skin from damaging sun-burn, so that a girl of high position often has as fair a skin as that of a European.

To attain the desirable fatness before making their *début* at the next grand dance, favourite children, whether boys or girls, were regularly fattened and imprisoned all day, a little gentle exercise being permitted at nightfall. If refractory, the guardian would even whip a culprit for not eating more, calling out "Shall I not be put to shame to see you so slim in the dance?" It was a point of honour to be the fairest and fattest of any young people present. The Rev. W. W. Gill, in his "Myths and Songs," says: "I know of no more unpleasant sight than the cracking of the skin as the fattening process proceeds; yet this calls forth the admiration of the friends."

Ellis, in "Polynesian Researches," also mentions this beautifying process, which in the Society Islands has the name of *haapori*. There was a particular resort for females of the higher class, "for the purposes of increasing the corpulence of their persons, and removing, by luxurious ease under the embowering shade of the coco-nut groves, the dark tinge which the vertical sun of Tahiti might have burnt on their complexions." So favoured was this spot formerly that a hundred canoes have sometimes been seen at one time on the beach.

The hair also receives a great deal of attention. It is dressed in various ways, perfumed with scented oil, combed, adjusted and decorated with flowers. Ellis describes the groups of women "sitting under the shade of a clump of wide-spreading trees, or in the cool mountain-stream, employing themselves for hours together in arranging the curls of the hair, weaving the wreaths of flowers, and filling the air with their perfumes." So important was the arrangement and adorning of the hair considered, that there was a god of hair-dressers, or combers, called Totoro-potaa, whose aid was invoked at the toilet.

On special occasions lime, made from burnt coral, is largely used in hair-dressing. The lime is mixed with water, and the head dipped in and then allowed to dry. The process is repeated several times until the hair is thoroughly coated with the mixture. This has the advantage of keeping the head in a clean condition, and it also dyes the hair a light brown, which has a curious effect.

By courtesy of Mr. J. J. Lister.

GIRL FROM SAMOA WITH HIBISCUS BLOSSOM IN HER HAIR

The illustration on p. 41 represents a Tongan woman on Saturday night, with her hair all plastered with lime in preparation for her Sunday toilet.

Some women favour the raised style of hair-dressing, which is especially characteristic of Fiji. For this the hair is cut fairly short, and stiffened with a mixture of scented oil and the gum of the bread-fruit tree; others prefer to wear their hair long in sleek oiled tresses. The contrast is well shown in the two Tongan girls on p. 40.

An unmarried girl generally has a "maiden lock" hanging over her shoulder, like a seventeenth century love-lock, and the cutting of it off often forms a part of the wedding ceremony. The girl illustrated on p. 38 has two such locks. A widow has her hair closely cropped.

Physical Deformations. As usual Art is called in to aid or counteract Nature. In many of the islands the skulls of the babies are artificially deformed by pressure with stones or slabs of soft wood, applied before and behind. More curious is the artificial flattening of the nose, performed on girls alone. The mother presses the plastic nose of the infant so as to spread out the nostrils on either side, and produce a shape in consonance with native ideas of comeliness, "unlike the thin starved nose of the white race," as a woman was heard to say.

The ears of the children are sometimes pierced with a fishbone, and enlarged with Gardenia twigs, so as to admit a fresh plucked flower. The hole is often large enough to hold a bunch of scented leaves, which serves at once as decoration and perfumery.

Tattooing.

The most striking type of decorative deformation is seen in the tattooing, a custom prevalent throughout the greater part of Polynesia. The method employed is practically the same throughout the whole area. The instrument consists of a row of fine teeth usually of bone (either human, or the bone of a bird, turtle, fish, or small animal), or of thorns or pins, fastened to a light handle. A heavier stick is used as a mallet, to drive the sharp points through the skin. The figure to be traced is generally sketched out with charcoal, but even the most elaborate devices are carried out by the more skilled workers with no other guide than the eye. The colouring matter, into which the instrument is dipped, is made from the kernels of the candle-nut (*Aleurites trilobata*), baked.

By courtesy of Mr. J. J. Lister.

TWO TONGAN GIRLS.
Showing different styles of hair-dressing.

charred, pulverised and mixed with oil. Soot from the seeds of *Calophyllum inophyllum*, mixed with oil from the same

By courtesy of Mr. J. J. Lister.

TONGAN WOMAN ON SATURDAY NIGHT.

With her hair plastered with lime, in preparation for the Sabbath toilet.

seeds, is also used as pigment, and occasionally a purple stain is composed from the scraped roots of a tree, mixed with lime.

The operator, immersing the points of the sharp bone instrument in the colouring matter, which is a beautiful jet, applies it to the surface of the skin, and, striking it smartly with the elastic stick held in the right hand, punctures the skin, and injects the dye at the same time, "with as much facility as an adder would bite and deposit her poison."

Ellis adds "that the operation was continued as long as the person could endure the pain, but it was seldom that a whole figure was completed at once, and the scheme of decoration often extended over several years."

In some islands both men and women are tattooed; in most, the women are more sparingly decorated than the men, and their faces are seldom marked. A prevalent fashion in Tahiti was the tattooing of the feet in a pattern suggesting a lace-work boot, reaching to just above the ankle.

Patterns generally vary between the sexes, one type of design being characteristic of male decoration, and others of female. In Rotuma a favourite design for the men is the *perero*, supposed to represent a strong-smelling flower which the young men give to their sweethearts. The women's proper marks are circles enclosing designs, placed three in a row on each arm, diagonal marks along each finger joint, and small blots on the hand below the base of the thumb between the palm and the wrist. Only the women with their hands thus marked were able, in times gone by, to peel the vegetables for the chief.

In many of the groups tattooing is now discontinued, owing to the influence of the

By courtesy of Mr. J. J. Lister.

TAUPOU, OR OFFICIAL MAID, OF APIA, SAMOA.

missionaries, and its connection with heathen customs. In Huahine (Society Isles), native law decreed: "No person shall mark with *tatau*, it shall be entirely discontinued. It belongs to ancient evil customs. The man or woman that shall mark with *tatau*, if it be clearly proved, shall be tried and punished. . . . This shall be the woman's punishment: she shall make two large mats, one for the king and one for the governor." . . . . "The man and woman that persist in *tatauing* themselves successively for four or five times, the figures or ornaments marked shall be destroyed by blacking them over." It is not told how the obliteration was to be accomplished.

In other groups tattooing still flourishes by the side of Christianity. Robert Louis Stevenson, when describing the Samoans, said: "They are Christians, churchgoers, singers of hymns at family worship, hardy cricketers; but in most respects they are the contemporaries of our tattooed ancestors who drove their chariots on the wrong side of the Roman Wall." Samoan damsels will not look at a man unless he is tattooed, although the best part of the decoration is now covered by clothing.

Dress.

The ancient costume of Hawaii was said to consist of "a smile, a *malo* and a cutaneous eruption," and the children wore even less, being clad, as Mark Twain described it, "in nothing but sunshine—a very neat-fitting and picturesque apparel." Nowadays, in the same island, every child trots to school morning and noon in print frock and pinafore, or coat and trousers, according to its sex.

Complete nakedness was never a Polynesian fashion, and though the climate renders clothes almost unnecessary, artistic taste in costume is characteristic of the people, and they seem to possess an instinct for the becoming. But it must be confessed that this instinct is being rapidly eradicated under the influence of civilisation and Manchester goods.

Owing to the absence of all indigenous mammals except rats and mice, and owing to the ignorance of a loom, the native dress materials are all derived from the vegetable world. The simplest costume is a covering of *ti* leaves (*Dracaena terminalis*), forming a petticoat from waist to knee. This was the ordinary Samoan garment, mats and native cloth being worn only on special occasions. In Tahiti native cloth was worn by all, and "prince and peasant, warrior and voluptuary, were clad in vestments of the same material." But on coral atolls, where fibre-producing trees and plants are unknown, petticoats are made of split *Pandanus*, or coco-nut, leaves coarsely plaited.

One of the prettiest of native garments is the fringe made of various plants and leaf strips, called in Tonga the *sisi*, worn commonly round the waist, over a skirt of *tapa*, or else round the neck as a decoration. The women may often be seen sitting under the shade of a tree, chatting together while weaving the fragrant fringes of *Pandanus* strips, and fruits, nuts, flowers, and bunches of sweet smelling leaves. (*see* p. 44.)

Tapa and its Manufacture.

Native cloth, commonly called *tapa*, *i.e.* the beaten, is one of the most wonderful products of Polynesian industry, and the art of manufacture is brought to a remarkable degree of perfection.

Various kinds of bark are used for its preparation, that of the paper mulberry (*Brousonetia papyrifera*) makes the best cloth, and shoots of the tree are specially grown for the purpose. The legend of its origin is thus told in Samoa:—

There were once two brothers, Tutunga, the paper mulberry, and Salato, the stinging tree, and each had his plot of ground and a distinct boundary. One morning Tutunga crossed over his boundary and encroached on the land of Salato, who thereupon complained, and, unable to obtain satisfaction from the trespasser, referred the affair to their parents. These decided that the two brothers should separate, that Salato should go further inland, and be sacred and respected; and so it is, for no one dares to touch it. On the other hand Tutunga was to be punished for his aggression. He was to be cut, and skinned, and beaten, and painted, and made to cover the bodies of men. Then to rot, and then to be burned. And this is his fate to this day.

Photograph by J. W. Waters.

SAMOAN GIRL SITTING CROSS-LEGGED.
The hair is dressed in European style.

The poorer people, who cannot afford paper mulberry, use the bark of banyan, hibiscus, bread-fruit, and varieties of lianas in its place.

The making of the *tapa* is one of the most important labours of the women, and though to a great extent the native material is superseded by European cloth, it still forms the characteristic clothing in many parts.

The method of cloth-making is as follows :

First the bark of the shoots is stripped off, soaked, the hard outer rind scraped away, and the inner fibrous surface steeped in water ; when thoroughly soaked it is laid on a piece of wood hollow beneath, or raised somewhat from the ground, with a convex surface above. On either side of this sit the women, each one armed with a mallet of heavy wood with which she beats out the cloth (*see* illustration on p. 48). The mallets are square, with rounded handle ends, and the sides are incised in different modes, one surface having coarse ribs, another fine grooves, and another a chequered pattern, to give variety to the beaten fabric. The beating spreads the fibrous material into a broad sheet, as thin as tissue paper, and about as strong ; it is kept saturated with moisture during the whole process of manufacture, and the fibres of bark become completely interwoven. The women hammer away, hour after hour, gossiping and laughing, and after several days or weeks, by beating out the strips, and joining strip to strip, large pieces of cloth are produced. A single piece is often two hundred yards long and four yards wide, though the strips of bark are rarely more than four to five feet long, and not more than one and a half inches broad.

When the piece is finished it is spread out to dry in the sun, which bleaches it to a beautiful white. Cloth made of other kinds of bark does not attain the whiteness of that made of paper mulberry.

The next process is that of decoration, which is carried out by the aid of various dyes rubbed over patterns cut out of banana leaf, or made of ridges of fibre, or by ferns or flowers dipped into the dye, and then pressed on the cloth; finally a certain amount of durability and imperviousness to rain is attained by a layer of gum or resin to form a varnish. Only the most highly glazed textures are proof against wet, and a really strong well-made garment of native cloth will only last a few months. Cloth-making was at one time an almost incessant task, in which the women of all ranks were employed, from the queen and ladies of highest rank downwards. "The queen," as Ellis relates, "would have felt it derogatory to her rank if any other females of the island (Tahiti) could have finished a piece of cloth better than herself, and each lady of rank strove to excel in some particular department, either the elegance of the pattern, or the brilliancy of the colour."

By courtesy of Mr. J. J. Lister.

TONGAN WOMEN PLAITING *SISI* OR PETTICOATS.

The women generally work in parties of a dozen or more together, in the cloth house built for the purpose. Ellis describes his entering a large house in Eimeo, where sixteen to twenty women were all at work, "and the noise of sixteen to twenty mallets going at one time was almost deafening."

The queen sat in the midst and worked as diligently and cheerfully as any present.

The cloth is worn in various ways to form graceful draperies, and it is also cut up, according to patterns supplied with English fashion papers, and made into what the natives call "pinafores." The most effective garment is the Tahitian *tiputa*, which resembles the South American *poncho*.

It is made by beating together a number of layers of cloth so as to form a stout material. A thick piece of bread-fruit bark is chosen for the outer layer, and the inner layers are attached by slightly moistening them with arrowroot, and the whole is beaten together. When finished a hole is cut in the centre, through which the head is thrust and the cloth falls in ample folds to the knees.

Samoan Mat-clothing.

But great as was the pride taken in cloth making, almost more importance was attached to the mats which formed clothing, house furniture, and in some islands wealth and currency. In Samoa the fine mats are still considered the most valuable clothing. They are made of the leaves of a species of *Pandanus*, scraped clean and thin as writing paper, and slit into strips about the sixteenth of an inch wide. A special house has to be built for the work, as the growing mat must not be exposed to the domestic dangers of an ordinary house. It is not on every day that the maker may work, the weather must be fine and fair, or the weaving is blemished. The mats when completed are from two to three yards square, fringed, and sometimes ornamented with small scarlet feathers inserted here and there, and they are almost as flexible as a piece of calico. Few of the women can make them, and many years are often spent over the making of a single mat which is worth a few pounds when finished. These are preserved with great care; some are treasured through many generations, being valued all the more as their age and historic interest increase. One of these mats forms the full dress of the *taupou*, or official maid of the village.

HAWAIIAN "TAPA" OR NATIVE CLOTH MANUFACTURED FROM BARK.

Hibiscus bark, prepared with great care, is made into mats about three to four feet wide and nine to ten feet long. These are worn by the men either wound round the loins, or with a hole in the middle, as a *poncho*, or as a mantle thrown over the shoulders. These mats are remarkably durable, and are very light and elegant in appearance.

Ornaments are far more sparingly worn in Polynesia than in Melanesia, if we except the almost universal custom of the people of decking themselves with flowers, which adds a peculiar charm to the already attractive appearance of men, women, and children. A typical Polynesian girl always wears flowers in her hair, and the pure white with the dark centre or the rich scarlet of the *Hibiscus*, the pink of the oleander, the yellow of the alamander or the stars of the jessamine, show up well against the dark gloss of the hair. If the ear is perforated, it is to receive a flower, and wreaths of flowers are worn as garlands for the head, as necklaces, and as girdles on every occasion.

Ornaments.

Ornaments, except for floral decorations, are mainly confined to necklaces, bracelets, and frontlets of various descriptions. As in Melanesia (and probably indicative of Melanesian influence), one of the most highly prized ornaments is a nearly circular boar's tusk, worn as an armlet, or as a pendant round the neck.

The most valuable form of necklace is made of sperm-whale teeth, and such is the value with which they are held in Fiji that it is not safe for a common man to be known to have a tooth in his possession. The teeth are cut up into small curved pieces an inch or two long, which are strung together so as to project like a spiked collar round the neck.

Frontlets are made of shells, seeds, or beads, forming a band, worn across the forehead; but these are mainly reserved for official occasions. The *tuinga* or headdress of the Samoan *taupou*, or maid of the village, is a most complicated affair. Mrs. Churchill, in "Samoa Uma" gives a good description of its formation: "It is part wig, part frontlet of Nautilus shell, part bright plumage, and part scaffold of three sticks. It is not an easy thing to put on, for its component parts must be assembled piece by piece every time of using. It is productive of constant pain while it is worn, and is taken off with a feeling of relief, yet the sway of custom is so rigid that a *taupou* would scarcely feel herself clad without her *tuinga*. As this mass of hair and sticks is exposed to somewhat rough treatment and violent motions it must be firmly attached to the head. The foundation is a strip of cloth which is wound around the head at the roots of the hair and which serves to draw all the hair into a bunch at the crown, where it is allowed to stand up to its full length of three inches, which is the usual length. Upon this one lock is tied the wig of natural hair set in a frame of cloth or fibre netting. When that is attached so securely as not to be dislodged, the scaffolding of three twigs and a cross piece is tied in front and made fast to the cloth covering just above the forehead. Tresses of the green and red feathers of the tiny parakeet are attached to the wig and to the framework. The *tuinga* is completed by tying across the forehead a band of several rows of the partition plates of the Nautilus."

No wonder that the toilet of the *taupou*, before a dance, occupies several hours.

Birth and Childhood.

The Polynesians are often compared to a race of children, and the attitude of a Polynesian mother to her child frequently suggests that of a little girl to her doll. There is the same impulsive affection and the same heedless forgetfulness; periods of devotion alternate with periods of apathy and neglect, which have results as disastrous as deliberate cruelty.

Infanticide.

The custom of infanticide is attributed largely to natural indolence, an unwillingness to take trouble, and a carelessness regarding everything but immediate personal ease.

In some parts the first three children were always destroyed, and families of more than two were rare. In Tahiti a father with three or four children (which was a rare occurrence) was called by a special name, meaning a man with an unwieldy or cumbrous burden.

Economic considerations formed another motive for infanticide, which was also greatly influenced by the licentious tone of society. In the small island of Vaitupu only two children were allowed to a family by law, for fear of famine; while in Samoa, where food is abundant, infanticide was practically unknown. Samoa was also

SAMOAN DANCERS.

noted for its strict insistence on pre-nuptial chastity, at least in the higher ranks of society, while in the isles to the east such a condition was unknown. One of the laws of the notorious company of the Areois of Tahiti, which Ellis describes as "a sort of strolling players and privileged libertines, who spent their days in travelling from island to island, and from one district to another, exhibiting their pantomimes, and spreading a moral contagion through society," decreed the killing of all the children that might be born to them in their life of luxurious and licentious indolence and crime. A candidate for admission to the society had to murder all his children as one of the ceremonies of initiation. Owing to the reverence accorded to rank, if a man married a woman of an inferior order, the children were not allowed to live, as it was supposed that they would endanger the dignity of the family.

Thus, though infanticide is a custom which occurs among almost all races and peoples, it has nowhere been found so prevalent as among some of the Polynesian groups, where two-thirds of the new-born population are believed to have been destroyed. This destruction was often contrary to the desires of the women; the father was the autocrat of the family, and his decrees were frequently carried out in spite of the pleadings of the mother. A Rachel weeping for her children might often be seen in Polynesia, and the women have welcomed Christianity largely on account of its prohibition of infanticide. If the child was not wanted it was always killed immediately after its birth, and if it was allowed to live for only a few hours, its life was safe, and it was tenderly cared for.

By courtesy of Mr. J. J. Lister.

TONGAN WOMEN BEATING OUT PIECES OF BARK TO MAKE *TAPA.*

Everywhere female children would have less chance of being spared than male, the reason given being that fishing, the priesthood, and war were the only purposes for which it was useful to rear children, and girls were useless for all.

Polynesian children seem to illustrate the truth in that very ancient maxim, for they are never chastised, and they are invariably spoilt. Stevenson speaks of "the spoiling—I might almost say deification—of the child," especially by the Paumotu natives, "children make the mirth and the adornment of their houses, serving them for playthings and for picture galleries."

Pampered Childhood.

They grow up in an atmosphere of careless affection, they are petted and pampered by their parents as the fancy takes them, and left to look after themselves when more amusing occupations absorb their elders. Mrs. Bishop noted that in Hawaii far more tenderness was lavished on the pet dogs which the women carry about with them, than on the children. A mother will be almost heart-broken at the illness of her child, but she will rarely persist for many days together in any treatment prescribed by the doctor.

A woman aptly described this native temperament to Mrs. Bishop in the following words :—

"We," she said, "are always happy ; we never grieve long about anything. When anyone dies we break our hearts for some days, and then we are happy again. We are happy all day long, not, like the white people, happy one moment, gloomy another ; we have no cares, the days are too short. What are the *haoles* (foreigners) always unhappy about ?" Mrs. Bishop adds, "She evidently thinks us a sour, morose, worrying, forlorn race."

By the courtesy of Mr. J. J. Lister.

TONGAN WOMEN MARKING OUT A DESIGN ON A PIECE OF TAPA.

II

Samoan Childhood—Adoption of Parents—Age of Betrothal—Marriage Customs—Hawaii—Tahiti—Polygyny—A Tongan Woman on Polygyny—Matrimonial Morals—Widowhood

Photograph by J. W. Waters.

SAMOAN WOMAN
And Chief's Head-dress.

MRS. CHURCHILL thus writes of childhood in Samoa: "This child of savages is born to the best of good treatment within the knowledge of the parents, and is encouraged to feel that father and mother are its willing servants. It is not an uncommon sight to see a small child imposing infantile commands on obedient parents; admonition, correction, and punishment of the young are extremely rare."

Samoan Childhood.

The devotion of Finow, the chief of Tonga, to his little daughter was very touching, and when she was taken ill, his anxiety was very great. She was removed to a sacred enclosure, to be safe from malicious influence, and hogs were offered daily to the god on her behalf, and his intercession implored. "Here thou seest Finow and all his chiefs—(then would follow their names)—thou seest them humbled before thee. We pray thee not to be merciless, but spare the life of this woman* for the sake of her father, who has always been attentive to every religious ceremony."

Perhaps the gods knew that this last statement was not true (for Finow was openly irreligious), since, in spite of the removal of the child from one sacred enclosure to another, and supplications to one god after another, she grew gradually worse, and died.

When the little girls are a few years old they begin to help their mothers in various ways, fetching water, learning to make mats and native cloth, and collecting shellfish. Girls of all ages may usually be seen on the shores at low tide fishing with hand nets, as is seen on p. 36.

Adoption is a common custom. Parents give away their children, especially if they are any trouble, and adopt others indifferently. In Samoa it was the usual custom for a father to give his child to his sister, and she and her husband gave handsome presents in return. Children may also adopt parents, even though their own are still living. The Rev. W. W. Gill calls adoption "the curse of family life." It makes discipline almost impossible. "A cross word will make the youngster run off to its adopted parents, who sympathise where they ought to scold. I have known parents take a present of food to the runaway, and humbly entreat his return; but all in vain!"

Adoption of Parents.

The age for betrothal varies in different islands. As a rule a girl is not betrothed until maturity is reached, at twelve or thirteen, or later, and an unmarried girl is in most of the islands allowed absolute liberty. It was a cause of grievous complaint to the Tongans, used to the easy habits of their island, to find at Fiji that "there was no woman but who was under the protection of a jealous husband." The jealous husband is not typical of Polynesia. When, among people of high rank, infant betrothals were made for political reasons,

Age of Betrothal.

* The child was only about six years old, but the ceremonious word had to be used in addressing the god.

By the courtesy of Mr. J. J. Lister.

SAMOAN GIRLS FROM TUTUILA.

Showing costume and ornaments.

the girl spent all her time within doors on a small platform, in her parents' house, and she was guarded by some member of the family night and day, and never allowed outside the house by herself.

Marriage Customs.

Marriage is not a matter of sale or barter, though, as usual, it is an occasion of much present-giving on both sides, and the suitor often ingratiates himself with the parents of his beloved by means of well-chosen gifts.

Marriages are usually arranged by the parents, especially among the higher classes, and the individuals are passively acquiescent; but among the lower ranks the young man generally chooses for himself, though he selects a friend to act as go-between to conduct negotiations.

Women of rank had the right to make proposals to men of equal or inferior grades, and in Tahiti, if the wife was of superior rank to her husband, she was at liberty to take as many other husbands as she pleased,

By the courtesy of Mr. J. J. Lister.

TYPICAL CROSS-LEGGED ATTITUDE OF SAMOANS.

The woman's dress is of native tapa, but is cut in European style.

though still nominally regarded as the wife of the man she married first. The wedding ceremony usually included a feast, in which bride and bridegroom ate together, and a giving of presents by the family of the bride to the bridegroom, and *vice versa*. In Samoa the bride's relations and friends would contribute fine mats and native cloth, which were looked upon as the bridal dowry, and the friends of the bridegroom would give canoes, pigs, or trade goods in return.

By the courtesy of Mr. J. J. Lister.

SAMOAN GIRL.

With banana leaf neck wreath.

But the cost of such a ceremony made it prohibitive for all but wealthy people. Poorer folk dispensed with the display, and merely gave a feast to the relatives and friends on both sides. An elopement was the least expensive form of all, and was frequently resorted to when the consent of the parents was doubtful.

Sometimes the dowry of the bride was attached to her person. Mariner describes a Tongan bride who was decked out with about forty yards of mats of the finest texture, as soft as silk "so that her arms stuck out from her body in a ludicrous manner, and she could not, strictly speaking, sit down, but was obliged to bend in a sort of half sitting posture, leaning on her female attendants, who were under the necessity of raising her again when she required it." It was usual also to anoint the hands, feet, face and breast of a bride with a mixture of sandalwood oil and turmeric, producing a deep orange tint.

Hawaii.

In Hawaii it was generally the parents or friends of the girl who arranged the marriage, and there was practically no wedding ceremony. Sometimes the bridegroom threw a piece of *tapa* or native cloth round the bride, and a feast was spread in honour of the occasion.

Tahiti.

In Tahiti the sanction of the gods was considered necessary for the marriage contract. A temporary altar was erected in the house of the bride, on which were placed the skulls and bones of her ancestors. The bride and bridegroom, arrayed in wedding garments (which were afterwards considered sacred), stood a few yards apart, and the priest asked the man,

By the courtesy of Mr. J. J. Lister.

TONGAN WOMAN.

With necklace of Pandanus nuts.

"Will you not cast away your wife?" to which he answered "No"; then the bride was asked a similar question, and returned a similar answer. The priest then said to them both, "Happy will it be, if thus with you two." He offered a prayer to the gods in their behalf, imploring for them that they might live in affection, and realise the happiness marriage was designed to secure. Certain ceremonies followed, and the giving of presents. Sometimes the women relatives gashed their faces with shark's teeth, and collecting the blood on a cloth, placed it at the feet of the bride.

Polygyny.

Polygyny was a universal custom, limited only by the wealth of the husband, and the fact that in most of the islands the men were numerically in excess of the women.

A bride in Samoa was always accompanied by one or two maids of honour, either a daughter of her brother, or a girl of her mother's family, though they did not always become secondary wives. If a man of position married a slave girl, the younger sisters became his as a matter of course, and amongst those of equal rank a man often had two or three sisters to wife at the same time. But the Samoan has always shown a disposition towards monogamy, and, owing to the quarrelling which polygamy engenders, few men retained more than two wives, unless they were great chiefs.

A Tongan tale relates the adventures of Matandua the One-Eyed, who delivered his countrymen from a terrible giant and became King of Tonga, and took Tauki the Merry One, the fairest maiden of the land, to wife, and soon the great house had children rolling upon the mats. Only one wife did he take—her and no other. And when his foster-mother said to him, "You should take more wives, my lord, that you may get your *tapa* cloth made," he only shook his head and smiled. "*Tapa* is good, but peace and quietness are better," quoth he.

In Hawaii plurality of wives gave distinction to the husband, and was enjoyed by such as could afford it, but it was limited by the poverty of the common people, by the equality of the sexes (for the destruction of the female infants compensated for the men killed in war), and by the imperative demand of the common man for a mate.

By the courtesy of Mr. J. J. Lister.

WOMAN WITH TAPA SKIRT

Which shows beneath the velvet overall.

A Tongan Woman on Polygyny.

It is interesting to hear what the women themselves thought of this question. Mariner gives the naïve opinion of a Tongan girl concerning polygyny: "The custom of having only one wife is a very good one provided that the husband loves her, if not it is a very bad one, because he would tyrannize over her the more; whereas, if his attention was divided between five or six, and he did not behave very kindly towards them, it would be very easy to deceive him."

Matrimonial bonds sat lightly on the Polynesians. Neither husbands nor wives felt bound to regard them as binding any longer than suited their inclinations and convenience. But in the west, fidelity was the rule. In Fiji the jealous husband bewrays the Melanesian element. In Tonga, Mariner, during his long stay in the island, before it was known to civilisation, only knew of three successfully planned intrigues, and in each case the man was a chief, and fear may have prevented refusal. This was no doubt partly due to the facility of divorce, which merely consisted in telling a wife she could go, and she was free to marry again at once. In Samoa, though infidelity was common, public opinion sanctioned the injured husband in seeking revenge in blood. But, owing to the prevalence of the communal spirit, the husband was satisfied with killing a brother or other relative of the offender, and it was rarely the latter who suffered punishment.

Matrimonial Morals.

In the islands to the east, even before the coming of the whites, society was on the high road to decay, and civilisation increased its degradation, breaking down ancient restraints, making the people restless and reckless, and teaching them to sell their wives and daughters for gain.

SAMOAN GIRLS.
Showing costumes and ornaments.

Respect for the wives of other men seems only to be engendered by the personal fear of consequences; even the enlightened Finow, the Tongan chief, acknowledged no higher motive. He confided in Mariner that he would like to learn magic, *i.e.*, writing, and for all the women to know it, "that he might make love with less risk of discovery and not so much chance of getting his brains knocked out by their husbands."

Though conjugal love and philoprogenitiveness are not characteristic of the Polynesians, as is shown by the prevalence of infanticide and adoption, and the facility of divorce, yet instances of the most devoted attachment are not rare; and tales of the suicide of despairing lovers, of incorruptible fidelity, and of love triumphant over death, show that the same ideals exist here as elsewhere.

Mariner (whose reports have been called "the Bible of the Friendly Isles") tells of the killing of Nowfaho by command of Finow, and how with his dying breath he sent messages of affection to his wife, and how she, on hearing of his death, seized spear and club to avenge his murder.

Another woman at her husband's death "for six months scarcely ever slept but on his grave, washing it with her tears, and disturbing the silence of the night with her sighs."

Louis Becke records the pathetic romance of the girl of Niué (Savage Island), whose lover died while absent in the guano islands. Her parents wanted her to marry another man, but she preferred to end her troubles and to rejoin her lover by leaping over the cliffs into the sea.

By the courtesy of Mr. J. J. Lister.

SAMOAN GIRLS.

Widowhood.

When a man died, his brother, whether married or not, would naturally become the husband of his widow and the father of his children. If he did not want her, he might pass her on to a relation or friend. But if there were any unwillingness on her part she could return to her own people.

Mourning for a husband usually continued for some time, and it was marked in the eastern isles with great barbarity. The women, at their marriage, provided themselves with knives, made of five or six shark's teeth, fixed to a small cane, with which to cut themselves on their husband's death. Frightful wounds were often inflicted. Mourning costume consisted in the wearing of an old ragged mat, the more ragged the better; and half-mourning permitted a wrapper of *tapa* to be worn underneath the mat, not so as to be visible, but to save the skin from the painful friction.

Black and white pebbles are collected to decorate the grave. The white pebbles are strewn over the body and the black pebbles above, in an eccentric ellipse, about the length and breadth of a man. Finow's chief widow used to go every morning to his grave, accompanied by her women, and cut the grass short with knives and sharp shells, and sweep away the leaves with brooms of coco-nut stems. The illustration on this page shows a modern Tongan widow in mourning, with cropped hair, wearing an old ragged mat, pouring oil over her husband's grave.

By the courtesy of Mr. J. J. Lister.

TONGAN WIDOW POURING OIL OVER HER HUSBAND'S GRAVE.

By the courtesy of Mr. J. J. Lister.

TONGAN GIRL PLAYING NOSE-FLUTE (*p.* 63).

III

The Position of Women—Racial Influences—Geographical Influences—Sociological Influences—Paumotu—Hawaii—Tonga and Samoa—Kava—Taupou—Society Islands

IN Polynesia, as everywhere else, the position of women is determined by three main factors, racial, geographical, and sociological.

Racial Influences. First note the racial influences :—De Quatrefages describes the Polynesians as a race whose character has remained childlike while its body has matured. They possess both the happy and the unhappy qualities of childhood, the affection, the naïve credulity, the emotional temperament and love of pleasure in all forms ; also ungovernable passions, instinctive aversions, and careless brutality. Their weakness is another childlike character. They lack stamina both physically and psychologically. In spite of their fine appearance their bodily strength is not great, while the small amount of labour they undertake does not produce physical development ; and, notwithstanding their state of constant warfare, they cannot be regarded as a virile race. For this the geographical conditions are no doubt partly responsible.

Geographical Influences. Letourneau points out how the Polynesian islands were both too richly and too poorly endowed to allow man to make much progress. Too rich, because food was abundant and obtained with little labour, and want, that great spur towards progress, did not encourage man to work, either with hands or brain. Too poorly endowed, for the absence of metals set a bar to development of any perfected industry, and the absence of domesticable animals limited the possibilities of advance.

" It was literally an Eden in which men were living, as did Adam and Eve, stupidly, in their earthly Paradise."

But climate and soil and productions are not the same for all. There are the comparatively barren atolls, where there is no fresh water, and only a few coco-nuts will grow, and volcanic islets, where (though

By the courtesy of Mr. J. J. Lister.

SISI AND BOAR'S TUSK PENDANT.

the soil is fertile) the surface is covered with lava; and with these may be contrasted the islands of the Society group, of unparalleled fertility of soil and rank luxuriance of vegetation.

Another important geographical factor is isolation. Next to a tropical climate with its consequent inertia, this is perhaps the most serious bar to racial advance. Isolation of larger areas means stagnation; in the small islands of Polynesia it produces degradation.

In those groups, such as Tonga and Samoa, which have been in touch with other islands, a high grade of civilisation has been attained; and Easter Island, 1,100 miles east of Pitcairn (its nearest neighbour), perhaps exhibits in its "degenerate sons of worthy sires" the other end of the scale.

Sociological Influences.

Among the sociological factors may be noted the influence of religion, the institution of *tabu*, the customs of *kava* drinking, the deference accorded to rank, the very slight regard paid to the bonds of matrimony and the licentious tone of society in general. Since all these factors vary to a certain extent throughout Polynesia, so does the status of woman vary. We may note four typical grades.

Paumotu.

Disadvantageous conditions bear most heavily on the weakest members of a community, and the position of women is hardest where Nature is least benign. In some of the islands to the south-east of Polynesia the conditions of life are unfavourable. Paumotu (or Cloud of Islands) consists of innumerable atolls and islets extending over sixteen degrees of longitude. Many of the atolls have an altitude of only three feet, and in severe storms the sea breaks over them, drowning the inhabitants and making radical changes in the geography. Fresh water is everywhere scarce.

By the courtesy of Mr. J. J. Lister.

GIRL WEARING A SISI AND BOAR'S TUSK PENDANT.

TAHITI GIRLS.

The soil consists of sand and gravel, washed up by the waves. Coco-nuts and fish are the main resources of the population, but on some islets there are no coco-nuts, and only the pandanus grows. Here are some of the rudest and most savage people of the Pacific, and probably nowhere in the world are women more brutally treated. They work from morning to night to provide food for the men, spending all the time on their knees, pounding pandanus nuts, or on the sharp coral, collecting shell-fish and sea-eggs. Polygyny obtains to an unlimited extent; any man of the community might put away one wife and take another at pleasure, and without ceremony. Captain Beechey noted that the offspring of these unions seemed to be the only objects of the men's affection—certainly they had none for their wives. The women were below the common standard of height, and deficient in personal attractions. Tyrannised over, debased, over-worked, neglected, and strangers to social affection, no wonder that all those qualities which in civilised countries constitute the fascinations of women were wanting. It is a significant fact that the women had no ornaments at all, and that they showed no interest in the beads or trinkets offered them by Captain Beechey.

Hawaii.

Next note the influence of geographical conditions on social life in Hawaii. Hawaii consists of a series of islands sufficiently numerous and near together to influence one another decisively, yet far enough apart to make communication difficult. The isolation of the group and the small size of the individual islands tend to develop narrowness of view, energy of inherited habit, persistence of tradition, and conservatism of custom.

The climate is well described by King Kamehameha IV. in a speech at the opening of the Hawaiian Agricultural Society. "Who ever heard of winter on our shores? Where among us shall we find the numberless drawbacks which in less favoured countries the labourer has to contend with? They have no place in our beautiful group, which rests like a water-lily on the swelling bosom of the Pacific. The heaven is tranquil over our heads, and the sun keeps a jealous eye upon us every day, while the rays are so tempered that they never wither prematurely what they have warmed with life." The equability of the Hawaiian climate is shown in the fact that the language possesses no word for "weather."

The genial climate and abundant sunshine tend to beget a cheerful temper, and the Hawaiians are naturally a merry people. Mrs. Bishop describes the girls at school:—"I never saw such a mirthful-looking set of girls. Some were cooking the dinner, some ironing, others reading English aloud; but each occupation seemed a pastime. I cannot convey a notion of the blitheness and independence of manner of the children (to their teachers); to say that they were free and easy would be wrong; it was rather the manner of frolicsome daughters to very indulgent mothers or aunts." This reflects a different aspect of school-life from that in the early "female seminary" at Wailuku, where many girls fell sick, and not a few died. It is pathetic to hear the complaint of the grave New England teacher: "It seems impossible to restrain them from rude and romping behaviour, and confine them to those exercises deemed more proper for females, without serious injury to their health."

Where all seems favourable to man, one might expect Utopia, but Nature in Hawaii spoils her children. Tropical conditions are only favourable to social evolution up to a certain point, beyond this they become a hindrance by removing all spur to further advance. Flowers, music, ease, enough to eat, these constitute the Hawaiian essentials of life, and but little attention is paid to what, in more exacting zones, is called duty.

A tropical climate also tempts people to live mainly out of doors, and, by diminishing the importance of the house and home, tends to sacrifice the interests of the family to those of the community. The communal system thus evolved has the inevitable effect of removing all stimulus to exertion, and paralysing all individual effort. To work more is to be the more pillaged, to save is impossible.

Blackman, in "The Making of Hawaii," after reviewing the various influences affecting social life in Hawaii, says: "We should expect to find woman occupying a middle position, and so we do." On the one hand the descent of rank through females gave women a place of importance, and often elevated them to the topmost station in society, and as queen or regent they might exercise absolutely unlimited power. On the other hand they were hemmed in by conventions, restricted by *tabu*, and deprived of their liberty, merely on account of their sex.

Photograph by C. C. Pierce.

HAWAIIAN DANCERS.

Women were not allowed to eat with men; wives could not eat with their husbands, neither could their food be cooked in the same oven, and the highest lady in the land might not eat with the humblest man. Certain foods were forbidden them, they were not allowed to eat of pork, bananas, coco-nuts, turtle, or certain kinds of fish. Rank had no privilege.

When Kapiolani was a girl she resolved to eat a banana in defiance of the *tabu*, but her crime was discovered, and she was condemned to degradation of rank, perpetual poverty, and celibacy. The ban was, however, removed by the expiatory sacrifice of a young boy.

Although hedged in by oppressive prohibitions imposed by religion the consolations of religious worship were denied. The women were excluded from the *heiau* or temples (which dotted the settled parts so thickly that from the walls of one the next could clearly be seen), as their presence was thought to defile the sacred sites; neither could they, for the same reason, enter two of the six houses which formed the Hawaiian establishment, the house for the family gods, and the men's eating house.

At birth a girl was more unwelcome than a boy, and was less likely to be allowed to live; as a wife the woman was absolutely in the power of her husband, who could divorce her at will. The whole duty of women consisted in ministering slavishly to the pleasures of the dominant sex.

Woman reaches her highest social position in Tonga and Samoa.

Tonga and Samoa.

Samoa possesses all the advantages of climate and soil characteristic of Polynesia. It is healthy, and the means of subsistence are perhaps more easily obtained here than in any other part of the world. It is not subject to the disadvantages of isolation, which retard progress in other groups, and contact with neighbouring peoples has prevented stagnation. The fine harbours and safety of navigation in the sheltered waters developed the migratory impulse, leading to that widening of ideas which is essential to social advance. Though the Samoans now confine their voyaging within their own group, the number of colonies claiming Samoan descent which sprinkle the Pacific shows that this was not always the case, and tales recount intercommunication with Tonga and Fiji. A strong government had established law and order long before the coming of the whites, as is shown by the homogeneity of custom and language throughout the group, and the punctilious attention to etiquette and ceremony are characteristic of a high grade of culture. In habits of cleanliness and decency the Samoans are more advanced than the most fastidious of civilised nations. Their public meetings and discussions are carried on with a dignity and forbearance which Europeans never equal, and even in the heat of war they have shown themselves amenable to the influence of reason and religion.

By the courtesy of Mr. J. J. Lister.

A TONGAN MOTHER AND CHILD.

Tonga does not possess all the natural advantages of Samoa; it lacks the fine harbours, and it is surrounded by dangerous reefs, but this has not daunted the development of a fine race of boat-builders and sailors. The climate also is less healthy, and the land is in parts absolutely barren, as the result of recent lava flows. But the inhabitants have an advantage over the Samoans in another direction, for they appear to be a more mixed people, and to blend the culture of the Polynesians with the greater intelligence and vigour of the Melanesians. The less attractive character of their climate and soil has probably been a blessing in disguise; it has had the twofold result of encouraging native energy, and of discouraging too great an intrusion of whites, and the Tongans surpass all the other South Sea islanders in mental development.

Women are the gainers by this advance. They have considerable regard paid them on account of their sex, independently of their rank. As Mariner quaintly phrases it: "They are considered to contribute much to the comfort and domestic happiness of the other sex, and as they are the weaker of the two, it is thought unmanly not to show them an attention and kind regard. They are therefore not subjected to hard labour or any menial work. The men work, and the women do chiefly those offices which are requisite for domestic comfort and for the promotion of health and cleanliness."

Instead of women being shut out from the sacred rites which their presence would defile, we read of the "extremely religious and universally respected Foonagi," whose knowledge of all religious matters was so accurate that chiefs used to come to consult her on such topics, and her advice on political matters was also prized. Women often went to battle with their husbands, mainly to be of assistance if they were wounded, but if taken prisoners were well treated. Stevenson noted in Samoa how the women were respected in war: "They are suffered to pass between the hostile camps, exchanging gossip, spreading rumours, and divulging to either army the secret councils of the other." The Tongan women were not deficient in valour. Mariner records the impassioned speech of a woman of Vavau who, when the people were discussing the proposal to throw off the yoke of Finow in revenge of his murder of their chief, rushed into the assembly, demanding why they hesitated when honour pointed out the only course to pursue, "but if men are turned women, the women shall turn men, and revenge the death of the murdered chief; let then the men stand idly looking on, and when we women are sacrificed in the glorious cause, our example may perhaps excite them to fight and die in the same spirited endeavour to support and defend their rights."

Music and Dancing in Tonga.

The Polynesian love of pleasure manifests itself most characteristically in a devotion to dances, accompanied by songs and musical instruments, which play an important part in social life. But these are less conspicuous in Tonga than in Samoa, from whence a great number of the Tongan dances derive their origin, and the indigenous Tongan *oóla* was only danced by men. Among Tongan musical instruments is one of special interest, since it seems in certain islands to be played only by women, and also to indicate a culture drift from Asia to Polynesia. This is the nose-flute which occurs in various islands from Tahiti to Fiji and New Zealand, and which is illustrated, as played by a Tongan girl, on p. 57. It is usually made of bamboo, with three or more stops, and it is blown by one nostril, while the other is closed by the thumb. Professor Tylor suggests that the origin of this custom may be traced to India, where a high-caste Hindu will not touch with his mouth a pipe or flute which has touched the mouth of a lower-caste man who made it or may have used it, but it does not defile him to blow it with his nostril.

The Samoan Housewife.

The position of woman among the Samoans is, when all things are considered, not only satisfactory but enviable. The Samoan housewife is by no means the drudge and beast of burden which women in other rude communities are; she has a voice in affairs. In matters concerning the family well-being

By the courtesy of Mr. J. J. Lister.

TONGAN GIRL.

With hair cut and stiffened in Fijian style.

she is consulted ; she has the right to advise and vote on terms as free as those allowed to her brother. She may rise to a position of dignity and authority in the community. She may be chosen its *taupou* (or maid of the village), and as such is as much a part of the system of government as is the chief ; honours are her official portion. She is sought in marriage by the great, her nuptials cement alliances. The first of Samoans to attain supreme authority, to become possessed of all four royal names, was Salamasina, a woman.

Such are the chances of the woman in public life. Her domestic cares are summed up in the duty of the housewife. Hers the task to wade the lagoon for the smaller fish, to weave the mats, to beat the bark into cloth, to cook, to manage the affairs of the home. These tasks are not burdensome, and there is no idea of menial occupation. With all her dignities and honours the *taupou* may be seen on her knees pulling up the weeds in the pavement before the guest house where she exercises the rites of hospitality, and the wife of the chief of highest rank hunts for sea-urchins by the side of the wife of the meanest commoner.

The Samoan family rises at dawn, and the first duty of the housewife is to tidy the house by rolling up the mats and putting away the wooden pillows, which serve not only as head rests and to preserve an elaborate coiffure from disarrangement, but also to tether each sleeper to his or her proper place on the common mat. After the morning bath and breakfast she spends an hour or so weeding in front of the house, interspersed with gossiping. During the day she is employed in various ways, fetching water, making mats, or in the proper season beating out the bark for cloth, and, if the tide is low, searching the lagoon and reef with the other women of the village for shell-fish and sea-slugs. Or her wardrobe may require replenishing, and she will sit down to make a new *lavalava*, or a *faloka* ("Mother Hubbard" frock). Or her deft fingers may contrive a hat of native materials, which she will wear "with the gaudy humility of the converted soul," when next she goes to church, for that is the conventional sign of the woman who has got religion and joined the church. In certain seasons men and women spend from early morning to perhaps midday in the yam or taro patches or banana plantations, but this only occupies a few days in the year. All this with visiting and receiving of visits together with a good amount of solid sleeping, and the preparation of the evening meal, finishes the day.

No account of social life in Samoa is complete without a description of its central features, *kava* and the *taupou*. *Kava* (or *'ava* as the Samoans call it) is the necessary part of every ceremony, no festival is complete without it, no war may be fought or even determined on if the *kava* has not been rightly served, and the beginnings of peace are in the *kava* bowl. A visitor must always carry with him his three pieces to present to his host, who, in his turn, never fails to present *kava* to his guest.

Kava.

The drink is made of the roots of the *Piper methysticum*, and in old days it was "masticated by the pearly teeth of flower-clad maidens," but this practice has been stopped by the missionaries, and is now only to be found in out-of-the-way parts. Near Apia the *kava* pounding stones form prominent items in domestic furniture, as in the illustration on p. 66. At a ceremonial *kava*-drinking the root, reduced to a coarse powder and a mass of fibre, is placed in the large bowl, or *tanoa*, carved out of a solid piece of hard wood, and the *taupou* (the girl chosen to act as official hostess of the village) proceeds to the mixing of the beverage with the addition of water. This is stirred and squeezed and then strained with a bunch of hibiscus fibres, and the grace with which the wet mop of fibres is whirled round her head is one of the accomplishments of the *taupou*. When the *kava* is ready the master of the ceremonies begins his task, which is to call out the names of those to whom the drink is to be served in turn, and any slight mistake

WOMEN OF RENNELL ISLAND (POLYNESIA).
DRAWN BY NORMAN H. HARDY.

Facing on page 64

in the order, or in the complicated forms of address or other intricacies of etiquette, might entail grave consequences. As each name is called, the *taupou* fills the coco-nut cup by dipping the bunch of fibres into the bowl and squeezing it into the cup, held by her attendant, who carries it to each recipient. And so on, with each episode thickly overlaid with ceremonial, until all have partaken. *Kava* has been described as a perfect outrage to a critical eye, a turbid, yellowish-green liquid, with a dull earthy odour, a taste of soapsuds with a curious twang of ginger, leaving a not unpleasant sense of smoothness in the mouth. It seems to fail in sedative, stimulating, or intoxicating qualities, though some claim for it the virtues of a tonic. Large quantities of fresh *kava* taken in excess produce partial paralysis of the lower limbs.

The social influence can perhaps scarcely be over-estimated, and it has contributed not a little to the better qualities of Samoan social life. As a means of promoting peaceful relations, and cementing friendships between one tribe or one village and another, as an opportunity for friendly contact with neighbours and with strangers, as a ceremony in which both sexes had definite responsibilities, and played their parts with dignity, and as a national recreation accompanied by none of the common abuses of wasteful extravagance, intoxication, sexual licence, quarrelling or other relics of barbarism, *kava* drinking has no superior in the Pacific.

By the courtesy of Mr. J. J. Lister.

TONGAN DANCE.

The Taupou.

As has been seen throughout these pages the institution of the *taupou* or official maid of the village is a prominent feature in Samoa. Each village elects a girl, who must be the daughter of a chief, or occasionally certain great chiefs have the right of appointing some girl of high birth. The *taupou* has a large house provided for her in the village, and has control of all the women and girls in it. Here she resides more or less, with her court of young girls, and she never goes anywhere unless accompanied by an elderly woman. No man belonging to the village is allowed to enter the house.

In all the village festivities, and especially when visits are exchanged between villages, the *taupou* and her court play an important part. One of her chief duties is to receive strangers, to entertain them, and to make the *kava* without which no Samoan ceremony is complete. If a visit is paid to a neighbouring village, the orator heads the procession of girls, calling out the name and rank and titles of the official maid.

The *taupou* herself is a sort of village property, and a model of virtue to all the other girls. It is her duty to attract courting parties from other villages, with their many presents. Eventually she will be married to some young chief who presents so many hundred pigs, which are divided amongst the village, and in return her friends contribute so many hundred fine mats for the relations of the bridegroom. Dancing is one of the duties of the *taupou*. She is instructed in all the poses of the dance by her duenna; her scanty wardrobe is largely made up of material which shall adorn her for the dance, and the court of attendant girls are carefully trained to accompany her in the *siva*. She is not a soloist in these performances, for there is no distribution of parts, but she is the central figure of the group, and the leader of the concerted movements of the party. Her dancing is one of the things about which her village boasts in order to attract suitors, the poets of the village write verses about it, and sing them as they travel by canoe in front of other villages.

By the courtesy of Mr. J. J. Lister.

KAVA PARTY, TONGA.
With stones for pounding the root.

The *siva* is a dance of the upper body, which is danced sitting, and the feet and legs move only slightly to keep time. The number of possible motions of the body and arms is limited only by the flexibility of the muscles of the dancers and their ideas of what is graceful. A backward curve of the outstretched hand, such as is attained by

By the courtesy of Mr. J. J. Lister

SAMOAN DANCE, THE SIVA

The dancers sit : all the movements are made with the upper part of the body.

the dancer on the left of the picture on p. 47, is very much admired.

Society Islands.

A description of social life in Tahiti demonstrates how much mankind owes to Eve, and that it is not good for man to live in the Garden of Eden. All travellers agree in praising the island as a veritable paradise, in which a healthy and delightful climate brings to maturity all the products of the tropics, which are nowhere to be found in greater luxuriance and perfection. The men suit well with the landscape, for they represent the most beautiful type of Polynesian, but it is noticeable that the gentle Hawaiians are called manly in comparison.

Indolence and sensuality are the curse of the inhabitants. "Why should we work?" they said to Captain Beechey. "Have we not as much breadfruit, coconuts, bananas, etc., as we can eat? It is very good for you to work who want fine clothes or fine ships, but we are content with what we possess."

The clubs or secret societies of the men are often found to reflect the dominant interests of the community, and it is significant that the objective of the most important society of the group, the Areois, was indulgence in sexual excesses.

When women are valued merely for the sake of their sexual attractions, their position is not likely to be one of dignity, though their lives may be free from hardship; and in the eyes of a moralist the Tahitian women exemplify the lowest stage of degradation to which Polynesian women could sink. This is where civilisation found them, and it is doubtful if it has brought them much benefit. The prevention of war, and a perhaps injudicious prohibition of all forms of native entertainment, have quenched the only outlets for Tahitian energy, and idleness and sensual indulgence are the only means of recreation. The men have lost much of their cheerfulness,

Photograph by Kerry, Sydney.

SAMOAN TAUPOU, OR CHIEF GIRLS.

and the women much of their beauty, while manners and morals remain much the same.

Under these circumstances the race is doomed. The birthrate is low, sterility is common, and epidemics and intemperance have slain their thousands. As a native proverb says, "The coral waxes, the palm grows, and man departs." Too often the native races may be likened, in the words of Stevenson, to "a shopful of crockery, launched upon the stream of time, that now fall to make their desperate voyage among pots of brass and adamant."

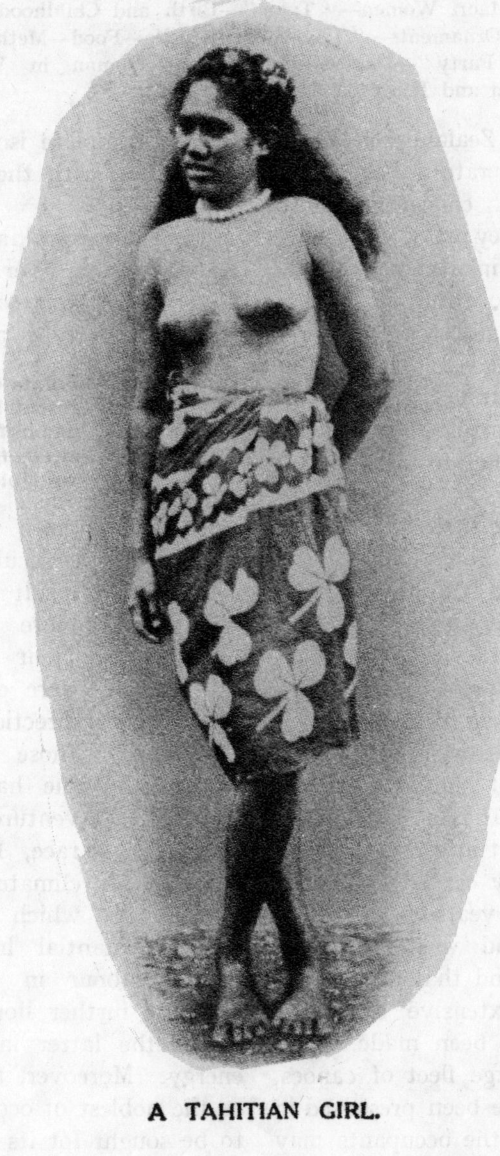

A TAHITIAN GIRL.

NEW ZEALAND

By T. ATHOL JOYCE

New Zealand and the Polynesians—Points of Resemblance and Difference between the Maori and Polynesians—Position of Maori Women—"Tapu"—Birth and Childhood—Tattoo—The Sacred Art of Weaving—Dress—Ornaments—"Tiki"—Daily Life—Food—Methods of Preserving and Cooking—A Maori "Party"—Dances—Cannibalism—Woman in War—Marriage Customs—The story of Tutanekai and Hinemoa

New Zealand and the Polynesians.

THE natives of New Zealand, or Maori, have been—at any rate as far as historical times are concerned—Polynesians; and though they have very much in common with the inhabitants of the islands to the north-west, their culture, nevertheless, exhibits such important peculiarities that they demand a chapter to themselves.

The date at which the first representatives of the Polynesian race arrived in the islands cannot, of course, be determined with accuracy; but one authority, drawing his arguments from a mass of tribal tradition and history collected in all parts of the Pacific, believes it to have been about 850 A.D. At any rate, it is comparatively certain that during the years 1250-1325, New Zealand was frequently visited by Polynesians, and that about 1350 took place the most extensive colonising movement that had yet been made. This was the arrival of a large fleet of canoes, the names of which have been preserved in tradition, and of which the occupants may be regarded, for all practical purposes, as the founders of the Maori nation. From that date until the arrival of the European the settlers lived in complete isolation, holding no communication with the rest of Polynesia.

Photograph by Muir & Moodie, Dunedin.

MAORI GIRL.

Seated by the central pillar of the verandah of a house.

Points of resemblance and difference between the Maori and Polynesians.

The Maori, speaking generally, very closely resembled the other Polynesians, yet there was considerable variation of type amongst them, and the hair showed a tendency to curliness (*see* p. 71); they were also more finely built and more muscular, probably as the result of lives spent under more strenuous conditions. Their psychological qualities were developed in a similar direction. Descended from those who must have been the hardiest and most adventurous of the Polynesian race, living in a temperate climate under circumstances which required them to build more substantial houses, and to expend greater labour in cultivation than their relations further north, they naturally surpassed the latter in initiative and native energy. Moreover, the glorification of war as the noblest of occupations, as something to be sought for its own sake, fostered the military spirit and rendered them fierce and, at times, cruel and bloodthirsty. Family and racial pride was a marked characteristic

Photograph by Muir & Moodie, Dunedin.

MAORI WOMEN AND GIRLS.

On the veranda of a house. The group shows the variation in type of hair.

of the aristocracy, but it was often accompanied by a certain nobility of character which would be praiseworthy in peoples at the highest stage of civilisation.

The Maori of To-day.

It will be noticed that in speaking of these people the past tense has been employed; this is because the march of civilisation, which has proved less fatal to the Maori than the rest of the Polynesians, has practically destroyed all their ancient customs. Indeed, families of pure race are rare, most have at least a slight strain of white blood in their veins. Their old industries have practically vanished, and even their dances have greatly deteriorated. Still, they have a stake in the fortunes of the country, in-so-far as they send members to Parliament. The women, however, unlike their white sisters, have not been admitted to the suffrage.

The position of the Maori woman in the tribe was unusually high for a primitive people, and her influence was correspondingly great. The women took an active part in all the business of life, sharing in the work and the amusements of the men, assisting in the defence of their fortified villages, and accompanying war-parties on expeditions. Moreover, their advice was sought on all matters, public as well as domestic; in fact, it was by no means reckoned extraordinary for a woman to take part in the deliberations of the war-council. Women of high rank were particularly important, since they brought both position and wealth to their husbands. In default of a male successor, a woman could become chief, transmitting the dignity to her children.

Position of Maori Women.

Maori women were very affectionate as sisters, wives and mothers, and suicide upon the death of a husband or brother was a very common occurrence in the old days. But they were also passionate and jealous; and it is to be feared that they were often cruel in their treatment of their slaves for this reason: cases have even been known where a woman has killed her baby to spite her husband.

Before passing to a consideration of woman's life in detail, a few words must

Photograph by Muir & Moodie, Dunedin.

TYPICAL MAORI WOMAN.

be said about an institution which played a most important part in Maori life in general—the institution called *tapu*. To say that persons, objects, or places were *tapu* means that they were sacred, but with a peculiar and dangerous form of sanctity; they became under certain conditions charged with holiness as with electricity, which was communicated to any person who touched them, and either rendered him equally *tapu*, or even—in the case of persons of lower rank—killed him outright. In this way the high chiefs were always *tapu*, and for a common man to touch any of their possessions spelt death. So firmly fixed was this belief that cases are known where individuals who had unwittingly used some utensil belonging to a chief died of sheer fright when their mistake became known to them. Everything connected with death was invested with a very strong form of *tapu*, and those who had taken part in a funeral were isolated until the *tapu* was removed by a priest.

"Tapu."

Priests and chiefs could lay the *tapu* on persons, objects and places; thus *tapu* became a most useful administrative weapon. For instance, all crops were *tapu* until they were ripe, when the *tapu* was removed and they could be reaped; individuals engaged in a particular piece of work, whether connected with agriculture, hunting or fishing, were made *tapu* so that they could neither leave the place nor engage in any other occupation until it was finished. Persons under *tapu* were usually fed by someone who was not, or had to pick their food off the ground with their mouths; they dare not touch it with their hands lest the *tapu* become communicated to the food, and the latter prove fatal to them.

It is impossible to follow the ramifications of this interesting belief into all the departments of life in which it was active; enough has been said to give a general idea of its character and to show the important place it held in the Maori world.

Birth and Childhood among the Maori.

To return to the Maori woman. As a baby, her advent into the world was not always regarded as a subject for rejoicing; as among so many primitive peoples, and others also, the parents were usually disappointed because she was not a boy. In fact, under certain circumstances, a girl was not considered worth rearing, and the unhappy infant was not permitted to live. If she were spared, she was dipped in the sacred stream outside the village by the priest; this ceremony rendered the mother and child *tapu*, and they were isolated for a few days in a special hut, called by the poetic name of "nest-house." Then a similar ceremony, accompanied by invocations, were necessary to remove the *tapu*. Later a third "baptism" was performed, at which the baby received her name.

As a child and young girl her lot was usually a happy one; she was treated with affection and kindness and even "spoiled" by her parents, and spent much of her time in playing various games with her companions, boys and girls together. Some of these amusements bore a close resemblance to games well-known in Europe; for instance, peg-tops, cats-cradle, giant-stride, skipping, stilts, hide-and-seek, and a kind of "up Jenkins." There was also a game played with the fingers, resembling somewhat the Italian game of *mora*; it was played by two persons, and the object was to hold up certain fingers on the pronunciation of certain words by the opponent. Another game, called *poi*, was played with balls attached to strings, the players were seated, and various evolutions were performed to the accompaniment of singing. In fact, many games were played to an appropriate song; and one of these is quoted by Taylor,* the well-known writer, in his description of a game called *puni-puni*, "a game played with the fingers whilst the following words are sung:—

'By the great water,
'By the long water,
'The sea-gull and the penguin cry,
'Where is the entering,
'Where is the closing,
'For the resting.'

If the fingers enter each other whilst these words are being uttered, the game is ended; if not, it is again repeated."

But more serious considerations enter early into the life of a New Zealand

Photograph by Muir & Moodie, Dunedin.

A CHIEF AND HIS WIFE.
The latter being of the curly-haired type.

girl; if she belongs to a family of high position, she must be tattooed; and since tatooing is an important ceremony, and performed in a peculiar manner in this country, it deserves a special paragraph to itself. In the rest of Polynesia, as in other countries inhabited by a comparatively fair-skinned people, a number of small punctures were made in the skin and the colouring matter rubbed in; but in New Zealand the process was far more

Tattoo.

* *Te Ika a Maui.*

painful: regular grooves were cut by means of an instrument pointed with bone and shaped like a diminutive adze, which was struck with a small mallet. The blood flowed freely, and was wiped off with a

Photograph by Muir & Moodie, Dunedin

TYPICAL MAORI WOMAN OF HIGH RANK.

Showing tattoo on chin. Note the feathers in the hair.

tuft of flax, the pattern being indicated by dark lines drawn on the skin. After this the dark pigment, in the form of powder, was applied. Girls were tattooed on the lips and chin, as shown in the above illustration, and occasionally on the thighs and breast also. Though the process was far less severe in their case than in that of the men, the operation was productive of a great deal of suffering and inflammation. The subject was regarded as under a heavy *tapu*, and the work was accompanied by numerous incantations; in the case of the daughter of an important chief, a slave was sometimes sacrificed. The pattern of the tattoo was traditional and the various lines were cut in a definite order, each group being known by a particular name.

The education of the girl was left mainly in the hands of her mother, but there was one occupation which partook of a sacred nature, regarding which special arrangements were made. This was the manufacture of the various mats which formed the principal clothing of men and women alike. In New Zealand, says Hamilton,* "The Maori found provided a plant which served him almost as well as the *aute* and palms of his fatherland. In his ingenious and industrious hands it clothed him with mats and garments of bewildering variety, and so entered into his daily life that one of the early Maori visitors to England, when he found that the New Zealand flax did not grow there, wondered how it was possible to live in a land so unfortunate. From the records of voyagers and from native traditions we know that, even in the long ago, the fibre of the *phormium* (*harakeke*) was skilfully prepared and manufactured into all sorts of articles. For the mats of people of rank specially selected varieties were cultivated and prepared with infinite labour, until the resulting fibre was as soft and lustrous as silk."

The Sacred Art of Weaving.

Though men were occasionally trained in the complicated rules of weaving, the latter was essentially the work of the women, and, as such, a short description is necessary. Selected leaves of the plant were cut with a shell in winter, and carried home from the plantation to be scraped until only the fibre remained. Only a portion of the leaf was used, and the implement employed was a mussel-shell. The resultant fibre was alternately soaked in running water and scraped again and again until it was quite clean, when it was hung up to dry and bleach. "The observant and discriminating powers of the old Maori," writes Hamilton,† "are well shown when one examines the long list of some fifty or sixty kinds of flax known to them, and notices that the various qualities and strengths were all recognised and allotted to suitable and specific purposes." The fibres were beaten with mallets, and if a coloured pattern, such as frequently

* "Maori Art." † *Loc. cit.*

MAORI GIRL : NEW ZEALAND.
DRAWN BY NORMAN H. HARDY.

Facing on page 74

appears on the borders of mats, was desired, were stained red or yellow by means of different varieties of bark, or black by means of bark followed by immersion in a particular kind of mud. The fibres were formed into thread by being rolled with the hand on the thigh, and sometimes two threads were twisted together to form a two-ply cord. The material was then ready for weaving.

Instruction in weaving was, as has been said, of a sacred nature, and the services of the priest were in requisition to pronounce the necessary incantations, by means of which the mind of the pupil was supposed to become especially receptive. The sacred nature attaching to the occupation was never subsequently forgotten, and many were the rules which the operator had to observe under penalty of supernatural punishment. The apparatus was of the simplest: two sticks supported the threads which formed the warp, and the weft was manipulated by the hand alone. The process resembled plaiting rather than weaving proper, the cloth being of the variety known as "tied-cloth." The feathers of the Kiwi were often incorporated in the work, and, at a later date, those of fowls, the latter arranged so as to form patterns; or strips of dog-skin with the hair attached might be fastened along the exterior surface, or flax-stems to form a kind of thatch (*see* on the right of illustration, p. 79).

Maori Dress.

From the question of weaving we pass naturally to that of dress, which consisted almost invariably of two of these mats, one fastened round the waist, and the other round the neck to form a sort of cloak, which could be quickly discarded if the wearer wished to engage in any work. Practically the only difference between the dress of men and women lay in the fact that in the case of the former this upper mat was fastened on the right shoulder; in the case of the latter on the left (*see* p. 71). Children dispensed with clothing altogether until about eight years of age.

The hair of women was left to grow long (p. 72), though girls used to cut the locks on the forehead in a fringe level with the eyebrows (*see* p. 71); those of high rank often wore two of the tail feathers of the *Huia* bird in their dusky tresses. Such feathers were greatly prized, and were kept stored in finely-carved wooden caskets, of which specimens can be seen in most museums.

Ornaments.

The ears were pierced, and a great variety of ornaments worn in them, of which the most valued were those of jade (*see* p. 72), owing to the enormous time and labour expended in the preparation of a single specimen. Jade is one of the hardest stones known, and it must be remembered that the Maori possessed no metals until the arrival of the Europeans.

Photograph by Muir & Moodie, Dunedin.

NATIVE FOOD STORE.

Other objects so worn were the down of the albatross and gannet, the wings of smaller birds, sharks' teeth, flowers, and the teeth of husbands or valued friends or relations.

"Tiki."

Perhaps the ornament most characteristic of the Maori is the jade pendant known as *Tiki*, which was worn round the neck. These *Tiki* were grotesque human figures of a prescribed and somewhat conventional pattern, and were beautifully worked and polished (*see* p. 79). Each one of them must have taken literally years of patient toil to produce.

They were regarded as heirlooms, and were passed from father to son, and the sentimental value attached to them was enormous; though usually worn by men, they were frequently seen on the necks of females, especially heiresses or those of chiefly rank. The *Tiki* was suspended round the neck by a cord of woven flax, fastened at the back by a toggle of bone, either human or taken from the Moa, the gigantic ground-bird, somewhat resembling an ostrich, which has been extinct for many years. *Tiki* were occasionally made from part of the human skull, but examples are very rare.

Maori Daily Life.

As regards the general routine of daily work in times of peace, a passage from Maning * is well worth quotation: "In the morning, but not early, they descended from the hill *pa* (fort) to the cultivations in the low ground; they went in a body, armed like men going to a battle, the spear or club in one hand, the agricultural implement in the other; the women followed. Long before night (it was counted unlucky to work till dark) they returned to the hill, with a reversed order, the women now and slaves and lads bearing fuel and water for the night in front; they also bore, probably, heavy loads of *kumera* or other provisions. In the time of year when the crops did not call for their attention, when they were planted and growing, then the whole tribe would remove to some fortified hill, at the side of some river, or on the coast, where they would pass months fishing, making nets, clubs, spears, and implements of various descriptions; the women in all spare time making mats for clothing, or baskets to carry the crop of *kumera* in, when fit to dig. There was very little idleness, and to be called 'lazy' was a great reproach."

* "Old New Zealand."

Food of the Maori.

The preparation of food was regarded as almost essentially woman's work, and this subject might be extended to fill a whole volume by itself. The food of the Maori was mainly fish and vegetables; meat was a great dainty, but, beside the dog, the largest mammal found on the island in the early days was the rat. Later, after the introduction of the pig and goat by Captain Cook, the former was considered an especial delicacy. Most birds were eaten, the few that were spared being supposed to contain the souls of deceased ancestors; in fact, the extermination of the Moa is due to the ardour with which it was hunted by the natives. Practically all fish were eaten, and the large eels with which the country abounds were regarded with especial favour. Of vegetable foods, which are too numerous to mention in detail, one of the most important was the root of the edible fern. This was only eaten fresh in times of scarcity, and was usually stored in shelters above ground for a year. Before cooking, it was steeped in water and dried in the sun, then roasted on the embers, scraped with a shell and pounded with a mallet of stone or wood to loosen the fibres; in some cases the fibres were removed after pounding. Sweet potatoes also formed an important article of diet, and there is a long list of berries and other fruits which were prepared in various ways. So accustomed had the Maori become to regard the root of a plant as the edible part, that, according to Bishop Marsden, when corn was introduced, the natives became impatient of waiting for the crop, and tore up the green stalks in the expectation of finding the produce at the roots.

Cooking was usually performed by means of steam, in the manner general throughout Polynesia and illustrated on this page. A circular hole was dug, in which a wood fire was kindled, stones were thrown on, which, by the time the fire had died down, had become red-hot. They were then removed, and the embers scraped out. Then the stones, still glowing, were replaced, covered with leaves, and water sprinkled over them; on these the food was placed, meat or eels being wrapped in leaves to keep in the gravy; a layer of leaves plentifully sprinkled with water followed, then another of mats or old baskets; finally earth was piled on the top to prevent the steam from escaping.

Photograph by Muir & Moodie, Dunedin.

THE MAORI METHOD OF COOKING.

The food, wrapped in leaves, was placed on stones previously heated.

There were two meals in the day, except in times of plenty: one in the morning, the other just before sunset.

During the time the food was cooking, which rarely exceeded an hour, the women plaited baskets of green flax or leaves in which to serve the food. Chiefs had each a separate basket, but usually there was one to every four or five individuals. They eat in silence and rapidly, the women apart from the men, and slaves apart from their masters. If there were guests, they formed a separate group, since it was not etiquette for their hosts to eat with them. Fingers were the only implements, and the question of table-napkins was solved in a very simple manner—the back of the nearest dog provided ample accommodation for this purpose.

Methods of Preserving and Cooking.

There were various methods of preserving fish and birds; the former were dipped in sea-water and dried in the sun or smoked, and shell-fish were treated in the same manner. The so-called mutton-bird was cooked and preserved in its own fat in vessels of bark, and pigeons were boned and similarly stored. An important article of diet, especially in times of scarcity, was shell-fish; these were eaten fresh or were dried as other fish.

Where hot springs were found, boiling was also practised, and roasting was universal, though regarded rather in the light of a make-shift. If hot water was required for any purpose, and no hot spring was handy, water was boiled by means of hot stones dropped in the wooden water-vessels. Apart from the question of cooking, the hot springs afforded a quite luxurious form of hot baths, of which the natives were very fond (*see* p. 80).

A Maori "Party."

Apart from weaving and cooking, there is little which can be described as essentially the work of the women, but since they shared in the feasts and the various ceremonies which accompanied these festive occasions, the formalities which accompanied the visit of one friendly tribe to another may legitimately be described in this connection. The invitation was usually sent by a herald, great stores of food were prepared against the arrival of the guests, and sometimes large stages were erected on which the provisions were placed. We are told that in 1836 a feast was witnessed at which 8,000 baskets of potatoes, 500,000 eels, 800 pigs, and 15 casks of tobacco were counted.

Before the party entered the fort the women collected on some stage or hillock, waving branches and shouting the cry of welcome. They then walked to the chief open space, and the peculiar ceremony of the *tangi* was performed. This consisted of the visitors and guests sitting down in pairs, embracing and indulging in more or less prolonged lamentations. Such *tangis* always accompanied the reception of a returning war-party or, indeed, any individuals or body of friends who had been absent for some time. If the parting had been of long duration the women would cut themselves with shells or pieces of obsidian, often inflicting severe wounds. The *tangi* has been described as "the chief amusement of the females."

After the *tangi* the hosts proceeded to greet the guests in the customary fashion, by pressing noses together (*see* p. 79), and the distribution of food followed, which was either made by a "master of ceremonies," or the food was brought by a procession of women, including, if the guests were important, those of high rank. Presents of great value were sometimes distributed, which were received as if snatched from an enemy, but it was expected that their equivalent should be returned upon some future occasion.

Maori Dances.

Often such feasts were important political meetings, and were accompanied by long speeches on the part of the chiefs. Dances, too, formed a prominent feature of the ceremonies, as, indeed, at all festal gatherings. These were performed by men or women, or by both in common. They were usually descriptive. For instance, a canoe voyage might be acted; the launch of the canoe would be depicted, followed by incidents on the journey, the various vicissitudes experienced by the voyagers at the hands of the elements, and the safe conclusion of the journey. The principal feature of the dance was the remarkable time kept by the dancers, who ordered their movements with a precision almost incredible, and far surpassing the evolutions of the most highly-trained European troops. Dances were almost always accompanied by a song which formed a running commentary upon the actions of the dancers.

The dance-song, or *Haka*, was the chief amusement of the maidens and youths of

Photograph by Muir & Moodie, Dunedin

THE NATIVE FORM OF GREETING—PRESSING NOSES.
Note the *tiki* ornament worn by two of the women.

a village on fine evenings. Their hair decked with flowers and feathers, their faces with paint and flower-petals, they sat down in a row, and a few chosen voices would start the song, the rest joining in chorus.

Referring once more to food, the Maori were great cannibals, and two circumstances contributed to this. Firstly, the scarcity of animal food on the island; and secondly, perhaps chiefly, the idea that the greatest insult to be offered to an enemy was to eat him. But women usually abstained by custom from human flesh—at any rate, among many tribes, though the chief woman of the tribe sometimes partook ceremonially of the feast.

Cannibalism.

In war, the chief business of the life of the men, women played little part, except as an incentive. They accompanied expeditions as food carriers, but did not engage in fight. In the defence of a fort they had a more important function—that of guarding against the risk of fire. It was the custom for the assailants to attempt to set the fort in flames by means of red-hot stones cast from slings, and the women were employed to guard against this danger with calabashes of water ready to hand. But usually, if an opportunity

The Maori Woman in War.

Photograph by Muir & Moodie, Dunedin.

A NATURAL TURKISH BATH.

A hot spring at Lake Taupo.

offered, they were sent away to a safe place before the attack.

Less attractive was their share in the slaughter of prisoners. This was dictated by the law of recompense, an ordinance which, in every department of life, was carried to an extreme which often seems ridiculous to us.

As an instance of the common practice according to which any woman who had lost a relative or husband in battle could claim one or more victims among the prisoners, may be mentioned the incident quoted by Taylor. "When Hongi returned from a war expedition, the widow of one of his chiefs who had fallen in battle rushed down to the canoe as it approached, loudly demanding *utu* (satisfaction) for her husband's death. There were many captives on board. She jumped into a canoe with a hatchet in her hand, the poor fellows, knowing that their doom was sealed, without a murmur, of their own accord, laid their heads over the side of the canoe, and met their fate at her hands. Sixteen thus fell victims to her fury."

but the marriage of a high-born woman with a male slave was considered very disgraceful. Perhaps the reason was that a man became raised in status by union with a woman of superior rank, while the position of a woman remained unaltered by marriage.

Girls usually married within their own nation. If members of two different nations desired to become man and wife, the consent of both nations was necessary. In any

Photograph by Muir & Moodie, Dunedin.

A MAORI CHIEF'S HOUSE ON THE WANGANUI RIVER.

Of comparatively modern construction, though in the old style.

case, the brothers of the lady were the persons whose goodwill it was most necessary to cultivate. The most time-honoured method was for the man to assemble his friends and carry off his beloved, and even in cases where the affair had been arranged, a mock struggle ensued in which the lady must have had rather a bad time. Where the resistance was genuine the poor girl was often seriously injured out of spite, or even killed, by the members of the party who found themselves in danger of being overpowered. Sometimes the father simply told his intended son-in-law that he might come and live with his daughter, in which case the man became one of his wife's tribe; and it often happened that a man would lose his wife by refusing to comply with this condition. In any case,

Maori Marriage Customs.

And now for the question of marriage. It seems strange that among this people, where most events of daily life bore a semi-religious character, and were accompanied by incantations, marriage was purely a civil matter, and the services of the priest were not in requisition. Unmarried girls were allowed great freedom, and were permitted to have lovers, but married women were expected to remain faithful to their husbands. Among the higher ranks polygamy was the rule—indeed, the importance of a chief was, in a measure, determined by the number of his wives. Each of them had her own farm and retainers, according to her rank, and contributed to the maintenance of his establishment. Among these wives slaves were frequently found, the act of marriage was constituted by the man taking the girl to his house.

As a rule, girls married young, brides of ten years old were not infrequent, and the girl had little choice in the matter—the match was usually arranged by her relations. Love matches, however, were known, and there exist romantic stories, of which the most charming, a sort of inverted Hero and Leander tale, may be given in conclusion. It is the story of the loves of Tutanekai and Hinemoa, as related to Sir George Grey.*

The Story of Tutanekai and Hinemoa.

In a village on the borders of Lake Rotorua lived a maiden of high rank and incomparable beauty named Hinemoa. Proud of her and of their own standing, her relations had not affianced her to a chief, because they could not find one whom they considered worthy to be her husband. On the island of Mokoia, in the middle of the lake, lived a chief who had five sons, one of whom, called Tutanekai, was believed to be illegitimate. This Tutanekai was a skilled performer on the trumpet, and he was accustomed to solace himself with music in the night-time, seated on a balcony which he had erected on the high hillside. His companion on these occasions was his bosom friend Tiki, who was also a musician, an accomplished flute-player.

Now Tutanekai and his brothers each separately resolved to win the love of Hinemoa—they had opportunities of meeting her when the tribes were assembled together on festal occasions—but none of them knew that Hinemoa had fallen in love with Tutanekai at the first moment she set eyes upon him. Both of them were shy, and each feared to make the first advances. So matters stood for some time, and Hinemoa would spend the evening listening to the music of her beloved Tutanekai wafted across the lake by the soft night-breeze.

Tutanekai at last took courage and sent a message to Hinemoa, telling her of his passion, and found that his love was returned. Shortly after this, when Tutanekai's brothers were boasting each that he was the favoured suitor, the former could keep silence no longer, and exclaimed: "No, it is I whom she loves; I have pressed her hand, and she has pressed mine in answer."

His brothers ridiculed the notion, and taunted him with the stories which were current concerning his parentage. Fired by their jests, he sent a message to Hinemoa: "A trumpet will be heard sounding every night; it will be I who sound it, beloved. Paddle then your canoe to that place." But the suspicions of the maiden's family were roused, and when she stole down at night to the lake's edge, she found that every canoe had been removed. As she sat on the shore in despair, she heard the music of Tutanekai's trumpet, and her love shook her "as an earthquake," impelling her to fly to him. Rising up, she took six large dry gourds, which she fastened beneath her arms, three on each side; and, having removed her garments, boldly entered the water and struck out for the island of Mokoia. Half the night she swam, resting when tired on the surface of the water, supported by the empty gourds, cheered and comforted by the music of her lover's trumpet, which came to her through the night with ever-increasing distinctness, her sole guide in the darkness.

At last she came to land, just above Tutanekai's village, where was a hot spring and a bathing pool. Trembling with cold, and perhaps a little with fright, she slipped gratefully into the warm water.

Now Tutanekai was thirsty, and sent a slave to fetch water, and the slave brought the calabash cup down to the lake, close by the pool where Hinemoa was sitting. The maiden was frightened, and, imitating a man's voice, called out gruffly, "For whom do you fetch water?" The slave replied: "For Tutanekai." "Give me to drink," she rejoined, and when she had drunk she smashed the cup. "Why have you smashed the cup of Tutanekai?" asked the slave; but Hinemoa answered never a word. So the slave went back and

* "Polynesian Mythology."

told his master what had happened. "Take another calabash and fetch me water," said Tutanekai. So the slave did so. Again the scene was repeated, and again, several times, until all Tutanekai's cups were broken. Then he was angry, and, leaping up, rushed to the pool to take vengeance upon the mysterious occupant. And Hinemoa heard him coming, but shyness seized her, and she shrunk back into the shelter of the overhanging rocks by the hot spring. Her lover, seeing no one, went about the banks feeling under the rocky ledges, and finally seized her hand. "Who is there?" he cried. "It is I," said Hinemoa softly. "Who are you? Who is 'I'?" he repeated. "I, Hinemoa," said the maiden, softer still; and Tutanekai was silent in the joy of his good fortune. "Will you come to my hut?" he asked at last. "Yes," whispered she. And she rose up in the water as beautiful as the wild white hawk, and stepped upon the edge of the bathing-pool as graceful as the shy white crane; and he threw garments over her and took her to his house." So they were married; and later Tiki, the friend of Tutanekai, took to wife Tupa, the sister of Hinemoa.

Photograph by Muir & Moodie, Dunedin.

A MAORI VILLAGE

WOMAN FROM THE ANCHORITE ISLANDS.
Wearing the oahi or double apron made of turmeric leaves (*see p.* 90).

Photograph from Museum Godeffroy Album

MELANESIA

By A. HINGSTON, M.A.

Geographical Position—Physical Type—An Island of Women—Personal Decoration and Ornament—Ornament and Sex—Tattooing—Scarification—Physical Mutilation—Cranial Deformation—Blackening of the Teeth—Floral Ornaments—Personal Ornaments—Dress

Geographical Position.

THE portion of Oceania called Melanesia ($\mu\acute{\epsilon}\lambda\alpha\varsigma$ = black, $\nu\tilde{\eta}\sigma o\varsigma$ = island) stretches from New Guinea on the north-west to Fiji on the south-east, over an area of several thousand miles (*see* map on p. 37). It includes, besides New Guinea and Fiji, at least seven distinct groups of islands: 1. Admiralty Islands. 2. Bismarck Archipelago. 3. Solomon Islands. 4. Santa Cruz Islands. 5. Banks and Torres Islands. 6. New Hebrides. 7. New Caledonia and the Loyalty Islands. These groups of islands are occupied by peoples possessing a sufficient number of common characters to warrant their being classed together under the race name of Melanesians.

Physical Type of Melanesians.

Their head-form is in general the same, prevailingly long and narrow, with a large, square, or lozenge-shaped face, and a broad and short nose, straight and up-turned. The skin colour reflects all shades between *café au lait* and *café noir*, sometimes glowing with a warm reddish tinge, like rusty iron. The hair is always naturally black, growing in little tight spirals, seldom attaining any great length, but longer and less woolly than that of the African Negroes.

In spite of these general resemblances throughout the whole island area, each group has to a certain extent specialised in various directions.

The lack of sea-faring ability or ambition, and the fierce and quarrelsome disposition, characteristic of the Melanesian race, have made friendly relations between the groups impossible, and very little voluntary intercourse springs up even between neighbouring islets.

Involuntary visits are not infrequent owing to the drifting of canoes out of their course, and traditions preserve records of a number of these. In some instances the newcomers made a settlement, and so brought about an admixture still traceable in the population; but more often the whole boat-load was murdered on its arrival, for every stranger was looked upon not only as a dangerous enemy, but also as a welcome addition to the scanty store of animal food, in a land where the largest indigenous mammal was the rat.

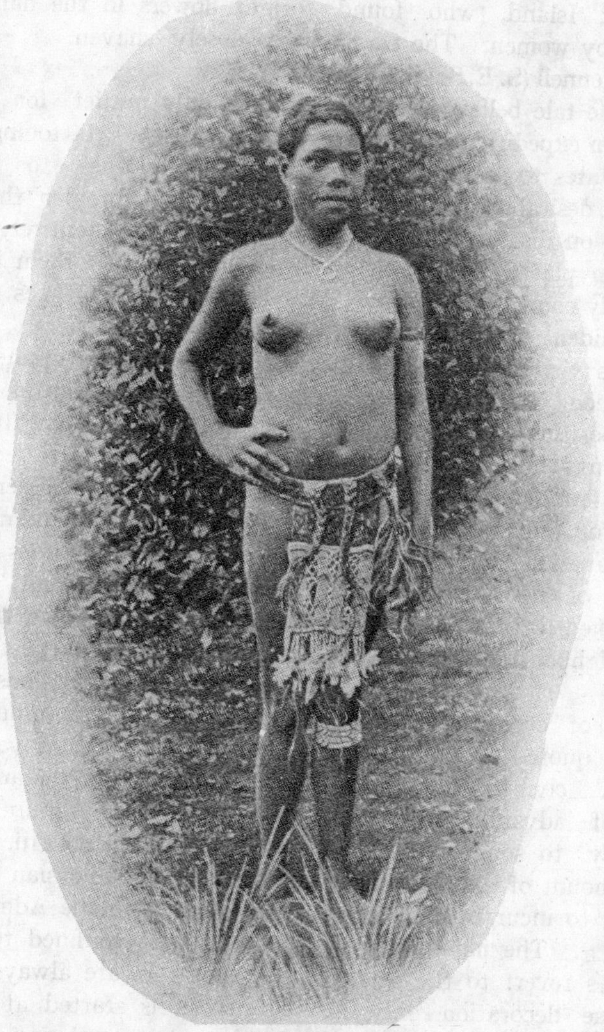

GIRL FROM THE ADMIRALTY ISLANDS.
Showing necklace, shell-bead apron, and other ornaments.

Since these were the conditions prevalent in Melanesia before the advent of civilisation, and since in many of the islands civilisation has but touched the shores, it is not surprising to find a lack of uniformity in personal appearance, dress, ornament, customs and habits throughout the whole area. The result is that, though generalisations are possible, nonconformity is seen to exist in almost every direction, and in no case is our knowledge of Melanesia so complete as to warrant an assertion that a certain feature is to be found throughout, or that another feature is entirely missing.

Moreover, civilisation is making such rapid and radical changes in manners and customs that what is true one moment may not be true the next, and in the following pages the present tense should often, in strict accuracy, be replaced by the less graphic past.

Under these circumstances the study of man is difficult, and the study of woman even more so. For the men are extremely jealous and suspicious, and the women particularly shy and modest. Travellers frequently relate that on reaching certain villages the women were all hidden in the bush, only men were to be seen, and not until after the visitors had proved themselves to be human (for at first the pale-faced Europeans were taken for ghosts), and their intentions recognised to be peaceful and trustworthy, did a few of the older women venture out of their seclusion.

But there is one island in Melanesia where the rule seems to be reversed, where the women alone are visible, and no men are to be seen, and it is particularly interesting from the fact that tradition credits it with an exclusively female population.

An Island of Women.

According to the story the Land of the Pandanus Tree—that is the name of the Adamless Eden—was visited by Kaidakita, the Ulysses of Stewart Island, who found it occupied entirely by women. The tradition was located in Rennell (S. E. Solomons), and so firmly was the tale believed in that some few years ago an expedition was fitted out in the United States to search for and take possession of the desirable island, and it was only abandoned on discovery that the area had already been placed under British protection. Curiously enough, on two occasions when the Resident Commissioner of the Solomon Islands visited Rennell, only women were to be seen. He accounted for this fact by the supposition that the women worked in the gardens while the men were away fishing. The fact is also explicable on racial grounds, for the inhabitants are Polynesian, not Melanesian, and the difference in the attitude of their women forms one of the most marked features of contrast between the two neighbouring races.

Ornament and Sex.

The distribution of ornament between the sexes has been quoted as one of the tests of civilisation. "The grade of advancement of a race may, to some extent, be measured by the amount of expense which the men are willing to incur in decorating their wives. . . . . The males in highly civilised communities revert to the savage condition of profuse decoration only as warriors or officials or on state occasions."

In Melanesia the opposite obtains. The woman may, on grand occasions, be dressed up in all the family possessions, to display the wealth and importance of her husband, but in ordinary life the greater share of the ornaments is worn by the male. Many a gallant sailor has been mortified to see the necklaces or bracelets which he had bestowed on some dusky belle appropriated without ceremony by one of her male relatives.

In the Admiralty Islands the decoration is confined almost entirely to the men. Young girls sometimes have a necklace, arm-band, or leg-band, as is seen in the picture of the girl on p. 85. Old women have no ornaments at all. The women are even debarred from indulging in the universal South Sea method of decoration—wearing bright flowers in the hair, for their heads are closely shaven.

Tattooing.

The only outlet for their decorative impulse is in tattooing—"Having no clothes to embroider, they embroider their skins." Tattooing is almost entirely confined to the women, and with them it is universal.

There are three types of skin decoration in Melanesia.

1. Tattooing by puncture or incision, with the introduction of colouring matter.

2. Scarification or cicatrisation by gashing or burning, leaving raised scars.

3. Ulceration by blister-producing plants.

The Admiralty Island method of tattooing is by a series of fine lines or cuts, made with some sharp instrument, the pattern being formed in rings all over the face and in diagonal lines over the chest. Dark pigment is rubbed into the incisions.

Owing to the dark colour of the Melanesian skin, tattooing is not very effective, being invisible at a short distance, and it has only been noted in the Admiralties, the Solomons, New Caledonia, and Fiji. Possibly it everywhere shows Polynesian influence.

In Fiji, as in the Admiralty Islands, the decoration is confined to the women, and the operators are always of the same sex. The work is started at an early age with a view to its being completed before betrothal, as, owing to the painful nature of the process, only a little can be done at a time. The operator generally works until the pain can no longer be endured, and the more elaborate patterns take several months to complete. Sometimes the tattooing is not performed until after the first child is born, and further patterns may be added from time to time. Tattooed spots at the corners of the mouth indicate, in some parts, that the woman has borne children, but often they are added merely to conceal the wrinkles of age. In the Fijian Hades the women that are not tattooed are chased by their own sex, who tear and cut them with sharp shells, giving them no respite; or else they are scraped up and made into food for the gods.

Scarification.

With a black skin, scarification is the most effective method of ornamentation, for by means of incisions, often augmented by the introduction of some irritant, the non-pigmented dermic layer is destroyed, and the scars show up light against the dark skin. Scarification is practically universal throughout Melanesia.

Scarifications may be seen on the bodies of the New Ireland women on p. 89. The one smoking a pipe, and whose hair is whitened with lime, has marks on her chest and right arm, and a symmetrical scarification is visible on the body of the woman two places further to the right in the same row.

In Guadalcanar the faces of the women are ornamented all over with circular or chevron-shaped cicatrices, carved with the claw of the flying-fox or fruit-eating bat. This has to be done by a professional man, and it is a costly and painful process. In Eromanga (New Hebrides) the women operate on each other, tracing designs of leaves, flowers, etc., on cheeks and chins. In Tanna no particular design is followed, but large scars are produced on arms and thighs. In New Caledonia raised scars are made by a peculiarly painful method. A small hole is made in the skin, and a dry stalk inserted and set alight, so that it burns the skin. This is repeated in some thousands of holes until a large area is decorated.

Physical Mutilation.

It has been observed that when few clothes or none at all are worn it is necessary to hang such ornaments as are desired on to the body itself, and this results in certain decorative mutilations, such as boring the ear and nose.

A Melanesian child generally has her ear-lobe bored while quite young, and a piece of grass keeps the hole from filling up; the aperture is gradually enlarged by the introduction of thicker rods or discs and by the attachment of heavy weights, until the lobe is distended and hangs down to the shoulders, and often below. The edge of the ear may also be bored and hung round with rings or other ornaments.

The cartilage of the nose is often bored a few days after birth, and a piece of grass inserted which is later on replaced by skewers of wood, bone or shell. Ornaments such as a claw, a bone pin with a few beads at the end, etc., are occasionally worn stuck into the sides of the nostrils (*see* p. 88).

The piercing of the nasal septum seems to have some religious significance in the Solomons. The ghosts on the way to the land of the dead are met by an official spirit with a rod, which he thrusts into the cartilage of their noses to see if they are pierced, and if they are, they may proceed by a good path; if not, they have to find another way beset with pain and difficulty.

Cranial Deformation.

Among the most extraordinary and conspicuous of ethnic deformations is the alteration of the shape of the head by means of pressure. In New Caledonia the head of the new-born infant is squeezed by means of the fingers, steeped in hot water. One tribe affects transverse pressure with depressed forehead, and another narrows the head until it is no wider than the neck. In another part there are different fashions for boys and girls. A boy's face is lengthened to make him look like a warrior, while that of a girl is rounded by raising the chin.

The most marked instance of cranial deformation is seen in Malekula. A band is wound several times round the head of an infant and kept in place by means of transverse bandages, and the head is not released from constriction until the age of from twelve to fifteen. The process is extremely painful, and the eyes of the child seem ready to start out of its head, but it appears to have no dangerous consequences except perhaps by favouring the outbreak of cerebral disease. A mother takes great pride in the shape of her child's head, and, where the girls are concerned, it influences their marriageable value. A girl whose head had not been properly shaped in her infancy would not be chosen as a wife for a man of position.

In Futuna a heavy roll of *tapa* or native cloth is placed on the heads of young children to give them the high and narrow shape which is considered ornamental.

Photograph by Meyer & Parkinson.

WOMAN OF THE GAZELLE PENINSULA, NEW BRITAIN.
With *cuscus* teeth necklace. (Front and profile views.)

Blackening of the Teeth.

Under mutilations may also be classed the blackening of the teeth, characteristic of the Melanesians from the Admiralty Isles to the New Hebrides. Areca nut, betel pepper leaf, and lime are chewed together, resulting in the accumulation of a black incrustation on the teeth. The habit is so universal that familiarity has bred admiration, and it is thought disgusting to have white teeth "like dogs."

Floral Ornaments.

Decorations of bright flowers and leaves made into necklets or girdles are not uncommon, but seem to be enjoyed more by the men than the women, and the tucking of sweet-smelling flowers or leaves into waist-belts or armlets is almost exclusively a masculine fashion. But the whole question of ornament is bound up with that of the relationship of the sexes, and the scents are undoubtedly worn to attract the females. It is interesting to note how, in a land where polygyny prevails, and there is no surplus female population, the coquettish wiles considered exclusively feminine in a civilised community form part of the outfit of the male. Not that the females in Melanesia represent "beauty unadorned," for, except in the Admiralties, it is rare to see a woman without ornaments of some description, and often they are overloaded with them; but in every case, where one sex is more profusely decorated than the other, the advantage lies with the male.

Personal Ornaments.

The personal ornaments worn by the women comprise necklaces, girdles, headbands, combs, armlets, bracelets, leglets and anklets, besides ornaments stuck in the holes in ears and nose. They may be made of wood, bamboo, leaves, berries, seeds, nuts, fibre, and grasses; of bones, claws, teeth, turtleshell, fur, hair, feathers, or tails; of stone or of shell; not counting trade goods of all descriptions.

Among the most effective of all Melanesian ornaments are those made of boars' tusks. The lower canines of a boar are removed, and the upper pair, having nothing to bite against, grow into an almost complete circle, sometimes entering the upper jaw again. These ornaments are highly prized, and in parts are the exclusive property of the men; but where pigs are plentiful, as in the New Hebrides, they may be seen on women as well, the ivory showing up finely against their dark skins.

A fashionable ornament for women in New Britain consists of human ribs hung round the neck, and the New Britain women sometimes wear bone or wooden spikes in the wings of the nose, projecting like tusks on either side. More picturesque and more valuable is the necklace of *cuscus* teeth worn

WOMEN FROM NEW IRELAND.

Showing costume, ornament, and scarification. (*See pp.* 87 *and* 91.)

by women of the Gazelle Peninsula (p. 88). Fifty of these teeth are worth a fathom of *dewarra* or shell money (about two shillings), and the necklace contains a thousand teeth. The women only wear them until enough have been collected to make the collar which forms the most prized ornament of the New Britain men, and an indication of their wealth and position.

The shell beads which preceded the glass beads of civilisation were the product of great skill and patient labour. First the piece of shell had to be chipped down to the required size for the disc, an operation involving a vast amount of time; then the holes had to be bored either by means of a drill with a sharp tip of obsidian, or by repeated tapping. The discs were then strung on a thread of fibre and all ground together to a uniform size, shape, and smoothness of edge. A special variety made in San Cristoval consisted of discs, one-sixteenth of an inch in diameter, fifty to the inch. This was used for money as well as ornament, for ornaments usually have a certain relative value and pass readily into currency.

SOLOMON ISLAND GIRL.
Showing costume and ornaments.

The women of Shortland Island are very clever in making dance aprons of beads by stringing them on to fibre. One made of shell beads gives great distinction to its possessor, and is rarely to be obtained. Shell-bead aprons also occur in the Admiralty Islands, and one is illustrated on p. 85.

Each nephrite bead of the necklace which the New Caledonian bridegroom presents to his bride represents several months of labour, so the strings are handed down from generation to generation as family heirlooms. In the same island the hairs below the ears of flying foxes or fruit-eating bats are plaited into cords, which are very highly prized. A special ornament of a cord on which a white cowry shell is strung is worn here by men alone. It is interesting to note that rank may, to a certain extent, compensate for disability of sex, for a chief's daughter is allowed to wear this decoration at certain *fêtes*.

Varieties of Costume.

The clothing of uncivilised peoples is influenced by so many factors, sexual, superstitious, social, economic and artistic, that it is not surprising if fashions in dress vary considerably in Melanesia, both for men and women: of some of the former it is often remarked that absolute nudity would be more decent, but the latter are usually sufficiently and artistically clothed.

In parts of the Bismarck Archipelago, the Solomon Islands and the Banks Islands, women may be seen entirely naked, but generally a girdle, fringe, or petticoat is worn, varying in material, width and ornamentation. The irreducible minimum is reached in New Caledonia, where the dress consists of a string round the waist, supporting a little rag scarcely the size of a penny; but the Eromangan woman wears an ample petticoat from waist to heel, and the Nitendi costume consists of a complete covering of mats from head to foot.

One of the most bizarre costumes is the *oahi*, worn by the women of the Anchorite Islands, consisting of two aprons made of the leaves of a species of turmeric. One wide piece folds round the body, almost meeting behind, and a back piece covers the join, reaching from the shoulder-blades to the ground. A girdle of plaited pandanus leaf secures the whole (*see* p. 84).

The simplest form of costume, and one that might have been worn by Eve herself, occurs sporadically throughout Melanesia. A piece of fibre or liana is wound round the waist and tied over one hip, and a bunch of grass fibre or leaves, etc., tucked in before and behind.

This type of costume which is well shown in the New Ireland group on p. 89, can be donned at a moment's notice, and a woman, paying a visit across an inlet or along the shore, would leave her own garment at home, swim to her destination, and provide herself with a new dress on landing.

In the Admiralty Islands this is the ordinary form of clothing, but decoration is introduced by a brilliant red dye with which the tufts of grass are stained.

In parts of the Solomon Islands a short petticoat of fibre is the fashion, varying from a depth of only four inches in Ulaua to a depth of a foot or more in Guadalcanar. In the Shortland group a special sort of sporran, called *bassa*, is worn, made with great care from specified plants, and both the plants and the garment are *tabu*. An ethnological collector, who spent some time in the islands, was very anxious to obtain a specimen, but he found that the women absolutely rejected all attempts at barter. At last, by means of persuasion and irresistible bribes, he prevailed upon a widow of the chief, Gorai, to part with one of these sacred garments, though the transaction was fraught with danger both for buyer and seller. She was afraid to come openly, so she brought the *bassa* at night, and insisted on seeing it packed away in a chest in her presence, with the promise that it should never be shown to a Shortland Island man.

Photograph by J. W. Waters.

TAPA BEATING IN FIJI.

The girls beat the moistened strips of bark, on a hollow tree-trunk, with wooden mallets.

In the Banks Islands clothes are seldom worn, but some of the older women have narrow plaited bands ornamented with crimson dye.

In Santa Cruz and the New Hebrides dresses are made of mats. These are plaited in strips of Pandanus leaf or fibre, or other flexible material, and they are worn, one before and one behind, attached to a plaited girdle. Special fashions prevail in the different islands of the New Hebrides. In Ambrym frills of coconut leaves give the women the appearance of ballet dancers; in Aoba a little double band, ending in fringed tufts, is made of plaited fibre; but the most peculiar type is found in Vate. Here a broad belt of matting is worn, worked in a diamond pattern, in red, white, and black, and to this is attached behind the singular appendage of a tail, made in grass or matting, with ends of a loose fringe, a foot and a half in length, reaching nearly to the ankles.

In the interior of Fiji, which is still almost untouched by civilisation, the short frill of bast or fibre may still be seen, but European dress is fast superseding native garments elsewhere, and silks and velvets take the place of bark-cloth among the higher ranks of society. Often the adoption of the new costumes does not entail the casting off of the old, and the two Fijian girls on p. 97 wear the native and the imported garments in somewhat incongruous juxtaposition.

Bark-cloth is made and worn in some of the islands, although it does not play such an important part in Melanesia as in Polynesia, nor is it so artistically treated. It only comes into common use in Fiji, where Polynesian influence is strong. Here its preparation is one of the most important tasks of the women.

Bark-cloth. Two Fijian girls are seen hammering out the piece of bark on p. 91, and the illustration on p. 101 shows a completed piece of cloth spread out on the ground, ready to be painted.

GROUP OF MOUNTAINEERS FROM KANDAVU, FIJI.

In the Solomon Islands the bark of the paper mulberry (*Broussonetia papyrifera*) is stripped off, steeped in water, hammered to the required size and flexibility, and worn in various ways. Commonly the narrow strip of cloth is wound round the waist, and the ends are first tied in front and then passed between the legs and fastened into the belt behind. In Ysabel the cloth is dyed a blueish tinge, and a broad strip wound round and round the loins, reaching nearly to the knee. The bark of the bread-fruit tree is also made into cloth.

Large pieces of bark-cloth are made in New Britain (Blanche Bay) and in parts of the New Hebrides, where they form an

SOLOMON ISLANDS GIRLS.

With fibre petticoats, and ornaments of beads and shells. Their hair, from being constantly plastered with lime, is bleached to a reddish hue.

important article of commerce between the islands. In the New Hebrides and also in New Caledonia the bark of the banyan fig (*Ficus prolixa*) is treated like the paper mulberry, and made into cloth. Pieces of bark-cloth are imported into Vanikoro (Santa Cruz), and worn in the following way. A piece of slit cane or rattan is polished highly to a fine black, and forms the belt by being twisted into a concatenation of small hoops. To this the piece of cloth is fastened to form a kilt reaching to the knee.

In New Caledonia a herbaceous plant is chewed and expectorated, and produces a violet dye for the bark-cloth. The wearing of this is the special prerogative of married women, who have a strip wound round and round their bodies, leaving only the chest and legs bare. They also wear mantles, made of a kind of plaited rush, in cold weather.

Woven Materials.

The most advanced type of native dress is found in Nitendi (Santa Cruz), where the women cover their bodies and heads with fine mats made in a loom. A loom is also found in Leueneuwa (S.E. Solomons), where the people are Polynesians, with a strong Micronesian element, and traces of loom-work are recorded from San Matthias and the Banks Islands, though no loom is now to be found. Nitendi is the only purely Melanesian island in which the loom is in use.

Nowadays the calico of civilisation is everywhere superseding the materials of native manufacture, and, under missionary influence, the picturesque native dresses are discarded for travesties of European costumes.

Superstition and Dress.

Undoubtedly a great amount of superstition is bound up with native dresses, and this may have justified the missionaries in insisting on their being discarded with the adoption of Christian belief, but it is a pity that the beauty of the inward conversion is not more faithfully imaged in the exterior. In the Solomon Islands a satisfactory compromise has been effected, and the dress of the regenerate is the *sulu*, a large coloured handkerchief, which is worn round the waist, and has a most becoming effect. It is possible that the *sulu* may have an important influence in the spread of civilisation.

Photograph by Muir & Moodie, Dunedin.

Photograph by Meyer & Parkinson.

FRONT AND SIDE VIEWS OF A NEW BRITAIN WOMAN.

Her only ornament is a strip of banana leaf tied round her neck.

II

Birth and Childhood—Treatment of Girl-Children—Preparations for Marriage—Betrothal and Marriage—Child Betrothals—New Britain Customs—Woman Proposes—Ambrym Girls Exchanged for Pigs—Marriage a Matter of Commerce—Polygyny—The Question of Morals—Widows and Widowhood—Murder of Widows

At the moment of her birth the little Melanesian girl-baby finds herself in a precarious position, for the first question is "to be or not to be," and her grant of existence depends on various circumstances.

Birth and Childhood. Should she be one of twins she will probably be left to die of starvation, or, more mercifully, be thrown at once into the sea or buried alive. This may be either because of the inability or unwillingness of her mother to tend and care for more than one infant at a time, or else because twins, being unusual, are looked upon with suspicion as something uncanny, and it is considered safer to put one or both of the potential sources of danger out of the way.

Twins are not everywhere regarded as necessarily maleficent. Their rare occurrence in parts of the Solomons is considered proof of their being due to special spiritual interference, and in the Banks Islands parents are boastfully proud of twins. In the New Hebrides women who want a child go to a sacred place in the hope that Tagaro, the Creator, will give them one, and sometimes he gives them two. This is looked upon as very auspicious, and great things are expected of the children.

When a girl-baby makes her way alone into the world she cannot be sure of a welcome. **Treatment of Girl-Children.** Girls may not be wanted in that particular district or family, or it may be the fashion to kill all the children as soon as they are born, as in parts of San Cristoval, and to save trouble and expense of infantile up-bringing by importing well-grown children from other districts. The birth of a girl is generally regarded as a family misfortune. Mrs. Paton tells of the news of the birth of a boy baby to Litsi, a favourite *protégée* of hers, about whom she had been very anxious. The girl's uncle brought the news, and Mrs. Paton uttered a very fervent "Thank God," to which the man responded earnestly, "O, Missi, that's just the very thing I said myself, for, you know, it might have been a girl." In New Caledonia the women are supposed to belong to a lower grade than the men, and the birth of a girl is considered of no importance; the child may be either exposed or buried alive, and the father takes no interest.

The island of Tucopia (Santa Cruz) is very small, and there all male children, except the first two, are strangled as soon as they are born, the reason given being that there is not room for a dense population, owing to the scanty resources of the island. But female children are never strangled, with the result that the females treble the males in the population.

In the Banks Islands also the female children are preserved rather than males, as being of greater value both to their immediate family and to the larger family group. The immediate family benefits by the presents made at betrothal and marriage; and, since descent is reckoned through the females, the number of female relations contributes to the importance and influence of the whole group.

In the Solomon group it is generally the grandmother who limits the number of children that the young and strong shall have to attend to. The old women have to do all the field work while the young ones are occupied with their children, and this they resent. Ariahurono, a chief of Boré (San Cristoval), thus related his infantile adventures. "My mama, when I was born, she no want piccaninni, so she dig hole, and put me in. But another woman, she want piccaninni, so she take me out and feed me."

The Rev. Lorimer Fison says: "The grave was to the Fijian what the workhouse is to our pauper class at home; and thither he sent, as a matter of course, the unproductive members of his family, not excepting his infant children if they came in his way by arriving at an inconvenient season, or if they were deformed, sickly, too numerous, or what he looked upon as the wrong sex, or otherwise displeasing to him. 'The children are there,' said an old chief, pointing to the corner of the house which was always hidden from view by a large screen of native cloth; and he went on to explain that, as near as he could remember, about fifteen of them lay buried there, a few of whom had died natural deaths, but the majority of them had been disposed of for some one or other of the above reasons. He had kept a harem of more than fifty wives."

In many parts of Melanesia infanticide seems never to have been practised, and in other parts only to have been resorted to under the influence of economic pressure; and the child, if allowed to live and admitted into the family, finds no lack of that parental love and care which are its natural heritage in all grades of civilisation throughout the world.

Small children have occasionally been offered for sale by their parents to Europeans, but this is due less to a want of parental appreciation than to the domination of the trading instinct, under the influence of which every man has his price. A New Caledonian father will willingly exchange his daughter for a gun, and, from a commercial point of view, he makes a good bargain.

But instances of the most tender affection are not wanting. One of the most pathetic letters received by Bishop Selwyn was from Soga, of Bugotu, Ysabel, on the death of his only child from whooping-cough. "My father, I cannot write a long letter, because grief has come to me, for my child is dead with me, and I continue wretched. I have not done anything against God."

The children on their part are said to show no particular sentiment with regard to their parents, especially their mother, whom they cannot always recognise when their father possesses numerous wives. But here, again, there are many exceptions.

Throughout Melanesia, as a rule, less attention is paid to the birth of a girl than to that of a boy, and the feasts and pig-killings or other ceremonies designed to attract spiritual favours or avert spiritual maleficence are generally omitted. In the New Hebrides a pretty custom exists. When the child is ten days old, and the mother is well again, the father goes down to the beach to wash the things belonging to the baby. If the child is a boy he scatters toy bows as he walks along, so that he may be strong and a good bowman; if the child

TWO GIRLS FROM FIJI.

Photograph by J. W. Waters.

They are wearing native petticoats over their European frocks. Their hair is stiffened by means of gum, and decorated with combs with long spikes. The upper one is a half-caste.

is a girl he scatters Pandanus fibres on her behalf, in order that she may be industrious in the making of mats.

Sometimes the mother names the child, generally after a relation; sometimes the father gives her a name, which she keeps throughout life; sometimes she has no particular name at all, but has a generic name according to her age and status; sometimes she only gains a name after marriage, when she is known as the wife of So-and-so.

LOUISA AND FANNY.
Mission girls from Motalava, Banks Islands.

Children soon learn to fend for themselves, and at a very early age they cultivate such garden produce as will make them self-supporting. The mothers instruct the girls in their daily work, and they soon develop into useful members of the family.

Preparations for Marriage.

But childhood in Melanesia is of short duration. At the age when English children are still in the nursery, playing with their dolls, the little Melanesian girl is already being prepared for the most important occurrence of her life—matrimony.

Girls reach maturity early, generally before they are thirteen, often by the time they are ten; but they may be married at even earlier ages, ten being the marriageable age in New Britain, while in Ambrym girls are often married between seven and ten.

There are diverse customs in the various island groups to indicate when the marriageable age has arrived, generally consisting in the outward and visible signs of the donning of clothes and decoration by tattooing. The tattooing is usually done by a professional, and all the family and friends contribute towards the expenses, being rewarded by a feast when the work is over. The ornamented areas swell and give great pain, but *il faut souffrir pour être belle*, and besides, no girl would be considered marriageable unless she were tattooed.

In parts of the New Hebrides when a girl attains maturity her upper front teeth are knocked out, either by several small taps or one hard blow with a stone. One girl, seen by Dr. Cailliot in Malekula, had refused to undergo the operation, on account of the pain. She therefore remained unmarried, and was the object of unanimous scorn. The custom, however, only occurs in one or two districts.

Miss Grimshaw says that the operation is performed by the old women of the tribe, who greatly enjoy the revenge they are thus enabled to take on the younger generation for the injury once inflicted by their elders upon them.

More curious are the customs in vogue in parts of New Ireland, which were seen and described by the Rev. G. Brown. The poorer girls wear a fringe crossed over their breasts and backs until they are marriageable, but those who can afford the expense keep the girls in tiny cages, from the age of eight or ten, until they emerge to be married some five years later. Several girls are generally kept together in a special house, in an enclosure, guarded by an old woman, and each girl is put in a separate cage made of the broad leaves of the Pandanus tree, sewn quite closely together, so that no light and very little air can enter

These conical structures are built on piles, and they measure about ten to twelve feet in circumference at the bottom and for about four feet from the ground, and above that they taper off to a point. There is only room inside for the girl to sit or lie down in a crouched position. Yet here the girls remain for four or five years, never being allowed out save once a day to bathe in a dish or wooden bowl placed close to their cage, and they are not allowed to place their feet on the ground.

By means of bribery Mr. Brown got permission from the chief to see the girls, though it is *tabu* for any men, not their own relations, to look at them; and the old woman who acted as guardian, and the girls themselves, were evidently afraid of the consequences of disregarding the prohibition. He tried to inspect the interior of one of the cages, but the atmosphere was so hot and stifling that he could scarcely put his head inside. He asked if the girls ever died during their long confinement, and was answered negatively; if they are ill they are not allowed to emerge.

Modified forms of the custom occur in different parts of the island and in New Britain, and an analogous custom is found in Fiji, though in none of these places does the confinement seem to be so severe.

Child Betrothals.

Melanesian girls who belong to families of importance are betrothed very early, sometimes even before they are born, for the father of a new-born son begins at once to look out for the birth of a girl who will be a suitable wife for him; and it may be arranged between certain families that the next girl born in one shall be promised to the boy in the other. As soon as the betrothal takes place a series of negotiations and giving of presents begins, which ends with the marriage. Often the tattooing of the girl is the sign to the prospective father-in-law that the time has come to conclude the bargain, to make the final payments in compensation to the family for the loss of the girl, and to claim the bride for his son.

In New Britain, when a boy is about fourteen, his uncle buys a girl of eight from her mother to be a wife for his nephew; and later on the marriage takes place, with the giving of feasts which form the necessary accompaniment in all orthodox weddings.

In the New Hebrides a girl of seven or eight is almost always married prospectively to a man of eighteen or twenty, who looks on her as his wife. But she does not always view the matter in the same light, and as she grows older she may run off into the bush with the man of her choice, leaving the families to wrangle over the financial complications that ensue.

In New Caledonia the marriages are all

Photograph by G. B. Nething.

NEW CALEDONIAN WOMAN.
In ordinary dress.

arranged by the relations, and we are told that the children "are rarely consulted. and always obedient"; but the girl of a wealthy family is allowed a free choice, which she exercises according to local custom in a dramatic manner. If there are several suitors, they all come to the girl's village, and the men stand in a row on one side, with the girl facing them. Between them is placed a leaf piled up with pieces of coco-nut, one piece for each man. Each man takes a piece, and bites a bit off it, and lays the rest down again on the leaf. If the girl likes a man, she takes the piece which he has bitten and eats it, and the man pays the money demanded by her relations and takes her away. Should none of the men please her, she remains unmarried.

Among the presents of the New Caledonian bridegroom to the bride must be a necklace of worked nephrite beads, without which no betrothal is conclusive, and no marriage is valid unless the bride and bridegroom have drunk out of the same cup a fermented drink made from chewed herbs.

When children are betrothed very young, it is considered advantageous for them to have every opportunity of making each other's acquaintance, and the little girl is often sent to the house of her *fiancé*, bringing her food with her, to stay for a month or so, and get on friendly terms with the whole family. Then, when the time for marriage comes, she goes willingly to her husband's people as to a second home. In the Northern New Hebrides the girl is brought up in the house of her prospective mother-in-law from such a tender age that the boy often believes her to be his sister, and he is very shy of her when he learns their real relationship. At Aoba the girl is taken at ten years old to the house of her future husband, where his mother teaches her the ways of the household, and she grows up with the other children. When she is old enough, her parents fetch her home to be tattooed and clothed, and when the negotiations and payments are complete she returns to her adopted home as a bride.

In New Britain betrothals generally take place at an early age, to enable the man to pay for his wife before old age overtakes him. The payments are made in instalments, and the enormous sum asked for a girl is not usually expected to be paid in full. When the betrothed couple are grown up, and a certain portion of the price has been paid, the man will build a little hut in the bush for his wife, and the two elope together. The father of the girl collects his friends and relations in great anger—real or assumed—and they set out to kill the bridegroom. As a rule the latter is not to be found, and they content themselves with burning down the hut, after which outburst of their feelings they return to the village, where the wedded pair has meanwhile probably settled. But if enough of the bride-price has not been paid the expedition is undertaken in earnest, and the young couple will not be allowed to return until satisfaction has been given.

New Britain Customs.

When a young man grows up unbetrothed and is allowed to choose a wife for himself, he is hedged in by numerous restrictions. First the permission of the chief is always necessary, but this restraint has also its compensations, for the chief will often buy a wife for a man who is too poor to procure one for himself. Then in every tribe there are two distinct sections, and a man may only marry a woman from the section to which he does not himself belong.

The normal procedure in New Britain is as follows :—

Suppose a young man to want a girl for his wife. She would, of course, belong to the section into which he could properly marry, for it would no more occur to him to marry into his own section than to marry his own sister. The first step would be to inform his father, mother, or the chief of the district, and then to run away into the bush and hide. This is to escape from the spirits of dead relations who are particularly malicious at this especial juncture. Meanwhile the negotiations proceed between the relations of the prospective bride and bridegroom, the one party offering a certain amount of *dewarra*, or shell-money, and the other demanding more, and much haggling ensues before both parties acknowledge themselves satisfied. Then a certain day is fixed for the marriage, and the girl's relations bring her to the house of the

Photograph by J. W. Waters.

TAPA PAINTING IN FIJI IN FRONT OF NATIVE HUTS.

man's parents, together with presents, and there is much feasting and dancing in honour of the bridegroomless wedding. When all the food is consumed, the girl's relations go home, leaving her behind, and the bridegroom is searched for in the bush, and he returns happily when all is over.

MAN AND WOMAN FROM THE NEW HEBRIDES.

Woman Proposes.

It is a general custom throughout the world that the man proposes marriage to the woman, but in parts of Melanesia the positions are reversed, and the girl has to take the first step, and make a proposal of marriage to the man.

Among the Sulka of New Britain the girl chooses her future husband for herself. She "lays her heart on the man of her choice," as they say. Her father, or other near relative in whom she confides, says to her, "Wait, we will invite him here, so that he may work for you." Then the mediator goes to the young man, conveying the proposal of marriage. If he be willing he is brought to the bride's home, and she, at his entrance, presents him with baked taro and a neck ornament. The acceptance of these constitutes an engagement, and a general exchange of presents ensues; the bridegroom gives the neck ornament to his parents, who give him presents in return, and these he gives to the bride, who has to bestow them on her parents. This is the private betrothal. The young man remains with his bride's family, and helps them by working for them, and during this time a plantation is made for the young couple.

When this is finished, a day is appointed for the ceremonial handing over of the girl by her father to her future husband, and this is a feast day for all the villages round. This constitutes the public betrothal.

So far the girl seems to have had the best of it, but then her trials begin. From henceforth, until the wedding day, she has to live the life of a hermit. She is shut up in a little cell at the back of the house of her future parents-in-law, together with some young girls, her sisters or nieces. She may not eat taro baked between stones, flesh, fish, or certain fruits, or drink water. She may not cook her own food, or even feed herself. The girls who are with her prepare the taro, baked on the fire, and feed her by putting pieces into her mouth. She has to avoid the sight of men, and if she goes out she wears a long cloak of banana leaves down to the ground, and whistles all the time, so that men shall keep out of the way. During this period of seclusion she is decorated with scarifications, either incised with obsidian or burnt with midribs of coco-nut leaves by women specially paid for their work by the bridegroom. He meanwhile is building his house. When all these preparations are over the wedding day is announced, and there is much feasting, dancing, and singing, after which the young pair go away to their new home.

The most pathetic description of marriage in Melanesia comes from Ambrym (New Hebrides). Here a girl is sold for pigs almost as soon as she can toddle, five or six pigs being paid in instalments. At an age between seven and ten the child-wife is delivered over to her purchaser, possibly an old chief. Sometimes she is allowed to remain with her parents until she is twelve, then, with tears and much crying, she is carried off to her husband's village. This may have to be done several times, and the whip, or even severer means, may be used to enforce obedience.

Ambrym Girls Exchanged for Pigs.

The essential part of marriage, as has been seen, consists in the payments made to the family of the bride in compensation for her loss, and the commercial aspect is the most prominent feature throughout Melanesia, for the feasting and dancing which accompany all orthodox weddings are also part of the bargain, and the families and friends on both sides contribute towards the expenses, as in civilised communities. Every man or woman is expected to marry, and economic and social conditions discourage independence in bachelor or spinster. As a rule only those men who are too poor to marry remain single, and only those women are unappropriated whose parents demand too high a price for them.

Marriage a Matter of Commerce.

In 1901 the *Vaukolu* (Parliament) of the Florida Islands (Solomons) met to discuss the price of wives. Women were so dear that only rich men could afford to marry, which resulted in a great deal of unhappiness. A native had sold his daughter for 150 strings of shell money and 1,000 porpoise teeth, and as he was a Christian and a teacher it was felt that his cupidity should be rebuked. At the meeting a resolution was proposed by a chief that no one should pay more than thirty strings for a wife, unless both bride and bridegroom belonged to a family of chiefs, in which case the price might rise to fifty strings. The resolution was carried, but the women were very

FAMILY GROUP FROM THE NEW HEBRIDES.
The woman has scarifications on both arms.

angry at being thus cheapened, and would not speak to the men for some time afterwards.

In the New Hebrides, where pigs form the currency, a wife may be bought for ten to twenty pigs, according to her capacity in the yam patch. Beauty has little market value, true worth (*i.e.*, industrial capability) being of more importance in the eyes of match-making parents. On the north-west coast of Vate, however, the æsthetic sense seems to be ascendant, for a wife costs ten pigs if good-looking, but only six if plain. In parts of Malekula, where pigs are scarce, a wife costs six to ten pigs, and this prohibitive price restricts all but chiefs to monogamy. In Tanna a wife can be bought in exchange for one pig, and pigs are plentiful.

In Eromanga semi-transparent circular rings of calcareous spar, five to six inches in diameter, and one and a half inches thick, are highly valued, and serve as currency. One of these, together with a spear or bow and arrow, constitutes the price of a wife.

The Loyalty Islanders, "*les Anglais du microcosme Calédonien*," are great shipbuilders, but their island does not supply the necessary wood, and they have to procure it from New Caledonia. On the other hand, Loyalty Island maidens are in great request in New Caledonia, on account of their many charms. So the Loyalty Island father paddles his daughter over to the mainland, and exchanges her for a cargo of wood.

In the Bismarck Archipelago the bride-price is usually paid in shell-money, but a wife may also be obtained in exchange for an iron implement.

It is interesting to learn how the wives themselves regard the question of payment. In Malekula in the New Hebrides it is, according to Miss Grimshaw's account, the one satisfaction in a hard existence:—

"'I cost twelve pigs,' Mrs. Frizzyhead No. 1 boasts to Mrs. Frizzyhead No. 4, who is a new acquisition, and inclined to be cheeky. No. 4, who is painting her forehead jet black with burnt coco-nut, and drawing a line of red ochre down her nose, pauses in her toilet to say contemptuously: 'I cost fifteen!' Mrs. Flatface, the sole joy of old Mr. Flatface, from the bush, here chips in: 'I cost twenty, and two of them were big, as big as a whale-boat from the steamer!' The Frizzyhead ladies subside, and wait till they can catch young Mrs. Blackleg coming up from the yam plantations, with a baby in her arms and a hundredweight of yams on her back, to revenge themselves by telling her that she only cost ten pigs, and is a low creature anyhow."

Under the influence of education the women are beginning to resent being paid for. One girl from the Banks Islands in particular was very proud of having been "given," not "sold." She said, "I do not like the custom of selling women like pigs. We are not pigs, we are women."

In many cases the price asked for a girl is merely "bluff," and the impecunious Lochinvar runs off with the damsel of his choice, and the irate father-in-law is pacified afterwards by a feast and a present.

Polygyny.

Since matrimony is thus regulated by financial considerations, polygyny becomes a luxury that can only be afforded by the rich and the elder men. Many men do not desire more than one wife, either on account of the real affection and esteem which grow up in most cases between a married pair, or else because they fear the discord that polygyny engenders, for a great number of wives is in all the islands a fruitful source of quarrels and bloodshed.

A peculiar custom obtains in Aoba (New Hebrides), where a man who has a young wife takes an older woman, generally a widow, for a second, to look after the first. Often, where a man is accredited with many wives, they are not of his own choosing. The custom of the levirate obtains throughout Melanesia, that is, the wives left by a man at his death are looked upon as family property, and pass to his relations, usually a brother or nephew. Therefore, as a man advances in life, and survives his male kinsfolk, the widows of his brothers, maternal uncles and cousins, tend to accumulate round him. Though these would all be his nominal wives, he is not the husband, probably, of more than two or three younger women, whom he has chosen for himself.

Owing to the custom of infant betrothal, a man often has his first wife chosen for him by his relations, and, as he grows older, and he and she together have amassed sufficient wealth, he selects a young wife for himself. This is often the bitterest tragedy of a woman's life, and it may result in the first wife putting an end to herself by poison.

In New Britain a special ceremony marks the relationship between the first and the second wife. On the second day after the new wife has been bought, the two wives fight or wrestle in public for two days. It is practically a sort of game, but it may entail hearty thumps, and the spectators thoroughly enjoy it. The two wives are painted red all over, and they go down to the sea-shore, and each tries to throw the other into the water. This is supposed to drive away any jealousy between the two. Generally the first wife rules the household, and, if the new-comer is too troublesome, she is sent back to her relations.

The advent of a new wife may cause great distress.

Mal, a chief in Ambrym, had three wives, and the favourite was Botingi, a handsome girl, to whom he was much devoted. But one day he took a fourth wife, a young girl of about twelve. At the marriage feast or reception Botingi had now to put out her own fire, and, taking an ember from the dying coals, creep along on her knees and light with it the fire of the young bride. It was terribly significant of a dead affection.

EPA.
A Christian convert from Pilene, Reef Islands.

The Question of Morals.

People are apt to regard Melanesia as a savage and lawless area where a very low code of morality prevails, "where there ain't no Ten Commandments," and more especially no Seventh. But there are perhaps few lands where adultery is more severely punished, while, as a rule, chastity before marriage is most strictly insisted on, and lapses are punished with death. The girls are generally watched and guarded very carefully, especially when betrothed, as their marketable value may be endangered by lack of surveillance. This is not always the case, for in parts of the Solomons the value of a girl is held to be enhanced if, on attaining maturity, she has distributed her favours freely to all comers. But should one of her lovers desire her in marriage, she becomes his sole property, and settles down as his faithful wife.

Considerable license is also permitted in other parts, and sometimes there is no supervision over the girls. Probably in all the islands there are certain families which are always well-conducted, and others where no particular standard of morality is set up, but the latter would always be held in lower estimation.

In New Britain any unfaithfulness on the part of the wife is severely punished; the woman is immediately speared, and the man, if caught, is beaten, and has his neck twisted, so that he dies in great agony after a few days.

On the north coast of New Britain it is the man alone who is punished, and the strength of the desire for money in the New Britain native is nowhere more clearly shown than in the fact that it overcomes the jealous instincts of an injured husband. Vengeance is only exacted in shell-money, several strings being demanded. If this is not paid, the culprit's house is burnt down, and sometimes the houses of his neighbours, so that they shall assist in extorting the money. If this is of no avail, the houses of the man's relations are burnt, and their plantations ruined, until one of the family probably pays the fine.

In the Solomons an unfaithful wife is

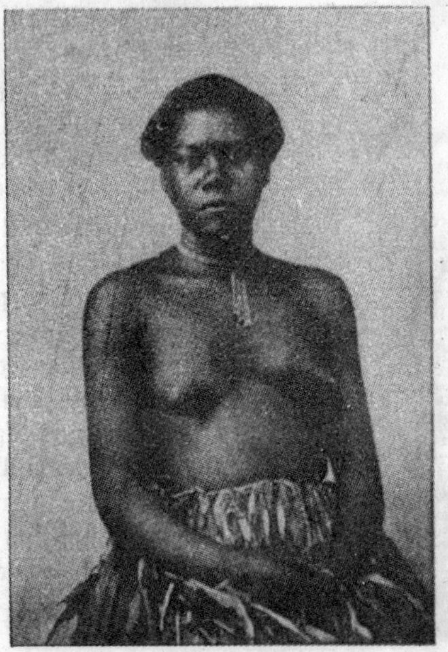

A FIJIAN GIRL.
With native petticoat and bead necklace.

killed, or else she is tied to a tree, and every man has the right to shoot an arrow at her. Should she survive, she is cleared of all dishonour.

Divorce is easy and common, and a separation may take place at the will of either party, though a man finds it easier to put away his wife than *vice versa*.

If a wife is ill-treated, she naturally returns to her own family, which has to repay the bride-price if the husband demands it, so another marriage is generally arranged for her as soon as possible. If the marriage had lasted for some time the whole of the bride-price could not be demanded, as the wife would be held to have paid some of it off by her work. As a rule no efforts are spared on either side to bring about a reconciliation.

The commercial aspect of marriage, and the power of the husband over the wife are seen in the fact that a man may hand over his wife to another man, and receive from him the bride-price, but this is not of common occurrence. Generally husbands and wives get on well together, and the children form a binding tie for life.

Widows and Widowhood.

When a man dies his widow does not regain her independence. Since the wife has generally been bought for the man by his relations, she still belongs to the family, and the family still hold marital rights over her. She naturally belongs to her husband's brother, but in case he does not want her she may be handed over to an uncle or a cousin of the dead man, or the family may dispose of her to an outsider in exchange for compensation. A woman rarely remains a widow long.

In Uripiv, however, off the north coast of Malekula, there was a widow of an original turn of mind, and a person of great consideration. She had been the wife of a chief, and she refused all subsequent offers and lived independently. She dressed with great magnificence, and at dances painted her face like a man, and danced with the best of them.

Murder of Widows.

In parts of the Solomons a wife, especially if the favourite wife, generally commits suicide by hanging, drowning, or stabbing herself, on the death of her husband.

In the New Hebrides widows were usually smothered or strangled, so that they might continue their wifely ministrations to their husbands in the next world. The process had to be effected as soon as the man was dead, and the wife's body buried with that of her husband, otherwise their spirits might miss each other on their way to the land of the dead. A conical cap, made of spider's web, which was used for smothering the New Hebridean widows, is illustrated on p. 108. The women were by no means anxious to escape their fate, even where escape was provided by aid of the missionaries, and the fear of reproach probably restrained any show of natural reluctance. This would be interpreted as a sign of unfaithfulness on the part of the wife, if not as a proof of her implication in the death of her husband, and she preferred death at the hands of her family (generally her son) to a life of dishonour and the risk of death at the hands of her husband's kinsfolk.

In Fiji widow-strangling is considered essential from the native point of view, for the following reason, described by the Rev. Lorimer Fison.

Photograph by Muir & Moo[illegible], Dunedin.

WAITOVA, NEAR LEVUKA, FIJI.

Two of the women have plastered their hair with lime.

A man is not considered to have attained complete manhood in this world until he has taken to himself a wife; and the same holds good of the next. When he is dead he has to start on his way to spirit-land, and some distance from the starting place stands a tree by the wayside, and at this tree he has to throw the whale's tooth with which his kinsfolk have provided him. No matter how good his aim, he is sure to miss if his

Fijian Justification for Widow-Murder.

friends have not strangled a woman to follow and tend him. If he hits the tree, he smiles a smile of satisfaction and goes on his way; if he misses, he proceeds a grumbling and discontented ghost. "Here's a fine state of things! Didn't I always take care of my father? Was I ever wanting in help to my friends? Why then have they not sent a woman after me?"

Photograph by H. Short.

CAP MADE OF SPIDER'S WEB.

(Now in the Exeter Museum.)

For smothering widows in the New Hebrides (*see p.* 106).

He has good reason for his discontent, for further on he has to pass a terrible guardian of the path, Nangga-nangga, who is utterly implacable towards bachelors, and who persists in reckoning every man a bachelor who comes to him without a female attendant. No excuse will serve, and there is no possibility of slipping by unnoticed.

The unfortunate man is seized, raised aloft and broken in two by being dashed down on a sharp-edged rock, but the ghost who is properly attended is allowed to pass.

This bachelor-hating guardian keeps a sharp look-out on women also, and demands a view of the marriage certificate, with which every woman who dies before her husband is carefully provided. This certificate is her husband's beard, which is cut off and placed under her left armpit when her body is being prepared for burial. When the ghost reaches Nangga-nangga, he asks, "How about your husband?" "His beard, sir, is this," she replies, producing her certificate, and she is allowed to pass.

Much devotion is shown by the widows of Malekula, who sleep on their husband's graves until their next marriage; while the New Caledonian widow carries about with her a basket, artistically woven, containing the skull of her husband, ornamented with odorous resin and scarlet seeds.

Old and incapable persons are usually put an end to by being strangled or buried alive; generally they are quite willing, and sometimes even clamorous for the privilege. It is interesting to note that in the Solomon Islands old men are put to death sooner than old women, since the latter are found to be useful to the community as scolds, to keep the younger men in order.

III

The Position of Melanesian Women—"Mother-right"—Three Dominant Factors—New Caledonia—Women as Workers—Bismarck Archipelago—Solomon Islands—Influence of Women—The New Hebrides—Fiji—Malekula—Castes in Ambrym—General Remarks

"MEN must work and women must weep," so sang the poet of civilisation, but the Melanesian thinks differently. Women may weep—that does not concern him, but he recognises no necessity for man to work. "Women may weep, but women must work," better expresses the Melanesian philosophy of life.

The Position of Women.

But this is not so unfair as it appears, and it is founded on the primary division of labour between the sexes. Man is the fighter; woman the feeder. The man is responsible for the security of the household from attack without, while the woman reigns supreme within.

In a state of savagery, when warfare, either aggressive or defensive, is the normal condition of existence, the man is fully occupied, and all his energies are required for his daily work; but when the influence of the trader and the missionary have introduced the blessings of peace, his employment is gone. At the same time the domain of the woman is practically uninfluenced, except that her work proceeds more uninterruptedly than before.

Under these changed circumstances the Western man might turn his weapons of war into agricultural implements, and amass wealth by working in the fields with the women, and trading in the surplus produce; but the typical Melanesian is a eudæmonist rather than a Mammon-worshipper, his goal is personal ease rather than wealth. Work is not natural to man, and it requires a sufficient stimulus to overcome his inherent aversion, especially in an enervating tropical climate. His women provide him with sufficient food, so hunger does not rouse him to exertion, and he has no incentive beyond the mere pleasure in physical exercise. Therefore he hunts and fishes for his own amusement, and eats and sleeps and plays the rest of the day; and the civilised world is horrified at the sight of women employed as labourers and as beasts of burden to support their idle husbands.

It is a common statement that the place accorded by man to woman in his society is a gauge of the civilisation of that society. But, like many generalisations, it does not always bear analysis. The status of woman is determined by various factors, and of these the vague abstraction called civilisation is doubtless of importance; but anthropology shows that woman often holds a higher place in a savage society than in one that boasts an advanced "civilisation."

At least two characteristic features of Melanesian social organisation may be noted as indicating the by no means insignificant position of women. These are the so-called Mother-right, and descent of property through females.

"Mother-right."

Under the system of Mother-right, descent is reckoned through the mother, instead of the father, and the mother's brother (*e.g.*, the maternal uncle) is considered a closer relation to the children than their own father. This system is still prevalent, but it is giving way before Father-right in many parts.

The custom of descent of property through females goes with Mother-right. Instead of the woman giving up all right to property on her marriage (as in England up to 1882), the sons inherit through their mother, while the father's property goes to the children of his sister. He may transmit some of his personal belongings to his own children, but there is usually some recognition that their claim on him is only secondary.

In some parts the daughters have an equal share with the sons in the inheritance of land.

Three Dominant Factors.

"Human history," says M. Taine, "may be resolved into three factors—environment, race and epoch"; the same three factors determine the position of women, and they may be defined as geographical, anthropological, and sociological.

Thus it is not sufficient to say that the subjection of woman in Melanesia is merely the result of the brutality or laziness of man. A certain uxorious ferocity seems to form a race character of the Melanesians, and the climate generally encourages physical inertness; but these influences are less potent than that of physical environment, especially when it results in economic pressure.

New Caledonia.

This is particularly clear in an extreme case such as is exemplified in New Caledonia. First note the environment. There are no wild or domestic animals, and scarcely any useful plants in the island. Climate and soil give nothing without labour, and the resources are poor and unstable. Paradise, in New Caledonian theology, is a place where a man can eat when he is hungry, and can really cram himself with yams. The women of New Caledonia are generally considered to be the most unfortunate of all Melanesians. They are scarcely looked upon as belonging to the same species as the men, but rather to an inferior creation. A boy, as soon as he is born, has the same rights as a man, but women have no rights at all.

They are described by M. de Vaux as veritable beasts of burden. They clear the land, dig it, turn it, and carry enormous burdens of yams or taro to the villages on their backs. If you have any fatiguing or pressing work in which a chief has promised you assistance, he will send you a troop of these miserable beings, to whom one can scarcely give the name of woman. While the men, well-built, carry their heads high, spend much time on their hair-dressing, and walk proudly upright, these unfortunates have shaven heads, and are deformed and bent double by hard work, and grow old before their time. At twenty-five or thirty they look twice their age. Even hunger is not a sufficient stimulus to make the men share the labours of the women. "*Souffrir pour souffrir,*" say they, "*nous aimons mieux avoir faim que de travailler.*"

It is easy to predicate the result. Professor Mason, speaking of the relationship between male and female in the human species, argues as follows :—"If one half of this species, the maternal half, in addition to many natural weaknesses, had been from the first the victim of malicious imposition and persecution at the hands of the other and stronger half, humanity would not have survived."

And the New Caledonians do not survive. They are a short-lived race, a man of seventy being a marvel, and they are rapidly decreasing. This is attributed largely to the poor condition of the women, who, physically and morally oppressed, cannot sufficiently nourish their children.

Thus it is seen that the degradation of women is to a large extent the result of environment, dependent on economic forces. Women are the comparatively weak members of the community, and are therefore the first to suffer under harsh conditions of life. Yet even in New Caledonia there is a brighter side to the picture, and the women are found to be not uniformly abject. In the question of marriage it was seen that the girl displayed a high-handed independence in choosing from among a crowd of suitors (p. 99). Captain Erskine was much struck by the freedom with which the women mingled with strangers, no restrictions being placed upon their intercourse. But the happiest time of their lives is that spent at the *pilou-pilou*, or *fêtes* at the annual celebration of the yam harvest and other

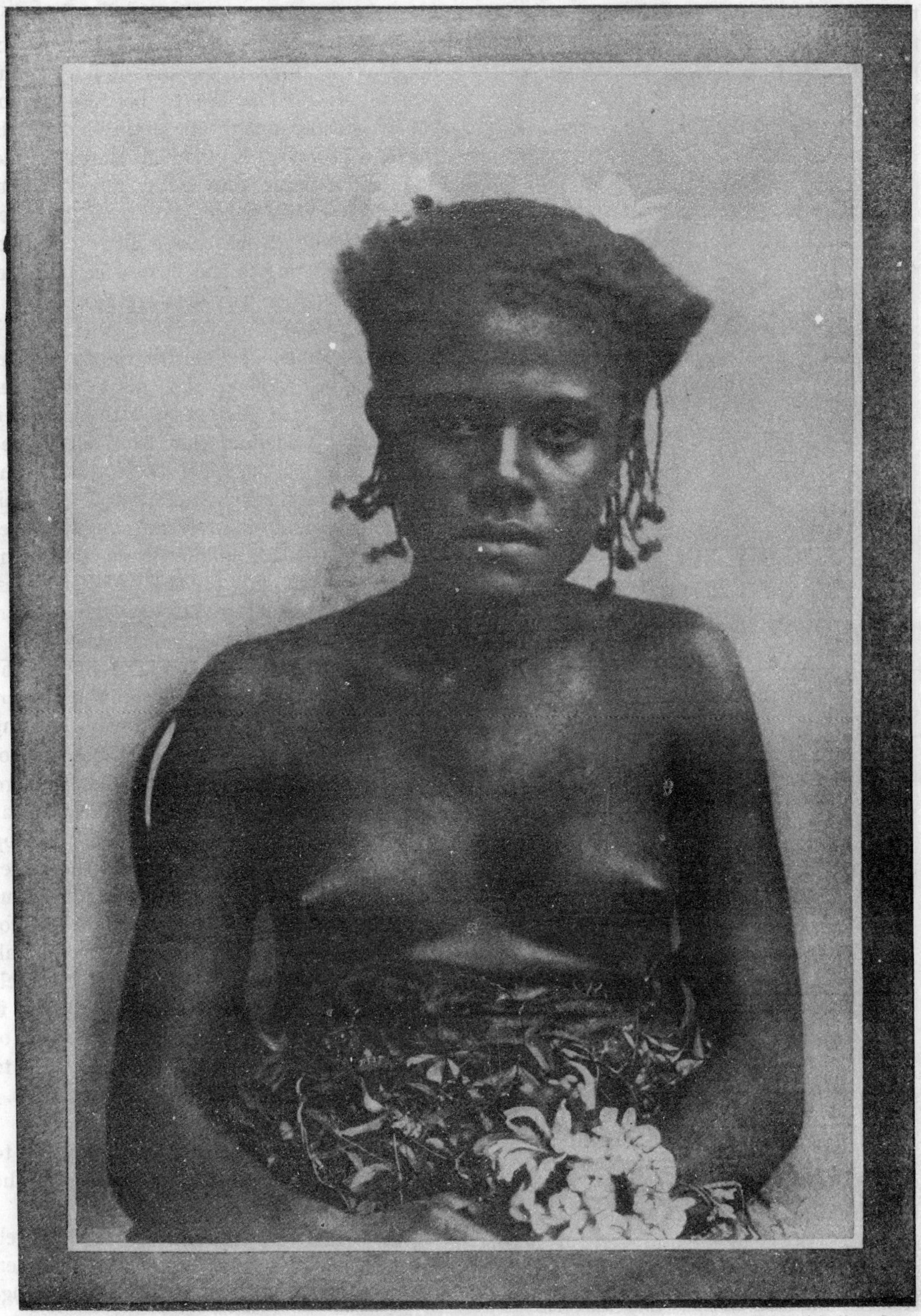

Photograph by Kerry, Sydney

FIJIAN NATIVE GIRL.

Her hair is stiffened on the top of the head, and plaited out to its full length behind, each plait ending in a frizzly tuft.

joyful occasions. Indeed, it is said that the main cause of infanticide lies in the unwillingness of the mother to be confined to her hut, unable to indulge in the enjoyments of the *pilou-pilou*.

The *pilou-pilou* lasts for several days,

Photograph by King.

FIJIANS CROSSING A BRIDGE.

sometimes eight or ten, which are spent in speech-making, present-giving, feastings, dancing, mock fights and general license. Ceremonial invitations in the form of knotted coco-nut leaves are sent to guests, and special huts are prepared for their reception. Preparations are begun a whole year before the event is to take place, and the chief who acts the host is usually insolvent for two or three years afterwards.

For the women, the *pilou-pilou* is the occasion for a great display of finery, and marvellous dresses are to be seen among the wives and daughters of invited chiefs. This, however, is only in the daytime. In the evening these trappings are abandoned for their habitual costume, but they wear round their necks a little bunch of keys, attesting to the possession of boxes in which their treasures are stored.

Women as Workers.

The women of Espiritu Santo are described as among the most degraded in Melanesia, although their degradation has not stifled a coquettishness that is one of their marked characteristics. In this island, too, it is not infrequent to see the men carrying the loads, while the women walk unburdened by their sides. This is unusual in any savage or barbarous society.

Missionaries new to island life in the Solomons would meet a woman staggering along a steep bush pathway, bending under a load of heavy bamboos full of water, whilst behind her came her lord and master, lightly clad in shield, spear and tomahawk. "It looks bad," Bishop Selwyn said, "but it is really the better plan. The women *can* carry burdens, but they *can't* fight, so the men go to protect them, with their hands free of all but their weapons." Moreover, the feeling never seems to be absent that it is a reflection upon the ability and skill of a woman, however weak she may be, to have her husband bearing her burdens.

Bismarck Archipelago.

Economic conditions are seen also to regulate the position of women in the Bismarck Archipelago.

New Hanover, though small, is well watered and extremely fertile. The men there are as a rule monogamists, and the wife possesses a good deal of authority. The women are referred to on occasions of bartering, and the men cannot part with articles without obtaining their consent.

In New Ireland the soil is poorer and less well watered; conditions of life are harder, and especially hard on the women on whom the field work falls. In most parts they are heavily overworked and entirely in the power of their husbands. A husband may kill his wife without the interference of her relations, who give up all claim to her at the marriage.

In New Britain sociological conditions of a peculiar character have influenced the status of the women to a remarkable extent, and have raised them in some instances to a position of great trust and responsibility.

New Britain seems to form an exception to the greater part of Melanesia, from the fact that a sufficient stimulus has there been discovered to overcome man's natural objection to work. This stimulus is the love of money (*i.e.*, shell money), which is an overmastering passion, and though the root of much evil, it is also productive of much good.

One result is that it produces industry. The men are not idle. A careful student of manners and customs after living eight years among the natives came to the conclusion that, comparatively speaking, they were as busy as Europeans. "Only those who know nothing about the New Britain people will call them lazy."

Another result, and one of great importance to the women, is the establishment of the right to personal property. The woman keeps for herself the money which she earns by her labours, and a wife may amass wealth independently of her husband. Unfortunately this often arouses the greed of the man, who seeks to get possession of the hoard. Force may not be used, that would be an invasion of the rights of property and an offence against the public conscience. "The husband perhaps gets up a charge of adultery against his wife, he becomes very angry, and threatens to do her bodily

Photograph by Muir & Moodie, Dunedin.

FIJIAN GIRL.

Showing method of dressing the hair before marriage.

harm unless she pays him so much money. Often she is charged with saying something derogatory to him. She is then made to pay for 'defamation of character.' She pays often to escape bodily harm at the hands of her husband. Often the charge is true, but often it is not. In either case the husband gets the money."

Still, the right to possess individual property marks a very real social advance, and leads to independent action on the part of the New Britain women. They enter into business engagements, and sell land without consulting their relations, who may even seek unavailingly to restrain them.

In the Solomon group conditions of life differ considerably. In some islands there is practically no firm government, and fighting and head-hunting keep the natives in a continual state of unrest. The women tend the gardens, and are over-worked and badly treated.

Solomon Islands.

In the islands of Bougainville Straits a strong government was established by the famous chief Gorai, and peace and prosperity came with more settled conditions.

The women, as usual, gain by the advance. They are better treated, and less of slaves than on the other islands, and they have great influence over the men. Wives are still looked upon as a working staff, and the main objection to missionary principles was the reluctance to reduce their numbers and diminish the profits. Gorai had eighty to a hundred wives, but they were well treated and enjoyed certain privileges.

In Bougainville the chiefs' wives do no field work. They are the companions, not the slaves, of their husband, and remain in the house to entertain him when he is at home, and are clever at various handicrafts. Some superintend the plantations, to see that there is sufficient food for the households, but, unless the husband himself condescends to work in the fields, the wives do no manual labour.

Without leisure there is small chance of advancement in civilisation, and it is noticeable that in the Solomon group certain arts and crafts practised by the women attain their highest expression. As has been mentioned, it is only here that bark cloth is made, but its unpopularity is scarcely surprising, for it is the most unsuitable material for garments in the wet climate. All the women and girls do plait work with grasses and strips of coco-nut and Pandanus leaves, adding dyes of native production. Mats for sleeping, for clothes, for ordinary occasions, and for protection from the rain, baskets and wallets, neck, arm and waist belts, reach a high level both in art and workmanship, and the women who excel enjoy great distinction, and make much money. The bead work of the Solomons, another feminine handicraft, also shows great skill and æsthetic appreciation.

The influence of the women has often been noted by travellers. Romilly says: "If an old woman once calls you 'her child,' she can be depended on to help you to the utmost of her ability, and would give you a timely warning were mischief intended." Often a present to an old woman is more effective than all persuasive arts. This influence may be due to esteem, but it more probably rests on the fear of magic with which women, and particularly old women, are so generally credited; for in a grade of culture where fear is the strongest deterrent to force, the mystery which surrounds a woman is often her most effective protection. In the Loyalty Islands the women are said to be on equal terms with the men, and to be most honourably treated. The slander of a woman's character would be considered a justifiable cause of a quarrel between two tribes.

Influence of Women.

Possibly both in the Solomons and the Loyalty Islands the gentler attitude towards women is due to the racial factor, for there is reason to assume Polynesian influence in both groups.

In the New Hebrides the geographical factor is again dominant. The climate is as a rule very unhealthy, and in some of the islands the natives live in daily dread of malaria. The life of the women is generally a hard one, and they are practically slaves. The field work and all the other work is done by the women, while the men fish or hunt, and when they fish from canoes the women do the paddling.

In the New Hebrides.

Miss Grimshaw describes the Malekulan women as bent and misshapen with the enormous loads they are obliged to carry, and with an expression if possible more degraded than that of the men, who were "the most ill-looking crew" she had ever encountered. She tells how she took up a basket of yams that one of the women was bringing home, which was amazingly heavy, and not an easy thing to handle, from its irregular shape. Her maladroitness in handling the yam basket appeared to be a great joke to the Malekulan husbands, or, as described by one of the boys in pigeon English, "All a Malekula man he say—'That fellow Mary (*i.e.*, woman) he no savee carry yam,' he plenty laugh," which, being translated, means, "What sort of a woman is this—what use is she, that she cannot carry yams?"

Malekula.

The life of the women is one of hard work. Pleasure of any kind is unknown to them. There is nothing for them to enjoy from the Pandanus plait cradle, slung over the mother's shoulder, to the grave, which is only a hole scratched in the surface of the earth, if indeed anyone takes the trouble to bury the poor little corpse at all.

The same writer tells of the effect of a present on a bush woman of Malekula, who had come down to the mission-house to sell yams.

"I gave her a pink ribbon, and tied it round her neck. A sort of sacred joy seemed to overflow her whole countenance and lift her far above things of common earth. She seemed to feel ennobled and exalted by this wonderful thing that had happened. That she should have had something given to her—she, a woman!—and that it should be this marvellous piece of loveliness, this nameless thing of beauty! Surely the skies were going to fall! She was all one ecstatic smile until she went away, evidently treading on air and feeling six inches taller; and I was glad to know that her husband could not take the treasure away from her, as anything that had been worn by a woman might never afterwards

Photograph by Kerry, Sydney.

TEACHER AND NATIVE GIRLS, SOLOMON ISLANDS.

The girls are wearing the *sulu*, a picturesque compromise between native and European costume.

Photograph by Kerry, Sydney.

A GIRL OF THE SOLOMON ISLANDS.

be allowed to disgrace the form of the superior sex."

The most striking feature in connection with female sociology in Melanesia is found in Ambrym, where the women have organised themselves into castes or grades of rank like those of the men. The men are divided into ten grades, starting from the common folk, who are of no rank at all. By influence, and payment of a certain number of pigs, admission to the organisation is obtained, and a man gains the status of *Berang*, the lowest step in the social ladder. By increasing influence and successive payments a man may slowly climb the hill of ambition until he reaches the topmost throne of the *Mal*.

Castes in Ambrym.

The women's organisation is on the same plan, but it contains only eight divisions of rank. It is significant that the topmost grade of the women's social ladder is that of *Berang-vir*, which is the lowest rung of that of the men. So that the best that can be said of the most influential and distinguished of the women is that she is on a level with the lowest rank of men.

One of the native customs of Ambrym compels a woman on meeting a man to kneel down and crawl past him on all fours. To this peculiar form of showing respect to the "lords of creation" Miss Grimshaw attributes the fact that the Ambrym mission hospital has had many cases of housemaid's knee to treat.

In certain respects the Fijians represent the highest grade to which women have attained in Melanesia, and here all three factors, geographical, racial, and sociological, are clearly discernible.

Fijian Superiority.

The islands are well watered, well wooded, and on the whole healthy, the soil is fertile, and the vegetation luxuriant. The people are a mixture of Melanesians and Polynesians, for the route of the early Polynesian migrations of the fourth century probably passed through Fiji, and colonies from Tonga and Samoa are known to have established themselves in the islands some two hundred years ago, and their influence is noticeable in physical type, customs and language. Lastly there was a regular system of government under the chiefs of tribes; great deference was paid to rank, and religion was a form of ancestor-worship, with a firm belief in a future state. This gave a stability to society and an incentive to energy and enterprise, and produced conditions of life which the old men speak of regretfully as "the good old times." Among the upper classes the women held a high position. Mr. Blyth (late Secretary for Native Affairs in Fiji) says: "The chiefs treated their ladies (*marama*) well. Their wives were of as high rank as themselves; and it might have caused serious complications with the families or tribes to which they belonged if the ladies had been ill-used or degraded to menial work. As a rule the chief was kind to the common women of his household, in whatsoever capacity they served him. The Fiji chief of those days was often a true gentleman." Where conditions of life were harder, the woman, as usual, suffered first, and became the drudge. As a rule, if there were a heavy weight to carry, she had to carry it. In some parts of Fiji the women took their share in the hard work of the fields; but in other parts, especially in those influenced by Tongan example (for the Tongans did not exact hard labour from their women), the women never went near the food plantations either to plant or dig food.

The women, like all Melanesians, were skilled in plait-work and basket-making. On p. 1 two Fijian girls are seen at work, the one on the right making a mat, the one on the left a fish-basket. One of these baskets is seen in use tied round the waist of the girl from the mountains on p. 118.

Fijian dances also show Polynesian influence. The dancers stand or sit, and the dancing consists in rhythmical movements and gestures. On p. 119 is illustrated a scene from the Lakalaka dance, as performed at Lekimba, by Fijians.

The Fijians always had a strong sense of law and order, and everything is accordingly regulated by courts and councils, *Mbose*. It is a significant fact that the women have their *Mbose*, in which they decide and determine what is their part in any function. It may be they have to decide what food they have to prepare or what property they shall give at some festival; but whatever the business, they always meet and do their work conscientiously and well.

But that the true Melanesian attitude towards women is not absent from Fiji may be seen in the following anecdote, related by Mr. Blyth: "A few years ago a magistrate was being rowed down a river in a downpour of rain. Looking out he saw what he thought was an umbrella on

Photograph by J. W. Waters.

ADI CAKAHAN.
A Fijian woman of high rank.

an approaching craft, and, on coming abreast of it, a raft was visible, made of bamboos. On the raft was an empty gin box, and on the box sat a native holding the umbrella. left hand. She was, in fact, dragging the raft up the river, swimming the while as only a native can swim. This woman was the wife of that man."

Photograph by J. W. Waters.

FIJIAN GIRL FROM THE INTERIOR.
With native costume and fish-basket.

The raft appeared to be moving up-stream, and yet no one was poling it or pulling it along the bank. After a minute's inspection the magistrate discovered a small black speck on the river, about a fathom ahead of the raft. This proved to be the head of a woman. She was striking out nobly with her right hand, and through her teeth was a rope fixed to the raft, and held by her

General Remarks.

Viewing the position of women in Melanesia as a whole, it can readily be seen that they lead no idle existence and play no insignificant part in social life wherever a certain amount of physical well-being is assured by natural advantages.

To begin with, there is the bearing and rearing of children, which forms no

Photograph by J. W. Waters.

THE LAKALAKA DANCE AT LEKIMBA, FIJI.

Fijian dancing consists merely of rhythmical movements of the body; the dancers either sit or stand.

inconsiderable item in an area where almost without exception every woman is married at an early age, where sterility is rare, and where lactation is prolonged for two or three years.

As a rule the woman has to do the greater part of the field work, though sometimes the men break up the ground. She digs, plants, weeds, and collects the harvest, often carries it to the store-house, and, if necessary, transports it to the market to exchange for other produce. She collects the food for the family from the gardens or the reef, prepares and cooks it, and fetches the water. For home work she plaits leaves and fibres for house furniture, baskets, clothes, etc.; where clay is procurable she makes the pots for cooking and for sale; and her deft fingers elaborate ornaments of plait-work, beads, feathers, fur, and an endless array of natural decorative materials.

Photograph by Kerry, Sydney.

GIRL OF RUBIANA, SOLOMON ISLANDS.
With characteristic shell armlets.

MICRONESIA

By A. HINGSTON, M.A.

Geographical Position—Racial Type—Dress—Tattooing—Ear Deformation—Ornaments—Marriage Ceremonies—Polygyny—Position of Women

Geographical Position.

NORTH of Melanesia and west of Polynesia lie countless little islands, sometimes forming large clusters, sometimes occurring singly, whose diminutive size has given to the whole area the name of Micronesia (μικρὸς small, νῆσος island). The most important of the groups stretch in a large curve outside the west-to-south bend of Melanesia. The Pelew Islands, or Western Carolines, are 600 miles east of the Philippines, and they, together with the Central and Eastern Carolines, stretch over an area of some 2,000 miles. To the north are the Ladrones or Mariannes. At the east end of the Carolines are the Marshall Islands, and, curving down towards the south-east, the Gilbert Islands and the Kingsmill Islands, while Nui, in the Ellice Islands, marks the furthest advance of the Micronesians towards the south.

Racial Type.

The islands are occupied by a very mixed population, probably based on an aboriginal Melanesian type, which has been constantly adulterated by subsequent infiltration of Malay, Polynesian and Japanese elements.

As a rule the Micronesians resemble the Polynesians very closely, differing from them in being more hairy and shorter in stature, with longer heads, but great varieties are found throughout the area.

The husband and wife, slaves, belonging to the Pimlingai tribe, illustrated on p. 122, probably represent the dark aboriginal population of Uap (Carolines). This type was described by Captain Morell with some enthusiasm as follows :—

"The women are small in size, and very handsome, with delicate features and a dark sparkling eye, expressive of tenderness and affection. They have round luxuriant chests, slender waists, small hands and feet, straight legs, and small ankles. In short they seem to be, in every respect,

By the courtesy of Dr. W. H. Furness.

WOMAN FROM UAP (CAROLINES).

With coco-nut bracelets, flowers in her ears, and *Hibiscus* bast dyed black tied as a necklace.

By the courtesy of Dr. W. H. Furness.

MAN AND WOMAN (SLAVES) OF THE PIMLINGAI TRIBE, UAP (CAROLINES).
Showing the dark aboriginal type.

admirably 'fitted for the tender offices of love'; and, setting aside our innate prejudices to certain complexions, their personal charms are of a very superior order."

But though the gallant Captain, when attempting to describe the fair Micronesian type, laments his lack of descriptive powers, and prays the reader to accept "the plain matter-of-fact observations of a seaman," he waxes eloquent :—

"A pair of long jet-black silken eye-lashes, with more than what we should consider a usual curve, are merely the drapery or window-curtain under which the soul peeps out from her palace through the crystal medium of a pair of bright penetrating black eyes. The women are of about the same size as ours, delicately formed, with very slender waists and exquisitely moulded busts. Their hands and feet are not larger

By the courtesy of Dr. W. H. Furness.

GIRL FROM MIGIUL: THE BEAUTY OF THE ISLAND. (*See* p. 124.)

than those of our children at twelve years of age, and I have frequently with both hands spanned the waists of girls of eighteen to twenty years old. They have small heads, high foreheads, large black eyes, full plump cheeks, handsomely formed noses, small mouths, and a beautiful set of teeth, which adds a thousand charms to each bewitching smile. Their ears are small,

By the courtesy of Dr. W. H. Furness.

GIRL FROM MIGIUL: THE BEAUTY OF THE ISLAND.
Profile view. (*See* p. 123.)

their necks very delicately formed, back of which flows their long black hair. They are extremely modest and sensitive, and blushes can frequently be seen playing through the darkness of their complexions. Their countenances ever express vivacity and cheerfulness, their movements are elastic and sylph-like; even the Virginian Pocahontas, on the score of personal attractions and tenderness of disposition, would be thrown in the shade by a comparison with these fascinating females."

An example of this type and some justification for the Captain's enthusiasm may be seen in the accompanying portraits of a girl from the bachelor's house at Migiul, acknowledged by common consent to be the most beautiful girl on the island. She is described by Dr. W. H. Furness as a nice, modest, gentle girl, and famous for her singing.

According to the prevailing custom her teeth are jet black with the encrustation resulting from betel chewing. A basket containing the areca nut, betel pepper leaf, and lime forms an indispensable companion.

The two girls from the bachelor's house on the north end of Uap (p. 125) carry their betel baskets under their left arms, and one has on her right arm a bundle of turmeric, which passes as money.

In some of the Micronesian groups betel is not fashionable, and in the Marshalls in particular the young folk are all noted for their beautiful regular rows of shining white teeth, in which they take great pride.

The women usually wear their hair long, flowing loosely down, but new fashions in hair-dressing are readily adopted. A traveller in the Marshalls tells how his cook was the first pig-tailed Chinaman to be seen in a certain island, and how the whole population crowded round his house to gaze at the novelty. The next day a whole row of girls were seen strutting about with their hair in pig-tails.

Dress.

The dress of the women varies in the different groups. In the Northern Pelew Islands the women are usually naked. In the Gilberts the costume consists of what Stevenson calls "the perilous hairbreadth *ridi*," a cutty petticoat or fringe of smoked fibre of coco-nut leaf, not unlike tarry string; the lower edge not meeting the mid-thigh, the upper adjusted so low upon the haunches that it seems to cling by accident.

In Nukuor and Ruk (Carolines) a *poncho*-like mantle is woven of banana and *Hibiscus* fibre, and a hole made for the head, bordered with shell decoration (*see* p. 128). The most highly prized article of clothing is a girdle of grass and lengths of young coco-nut, Pandanus or other leaves. split with a shell into strips of varying widths (pp. 122 and 123). That worn by the slave on p. 122 is made of grass and dried croton leaves, and constitutes the badge of an adult Uap woman.

The occurrence of the loom distinguishes Micronesia both from Melanesia and Poly-

By the courtesy of Dr. W. H. Furness.

TWO GIRLS FROM NORTH END OF UAP (CAROLINES)

Carrying their betel baskets, their indispensable companions, under their left arms. One carries on her right arm a bundle of turmeric, used as money.

of from fifteen to twenty-five strings of little discs of nut-shell ; 12,500 discs go to a girdle of twenty strings, so the labour and patience necessary for its construction are enormous.

In the Marshalls *tapa* mats are worn, reaching from waist to ankle, but bark-cloth is not found in the Carolines. The illustration on p. 126 shows the costume of one of the wives of a "king" on Jaluit (Marshalls), consisting of two woven mats, one worn before and one behind.

Skirts or deep girdles of woven grass are worn by the women from Ruk (Carolines), p. 127. The most characteristic costume of the Carolines is the full petticoat made nesia, but it is not in common use. In Kusaie (Carolines) both men and women wear a girdle woven of various coloured banana fibres, and in Ponapé the same kind of girdle is worn, but the patterns are different, and the work is much coarser.

Tattooing.

Personal deformation consists in tattooing, and distension of the ear-lobes, with occasional piercing of the cartilage of the nose. Tattooing is generally merely decorative, and patterns are taken from the interlacing of the coco-nut fronds in the native baskets. Sometimes it indicates rank ; slaves are not allowed to be tattooed, and, in the Marshalls, tattooed cheeks are the peculiar privilege of men of high birth. On Nukuor (Carolines) women have to live for three months in a sacred house, and bathe ceremonially in the sea. before the operation of tattooing, which

By the courtesy of Dr. W. H. Furness.

WIFE OF A "KING" ON JALUIT (MARSHALLS).

Wearing a costume of woven mats, one before and one behind.

only covers a small part of the lower part of the body. In Ponapé (Carolines) a tattooed girdle is begun at an early age, and continued in patches.

Ear Deformation.

Piercing of the cartilage of the nose is not universal, but distension of the ear lobes is fairly common. In the Marshalls the hole is enormously enlarged, and huge Pandanus leaf rings are worn, but in parts of the Carolines only a small hole is the fashion, into which tufts of red wool, flowers, etc., are thrust, and from which ear-rings of varied descriptions depend. Typical ear-rings are seen worn by three women from Ruk (Carolines) on p. 127. These are made of white conch shells and the black tips of coco-nuts, and the rings are split so as to be worn on the distended lobe.

For some time after the ears are first pierced coco-nut ear protectors are worn, until the wounds are sufficiently healed. Dakofel, daughter of a chief of Uap, on p. 129, is wearing these picturesque appendages. Under her arm she carries her betel basket, and also a sheet of *Hibiscus* bark, which serves as a seat.

Ornaments.

Necklaces of shell beads and rings of various materials are common, and a bunch of *Hibiscus* bast dyed black is often worn knotted round the neck with the ends hanging down in front, as is seen in many of the illustrations. The wife of the Jaluit "king," whose portrait is on this page, wears a necklace of red and white shell beads.

Circular pieces of mother of pearl shell and turtle shell, and polished discs of conch shell strung on human hair, are common ornaments.

Long narrow wooden combs are characteristic of Micronesia. They consist of ten to twelve teeth, and are decorated about the handle with rich feather ornament.

Marriage Ceremonies.

In most parts of Micronesia pre-nuptial chastity, even though ten to twelve is the usual age for marriage, does not exist, and the marriage tie is lightly regarded. A feast, eating, drinking and dancing, which may be continued for some weeks, constitute the characteristic features of Micronesian weddings.

In Ponapé (Carolines) the wedding ceremony is rather peculiar. The bride is brought into the house of the bridegroom's family, and her prospective mother-in-law rubs coco-nut oil into her back and shoulders, a garland of flowers is placed on her head, and the ceremony is concluded by a feast.

Turner tells of a curious custom of choosing a husband in Arorae, one of the Gilbert Islands. The girl sits in the lower room of the house, and over her head are her lovers, who let down coco-nut leaflets through the chinks in the ceiling. She pulls at one, and asks whose it is. If the reply is not in the voice of the young man she wishes to have, she leaves it and pulls another leaf, and so on, until the right man answers, when she pulls the leaf right down. The happy man then remains, while the rest slink away. The young couple go to their respective homes and prepare for the day of feasting, which is also the day of their marriage.

The ceremony is performed by the father of either of them. The two bow their heads before him. He takes hold of their hair with one hand and with the other pours on them a purifying libation of the juice of the coco-nut palm.

Divorce is easy, since there is no bride-price to be reclaimed, and as a rule it merely consists in the wife returning, either by her own choice or by the will of her husband, to her own people. A visitor to Nauru (Marshalls) met a young man of twenty-four, who had already had eleven wives, some of whom had deserted him, and some of whom he had deserted, because they did not please their mother-in-law.

By the courtesy of Dr W. H. Furness.

THREE WOMEN FROM RUK (CAROLINES).

With typical ear-rings of white conch shells and the black tips of coco-nuts.

Nevertheless family life is generally peaceful and happy, and genuine affection often unites husband and wife.

Polygyny.

The possession of many wives is as usual the privilege of the wealthy, and is enjoyed by the few. A tale told by Louis Becke suggests that this system is not so repulsive to the wives as one might suppose. The story relates the romance between Jelik, the brother of a chief in the Marshalls, and a young girl aged sixteen, in the service of a German trader in the same island. Jelik made his ladylove a present of a sewing-machine, then a novelty in the country, and a keg of salt meat, bought at about five times its value, both of which articles the girl naïvely sold back again to the trader for a few dollars, with which she bought

Photograph by Museum Godeffroy, No. 510, Pl. 23.

INOAR, FROM ETEN ISLAND, RUK (CAROLINES).

Wearing a poncho-like garment. Her ear-lobes are distended by the weight of rings.

tobacco and a clasp-knife for her lover. Instead of being offended at the fate of his gifts, Jelik was much touched at these proofs of her devotion. The marriage took place soon after, and the bridegroom announced his intention of putting away his two other wives, whom he had hitherto regarded with much affection and respect. The bride, however, strenuously resisted this plan, and made a most eloquent appeal, saying she would at once return to her home rather than consent to such injustice, and begged to be allowed to dwell with the other two wives under their husband's roof, and learn from them her wifely duties. Jelik gave his consent to her request, and they all lived happily together.

The women are usually well treated. *Muqul*, or "bad form," is the most potent restriction next to taboo in the Pelew group, and it is "bad form" for a man to beat or abuse his wife in public, and punishable with a fine.

Position of Women.

A linguistic peculiarity of the Carolines suggests that women are not held in very high esteem. The word *li* or "woman" is prefixed to words to give them a bad significance: for example *li-kum* = a lie, *i.e.*, a woman's fault; *li-porok* = curiosity, *i.e.*, a woman's peering; *li-pilipil* = favouritism, *i.e.*, a woman's choice; but *li-mpok* = sincere affection, *i.e.*, a woman's love.

The position of women is doubtless influenced by the fact that as a rule they do most of the work. It is said in the Gilbert Islands that the men are in such fear of breaking the Sabbath by mistake that they abstain from work, week in,

Photograph by Museum Godeffroy, No. 433, Pl. 27.

GIRL FROM PONAPÉ (CAROLINES).

With plaited head-dress of bast and discs in her ear-lobes.

week out, unless under the stress of absolute hunger.

Christian enumerates the labours of the women in Ponape. They make the mats and shutters of reed grass, plait baskets, bind the leaves of the sago palm into bundles for the thatch, make leaf girdles for the men, compound the coco-nut oil and fish-oil, and mix the cosmetic of turmeric, without which no Ponapé dandy's toilet is complete. They fetch water in calabashes, light the fires, build the stone ovens, prepare the food and perform all the household duties. When required they cheerfully assist in the outdoor labours. They prepare the copra,* filling the sacks and loading the boats with the accompaniment of so much fun and laughter that an onlooker takes it more for play than work. Finally, in time of war, they fearlessly accompany their husbands and relatives into battle.

* Dried kernel of the coco-nut, from which coco-nut oil is made.

By the courtesy of Dr. W. H. Furness.

DAKOFEL.

Daughter of a Chief of Uap. Aged about 12.

Her ears have recently been pierced, and she wears protections of coco-nuts. (*See* p. 126.)

ARUNTA WOMEN.
Showing headbands. They are usually netted of fine string, with close meshes, and smeared with red ochre.

AUSTRALIA*

By N. W. THOMAS

Physical Aspect of the Aboriginals—Clothing and Ornaments—Aboriginal Legends Relative to Children—Birth Customs—Mutilation of Girls--Education and Recreation—Betrothals—Pre-Marriage Mutilations—Elopements—Marriage Legends—Magic and Marriage—An Aboriginal Idyll—Monogamy—Abduction of Married Women—Relations of Husband and Wife—Wives as Loans—Tribal Etiquette—Woman's Work--Domestic Habits—Food Restrictions—Women as Fishers—Troubles of Widowhood—Death—The Corroboree—Australian Witchcraft—Burial Customs—Present Position of the Aboriginal.

Physical Aspect of the Aboriginals.

THE charms of the dusky belle of Australia have been sung, if at all, at most by aboriginal bards; for if the truth must be told, she is very far from being a belle when she frequents the neighbourhood of the white man and adopts whisky drinking and other civilised habits. In her native wilds she is a more presentable person, and Eyre, in his "Journals of Travel," goes so far as to say that he had met females in the bloom of youth whose well proportioned limbs and symmetry of figure might have formed a model for the sculptor's chisel. But such cases are the exception, for whether it be from centuries of the hardest labour or from a deficient appreciation of beauty on the part of the male portion of the community, or both, the native Australian woman is seldom good-looking. Her charms, such as they are, fade rapidly at an early age, and both physically and mentally she is inferior to the sterner sex; in fact the women are disproportionately small, and their limbs are not so well formed even as those of the men, which are remarkably slightly developed.

The aboriginal woman is as a rule five

* The aboriginal races only are here dealt with

feet high or a little more; her hair is generally said to be black, but whether this is not universally true or whether a liberal application of red ochre conceals the true colour, many of the specimens which reach England are rather reddish brown than black. As regards appearance, the hair is sometimes silky, but more often a tangled mass, matted with grease and ochre; it may be lank and straight or wavy and even curly as some of the illustrations show. The woman's head is usually easily distinguishable from that of the male; among other features the great bony projections are wanting above the eyes of the woman, though she resembles the sterner sex in the deep depression of the root of the nose. Her eyes, as the illustration on p. 144 shows, are often beautiful; they are usually dark brown.

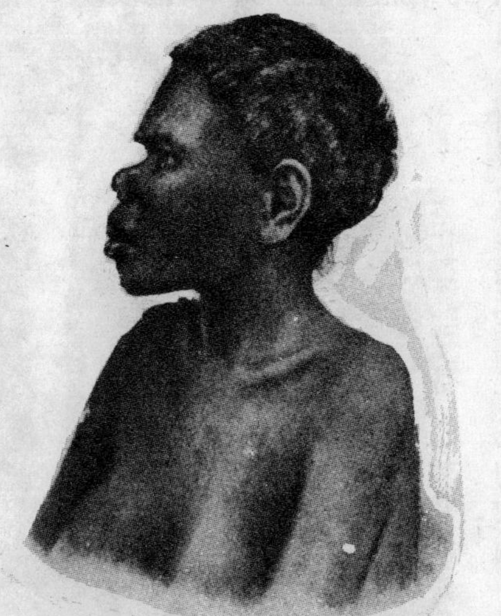

VICTORIAN ABORIGINAL WOMAN.
Showing depression at root of nose. The eyes of the Australian are nearly always deep-set.

Clothing and Ornaments.

A catalogue of her ornaments in various parts of the Continent, of her modes of hair-dressing, or of her clothing, such as it is, would be of little interest, and only a few points are here selected for notice. The inclement climate of the south compels the women to adopt some covering from the weather, and the opossum or kangaroo skin cloak was an effective one; the substitution of European blankets for it was a fatal error, and helped to extinguish the tribes of the south-east. Further north clothing is worn less for purposes of warmth than for decency, though native requirements in this respect are but slight. Observers have noted that in some parts the younger women were equally at ease with or without their narrow apron, though they objected to be seen at their toilet; in another case a white man hung a small mat apron-wise upon an otherwise unclothed girl, who was utterly unembarrassed in her natural state; her confusion when the "dress" was put on her was so pitiable that it was promptly removed again, to her great relief.

The apron or belt, worn in some cases only by unmarried or lately married women, is a fringe of opossum or other hair depending from a hair girdle. For decorative purposes armlets and necklaces, head fillets and pendants may be worn; nor must the nose-bone be forgotten, which on state occasions is replaced by a green twig. Lumps of gum or dog's teeth may hang from the woman's hair, and in some tribes the belle, got up regardless of expense, wears artificial whiskers, formed of locks of hair cemented with beefwood gum; these hang some two inches below the jaw. Sometimes a forehead net is worn; flowers or birds' down may also add to the effect; and a black or rather chocolate brown skin, polished with iguana fat, completes the toilette, save for the indispensable red ochre in the hair.

Aboriginal Legends relative to children.

The Australian woman, like the rest of mankind, begins life as a baby; and as the uncivilised are curious above every creature on the earth, except perhaps the civilised child, and are given to inventing explanations where they cannot discover causes, the Australian black has much to say on the origin of babies. In the north of New South Wales on the Narran River they say it is the moon who plays the principal part in the creation of girl babies, and sometimes the crow lends a helping hand; when, therefore, a small black boy quarrels with his girl friends, he taunts them with this fact, regardless of their effective *tu quoque:* "A lizard made you." But as women of the crow's creating have the reputation of being noisy and quarrelsome, perhaps the victory rests with the stronger sex after all.

It is somewhere on the Culgoa River that Bahloo, the moon, makes the girl babies; his work-table is a big stone, which lies at the bottom of a hole in time of drought, but at other times rises from its place and just keeps its top above the water. When Bahloo's share in the manufacture of babies is at an end, he hands them over to a birth-spirit named Waddahgudjaelwon, and he hangs them about on trees to wait till some woman passes beneath; then they seize upon her and are in a fair way to make their appearance on the earth. If, however, the baby is to live, it must manage to find an earthly father too; those for which Bahloo, the moon, is alone responsible, are born with teeth.

Another way in which a baby may find a mother is by being snatched up in a whirlwind by the evil spirit Wurrawilberoo; and the woman thus discredited by her enemy may even in bad cases become the mother of twins. Needless to say, twins are not looked on with favour where life is such a hard struggle as in Australia; and even where they are born without teeth, the father refuses to recognise more than one. Yet after all the poor mother is perhaps guiltless, for do not spirit babies hang themselves in pairs upon a single branch of the Coolabah tree and cruelly incarnate themselves in one unhappy mother, who is thus exposed to the opprobrium of the camp? And to put its malice beyond dispute the first born of twins comes into the world with its tongue stuck out in mockery of its miserable parent.

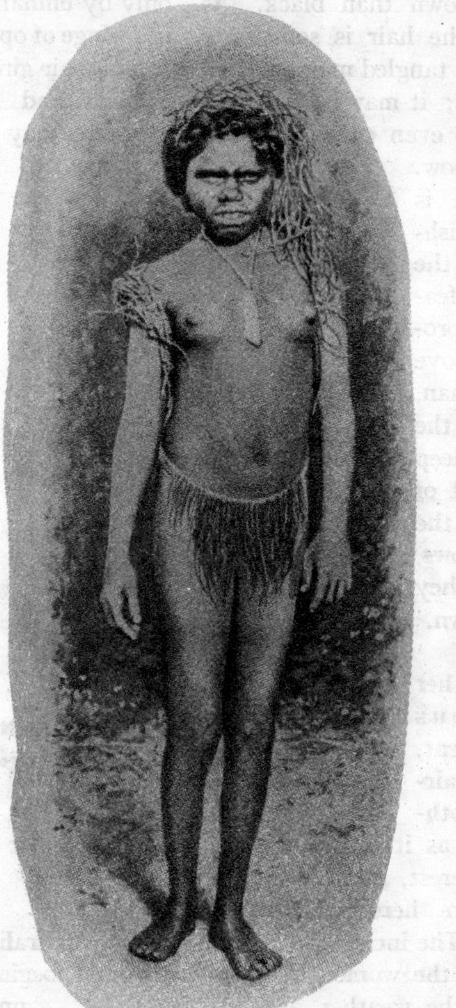

By courtesy of Dr. Seligmann.

GIRL FROM CAPE DIRECTION.

Undress. Under ordinary circumstances few ornaments are worn.

Some unlucky babies hang themselves on trees beneath which there is no traffic; waiting and wailing for a mother they get on the nerves of the spirits, who transform them into mistletoe, and form its orange red flowers from the blood of never-to-be born children. Usually the spirit baby is newly made for each mother; but if a child dies very young, it may be reincarnated; and the babies that are pleased with their first mothers choose the same again, otherwise they are allowed to go to some other acquaintance.

In the north of Queensland the blacks are equally ingenious if less convincing in their explanations. On the Tully River a woman expects a child if she sits over the fire on which she has roasted a kind of black bream, or if she has caught a kind of bull frog, or if she has dreamt of having a child, or, finally, if some man has told her she is to have one; another tribe says that a magician tells the mother to have a child, and ascribe twins to the malice of the medicine man of a hostile tribe.

At Cape Bedford spirits in the scrub

make the babies, which begin by being full grown; girls take the form of plovers to fly from their home in the west to their future mothers; arrived at its destination the bird is transformed into a baby, so when they hear the curlew at night, the blacks say "Hello! there are babies about." On the River Pennefather, Anjea fashions the babies of swamp mud, and before they reach their mothers they have to wander in the bush; when therefore a child has a club foot or any other deformity, it is clearly because it has caught its foot in a log in its prenatal journeys. Another tribe say that babies are made of Pandanus roots and reach their mothers when the latter are bathing; happily this does not seem to hinder them from their ablutions.

By courtesy of Dr. Seligmann.

GIRL FROM CAPE DIRECTION.

Full dress. For a corroboree or other ceremonial occasion armbands, legbands, chestbands, etc., are donned.

Birth Customs.

As with the women of most uncivilised peoples so with the Australian mother, birth is an easy matter. Ceremonial regulations, based on the fear of evil magical influence, compel her to retire from the camp; she may stay away only a few hours, or custom may demand that she shall be secluded for eight or ten days. On the Narran River, where the babies hang on the Coolabah tree waiting for a mother, they are born with a leaf in their mouths, and the first duty is to take this out, otherwise it would carry the baby back to spirit-land; then hot gum leaves are pressed on the bridge of the baby's nose, to make it flat, for a thoroughly flat nose is essential to good looks. In some tribes the baby is washed or rubbed with sand, in others it is only smeared with iguana fat, and some powdered ashes rubbed on its head.

Sometimes the happy father announces the birth of his child by special messenger to all his friends and relations, who hasten to make him presents of shirts, knives, and other valuables. In the central tribes the father, together with his wife's father, maternal grandfather and great-uncle, is forbidden to speak after the child is born—if he broke the *tabu* the child would be injured; later the woman goes from her camp to her husband's and shows him the child, saying that it is his, and then he is released from his bond of silence. The coming of a little stranger is by no means an occasion of unmixed rejoicing, and, though a woman may bear six or seven children, she rarely rears more than two. The remainder are not accounted for, as with us, by a gradual process of semi-starvation, by doses of gin, or by any of the other numerous civilised methods of reducing the too numerous mouths in the family; a superfluous baby is put out of the way as soon as it is born, either by actual violence or by the less humane method of withholding all food; but no half measures are allowed. In many parts the corpse was eaten by the brothers, sometimes by the grandparents.

But it must not be imagined from this that Australian parents have no affection for their children; on the contrary, they are as fond parents as can be seen anywhere. They rarely chastise them, and a mother will give all the food she has to her children, going hungry herself in times of scarcity. They will endure abuse and even blows from their children, and finally suffer themselves to be coerced.

ABORIGINAL WOMEN AND FISH.

Fishing with the line is the work of women; men use the spear; both sexes use the net.

A young mother is concerned for the bodily development of her children, and for their character, no less than for their protection against magic. In some tribes, if a child woke at night, its mother would warm her hands at the camp fire and rub its joints that it might grow lissome and shapely. When the child began to crawl, she would take a centipede, half roast it in the fire, and then beat the child's hands with it, crooning a charm to prevent it from stealing in later life. A baby's mouth would be carefully closed, to prevent some magician from sending a disease spirit to trouble it, and all sorts of precautions had to be taken when magpies or crows were seen, for they are counted evil spirits.

Very young children are carried in one of the boat-shaped water-vessels; when they are older, they may sit on the mother's shoulder, holding on with legs and arms; they may bestride the mother's neck and cling to her hair, or she may wear an opossum skin cloak or a big round mat on her back, and pop the child into the pouch thus formed. A mother seldom sings a lullaby to her child, though she may make a droning sound to send it to sleep; she slaps it in the European fashion, and sometimes makes faces to frighten it; an approved method is to pass a string through the hole bored in the cartilage of the nose and pull it upwards. Children are often weaned very late, and two may often be seen at the breast at the same time. As they get older they enjoy a diet of honey, opossum, and kangaroo flesh.

Mutilation of Girls.

Mutilations of various sorts are inflicted on the Australian girl. Sometimes she loses one joint of her little finger, sometimes she has a front tooth knocked out in imitation of the men, more often she has a bone or feather thrust through the cartilage of the nose, and this custom once gave rise to a pretty contest of wit between white and black. A European girl asked why a black woman wore a bone in her nose, and said that white women did not do that. The black gin looked her censor up and down and fixed her eyes on her earrings. "Why you make hole in your ears? No good that! Black gin no do that, pull 'em down your ears like dogs. Plenty good bone in nose, make you sing good. 'Sposin' cuggil (bad) smell, you put bone longa nose, no smell 'im. Plenty good make hole longa nose, no good make hole longa ears, make 'em hang down all same dogs!" And with that the old black went off laughing, pulling down the lobes of her ears and barking like a dog. In nimbleness of intellect the blacks can hold their own with us.

The education of the Australian girl begins early, she soon knows how to help her mother in the quest for food, grubbing up roots, preparing yams, capturing small lizards, extracting larvæ from beneath the bark of trees, and, in some of the tribes, accompanying her on fishing expeditions.

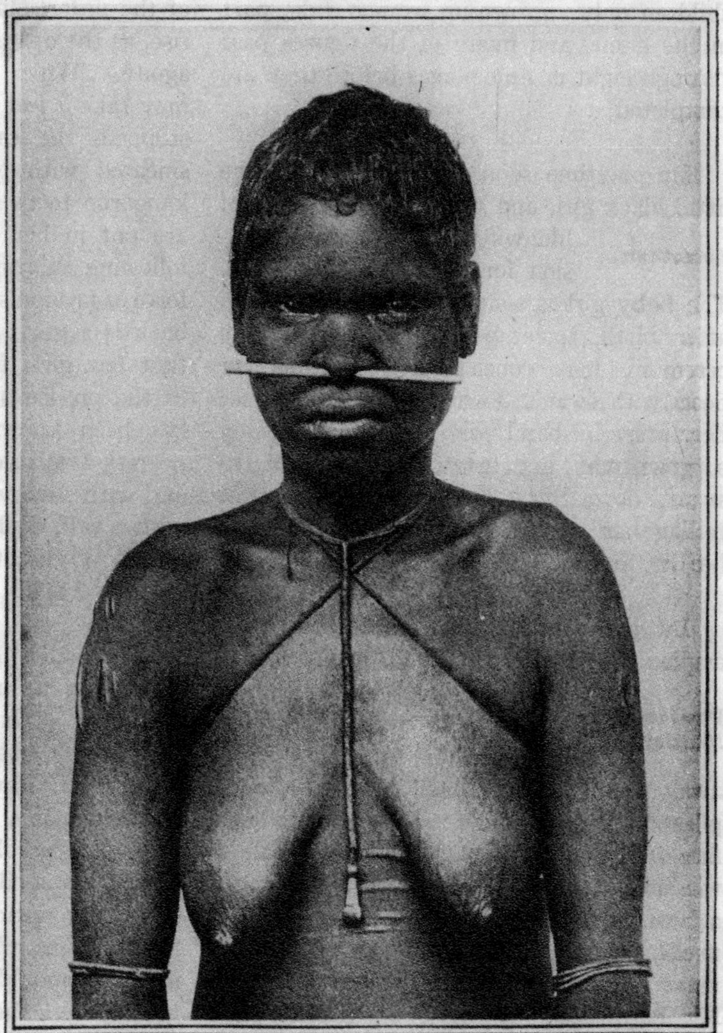

Photograph by King & Co.

ABORIGINAL WOMAN OF NORTH AUSTRALIA.

Wearing nose-bone, chestlet, etc., with scars on the shoulders and chest.

But even in black Australia, life is very far from being all work. Black children as well as white have their games; in some parts dolls are made of cane, split half way up to represent the legs, and the split part doubled to represent the knees. As the Australian is usually innocent of clothing in his or her youth, dressing dolls is a less absorbing occupation than with us; but sometimes pieces of bark are wrapped

Education and Recreation.

in grass and made to do duty as dolls, and perhaps, if we only knew it, the little black girl loves her doll just as well as the best brought up child in England. Cat's cradle, too, is a favourite diversion, and not for children only; grown-up women take part in the game, and many of the figures pass through eight or nine stages before they are completed.

Betrothals.

But playtime soon passes away for the little black girl, and the serious business of life, wifehood, the only profession for women, is taken up. The baby girl is sometimes betrothed soon after birth, sometimes a little later; the ceremony may consist in decorating her head with swan's down, taking her to see her future husband, who is perhaps already a grown man, and transferring some of the swan's down to his head, at the same time telling her unconscious ears that he is to be her husband in fourteen years' time.

Pre-Marriage Mutilation.

But before she is married the girl who aspires to be *chic* and beautiful has to undergo various initiatory ceremonial mutilations. An old beldam takes the girl away from the camp, and as a preliminary plasters her with mud; then she lights a fire of leaves and makes the girl swallow the smoke, at the same time giving her advice as to her future conduct. The girl meditates on her lessons in private, and at most returns to the main camp once to see her betrothed; he must obstinately turn his back on her; so she throws leaves on his shoulders, and shakes him, then turns and runs her hardest to her solitary camp, which she only quits some time later to become his wife. The initiation ceremonies, however, may be more severe, and involve painful mutilations, which are fully described in scientific works. Among the least of them is the production of so-called " keloids " —raised scars on the body or upper limbs. When these are to be made the girl is taken out early in the morning, she squats with her back to her decorator, her head tightly held between the knees of an old woman seated on the ground. A male operator with a mussel shell makes cuts in rows across the back, a quarter of an inch deep, and an inch long; and as the butchery proceeds the blood streams in torrents from the back of the unfortunate girl, whose piteous cries rise, as the operation proceeds, into a yell of agony. When all is finished—the work may take a full hour—and the bleeding has stopped, the candidate for matrimony is smeared with grease and red ochre, two kangaroo teeth and a tuft of emu feathers are put in her hair, and she fasts till the following morning. But so strong is the force of fashion's demands—for a well-scarred back is a great addition to other charms—that few girls fought against the infliction in the pre-European days; sometimes one has been known to fix her teeth in the nearest available portion of the old woman, and with such vigour, that she has leapt up with a yell, while her captive, to her lifelong regret, no doubt, remains with a back only half decorated.

Elopements in Australia.

Betrothal is, of course, not the only way of getting a husband, for a girl may be bartered by her brother against another man's sister, by her father in exchange for another man's daughter, and so on; or she may be allotted to her husband by a tribal council, and neither of them may have any intimation of the approaching happy event till the girl's brothers take a piece of smouldering firewood to the bridegroom, and the same evening apprise the woman of the name of the man to whom she has to go. In some tribes the woman shows her willingness to accept her husband by making a fire in his hut, and it is a point of honour with the men to gain this mark of favour. Elopement with betrothed or unbetrothed girls is by no means uncommon, and the consent of the lady is not in any way essential. A young man whose fancy lightly turns to thoughts of love assembles a band of his intimates and they help him to carry off his bride, or he may take her single-handed. In either case he has to reckon with the anger of her family, for her male

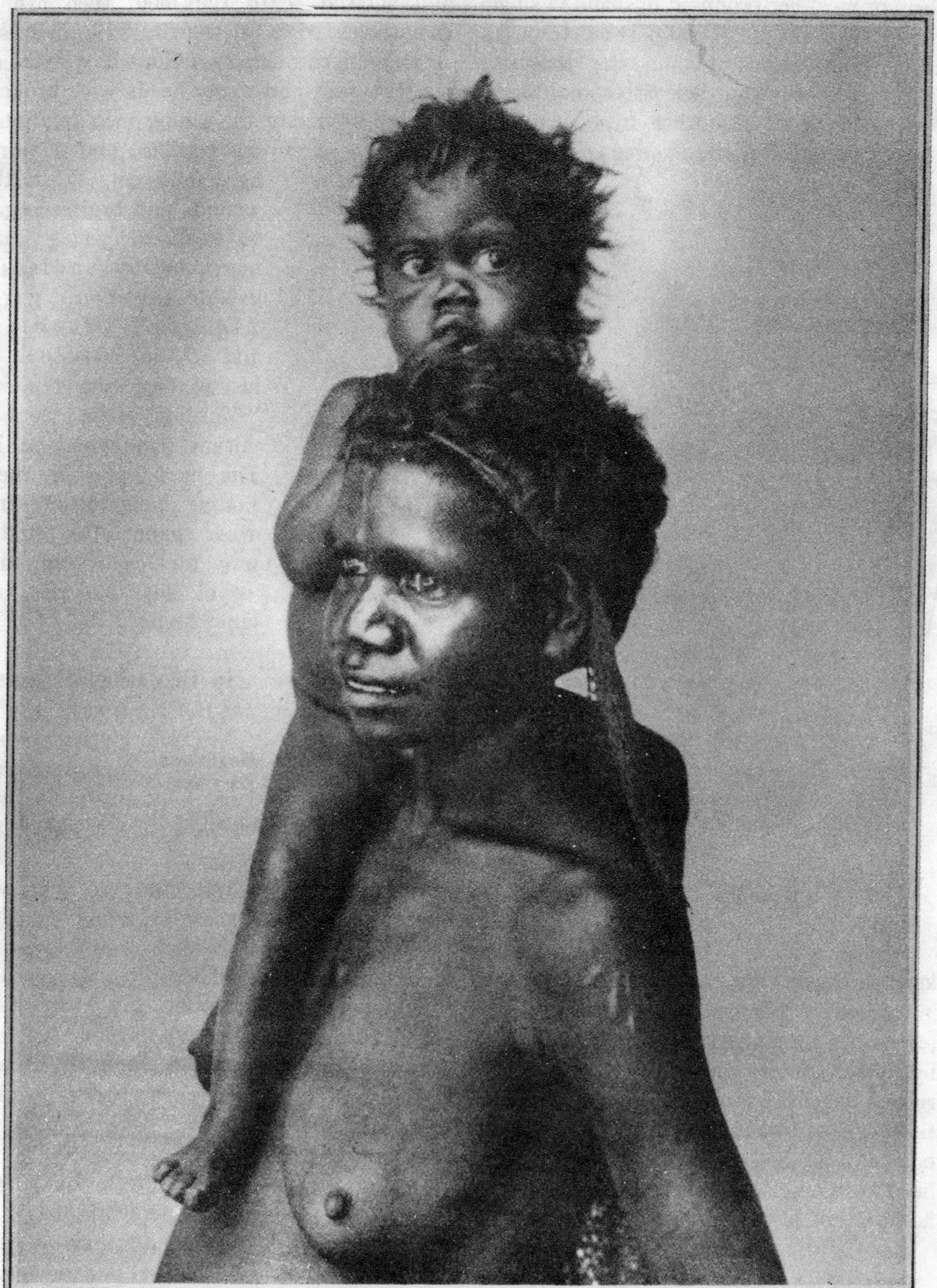

Photograph by King & Co

AUSTRALIAN ABORIGINAL MOTHER AND BABY.

When children are old enough to hold on they bestride the mother's neck and cling to her hair.

kindred pursue him; he may have to fight them or meet her promised husband in single combat, and she may be almost cut to pieces by her relatives, for of course the latter lose the woman for whom their sister would have been exchanged. In other tribes a milder custom prevailed; the eloping couple were knocked about, and the man gave a sister in exchange. The most serious fights take place when a man marries a woman to whom, by black marriage regulations, he has no right. Then the woman may be killed, and the man is attacked first with spears and boomerangs, then with knives; and even if he is the better man the lookers-on see that he does not have the best of it.

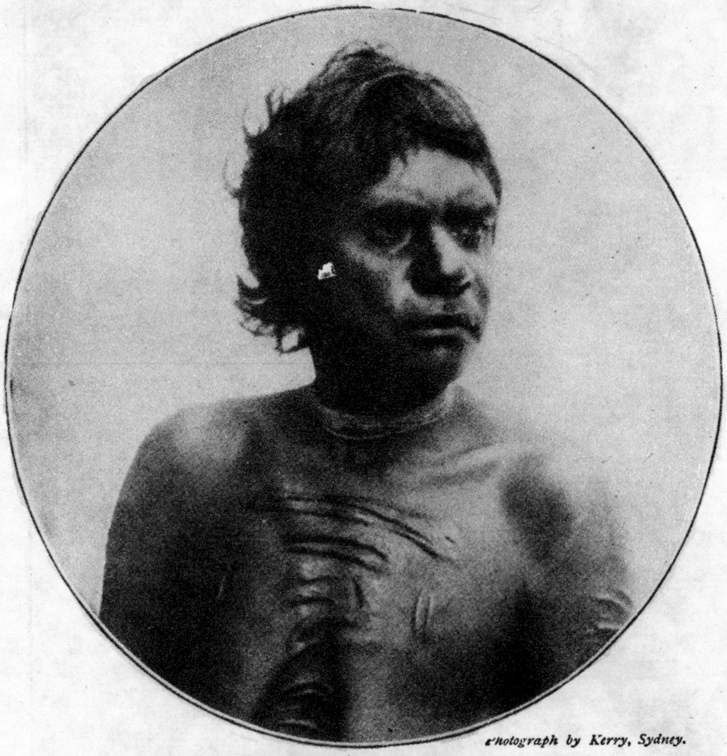

Photograph by Kerry, Sydney.

WOMAN OF THE WORKII TRIBE.
Showing scars on chest.

Marriage Legends.

One of the quaintest ways of getting married was practised in the south-east, where the males are believed to be the brothers of the emu-wren, while the women are the sisters of the superb warbler. If the young men were backward in coming forward, the women killed an emu-wren and showed it to the men, then armed themselves with sticks, the men likewise. A magnificent shindy followed, worthy of an Irish fair, and many heads were broken. On the next day the young men retaliated by killing a superb warbler, and a worse fight followed. When the wounds and bruises began to heal, a young man matrimonially inclined would say to a girl: "Djiitgun" (warbler), and if she consented to his wooing, she replied: "Yiirung, what does a yiirung (emu-wren) eat?" The man replied by mentioning kangaroo or some other game, the match was arranged, and they would elope on the first opportunity.

Magic and Marriage.

In this tribe elopement was the recognised way of getting a wife, and magicians made it their business to arrange marriages by elopement spells, which, however, were performed in public, so that the whole camp knew of the coming event. While the girl's parents, lulled by the incantation, lay wrapped in sleep, the wooer crept up behind the girl and touched her with a rod; if she was ready she gave it a tug; and then nothing remained but for the young couple to run off.

When the father woke from his magic sleep, he too proceeded to work magic in order to find out which direction the fugitives had taken, and then set out to capture them. If the young couple got away and remained away for some time, perhaps till a child was born to them, all went well when they returned. But if they came back too early, or if they allowed themselves to be caught by a pursuing party, the sub-

CAMP LIFE.

It is the duty of the women to collect wood, build huts, cook, etc.

if she wished to be ultra fashionable. Some seventy years ago a certain man Wawgroot had been promised Kilbangarroo to wife; when the time came he already had one pretty *lubra* in his *miamia*, and she was sulky at the thought of a rival. Two hours before nightfall Kilbangarroo's father suggested to her that it was time to go to her husband, but at dusk she was still lying at her father's fire wrapped in her opossum skin, and pretending to be asleep. A hint by proxy—unmerciful punishment of a disobedient dog—from her sire had no effect and he began to raise his voice; an hour passed and still no result. Picking up his club her father gave Kilbangarroo a rude thrust with the point, and then she could no longer feign sleep. Sitting up, she put on a sublimely sulky air, whereat, letting fly a string of aboriginal expletives, her progenitor pushed his advantage. But still the maiden made no move, and the heavy *nulla-nulla* was about to descend on her head when the mother intervened, raised her girl

sequent proceedings went very far beyond a joke. The girl was beaten with digging sticks by her female relatives, who had perhaps all got their husbands in the same way; and her father might spear her through one or both feet, to prevent her from running away again. The man had to meet both men and women in combat, and the latter tried to stab him in the stomach with their digging-sticks. Last but not least the couple did not even have the satisfaction of being able to settle down to married life; for the whole business of elopement had to be gone through a second time. It says much for the depth of aboriginal devotion and the fervour of black passion that all married couples should run these risks, and if necessary run them a second time, in order to enjoy connubial bliss.

An Aboriginal Idyll.

In some tribes it was a point of honour for the bride to appear unwilling to join her husband, and even carry her resistance so far as to use her yam stick upon him,

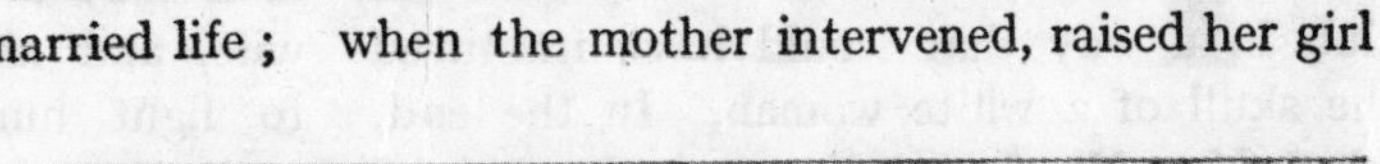

WOMEN DANCING.

The man on the left is using his shield to produce the music.

by the shoulders from the ground, and sent her on her way to serve her husband faithfully, if he could subdue her. But this is not always an easy matter. For the next day, in Wawgroot's absence, Mrs Wawgroot No. 1 abused her rival in her choicest Billingsgate, beat her soundly with her yam stick and drove her to take refuge in the bush; so Wawgroot, on his

WOMEN ABUSING EACH OTHER.

Quarrels are frequent, and the first stage is a free use of "language."

return, admonished his first love with his club in a way that would have fractured the skull of a white woman. In the end, when Mrs. Wawgroot No. 2 had received two or three severe beatings, the household settled down, and a year later even Mrs. Wawgroot No. 1 was getting fond of the new baby.

Monogamy.

As a rule the Australian male does not marry before the age of twenty-eight or thirty. In some tribes a wife would be cast off when she reached the age of thirty-five, and given to a younger man in exchange for his sister; for the young men are often trained up into matrimony by the old women, and sometimes have wives old enough to be their grandmothers. Conversely old men have very young wives, and as a man may have as many wives as he can get, there may be one old wife, one middle-aged, and one young one, all mated with the same man. In this case the young one has rather a bad time of it; for the old wife will rule her, and scold her, and carry tales to her husband about her goings-on with younger men, if she is foolish enough to speak even a word or two with one. Not only so but the young wife is not even allowed to bring up her children as she wishes, and leads a miserable life till someone abducts her, or the old wife goes the way of all flesh.

Abduction of Married Women.

It is by no means a recognised thing that a woman should cleave to her husband; on the contrary, especially if she is young and good looking (according to aboriginal standards), that is to say, plump and well favoured, she generally passes from master to master with considerable rapidity. This does not mean that she is always regularly abducted; for a man may take a fancy to some one else's wife, and challenge her lord and master to fight him for her; the latter does not accept unless he has good reason to suppose that he is the better man. If they fight, the winner carries off the aboriginal Helen, and holds her till a new champion enters the lists. A betrothed girl is watched with vigilance, especially if her future husband be advanced in years; but a young wife's lot is even harder, for her husband compels her to accompany him everywhere, whatever her state of health, and the barest suspicion of infidelity ensures her the most brutal ill-treatment—a crack on the head with a heavy club, or a spear through the fleshy part of the thigh or the calf are among the ordinary amenities of married life in Australia.

Even where a woman gives no encouragement to her admirers, her lot is by no means enviable. Plots are laid to carry her off;

AN ABORIGINAL WOMAN OF QUEENSLAND : AUSTRALIA
DRAWN BY NORMAN H. HARDY.

Facing on page 140

each of the combatants will order her to follow him, and her disobedience is punished by throwing a spear at her. Small wonder, therefore, that good looks do not bring happiness, for a beauty is soon scarred by the furrows of old and new wounds, her married life is as kaleidoscopic as that of women in some American states, and she may be carried off hundreds of miles before her troubles are at an end. Well is it for an Australian belle if she lives in a tribe where these rude manners are unknown or severely put down.

Relations of Husband and Wife.

The husband is the absolute owner of his wife; he may in most parts punish her with death in case of grave dereliction of duty, and simple chastisement will never cause her relatives to interfere. If, however, the husband kills his wife for any reason not recognised as sufficient by the native code, custom demands in some parts that he should give up his own sister to be killed by his wife's relatives, which seems a less than fair proceeding. But as it is by bartering his sister that a man gets a wife, the punishment is really more severe than it appears—in fact, it fully equals the penalty meted out to the English husband who beats his wife within an inch of her life.

Wives as Loans.

As the owner of his wife the husband is entitled to lend her to his friends, and she may not refuse; tribal meetings are often marked by the exchange of wives, and in certain tribes there is a curious system commonly known by the Dieri name *pirrauru*. According to this, a wife has a regular husband; but when he is away or at tribal meetings she passes to a man who may be called her secondary husband. Very often brothers arrange these *pirrauru* marriages, and, as a woman could with ease be abducted in the absence of her husband, it seems possible that the practice of *pirrauru* is really a kind of insurance against matrimonial accidents. As a man can have a *pirrauru* wife before he has an ordinary one, it is no doubt due in part to the scarcity of women.

Tribal Etiquette.

It is not always easy to find a wife or marry one in Europe, but for the black fellow the difficulties of entrance into the state of matrimony are far greater. Not only must the maiden be wooable and moderately willing, she must also be of the right tribal status, and woe betide the unlucky couple who fly in the face of native codes of morals; we have seen something of their fate above. Nearly all Australian tribes are divided into two great classes, whose original purpose, now falling into desuetude, was to control the matrimonial arrangements of their members. Not only must the woman belong to the right class, but in some cases it is even prescribed in what degree of relationship a man must stand to the person he is to marry; a Dieri man, for example, must marry his mother's mother's brother's daughter's daughter. This rule is, however, less alarming than it seems: a man must marry his cousin, and as in Australia the term translated "brother" includes about half the males of a given generation, instead of being confined to the male children of the same father and mother, there are sure to be some women available. However, only about one-eighth of the women of a tribe are eligible mates for a man, so that at best it is not always an easy matter for a young man to get married when the old men have first pick.

In some tribes these regulations are carried further, and all the members of the tribe are divided not only into two moieties, but, further, each moiety is subdivided into two or four classes; under normal circumstances a man is limited in his choice to the women of one of these classes, though at the present day these regulations are breaking down, and a man may marry any woman of his own generation.

In connection with these classes there is sometimes a singular and complicated system of etiquette. All over the world there are curious customs of avoidance, a son-in-law may not speak to his mother-in-law, nor a daughter-in-law to her father-in-law; sister avoids brother, and, more curious still, as we have already seen, betrothed couples avoid each other. These individual *tabus* are complicated by more general *tabus*, and the men's meeting ground is forbidden to women in Australian tribes, while the women's ground may not be profaned by the foot of a male. At night the girls and the boys under seven sleep round the family fire with the father and mother; but the older boys are banished to the camp of the unmarried men; sometimes there is also an unmarried women's camp under the command of an old woman.

Over and above these observances there is in Central Australia a strict regulation as to who may and who may not be on the visiting list, and the basis of the rules is the four-class system mentioned above. If we suppose that the four classes are named Bat, Crow, Emu, and Hawk, then a Bat man marries an Emu woman; Bat and Crow men are on calling terms with Mr. Bat and his wife; likewise Emu and Hawk women, any of these may call at will. If, however, a Bat woman wishes to pay a visit to the wife of a Bat man, she must choose a time when Mr. Bat is absent; more curious still, Crow women may not even enter his camp during his absence. Mr. Bat, on the other hand, may not speak to, look at, or go anywhere near a Hawk woman. It is perhaps as difficult to move in society in Australia as it is in England.

But it must not be imagined that these regulations entirely cut off all communication between the parties who practise avoidance. In West Australia the huts are placed some distance from each other, and at night the young men sit round their fire, relating their love adventures, when suddenly a deep, wild chant may rise, in which a new arrival relates the incidents of his journey or an old man calls to remembrance scenes of other days. Another will reply in the same tone, and the interchange of remarks conducted in this manner end by becoming general; probably woman is not behindhand in contributing to the conversation, for at night her work is over.

Woman's Work.

Broadly speaking, the wife has to do all the hard work while her lord and master occupies himself with the pleasant business of hunting. To the woman's lot falls the provision of wild roots and vegetables, the building of huts, the transportation of burdens, and children on the march, and so on; her load may amount to a hundredweight, no light weight for a traveller who has to cover twenty miles. Following at a respectful distance behind the father of the family, she carries in one hand her "yam stick," long and fairly thick, which is at once her weapon and her tool. In her bag or on her shoulders is a child or two, and the rest of her load is worthy of particular enumeration. It constituted the worldly wealth of an Australian household in the days when Grey explored West Australia. The list as given by him is curious and interesting: A flat stone to pound roots with; earth to mix with them; quartz to make spears and knives with; stones for axes; cakes of gum to make or mend weapons; kangaroo sinews to do duty as thread; needles made of the shin bones of kangaroos; opossum hair for waist belts; shavings of kangaroo skin with which to polish spears; a mussel shell to be used in hair-cutting; pipe clay, red and yellow paper bark as a water vessel, banksia cones or fungus tinder for fire lighting, and skins waiting to be dressed. She may carry her husband's spare weapons, or the wood from which they are to be made; she has, of course, the roots she collects during the day, for her lord and master must be fed after his hard day's travelling; and there are also knives, axes, grease, etc., etc.

If it should chance to rain, the wife, before the journey is at an end, collects suitable sticks. Arrived at the camping ground, she makes with her digging stick eight or nine holes in the earth, and plants in them the ends of the poles she has collected; the other ends meet in the centre, and keep their places without being tied in any way,

WORK IN THE CAMP.

The woman standing up is winnowing grass seed by blowing, the one on the right is grinding seed.

thanks to her art in building; then smaller sticks are laced through the poles, and over them comes a layer of bark or, it may be, grass or leaves intertwined.

The hut made, the wife may have to begin the preparation of the vegetable food, for the culinary processes are surprisingly lengthy, and in the case of poisonous or bitter food-stuffs may involve hours of work. In some parts of Australia grass seeds are an important article of food, and it is the woman who has to prepare them; the grass is put into a hole some twelve inches in depth, and she stamps upon it with a twisting motion till the seed is knocked out, and has worked down to the bottom; it is then transferred to a wooden bowl, and winnowed with the breath or a current of air; the next process is to grind the seed moistened with water upon the proper stone, which may have been brought hundreds of miles, and in such a case the carrier is always the woman, though the mass is eighteen inches square and several inches thick — no light load even for a man. As the meal is ready, it is scraped off into a bowl, and may be eaten raw or cooked.

Domestic Habits.

The stock description of the Australian black eating his fill and throwing the bones over his shoulder to his wife and family is only in part true; for by a curious custom the husband is not in all parts required to provide his family with food—in fact, it is rather the wife who is the prov der. Animal food is divided by the hunter in certain proportions, some of which go to his wife's parents, others to his own parents, his brothers and sisters, the bachelors of the camp, and so on. The support of a man's own children may fall to the lot of their grandparents, so far as animal food is concerned, while the vegetable food collected by the wife is reserved for herself and her children. The throwing of food over the shoulder is not necessarily a mark of contempt; there is a deep-seated objection to

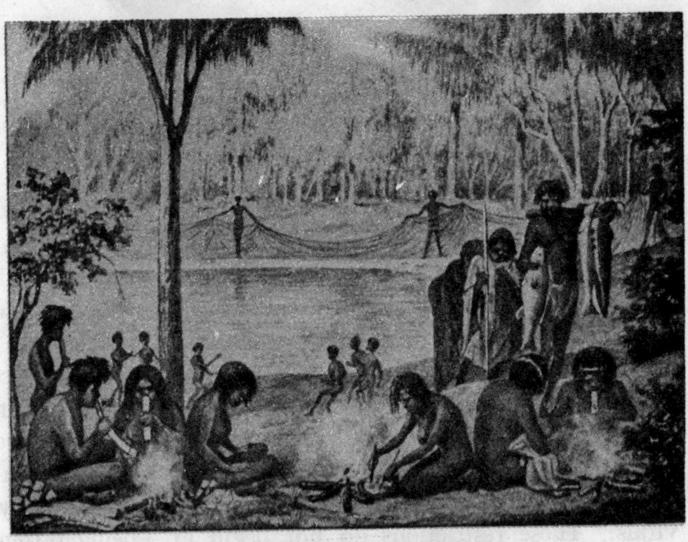

AN AL FRESCO MEAL.

Fish are often eaten half-roasted as soon as they are caught.

receiving food at the hands of another which may go far to explain the man's action; for with food may be conveyed magical force from one person to another; and who so likely to suffer as a person of different sex from the giver?

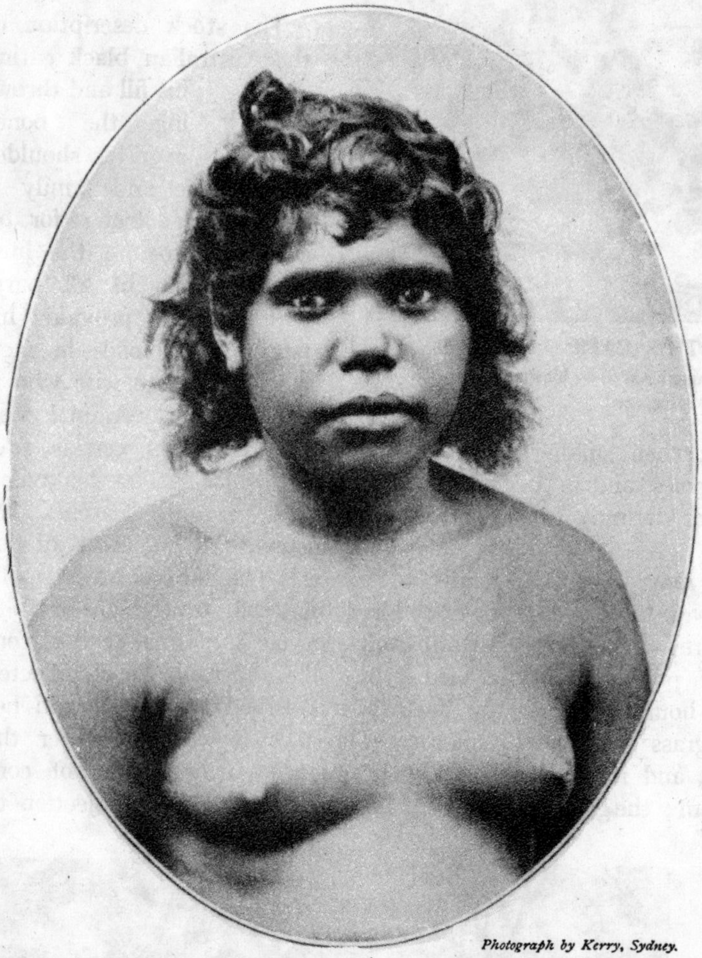

Photograph by Kerry, Sydney.

A BEAUTY OF THE MORUYA TRIBE, N.S. WALES.

The eyes of the Australian Aboriginals are sometimes strikingly beautiful.

Food Restrictions.

In connection with animal food another custom must be noted. All persons were not equally free to eat of certain animals; emu, black-headed snake, and porcupine were forbidden to young women in the Wakelbura tribe, and transgression meant that the offender would pine away, uttering the cry of the creature she had eaten; for its spirit would enter her and devour her vitals. These restrictions do not begin at once. Up to the age of nine or ten a boy or girl may eat pretty much what he or she pleases; then various foods are forbidden, and these are usually those which older people like best. Many more kinds of meat are forbidden when a woman is full grown—opossum, red kangaroo, duck, turtles, emu, bandicoot, dingo, and many other articles of diet must be looked at and longed for. In some tribes fish taken by diving are forbidden to all women, and at certain periods any kind of fish. With old age comes the good time, not only for old men, who then attain great power and authority in the tribe, but also for old women, at any rate in many cases. Then there are few articles which she may not eat, if she can get them; at the mouth of the Murray they did not partake of a kind of toad, nor yet of the young of the wombat before its hair had developed; otherwise they were free of all animal food.

Women as Fishers.

Where fish and mussels are an important article of diet, much of the work of collection falls on the women; at Lake Alexandrina a kind of mussel was eaten with bullrush root, and women dived for it, a net round their necks, which they brought up full after remaining three or four minutes under water; they used to work from a raft on which was a small fire on hearth of wet seaweed; this served to cook the catch which was often eaten half-raw. For eight months in the year the women collected crayfish, groping for them in the mud with their toes; they immediately crushed the claws to escape being bitten.

Another way of catching fish was for

women to work a small net in pairs; and in New South Wales the woman also fished from the canoe; at Port Jackson on her way to the fishing grounds she placed her child on her shoulders; it twined its legs round her neck and held on to her hair. Dropping on her knees, the woman sat on her heels and jammed her knees against the sides for steadiness; a small fire was kept up in the canoe, as on the raft, for cooking, and in the course of her two or three miles' paddle the unfortunate woman would have this so close to the small of her back that burns and frightful scars often resulted; fishing under such conditions can hardly have been regarded as an amusement.

Troubles of Widowhood.

Hard as is the life of the Australian wife her troubles are not at an end when she becomes a widow; for marriage is the natural state of woman, and in a few months she passes, willy nilly, to another husband, very often a brother of her "late lamented." In some parts she is required to mourn for her husband for a considerable period; in the Central tribes she must cut her head open, and is under a vow of silence till her period of mourning is ended, and two full years sometimes elapse before she regains her freedom of speech; meanwhile all her communications must be by gesture, language which in these tribes has been brought to a high state of perfection. In the east of Australia the widow was often required to sit in a hut erected upon the grave of her dead husband, her head covered with a cap of *kopi* (plaster of Paris), weighing eight or more pounds. Stranger still, but readily understandable when we remember the passionate love of an Australian mother for her children, is the custom of carrying the body of a dead child for months, and sometimes years; fortunately it is often well smoke-dried first.

Mourning customs are incumbent on other female relatives; in West Australia, if a man returned to the camp after a death had taken place, the nearest female relative of the deceased had to kneel before him, embrace his knees with her left arm and scratch his face with the nails of her right hand till the blood came; then she would sit down beside his wife, and they would rest their heads on each other's shoulders, and scratch each other's faces, crying and wailing all the time in heartrending tones. The same ceremonies were carried out when parties casually met in the bush, and five or six women could sometimes be seen kneeling to a boy of six or seven years old, lamenting most bitterly, the little fellow meantime preserving in his countenance and bearing all the gravity and dignity of a man.

AUSTRALIAN ABORIGINAL WOMEN FISHING.

Two women work a small net in shallow water.

Death.

Death in Australia is usually attributed to witchcraft, and it is the duty of the survivors to avenge it. It was the women who roused the men to sally forth, and an old hag would often chant on these occasions till she dropped from exhaustion. Standing with her legs

AUSTRALIAN ABORIGINAL WIDOWS SITTING ON THE GRAVE OF THE DECEASED HUSBAND.

Each wears a plaster of Paris (*kopf*) cap weighing 8 or 10 lbs.

curious duel goes on till one or the other has had enough.

Old women, when men fight, sometimes gather round the defeated champion and protect him, parrying the blows with their yam sticks. In a few cases old women seem even to have occupied a high place in the councils of the tribe, and were raised to the position by a special ceremony.

This is not the only part which the women play in the public life of Australian tribes. Though they may hear little or nothing of

wide apart, she waved her yam stick in the air, rocking her body to and fro, as she poured forth a wild stream of maledictions, her skin cloak floating behind her in the wind as she did so.

But the women did not confine themselves to inciting the men. On the Adelaide River an old woman has been seen leading the avenging party, a heavy club in her hand. Where the husband has to risk his life in the duel, his spouse stands at his side and endeavours to shield him from the missiles with her yam stick. The women, too, do their share of fighting; sometimes it is a kind of quarter-staff combat; sometimes it is a ding-dong affair, in which the wrongdoer has to receive the first blow; then her victim stoops down, her hands between her thighs, holding out her head to the blow of a four-foot yam stick, thicker than a broom-stick, which, thanks to the matted hair and general hardness, seldom knocks a woman out, and does not always knock her down; the first blow struck, it is the turn of the wrongdoer, and so the

religion, and though, as a rule, it is forbidden to reveal to them any detail of an initiation ceremony, women nevertheless play a part in the rites, but their share would hardly be intelligible without a longer description than can be given here. In the *corroboree* or dance their assistance is often invoked as musicians, their instrument being a folded opossum cloak which serves as a drum, failing which a portion of their person is made to produce a loud reverberation. They, no less than the men, chant in

The Corroboree.

AUSTRALIAN ABORIGINAL WOMEN FIGHTING.

They settle their quarrels in a kind of quarter-staff combat.

chorus, and in many cases take an actual part in the rhythmic movements of the dance. Sometimes women perform alone, and in one singular figure they stand with the feet close together, the hands joined above the head, throw the legs outward from the knee without moving the feet, and then sharply close them again. In another figure they keep the feet close together, and without lifting them from the ground advance by a peculiar movement of the limbs and describe a short semicircle. But space prevents our giving an account of all the varied movements.

Australian Witchcraft.

If the Australian woman plays no part in religion, she is sometimes enrolled among the magicians of the tribe. Her office may be maleficent or curative, and Mrs. Langloh Parker tells a story of her power in the latter direction. A European visitor to Mrs. Parker's house was suddenly and unaccountably taken ill, and to amuse her it was agreed to ask the witchwoman, old Bootha, to discover the cause of the illness. After a performance, apparently of the nature of ventriloquism, in which she professed to get replies from the spirits, Bootha announced that the young lady had offended the spirits by bathing in the shade of the Minggah (spirit) tree, in which they dwell. In this were, so Bootha said, swarms of spirit bees, which had put some of their wax on the liver of the sufferer, and had also stung her back. As the visitor had native girls as her companions in her bathing expeditions, Mrs. Parker regarded the diagnosis as mistaken; but on inquiry her visitor admitted having taken her dip beneath the Coolabah tree in question one day when she was too late for her usual party; not only so but she actually had an eruption on her back corresponding to the stings of the spirit bees. Bootha undertook to charm the bees away, and the patient rapidly recovered, though she ungratefully refused to be converted to the Australian view of her indisposition.

More notable still was a piece of rain-making on Bootha's part. Mrs. Parker's

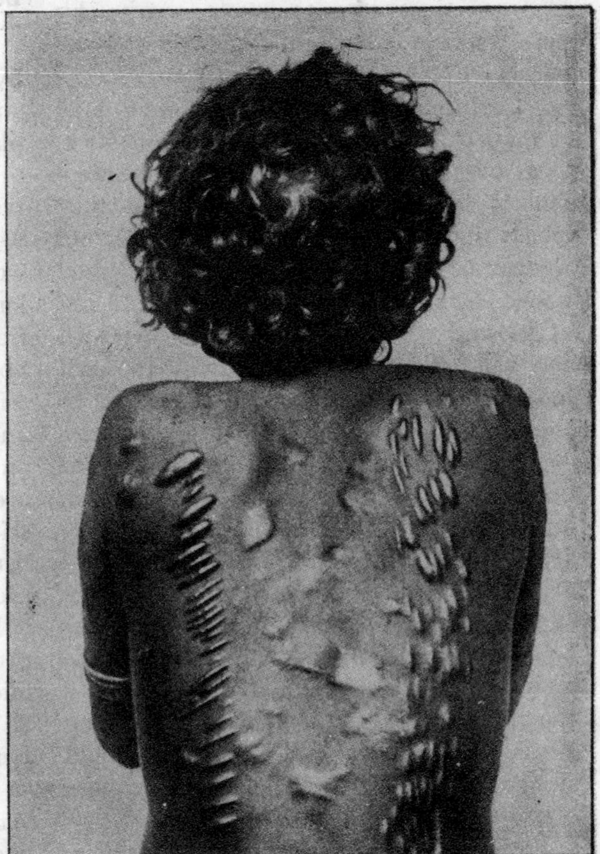

Photograph by Dr. Ramsay Smith & P. Foelsche.

WOMAN OF THE LARRAKIA TRIBE.

The scars on her back are a sign of widowhood.

rose garden was withering for want of rain, so she persuaded Bootha to bring some, and tied her down to a day. The day came, a heavy storm broke over the garden, and two inches of rain fell; within half a mile of each side of the garden the dust was barely laid, so Bootha got a new dress and some "bacca." Next time she failed signally; but then, of course, there was a great magician up the creek who was working against her because he was angry with the white people.

But to do magic a woman does not need to be a regular magician; any love-sick maid or slighted beauty can have recourse to its aid. If a woman wants to injure a man, she blows on her fingers, and then claws the air, moving her hand up and down with jerks towards the man as he leaves the camp, taking good care, of course, that she is not detected. This is said to cause him to waste away; his eyes sink into his head, and his muscles wither till he is a mere skeleton.

To injure another woman, an older wife, it may be, a woman takes her yam stick, sings over it, moves it about as if she were pulling something towards her, and then leaves it hidden in the scrub. The old woman becomes ill and can only be cured if her enemy anoints her with fat and red ochre, and at the same time rubs her with the yam stick, as if to extract the evil magic. Sometimes a woman undertakes to avenge an injury done to one of her kin; she is rubbed all over with grease and red ochre, and decorated with white down, stuck on with her husband's blood. She sets out at night and carries a club and a charmed stick; if the latter is thrown at the foe they say it enters his or her body in small pieces, and renders the victim insensible. While she is away the husband fixes one of her digging sticks upright in the ground; should she be killed, the stick falls to the ground of its own accord.

Love charms are, of course, not unknown, and a man may charm his head-band for a woman or a woman do the same for a man; another means is to take the *lonka-lonka*, a shell ornament, which is traded down from the north-west coast to the central tribes; the man charms the lightning into it and when the woman sees it flash "all at once her internal organs shake with strong emotion," as the native account assures us, and she takes the first opportunity to run away with him. On the other hand there are magical means of preventing a woman from misconducting herself; this is a knout of thirty or more strands which the men carry secretly in their wallets. The very sight of it is supposed to bring a woman to her senses, while a blow may be fatal; even at a distance it is effective, for when it is cracked the evil magic streams from it through the air.

Burial Customs.

Perhaps it is because a woman is of small account in magic that little trouble is taken with her when she is dead, for many burial customs mean no more than that the living are afraid of the spirit of the dead; and if the dead be weak, why trouble about placating them? But here, as in many other respects, the customs differ with the tribe. In some of the central tribes old women are buried at once, while young women and men are hung in a tree for a longer or shorter time; they say quite frankly that it is not worth bothering about the old creatures. Some of these tribes believe that a woman has no spirit, and this is naturally not without influence on their customs. In other cases women are laid in an open trench dug with a yam stick, and the body is exposed with the legs bent upwards; after a time the remains are transferred to a tree.

In the old days at Port Jackson young people were buried; those who had passed middle age were burned; and Collins gives an account of the cremation of the wife of Bennilong in 1796. The corpse was placed on a pile of wood, its head to the north. With her was a basket containing her fishing line and other implements, and her husband having put some logs on the body the fire was lighted. The next day the husband raked the ashes together with his spear, and raised a tumulus of earth on which he placed his bark spade.

Mrs. Parker describes the burial of an old friend of hers on the Narran River. All night long relatives sat round the corpse of Beemunni, to keep off the spirits, and then the body was put in its bark coffin, taken in a single piece from the whole circumference of the tree. On the way to the grave they heard a small bird cry, and Mrs. Parker was told that this was the soul of the dead woman. At the grave a fire was lighted to smoke the mourners and keep the spirits away. After lowering the body into the grave the women raised the death wail;

then came an address from one of the men, then more wailing; finally old women danced slowly round the edge of the grave, and men began to throw the earth in. As this was done, the dead woman's daughter shrieked "Mother, mother!" and hit her head with a sharp stone till the blood gushed out, and sat rocking her body to and fro, wailing all the time.

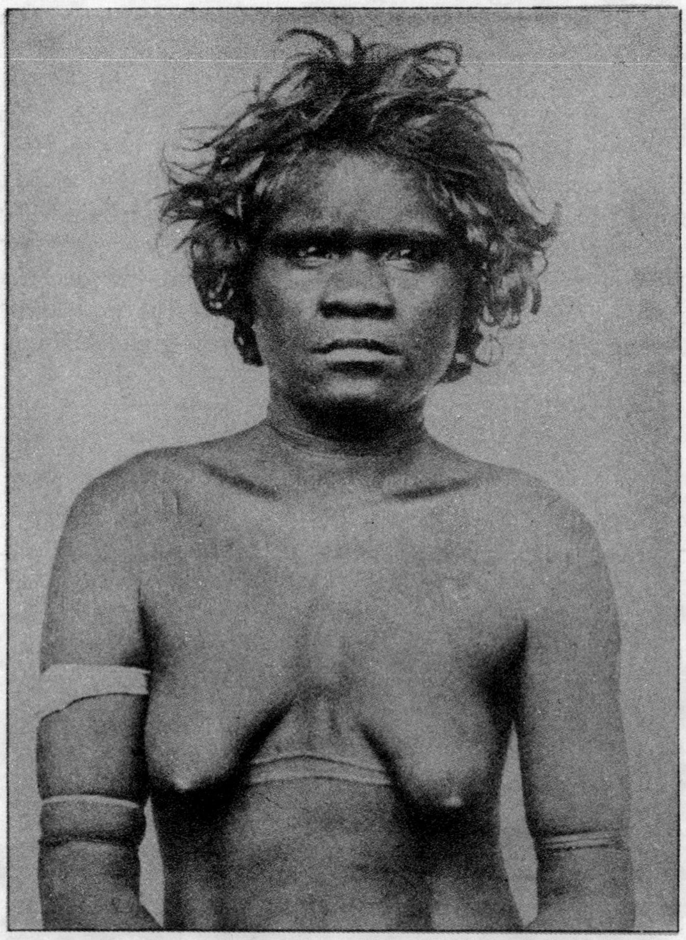

Photograph by Dr. Ramsay Smith & P. Foelsche.

WOMAN OF WOOLNA TRIBE, NORTH AUSTRALIA.

The nose of the aboriginal is sometimes nearly as broad as it is long.

At the funeral was the old witch woman, Bootha, and Mrs. Parker asked her when the drought would break. Coming very close Bootha whispered: "In three days I think it; old woman dead tell me when she dying that sposin' she can send rain, she send 'im three days when her yowee bulleem-rul—spirit breath—go long Oobi Oobi" (the sacred mountain). Beemunni had died on Wednesday night, and at bed-time on Saturday the sky was as cloudless as it had been for weeks; but in the middle of the night Mrs. Parker was awakened by the patter of raindrops on the iron roof; all night it rained, and all the next day. The blacks say that a dead person will always send rain within a week of his death to wash out his tracks on earth.

Of the future life of women there is little to say, for Australian ideas as to a future life are very undeveloped. But mention must be made of the beliefs of some of the central tribes, who hold that all human beings are reincarnations of mythical half animal ancestors; some, it is true, say that women have no souls, and are not reincarnated; but others say that the sex is changed with each incarnation.

Present Position of the Aboriginal.

And so the Australian woman goes on her way weeping, rejoicing, toiling, loving; she is far from being the lowest or unhappiest of her sex. If her ideas of sexual morality are not ours, it must be remembered that infidelity is, according to the tribal code of morality, merely an infringement of the husband's rights of property. She loves her children with more than common affection, and cares for them in a manner that many mothers in our boasted state of civilisation would do well to imitate. Kept in subjection by the men, she seldom hears anything of religion, and but rarely plays a great part in the public life of the tribe. If her husband often misuses her, she suffers far less than her civilised sister does from man's brutality; there is sometimes real affection between husbands and wives, and when one of them dies, the survivor's mourning is no mere formal display. In her old age the Australian woman may reach a position of importance in tribal councils; or she may be neglected or even cast forth to die, as one that is no longer of use to her fellows. More often, perhaps, she is kindly treated without being looked up to, and her declining days are made happy by the prattle of her grandchildren and great-grandchildren.

Photograph by Kerry, Sydney.

AN ABORIGINAL ENCAMPMENT, NEW SOUTH WALES.

TORRES STRAITS AND NEW GUINEA

By C. G. SELIGMANN

Papuans of Torres Straits—Extinction of the Race—Clothing—"Coming of Age" Celebrations—Courtship Customs—Motherhood in Saibai—Women of New Guinea—Eastern New Guinea—Tattoo—The Significance of the Petticoat—Courtship and Marriage in the Hood Peninsula—New Guinea Widows—Woman's Work in New Guinea—Women as the Cause of Strife—The "Gapa"—The "Iropi" Dance—Initiation of Girls—Methods of Cooking

THE Torres Straits, which stretch between Australia and New Guinea, comprise a shallow and reef-strewn area dotted with islands, which for political and administrative purposes are regarded as belonging to Queensland, though the natives, once the islands within easy paddling distance of Australia are left behind, cease to show Australian characteristics. The inhabitants of the islands of Torres Straits are, in fact, thorough Papuans, and differ but slightly in general appearance and habits from those of New Guinea in the neighbourhood of the mouth of the Fly River, with whom some of them intermarry. For the last twenty or thirty years the importance of the pearling industry has caused the Straits to be overrun by folk from the whole of Eastern Asia from Ceylon to Japan, and including the inhabitants of many of the islands of the Pacific.

Papuans of Torres Straits.

As the result of this invasion, combined with the influence of traders and missionaries, old habits of thought have died out, the old solidarity has broken down, foreign diseases have been introduced, and the natives are everywhere rapidly dying out; scarcely the memory survives of the condition of things which prevailed half a century ago when an iron knife or a glass bottle were of the same value as a necklace made of dogs' teeth, and any one of these articles was the usual price to pay for a wife. Some islands are already destitute of inhabitants, and in others scarcely half-a-dozen old men and women are to be found; while the number of the latter still living who bear upon the small of their back the scars cut in their youth to represent their old totem animals, such as the dugong, the shark, or the snake, can be counted upon the fingers of one hand. The back of one of the very few surviving women bearing this interesting clan badge is shown in the illustration on p. 152, which represents an old woman of Mabuiag. The two raised scars above her hips represent the snake, the chief totem of her clan. Breast marks, deeply cut scars made between the breasts, often wrongly regarded as designed to hold up the breasts which tend to become pendulous as child-bearing and hard life ages the women, and for the existence of which the natives themselves have forgotten the reason, are almost as rare.

Extinction of the Race.

In the old days the costume of the women of Torres Straits was a petticoat made of strips of the shredded leaves of the sago plant, and often dyed brown and black; but at the present day this simple and cleanly costume is utterly

Clothing.

extinct, and every woman now wears a hideous loosely made chemise-like gown, often of the brightest trade calico, clean only when it is first put on. For since fashion nowadays decrees that no woman shall be seen without one of these, and as few women have more than one, or at most two, of these garments, their usual condition of dirt and dinginess can be more easily imagined than described.

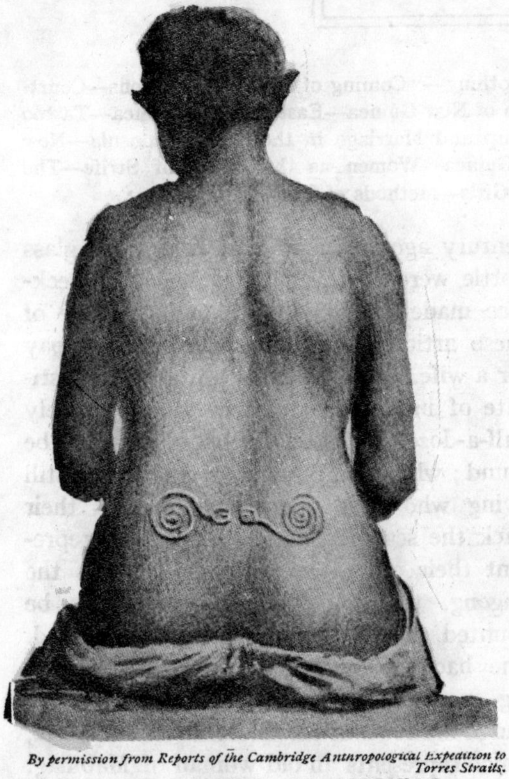

By permission from Reports of the Cambridge Anthropological Expedition to Torres Straits.

AN OLD WOMAN OF MABUIAG.

Showing the raised scars of her clan mark on her back.

"Coming of Age" Celebrations.

In all the islands lying in the western portion of Torres Straits between Australia and New Guinea, it was formerly the custom to celebrate a girl's arrival at womanhood by a long and complicated ceremonial, the chief feature of which was that she underwent a period of seclusion designed to prevent her injuring others, or being herself injured, at this most critical period of her life. Space permits of only a brief account of one ceremonial of this kind, that which until recently took place on Mabuiag (Jervis Island). A circle of green twigs and bushes would be made in a dark corner in the house of the girl's parents, and in this the girl squatted, fully decked with native ornaments, including nautilus shell pendants in her ears, surrounded by the greenery, which was piled so high round her that only her head and the upper part of her body were visible. There she sat all day for three months. The branches were changed nightly, at which times she was allowed to slip out of the hut to get a little fresh air. During the whole of her seclusion she was attended by two old women, generally her aunts, who looked after her and cooked her food, for during this time she might not even feed herself; all her food was actually put into her mouth by one of her attendants. It was most important that during the time of her seclusion the sun should not shine on her, and it was believed in the neighbouring island of Saibai that if a ray of sunlight fell upon her the girl's nose would rot. At the end of the three months' seclusion the girl was carried by her aunts to the mouth of a creek, special care being taken that no part of her body touched the ground. After the girl's ornaments had been removed, the aunts and the girl bathed together, the other women of the community making a point of splashing water over all three of them. On coming out of the water the girl was decorated in native finery, after which her aunts led her back to the village, where a feast in which she took part had been prepared. This was followed by a dance, and the girl, now regarded as a woman, henceforth took her full part in the life of the village.

Courtship Customs.

On almost all the islands of Torres Straits a girl formerly made the first advances, though a young man who desired to create an impression on any particular girl would take every opportunity of showing off in the village dances and otherwise posing before her. And, if the times were not too peaceable, he would make every attempt to procure a human skull, a feat of valour which no girl could resist. He would also probably prepare "medicine" by chewing up the leaves of various trees—some, at least, of which would be scented—and mixing these with the oil expressed from the leaf of a coco-nut. A little of this mixture would then be rubbed over his body in order to fascinate and attract the girl. If he were successful the young woman would take an early opportunity of sending him a string by some younger girl, often a sister of his own, as token that she wished him to come to her. The young man, who would probably be sleeping with his companions in the bachelors' quarters, would keep awake after his comrades had gone to sleep, and would then go to the girl's hut, where she would be ready to receive him. This state of affairs would go on for some time, the lover meanwhile making himself useful as occasion arose to the girl's father. At first the father would not be supposed to know what was going on, and later, when the matter was more or less officially brought to his notice, he would not be angry, but the mother of the girl and her people might feel it incumbent upon themselves to make a fuss, which usually ended in a brawl between the families. This, however, ceased as soon as a member of the bridegroom's people had been "marked"—that is to say, as soon as a little blood had flowed; it was felt then that enough had been done to show the value the girl's family put upon their women. After this, the girl—now considered a bride—and the bridegroom were dressed in their best, and were seated at opposite ends of a mat, while an exchange of presents of food took place between the two families.

Motherhood in Saibai.

On the island of Saibai, which is only twelve miles from the New Guinea coast, each woman went through a most interesting ceremony when it was recognised that she was about to become a mother for the first time. A peculiar ornament, called *bid*—which, in fact, is a primitive representation of a child—was made, and this the woman wore while she ceremonially paraded about the village. The body of the *bid* was made of strips of sago leaf, a bamboo loop at one end represented the nose and

By permission of Captain G. W. C. Pim and the Council of the Royal Anthropological Institute.

MERAUKE WOMEN.

Showing neck ornaments and method of dressing the hair.

two bamboo knots the child's eyes. The whole thing was about twenty inches long, and was worn hanging from the neck, so that the head end rested over the lower part of the chest bone; the two pieces of string which were knotted round the neck to prevent it falling represented the arms of the child, while two other pieces, which were passed round the waist and knotted behind to prevent the *bid* slipping round to the side of the body, represented its legs.

On leaving the islands of Torres Straits for the mainland of New Guinea, a vast, scarcely explored region of low, swampy, and very unhealthy country is reached, and but little is known concerning the habits and customs of the natives of this part, the most interesting of whom are the Tugeri.

Women of New Guinea.

This is the common name for a number of tribes living in Netherlands' New Guinea, who have for years raided the western portion of the British Possession, where they have succeeded in almost exterminating the coastal tribes. As the result of numerous punitive expeditions more is known about the weapons and canoes of these interesting people than of their other characteristics; but the illustration on p. 153 shows that their women are rather unusually well built for this part of the world, and, instead of cropping their hair, as is common about the neighbourhood of the Fly River in the British Possession, wear it in long, frizzled ringlets. The abundance of ornaments worn by these women is also rather noteworthy, since in New Guinea it is generally the men and not the women who are most decorated.

In the neighbourhood of the estuary of the Fly River, instead of the villages consisting of a number of family houses, a whole village may be represented only by four or five houses each 75 or 100 yards long standing on piles seven or eight feet high. In many of the villages in which these "long houses" occur, the sexes are separated; all the men of a clan, or sometimes of a number of clans, live in one long house and the women and children in another; but although the women may on no account come into the men's houses, each married man may visit his wife in the woman's long house, which is divided on each side of the central public gangway into a number of spaces, each with its own fireplace belonging to a family group. But when a man is ill, or about to die, he is, in some cases, removed to one of the fenced-in spaces under the floor of the women's house, where stores are kept and the family cooking is often done, and where such little privacy as is possible may be obtained.

Passing eastwards from the mouth of the Fly River, comparatively dark and always frizzy-haired people continue to be met as far east as the low jutting promontory known as Cape Possession. Eastward of this, for a distance of about 150 miles, a series of people are found presenting marked differences from the more westerly folk. Both men and women are lighter-skinned, and their hair, instead of being invariably frizzy, is not uncommonly curly or even wavy. Some of the younger girls have skin of a moderately light *café-au-lait* colour.

Eastern New Guinea.

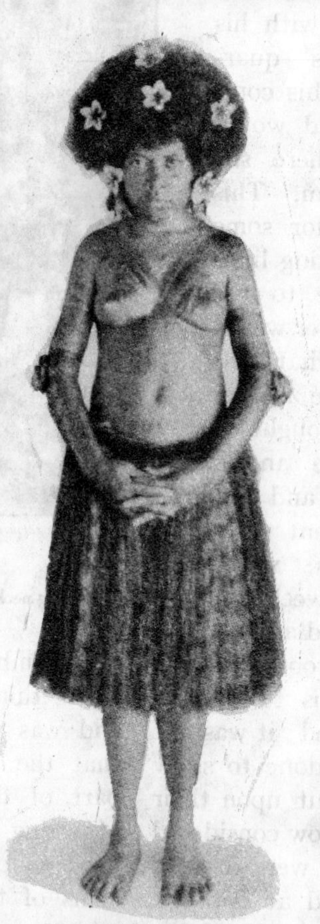

A MOTU GIRL.

Showing the V-shaped tattoo mark between the breasts which proclaims the girl of marriageable age.

Some, if not all, of the western people are cannibals, and the majority of them are, or were, intensely keen skull collectors; but cannibalism does not seem to occur among these more easterly people, who do not, except over a limited area, collect skulls.

Tattoo in New Guinea.

The women of the coastal tribes, instead of resorting to scarification, beautify themselves by covering their bodies with tattoo. The illustration on this page represents a Motu girl from the neighbourhood of Port Moresby, and gives some idea of the intricacy of the patterns employed. It fails, however, to convey any idea of the really pleasing effect produced by the dark blue patterns upon the brown skin of the body. Tattooing is begun at an early age—perhaps as young as six or eight—

and is continued gradually until shortly before the girl becomes marriageable, when the **V**-shaped mark, called by the Motu *gado*, the point of which is situated between the breasts, is pricked in. It is only after puberty that the lower part of the abdomen is tattooed, and it is said that without such tattoo a girl would not find a husband.

The Significance of the Petticoat.

Among most of the tribes of the Central Division an unmarried girl can be distinguished from a married woman by her hair being long, by the fact that she wears ornaments, and often by the ornamental character of her *rami*, or petticoat, the only covering she wears. A girl may wear as many petticoats as she pleases, and often does wear an extra one or two beneath her outer *rami*, as this is supposed to enhance the attractiveness of her figure.

The dancing petticoat, worn on ceremonial occasions, and when a big feast is toward, is an elaborate and really beautiful affair, composed as it usually is of a number of shreds of palm leaf dyed various colours, among which are interposed broad strips of the same material bleached to a whitish colour. Such a petticoat reaches from the waist to below the knee, and its right side is left open, so that as the petticoat is flirted in the dance a certain amount of the tattooing of the right buttock and thigh is visible.

Courtship and Marriage in the Hood Peninsula.

The following description of courtship and marriage customs applies especially to the tribes of the Hood Peninsula, but with slight modifications the same manners and customs prevail throughout the greater part of the Central Division. A boy who has found favour with a girl visits her after dark in her parents' house; no especial secrecy is observed, although there is a pretence at this—that is to say, the lover will not enter the house until its occupants are supposed to be asleep. At the same time no mystery is made about the matter, as the customary method of courtship throughout the Central Division is for the lovers to pass their nights together. The man is meanwhile busy collecting the arm-shells, dogs' teeth necklaces and pearl-shell ornaments, which are the most valuable property of the district, and with which he must pay for his bride. When he has collected enough he hands them over to the girl's father, who does not, however, keep any very considerable portion of the bride-price for himself, but divides the greater part of it among his kinsfolk. This may be regarded as a survival from the time when a girl was considered less as her father's daughter than as a valuable asset to the whole of her clan. A number of ceremonial visits between the families of the young couple, and exchanges of food and presents, take place, and for the first three days or so of her married life the girl almost continually wears her dancing petticoat and all the ornaments that belong to her, and any others that she has been able to borrow from her family. Then her ornaments are taken away, and although she retains her dancing petticoat for a few days longer—during which time she is still considered a bride—this too is taken away at the end of a week or so, and she now assumes the homelier petticoat worn by married women. Her head is shaved, generally with a piece of a glass bottle, and she does not, unless she wishes to make herself an object of ridicule, any longer join in the dance.

New Guinea Widows.

When a woman's husband dies she naturally goes into mourning for him, and the mourning of a widow in the Central Division of New Guinea is no quiet, real, or fictitious sorrow for the loss sustained by death, but an extremely elaborate series of ceremonies which have to be gone through completely, and in due order, if the risk of offending the spirit of the deceased is to be avoided. At the first feast for the dead, which takes place a few days after death, the widow's head is shaved and she is blackened from head to foot; she wears a long petticoat devoid of all ornament, which reaches to her feet, while a second similar petticoat is often placed round her neck so as completely to hide her body. Whether she wears this second petticoat or not, she dons a sort of waistcoat made of netting, and a netted mourning cap. She is also decked with a good deal of shell jewellery, and must wear round her neck her husband's perineal bandage, tightly twisted upon itself and covered with blackened string. To this is often attached the broken pieces of his lime gourd, his coconut shell drinking spoon, and other small personal effects. A widow wears these until, at the last mourning feast, a relative of her husband—usually his sister—cuts short her petticoat and rubs the black mourning paint off her body, after which she bathes in the sea and can, if she wishes, re-marry.

Woman's Work in New Guinea.

Throughout practically the whole of New Guinea, a woman does what to the European seems more than her fair share of household work. In the morning she must fill the water jars or bamboos, and prepare the snack of food which does duty for a Papuan breakfast; then, after making such disposition as she may for the comfort and safety of her children, she goes to the gardens, often carrying her youngest child with her, to gather the yams or bananas that form the staple diet of the natives. If it be the planting season she plants the seed-crop, and does the whole of the garden work, except the fencing and the first breaking up of the soil, which is done by the men. It is also her business to provide all the firewood requisite for the household. Usually she will not get back from the garden till considerably after midday, often not till early in the afternoon, when she must set about preparing the evening meal, which is eaten at twilight, and which to the Papuan is *the* meal of the day.

Women were, and—in spite of the efforts cf the Government officials—still are, a constant source of brawling between the different sections of the same village, and although these brawls usually do not lead to killing, a good deal of trouble is caused by them. It is rather strange that women do not seem to have been a common cause of war between different communities; perhaps they were valued too little. It would happen, every now and again, that a woman, considering herself badly used at one of the markets so often held for the purpose of bartering fish for vegetables, half-way between the coast and inland villages, would tell her relatives that she had been insulted or cheated, and the usual result of this was that a small fight would take place on the spot, and, since the combatants came to blows close to each other, there was more chance than is usual in Papuan warfare that somebody would be hurt. One curious custom for which the natives can give no reason is stated to have been observed. Should any woman or women throw a petticoat or petticoats over a wounded man or prisoner, he would be safe from all further molestation, although the women's relatives might be as desirous as ever of killing him.

Women as the Cause of Strife.

The "Gapa."

The importance of feasts and the dances which accompany them has already been referred to, but the most important feast of all, which is called the *Gapa* over a considerable area of the coast of the Central Division, deserves special mention. The preparation for the *Gapa*, and the more or less distinctly festive ceremonial connected with it, may last as long as six weeks or two months, and it is during this time that the biggest dances take place and perhaps the majority of marriages are celebrated. The first preliminary of the feast is to make sure that the gardens are bearing well, then, when it is found that there is a plentiful supply of food, the villagers giving the feast go the round of the friendly communities in the neighbourhood and borrow young pigs, coco-nuts, or whatever else they may need. Usually little but pork is required. This ceremonial borrowing

WOMAN OF THE RIGO DISTRICT : BRITISH NEW GUINEA.
DRAWN BY NORMAN H. HARDY.

Facing on page 156

is a more or less necessary precedent to the feast, since it is at the same time a convenient way of insuring that there shall be a worthy show of pork when the great day arrives, and the formal invitation to all the women of the neighbouring friendly villages to come to the feast, bringing with them empty baskets, which will be filled with food for them to carry away. Scaffoldings are built on the verandah of every house, and often a breast-high railing is erected all round the village. The *dubu*—that is, the carved ceremonial, one might almost say sacred—platform belonging to the clan in whose name the feast is given is thoroughly tested, and if it is found to be untrustworthy new planks are put in, or the whole may be rebuilt. It is next decorated with greenery, and great masses of coco-nuts are piled upon and under its staging, while huge bunches of bananas are laid along its edge, or hung from a special railing prepared for the purpose. Streamers, to every six inches of which are tied a yam or coco-nut, hang from its tallest poles, or are carried to the neighbouring verandahs, which are themselves hidden under a mass of vegetable food and green branches, as is the railing which, as has already been mentioned, is generally built round the village.

At last the ceremonial begins, men and women from all the neighbouring communities troop in; and since among so many strangers —who naturally in the old days did not come unarmed—a few blood debts might be outstanding, there was in some villages a special ceremonial observance in which peace was invoked by men carrying lengths of sugar-cane, and swinging these horizontally above the strangers' heads when the latter first entered the village. The dancing costumes on these occasions are really beautiful, especially those of the women. Frontlets of a valuable red shell are worn low on the forehead, a portion of the scalp being sometimes shaved so as to set off a second frontlet of white shells. In some tribes a dancing head-dress of feathers made from the yellow-red tail feathers of the female of a parrot called *audubora*, belonging to the genus *Eclectus*, is worn. These feathers are arranged on a strip of cane so as to radiate outwards from the head, around which they form a halo of brilliant colour, while projecting through the cane on which they are mounted rises the frizzy mop of hair of which every Papuan girl is so proud, and in which she probably wears sweet-

A MOTU GIRL

Carrying firewood. Showing petticoat and ornaments.

smelling flowers or more feathers. Round the girl's neck are shell ornaments, boars' tusks, necklaces of dogs' teeth, and, most brilliant of all, a moon-shaped ornament cut crescent-wise from the largest pearl shell obtainable.

The "Iropi" Dance.

On the Hood Peninsula the feast proper really lasts for two days. On the first day the initiation of the girls who have become marriageable during the year takes place, and this ceremony is carried out upon one of the *dubu* or platforms already alluded to. Before ascending the *dubu* the girls who are to be initiated, and who have, of course, been freshly tattooed for the occasion, perform a particular dance called *Iropi*, and for this a special petticoat, which allows a good deal of the buttock to be seen, is often worn. The whole ceremony has been so well described by the late R. E. Guise, who for a long time lived on the Hood Peninsula, that it is permissible to quote his description at some length. Speaking of the *Iropi* dance, he says: "To the centre of the string which upports the petticoat and immediately at the centre of the small of the back is attached a string about two feet long, with an old knitted bag on the end as a weight. The girls form up in a row one immediately behind another. Each girl holds the string in her right hand about six inches from the bag. To the slow beat of the drum she takes one step forward with her right foot, at the same time swinging the bag behind her and over her left shoulder, where she adroitly catches it with her left hand, and to another beat of the drum swings it over her right shoulder, recovering it in the right hand and taking another step forward."

This goes on for about twenty minutes, and then come other dances, in which all the villagers take part. There is a good deal of eating and chewing of betel nut, but the really important part of the festival, the ceremonial distribution of food, the full initiation of the girls, and the challenging

THE *IROPI* DANCE, HOOD PENINSULA.

This dance is one of the features of the ceremony connected with the initiation of girls of marriageable age.

PREPARING A FEAST IN A SINAUGOLO VILLAGE.
The women are cooking the food in native ovens.

of another clan to hold the same feast next year, only occurs on the next day.

The Initiation of Girls.

Some time in the afternoon the girls who are to be initiated ascend one of the *dubu*, accompanied by an old woman who carries a drum. The initiates stand side by side, and at a signal beat of the drum untie their petticoats and throw them behind them. The father of each girl who is being initiated has previously given one or more pigs to the feast, and these, which have generally been caught in readiness, are hung to the edge of the platform in front of the girls, or securely tied up or laid on the ground in front of them. A number of old women then advance and place on the *dubu* in front of each girl a basket containing some yams, a small knife, and a quantity of areca nut. On this occasion only, a girl, provided that her father has taken human life, may wear his head-dress of bird of paradise plumes so mounted and weighted as to wave whenever the head is slightly moved. "An old woman now advances and anoints each girl on the breast, and the whole of the front of the body with melted pigs' fat or coco-nut oil. . . . Two or three married women or widows seat themselves behind the girls and beat drums with slow and rhythmical measure. Each girl takes a yam in her left hand and the knife in her right, and at each beat of the drum cuts off a piece of the yam, bends her knees, and slightly bows her head, causing the weighted head-dress to sway forward. . . After each girl has cut up half a dozen yams, she, on the cessation of the beat of the drum, which is announced by two sharp claps, seizes the basket of areca nut and pelts the crowd."

Methods of Cooking.

Although only unmarried girls take part in dancing, married women as well play an important part in preparing and serving the food consumed at feasts. Pigs are killed and cut up by men, but in the Central Division it is the women who fetch the greater part of the vegetable food from the gardens and who cook this and the flesh of the pigs.

The photograph reproduced on p. 159 was taken in a village of the Sinaugolo tribe during the preparation of only a moderately important feast. The rail with bunches of bananas hanging to it, which runs entirely round the village, is seen immediately in front of the houses which form the background of the photograph. The foreground is occupied by women and girls, the latter not yet wearing their dancing petticoats and attending to the food which is cooking in the native ovens over which they are bending. These "native ovens," in which, when they are properly arranged, flesh and vegetables are alike cooked to perfection, are prepared as follows.

A shallow excavation is made in the ground and its bottom lined with stones; upon these a fire is made which is not raked away until the stones have become not far short of red-hot. Damp banana leaves are placed upon the stones, and upon these are put the pieces of meat to be cooked—vegetables are more usually simply boiled—wrapped in more banana leaves. More stones are piled over the food, and as these are being arranged, and in turn covered with leaves, a little water is dropped into the "oven," the steam from which is in great part kept in by the stones and banana leaves on top. The result is that the food is only slightly cooked by the direct heat from the stones at the bottom, the greater part of the effect being due to the steam which penetrates the leaf packets in which the food is wrapped. When it is considered that the meat has been long enough in the oven the stones are removed, and the packets with their deliciously cooked contents are removed and distributed.

Photograph by G. Lambert, Singapore.
BATTAK WOMAN.
Showing tin ear ornament.

Photograph by G. Lambert, Singapore.
ACHEHNESE WOMAN (SUMATRA).
Wearing Malayan costume.

THE NON-MALAY TRIBES OF THE SUNDA ISLANDS AND CELEBES

By R. SHELFORD, M.A., F.L.S.

I

Origin of Indonesians—Physical Features—Position of Women in Malaya—Marriage Customs—The Law of Divorce—The Achehnese—Curious Aids to Beauty—Achehnese Marriage Customs—Polygamy and Divorce in Acheh—Battak Marriage by Capture—Marriage by Purchase—Birth Customs in Acheh—Sumatran Children

Origin of Indonesians.

THE true Malay appears upon the scene in relatively recent times; before his advent the Malay Archipelago was peopled, in part at any rate, by tribes that now are known to anthropologists as Indonesians, a race typically of Caucasic affinities. The division of the inhabitants of Malaya into Malays proper and Indonesians is convenient rather than strictly accurate, for some of the non-Malay tribes speak languages that are evidently of Malay origin, and in their physical features conform to the broad-headed Malay type. Such are the Sea-Dayaks of Borneo, and for such tribes the name Proto-Malayan is perhaps more appropriate. The origin of all these tribes is buried in obscurity, but it appears probable that they spread over their present area of distribution from more than one centre, and it is practically certain that they did not arrive synchronously. Be that as it may, they now form a complex of tribes that have at least one feature in common, viz., that they are not the same people as the true Malays, and it is of these non-Malay tribes, whether showing pronounced Caucasic affinities or equally pronounced Malayan affinities, that the following account treats.

Physical Features.

The physical features of the Indonesian tribes present few points of difference that can be appreciated by any but the trained anthropologist or those who have lived for some time with the people. The women are of short stature, compact and plump rather than elegant in figure when young; their complexion varies from a pale yellow to a shade that has aptly been compared to the colour of a new saddle, though still darker people occur in Central Celebes and amongst the Kalangs of Java. Beauty, according to European standards, is rarely if ever attained, for the high cheek-bones, the absence of a distinct bridge to the nose, the thick and somewhat everted lips, forbid this, but the general cast of countenance is frequently gentle and pleasing, and the dark brown eyes and normally abundant hair are good features. The habit of chewing betel-nut dyes the lips a brilliant scarlet, and the teeth are usually artificially blackened, so that the mouth looks larger than it really is; white teeth are not regarded by all the tribes as an accessory to beauty, and the teeth of Europeans have been contemptuously referred to as being "like the teeth of a dog" by more than one Indonesian belle.

Position of Women in Malaya.

The dress and ornaments, manners and customs of the various tribes differ so much that they may be discussed more conveniently under geographical sections. But before passing on to this, a word or two may be said on the position which women occupy in Malaya. The European traveller, seeing women toiling in the fields, carrying heavy loads, and working as hard as, and even harder than, men, will not unnaturally conclude that woman in these lands is little better than a drudge, and that her position in family and village life is purely subordinate to that of man. As a matter of fact this estimate would be incorrect, for on longer acquaintance it would be found that amongst most Indonesian tribes woman occupies an important and well-recognised position. In some of the islands she takes a part in village councils—individuals have been met who actually directed the management of the affairs of the village—whilst in the family her voice is often supreme, and Dr. Hickson cites an instance of a man in Minahassa, Celebes, who actually consulted his wife before concluding a bargain dealing with the sale of an egg. It is true that the women work hard, but in many cases the farm that a woman cultivates is the joint property of herself and her husband, so that it is to her interest that as much gain as possible be derived from its cultivation. Moreover, in no part of the world is the dignity of labour more considered, though quite unconsciously, than in the Malay Archipelago, so that she who sits at home idle and at ease reaps a harvest of scorn and contumely from her more industrious sisters.

Marriage Customs.

If we glance at the marriage customs of some of the tribes we shall gain a clue to the important position occupied by Indonesian women. Among the Menangkabau Malays a man is compelled to marry a girl of some other village than his own. When he has married her he must leave his home and take up his abode with his wife in the house of his parents-in-law; he is regarded so much as an intruder and interloper that his parents-in-law ceremonially ignore his presence, and he must ignore them; he has no voice in the up-bringing of his children, this office being performed by his wife's brother; his property on his death goes to his sister's children; finally, descent is reckoned through the maternal line. Here we have what is termed the Matriarchal state, or Matriarchate at the height of its development. In Acheh, Sumatra, the laws are somewhat modified: a man need not always marry out of his own

Photograph by G. Lambert, Singapore

BATTAK WOMAN (SUMATRA).

Showing head-dress.

village; he is allowed to bring up his children, and his property, on his death, goes to his wife and children; but he is compelled to live with his wife, or wife's parents, and he must ceremonially "cut" his parents-in-law.

In Borneo and the Minahassa district of Celebes the Matriarchate is in a degenerate condition, but there is evidence to show that once it was more fully developed. In Borneo, at the present day, there is no fixed rule as to exogamy: a man, as often as not, selects his wife from his own village or communal house, and she either lives with him, or he with her and her parents—that being a matter for mutual arrangement. It is forbidden for a man to mention the name of his parents-in-law, but he does not ignore them. After the birth of a child a Kenyah father loses his name, and is endowed with a new one which means "Father of X——" (his child). In the Minahassa district of Celebes a young married couple set up house for themselves, and the only trace of a former Matriarchal state is found in the custom which forbids a man to pronounce in full the name of his mother-in-law; *e.g.*, if her name is "Wenas" the son-in-law must abreviate it to "We," if "Mainalo" to "Maina."

The Law of Divorce.

According to Mohammedan law a woman cannot claim a divorce unless she can prove that her husband is unable to support her; he may desert her, and leave her without visible means of support, but still she has to prove that he is penniless himself before she can be freed. In the popular opinion of many Mohammedan countries of the East Indian Archipelago it has been felt that under this law the position of married women is rendered too precarious; and a new law has been grafted on the old one, whereby a man before making a marriage contract definitely promises to support his wife, and empowers her to claim a divorce if he fails to do so, if he deserts her, or if he takes to himself another wife: the promise is known as the *talik*. In Acheh the *talik* is omitted, for the reason that the woman loses nothing if deserted by her husband; she may be rendered unhappy, but she still has her home and her property, and her parents will provide for her if the produce of her property is insufficient; so that in this country it is the husband who is the chief loser by a divorce or separation.

The foregoing account will serve to show that where the Matriarchal state holds good, or did once hold good, there the position of woman is of some dignity and importance, and it need cause us no great surprise to learn that in former times queens ruled for brief periods both in Acheh and in Celebes; in the latter country at any rate they appear to have ruled in a masterly manner, and to have won their power not only by virtue of their descent from previous rulers, but through sheer force of character and highly developed instincts of power.

SUMATRA

The Achehnese.

The principal non-Malay tribes of Sumatra are: the Achehnese in the North, the Battaks in the North-East and East, the Rejangs and the Lampongs in the South and South-West.

The dress of the women consists of a petticoat which may reach to the feet or no lower than the knees; the upper part of the body is clad in a jacket which is discarded during work on the farms. The Acheh women wear, in addition to the petticoat or *sarong*, wide trousers, and across the body over the jacket a wide scarf, which also covers the head when necessary. Much of their cloth is woven by themselves, but Manchester piece-goods are bought from the ubiquitous Chinese trader. The hair is dressed in a variety of ways, and at festivals is adorned with pins and combs of admirable workmanship.

Curious Aids to Beauty.

The Rejangs flatten the noses of their children and manipulate their ears in order to get them to stand out from the head; the front teeth are either filed almost flush with the gums or else are sharpened to points. Metal bracelets and belts are worn, and in addition the women of the Padang highlands adorn the lower part of the leg with a series of tightly-fitting brass rings. Enormous ear ornaments of tin are worn by the Battak women. The tin is cast in bamboo cylinders of suitable diameter, and cut to the required length; the cylindrical rod so obtained is passed through a large hole pierced in the upper part of the ear and bent into a loop, the free ends of which are rolled up to form flat coils. Each ornament is about six inches long, and several ounces in weight; to prevent them from knocking against the face during active movement, they are clipped to the peculiar cloth head-dress worn by these women, a fold of the cloth passing between the limbs of the loops of flexible tin.

The ear ornaments worn by the Rejang women are discs of filigree work fastened with a screw and nut attachment, and worn in the ear-lobe. Amongst the Achehnese the boring of the ears takes place at the early age of six or seven years, and the operation is attended with a good deal of ceremony, the child being taken in procession to the tomb of some saint, in order that the blessing of the saint may rest on the act. After the child has been sprinkled with flour and water, and rubbed behind the ears with a glutinous kind of rice, stained yellow with turmeric, the lobe of the ear is pierced either with a golden needle or a thorn.

Achehnese Marriage Customs.

Achehnese girls are married when they are eight to ten years old, and "one sees children whom we should deem of an age to be taken on the knee making purchases in the market in the capacity of matrons." * The following account of the marriage ceremonies applies to the Achehnese only. If a suitor does not present himself when a girl has arrived at the marriageable age, it is supposed that evil spirits are at work, and ceremonies are undertaken to counteract these influences. A girl is not supposed to marry beneath her station in life, and it is not considered fitting that she should be married before an elder sister.

An engagement in an Achehnese village is a very public affair, for the headman of the village has to be consulted as to the advisability of the match, the engagement presents, which generally take the form of a gold ring or hair ornament, and which are regarded as tokens of good faith, are delivered by the prospective bridegroom to the leading men of the village to be handed on by them to the parents of the bride. An engagement may last for one month or for twelve. At some time during this period the marriage contract is agreed upon and signed, and finally a day is fixed for the wedding.

The wedding day is preceded by three nights of feasting in the house of the bride's parents, and on the third night an important ceremony, known as the *andan*, takes place. This consists of shaving off some of the bride's hair, and is important because the bride, by submitting to it, openly declares that she is relinquishing her maiden state for married life. As long as she is unmarried a girl's hair is all drawn back off the forehead to the top and back of the head, but in the *andan* ceremony the shorter hairs are combed forwards and shaved off to the depth of one finger's breadth. Next evening the bridegroom is escorted to the bride's house by a body of his friends, and at the threshold is met by the bride's relatives; after a good deal of ceremonial cross-questioning and recitations, the bridegroom, who meanwhile has been hidden behind his friends, steps forward and enters the house. The bride is awaiting him in the inner room of the house, and the bridegroom takes his seat beside her on a mattress covered with cloth and finely woven mats. The maiden is supposed to be so bashful that her face is constantly concealed from view by a fan held by an ancient mistress of the ceremonies. She gives now a token of wifely obedience in the form of a long obeisance before her husband, who thereupon hands to her a small present of money.

The wedding-guests and fellow-villagers, who during all this time have been gaping with open-mouthed interest at the

* "The Achehnese," by Dr. Snouck Hergronje (English Translation).

Photograph by G. Lambert, Singapore.

BATTAK WOMAN (SUMATRA)

Carrying water vessels of bamboo. Note the ornaments in the upper part of the ear.

proceedings, are then served with a feast in the outer verandah of the house, whilst the young couple partake of a meal out of a common dish in the inner room. After the meal both are smeared behind the ears with glutinous rice, the idea of this ceremony being to confirm them in well-being and to ward off evil influences.

Throughout the Malay Archipelago happiness and goodness are associated with coolness, evil with heat, and under many circumstances heat, which is synonymous with evil, is averted by cooling the object or individual likely to be subjected to it with libations of water, or anointings with clay, or a peculiar glutinous rice.

Towards morning the bridegroom leaves the house and returns to his own home; he is not permitted to share the couch of his bride till the following night, and it is some time before he takes up his permanent abode in the house of his wife's parents.

Polygamy is unusual in Acheh, and it is only the rich who can afford it. If a man of rank and importance in a certain village marries a girl of some other village, it is impossible for him to live always with her, for this would entail the neglect of the duties and business which demand his attention in the home of his birth; it is contrary to law for his wife to leave her village and live in her husband's. The result of this state of affairs is, that a man with a wife in a distant village consoles himself for his frequent and enforced absences with one or more wives nearer home.

Polygamy and Divorce in Acheh.

Divorce is a simple process. If a couple desires to separate, the man takes three pieces of betel-nut, and hands them one by one to his wife, saying, "One divorce, two divorces, three divorces, thou art to me but as a sister in this world and the next." Notice of the divorce is then given to the head-man of the village, and the matter is at an end. The betel-nut is so intimately associated with divorce, that a woman in a

BATTAK WOMAN (SUMATRA). *Photograph by G. Lambert, Singapore.*

The houses are built on piles. This woman is seated on the front door steps.

passion with her husband will exclaim, "Give me then the three pieces of betel-nut."

Battak Marriage by Capture.

Amongst the Battaks, whilst exogamy is insisted on, marriage by capture is the universal custom, and a man will steal his wife by night from some neighbouring village, and carry her off to his own home, leaving behind him a small sum of money as a compensation for the theft. Nowadays the whole operation is purely ceremonial, and the parents of the girl are well aware when her abduction is planned, and when it takes place.

Polygamy is the rule rather than the exception, and a man may have as many as six wives, who all live in one large room; to each is allotted a separate cooking place and cooking utensils, and it is their duty to prepare in turn the meals of their sovereign lord and master. Amongst these people the position of women is not nearly so advantageous as in other parts of the archipelago, and men frequently sell their wives and children, and at all times treat them as little better than slaves. The Lampongs regard this form of marriage as disgraceful.

Marriage by Purchase.

Marsden, in his "History of Sumatra," states that amongst the Rejangs two forms of marriage exist, one which is similar to that found in Acheh, the other in which the bridegroom pays compensation for his wife, as with the Battaks: in the latter case the bridegroom, when escorting the bride to his house, takes care to tread on her big toe to signify that she is his property.

Birth Customs in Acheh.

In Acheh a pregnant woman is forced to observe all sorts of taboos. For example, she must not sit at the top of the steps leading up to the house lest her labour be difficult; nor should she be allowed to see monkeys, lest her child resemble them; if her husband goes out in the evening he must not return direct to the house, for if he does so the *burong*, an evil spirit that once dwelt in the body of an unchaste woman, will follow him in.

Great precautions are taken to prevent the entry of the *burong* to a house in which lie a woman and her new-born child; the stairway is guarded by ropes of rattan or palm fibre, and charms and pieces of malodorous bark are hung round the bed of the mother.

Directly after the birth of a child, the mother is laid on a platform under which is an oven that is kept supplied with fuel for forty-four days. The unfortunate patient endures agonies of thirst during this period of torture, but is only allowed to drink a little tea or pineapple juice; water must on no account be given to her. At the end of the forty-four days she is allowed to rise and is given a bath, to which is added the juice of sour oranges. On account of their early marriages Sumatran wives bear children long before they are twenty years of age, and at thirty they are too old to expect further additions to their families.

Sumatran Children.

A child is carried straddling across one hip of the mother, and supported by a cloth band which passes across the body of the mother and is knotted on the opposite shoulder. Children are suckled till they are two or three years old, but are soon taught to walk and to look after themselves; in fact, it may be said of them, as it has been said of Malay children, that they can walk, swim, and smoke before they are weaned.

Photograph by G. Lambert, Singapore.

BATTAK WOMAN (SUMATRA)

Resting on the notched log which serves as a ladder to the house. She holds a winnowing basket in her right hand, and has a basketful of rice on her head.

Photograph by H.H. the Ranee of Sarawak.

LAND-DAYAK WOMEN.
Wearing brass and shell armlets and leglets.

II

Types of Borneo—Mutilating Customs—Ear Ornaments—A Curious Corset—The Dayaks' Cylindrical Corset—Brass Ornaments—Dayak Necklets—Dress in Borneo—Tattooing in Borneo—Tattoo Class Marks—Woman's Work in Borneo—Women as Witch Doctors—Marriage Customs—Head Hunting and Courtship—Density of Population—Javanese Class Distinctions—Dancing Girls of the Harem—Other Dancing Girls—Women as Agricultural Labourers—General Position of Women in Java—Manners and Attractions of Javanese Women—Betrothal and Marriage—A Curious Tribe and its Wedding Customs—Balinese Beauties—Dress in Bali—Sacrifice of Widows—A High Code of Honour—Christianity and its Influence—Celebean Costume—Betrothal and Marriage in Celebes—The Importance of the Betel Nut—The Price of a Bride—The Women of Goa—Dress in Central Celebes—Weaving in Celebes—Papuan Influences

BORNEO

Types of Borneo.

THE numerous tribes of Borneo may be grouped for the sake of convenience into three main divisions: (1) a narrow-headed stock, typically Indonesian in their characteristics, and dwelling in the extreme north-east, the extreme north-west, and sporadically in the central highlands; (2) a broader-headed, Proto-Malayan stock, the Sea-Dayaks, whose headquarters are the centre of Sarawak; (3) the Kenyahs and Kayans, who may be regarded as intermediate in their physical characteristics between typical Indonesians and typical Proto-Malayans.

Mutilating Customs.

Fashion is a singularly hard task-mistress in Borneo, and there are few tribes whose women-folk do not mutilate some part of their persons or who do not wear some galling and irksome ornament. Amongst many of the Indonesian tribes, such as the Kanowits and Tanjongs, and amongst the Kenyahs and Kayans, distortion of the ears is carried to an excess. Girls at the tender age of two or three years have the lobes of the ears bored, and heavy weights are suspended from them, so that in course of time this part of the ear is pulled out into a slender loop of skin as many as seven inches long. The ideal aimed at is to stretch the loop until it can actually be passed over the head, but this is seldom attained, and often one of the loops breaks under the strain of the increasing weight of ornament. The broken ends may be spliced together and heal perfectly, but there is always a marked shortening of that loop, which is considered a grave blemish to beauty.

The ornaments worn in these elongated ear-lobes weigh anything from four to ten ounces, and are spiral coils of tin, copper or brass, or else pear-shaped ear-drops of the same metals or of stone. Some Indonesian women, *e.g.*, the Punans, Milanos, and Kadayans, wear plugs of wood, silver or gold one to two inches in diameter, in the distended ear-lobes; even an empty cotton reel, with one flange cut off, is often made to do duty as an ornament. Sea-Dayak women wear studs of copper or lead in the ears, but though the head of the stud is a disc of one inch or more in diameter, the shank and foot are small, and the orifice in the ear-lobe is not unduly distended.

Ear Ornaments.

The Sea-Dayak woman, if less of a martyr to fashion in the matter of ear-ornaments than her Kayan and Kenyah sisters, nevertheless finds it essential to wear on special occasions an ornament that must be, to the tyro at any rate, a veritable instrument of torture. It is known as the *rawai*, and consists of several circles of tightly rolled strips of Pandanus leaf on which are

A Curious Corset.

Photograph by H.H. the Ranee of Sarawak.

TANJONG WOMEN (SARAWAK, BORNEO)

Weaving baskets of bemban grass. The second woman from the right and the woman on the left wear heavy brass ear-rings, which have pulled the lobes of the ears into long loops.

threaded innumerable little brass rings; the circles are pinned together with brass rods, and the whole forms a more or less flexible cylinder, which is worn round the bust and waist. Sometimes this corset is

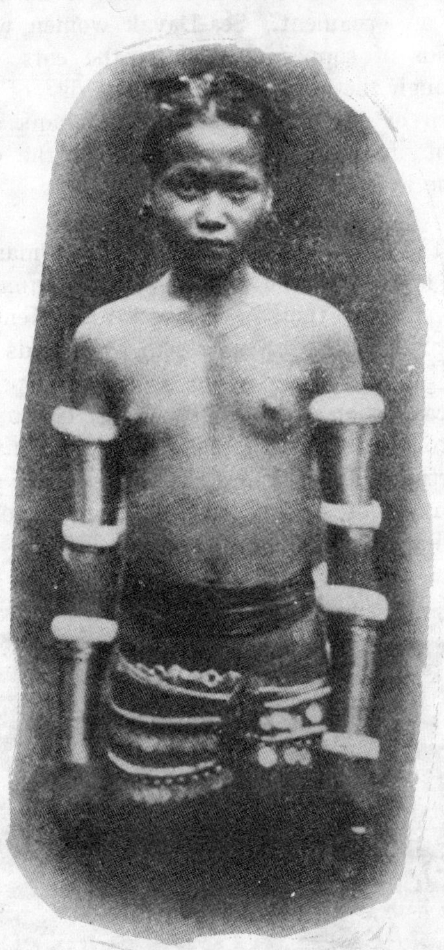

Photograph by H.H. the Ranee of Sarawak.

LAND-DAYAK GIRL (SARAWAK, BORNEO).
With brass wire and shell armlets.

made so as to open down the front, fastening by means of a simple form of catch, in which case the donning or doffing of it is a simple matter. But more often the corset has no such opening, and it must then be worked into position over the head and shoulders, the arms being held up above the head during the process. If the corset fits at all tightly the operation is a lengthy one, and a woman who has just undergone the pain and trouble of beautifying herself thinks twice about removing the embellishment until some days or perhaps weeks have elapsed. Since, in addition to the *rawai*, a Sea-Dayak belle will have also her arms and the lower parts of her legs encased in coils of brass wire, her dead weight is somewhat considerable when all her finery is worn, and it has happened more than once that such a brass-bound beauty, falling into a river from a bridge or through the capsizing of a canoe, has been drowned, notwithstanding her admirable swimming powers.

The Dayak Cylindrical Corset.

The corset worn by the Indonesian Land-Dayaks* still more recalls a strait-jacket, for it is a cylinder of bark, covered with vertical strips of brass wire clipped over the edges of the cylinder; it has no opening down the sides, front or back, and it is absolutely inflexible. It is only worn by unmarried girls, and once on it is seldom taken off; in fact, it is only when the prolonged chafing of the edges of the corset and of the ends of the brass wires has produced galls and open sores, that a girl calls on a friend to assist her to rid herself of her uncomfortable ornament.

Brass Ornaments.

Some of the Land-Dayak tribes do not wear this corset, but sheathe the arms and lower part of the legs in brass-wire rings with white shell armlets interspersed; the rings on the legs fit very closely, and in course of time produce considerable distortion of the calf-muscles. The brass ornaments are always highly polished, and with the glistening shell armlets impart a very picturesque appearance to the wearer; indeed, the writer can remember no prettier spectacle than that which met his eyes one evening when, as he and his crew were laboriously forcing their way up the rapid stream of the Upper Sarawak river, he was overtaken by a canoe containing half-a-dozen Land-

* The name Land-Dayak is rather unfortunate, since it leads to confusion with the very different Sea-Dayak. We owe it to the first Rajah of Sarawak, Sir James Brooke, who was one of the first to realise that the "Dayaks" of Borneo were not all of one stock.

Dayak women poling their frail craft with great precision and swiftness over the purling shallows and foaming rapids. With their beautiful brown skins glistening in the rays of the dying sun that sparkled on their brass and shell ornaments, they formed a perfect picture of young and vigorous womanhood.

Dayak Necklets.

Bead necklets are a common form of ornament, but with some Land-Dayak tribes they are, in addition, a badge of office worn by female witch-doctors or *borich;* all sorts of charms of wondrous magical properties are attached to the necklets, and hang down the back of the wearer. The Muruts of the Limbang river in north-east Sarawak are said by Spencer to wear round the neck "a couple of fathoms of brass wire, rising from the shoulders to the chin, forming what appears a stiff collar with a very broad base." This seems to be similar to the brass-ring collar worn by the Padaung women of the Shan States in Burma.

Dress in Borneo.

The dress of a Bornean woman, apart from her ornaments, is not elaborate, for it consists of little more than a skirt which may reach no further than the knees, as amongst the Sea-Dayaks, Muruts, Kalabits, and Land-Dayaks, or else to the feet. The skirt of the Kayan and Kenyah women is slit down the side, so that one leg is exposed to view during movements of any activity. Sometimes a short jacket is worn, but more usually the upper part of the body is uncovered. The Tanjongs and Milanos wear a long jacket cut low at the neck and with tight sleeves, along the lower part of which a row of gilt or silver buttons is sewn. Unmarried Dusun girls cover the breasts with a strip of cloth kept in position by coils of split rattan stained red with dragon's blood. When working on their farms large sun-hats, one to two feet in diameter, made of palm-leaf, are worn; they vary in shape from conical to flat discs, and are generally decorated with bead-work ornaments or plaited and dyed designs. To the centre of the hat on the inside is attached a cap of plaited material that fits the head. Seen from a distance women with this head-gear appear like gigantic animated mushrooms. The saucer-like sun-hats of the Brunei Malays are so huge that a woman, crouching in a canoe by merely tilting her head towards the observer, can conceal the whole of her person from a too inquisitive gaze.

Photograph by H.H. the Ranee of Sarawak.

SEA-DAYAK UNMARRIED GIRL.

Showing dress and ornaments. Note the tiara and brass rings round the neck; she does not wear the *rawai* or wire corset.

Tattooing in Borneo.

No account of feminine embellishment in Borneo would be complete without some reference to tattoo. The Kayan women tattoo most extensively and elaborately; the whole of the forearms, the back of the hands, the thighs and the upper surface of the feet being covered with intricate, and, in some cases, beautiful designs. The pigment used is a compound of soot and sugar-cane juice or water, and the designs appear in a dark blue colour, producing a likeness to skin-tight knickerbockers and mittens.

The process of tattooing is a lengthy one; it extends over three or four years, and as it is performed by means of rusty needle-points embedded in a wooden handle, and driven into the skin by repeated blows with a light hammer, most exquisite pain is caused. Frequently the operation has to be suspended, owing to the patient being thrown into a high fever. Since no antiseptic precautions of any sort are ever taken, it is remarkable that extensive ulceration of the wounded parts does not occur; but as a matter of fact the designs are seldom marred by the formation of scar-tissue.

Tattoo Class Marks.

The women of a Kayan tribe are divided into three classes, the relations of the chief, the free women, and the slaves, and the social status of a woman can be determined by the character of her tattoo designs—the more elaborate the design, the higher her rank. The Kenyahs only tattoo the fore-arms, hands and feet; Murut women tattoo the entire length of the arm to the finger-tips with fine longitudinal lines; Kalabit women tattoo weird geometrical designs on the shin and calf of the leg; the Long Glats of the central highlands tattoo representations of the hornbill's head and of the Argus pheasant's flight-feathers on the thigh and forearm. In fact the practice of tattoo is widely spread throughout the island, and the number of the designs is legion.

The origin of their tattoo is obscure, and the natives themselves, in attempting to explain it, can only put forward strange beliefs in its efficacy as a light to lighten their darkness in the next world, as a means of recognition after death, or as a passport to a magic river in the world beyond the grave, in whose bed many pearls are to be found.

Women's Work in Borneo.

As in the other islands of Malaya, the Bornean woman, unless she happens to be the wife or daughter of a chief in the feudal tribes of the Kayans and Kenyahs, works hard at tilling the communal rice-fields, clearing the ground, sowing the seed and reaping the harvest side by side with the men. A mother may frequently be seen amongst the labourers with her infant tied on to her back by a band of cloth, or seated in a wooden sling which is suspended by straps from her shoulders. If there is no work to be done on the farm, then it is a woman's task to husk the rice for the general consumption. The unhusked rice or *padi* is placed in a large wooden mortar and is pounded with a heavy pestle. Two women take part in the operation, pounding with alternate blows, and the thud of the pestle is one of the characteristic sounds in a Bornean house.

Water for drinking purposes is brought up from the river by the women. It is carried in lengths of bamboo held in a sling basket, and is poured into jars kept in the house.

The Sea-Dayak women weave from cotton thread of their own manufacture a strong cloth with a two- or three-colour design in it, the designs being produced by what is known as a "stop-out" process. The warp threads are stretched on a frame, and bundles of the threads are tied up here and there with strips of palm-leaf, the position of these tied-up bundles depending on the character of the desired design. The warp is then dipped into a red dye, and on removal from it the palm-leaf strips are cut off, and the design appears in the natural colour of the thread against a red background, or *vice versa*, according as the "stopping-out" has been arranged. If a third colour is required, the palm-leaf strips are not cut off on removal from the red dye, but more are added, and the warp goes then into a blue dye, which, of course, acts only on the uncovered portions of the warp threads. Finally, the warp is stretched on a simple loom, and an undyed weft is woven in. The illustration on p. 175 shows a woman tying up the warp-threads; frames holding the unwoven fabric in various stages are

KENYAH-KAYAN GIRL : SARAWAK, BORNEO.
DRAWN BY NORMAN H. HARDY.

Facing on page 174

in the background: the woman wears a petticoat of cloth of her own manufacture.

Amongst the Kayans and many Indonesian tribes, such as the Land-Dayaks, Long Wai and Trings, the witch-doctors are women, and by virtue of their supposed power over evil spirits, their services are much in request. All savage folk attribute most forms of disease to the possession of the patient's body by some demon that has taken the place temporarily of the patient's soul. The witch-doctors, by means of ceremonies, incantations, and charms, can exorcise the evil spirit and retrieve the wandering soul of the sick person, and this they are always ready to do for a fee which sometimes is exorbitant. The Sea-Dayaks employ male witch-doctors, but those who inspire most confidence are men who have assumed the dress, voice, and habits of women. These emasculated creatures occasionally take to themselves "husbands," and though the "husbands" are objects of scornful derision to the tribe, the witch-doctor's authority is increased by his entry into the state of pseudo-matrimony.

Women as Witch-Doctors.

Photograph by H.H. the Ranee of Sarawak.

SEA-DAYAK WOMAN (SARAWAK, BORNEO).

With *rawai* or brass corset, silver tiara and shell ornaments. She is preparing a warp of cotton thread for dyeing, as described in the text (p. 174).

Weddings are not attended with a great deal of ceremony, and are conducted very much in the same way as described in connection with the Achehnese of Sumatra. There is the same preliminary discussion of the terms of the marriage contract: the bridegroom is escorted to the bride's house by a band of comrades, or he receives the bride in his own home. The young couple are smeared on the forehead and breast with glutinous rice stained yellow with turmeric, and are exhorted by an ancient man or woman of the tribe to increase and multiply. At a Sea-Dayak wedding there takes place the ceremony of *blah pinang*, or splitting the betel-nut. One or two betel-nuts are divided into

Marriage Customs.

eight pieces, which are supposed to represent the husband's responsibilities, and these are laid on a plate. Another betel-nut is divided into seven pieces representing the wife's duties; these are put on the same plate, which is then covered with a cloth and placed on one side. After a decent interval the cloth is removed and the pieces of betel-nut are examined: should there be more than fifteen pieces, prosperity for the young couple is assured, but should there be fewer then disaster is prophesied. The whole proceeding is nowadays nothing more than a mere ceremony, and fifteen pieces of betel-nut are always to be found on the plate; but perhaps at some former time the officiating priest or priestess by sleight-of-hand added to or subtracted from the number, the action being determined by the nature of the fee that was paid.

Photograph by H.H. the Ranee of Sarawak.

LAND-DAYAK *BORICH* OR FEMALE WITCH-DOCTORS.

Bundles of curative charms are attached to their bead necklets. They are believed to control evil spirits and all diseases.

Divorce is common—sterility, incompatibility of temper, or even a dream of ill-omen, being sufficient cause for a separation. It is no unusual thing among the Sea-Dayaks for a young bachelor to visit at night the couch of his inamorata, but it by no means follows that immorality thereupon takes place. The lovers converse and play to each other on the jew's-harp, in the strains of which they fancy they can express more passionately their mutual affection. If a girl, as a result of these nocturnal visits, becomes pregnant, her lover is almost invariably ready to marry her; even if he were reluctant to do so, he would be afraid to face the storm of hostile criticism which would be raised by all his friends and neighbours.

Head-hunting and Courtship.

The possession of one or more heads of enemies slain in battle is a great asset to a young man when he goes a-wooing; his reputation as a man of valour is established, and the marriageable maidens of the district regard him with as much admiration as Mary Jane displays towards her Life-guardsman. A desire to excite feminine admiration has been sometimes given as an excuse by head-hunting culprits when arraigned before a court of justice, but it need not be supposed that in this desire is to be found the origin of the barbarous custom.

To recover the affection of a fickle lover, love-potions are concocted, the principal ingredient of which is coco-nut oil. This is smeared on the body of the man or on his bedding and clothes when he is asleep, and an incantation is uttered to invoke the aid of the spirits.

JAVA

Java is the only tropical island in the world with a dense, indigenous population. Thirty millions of people, not including

Europeans, Malays or Chinese, occupy this island of 50,000 square miles in extent.

Density of Population.

Hindu and Mohammedan civilisations existed here for long ages before the advent of the European, but in spite of that, and in spite of their Mohammedan religion, the people to-day exhibit in a thousand ways the primitive characters of the Indonesian race. The Sundanese of Western Java, the Javanese proper of Mid and Eastern Java, the Tenggerese of the Eastern highlands, and the decadent Kalangs scattered here and there throughout the island, are the component tribes of this vast population.

On account of its ancient civilisation we find in Java a sharp line drawn between an aristocratic ruling class and a servile plebeian class, such as we find nowhere else in the Malay Archipelago. Among the Bornean Kayan the chief owns slaves, rules his village with a rod of iron, and toils not in the fields, but he lives in the communal house of his tribe, and there is little to distinguish him in dress from his subjects. But in Java the sultans live in palaces, and maintain a very considerable pomp and majesty.

Javanese Class Distinctions.

Every sultan and a few nobles have large harems, some of the inmates of which are trained dancers, who perform on state occasions. The dance is called the *s'rimpi*, and is a figure-dance in which four performers take part to the accompaniment of an orchestra of gongs, harmonicums, and viols. The girls, none of whom exceed more than fourteen or fifteen years of age, are clad in gorgeous silk petticoats reaching to the ground, and fastened round the waist with a girdle of gold plates joined by slender chains; the upper part of the body is enclosed in a kind of corset passing above the bosom and under the arms, and confining the waist to the smallest possible compass. A silken sash is thrown over the shoulders, and is an important adjunct in the waving motions of the hands and arms in the dance. A tiara of gold studded with precious stones, richly chased armlets, bracelets, and finger-rings, complete the attire of these damsels. The music of the orchestra

Dancing Girls of the Harem.

Photograph by Mr. Shelford

KADAYAN WOMEN (BORNEO).

Note the tight-sleeved jackets with rows cf buttons.

is slow and solemn, and the dance consists of little else than graceful movements of the upper part of the body and arms, with an occasional change of the position of the performers. When the dance is at an end, the performers sink to the ground, and after a low obeisance to their sultan sit with downcast eyes, whilst elderly duennas put straight their dress and hair which may have become disarranged in the dance.

Other Dancing Girls.

The *bedaya* is a figure-dance for eight persons, and is performed by the concubines of a noble, though, as there are few nobles who can afford to maintain a sufficient number of trained dancers, the parts are often taken by boys. The *ronggeng* are the common dancing girls of the country, and are frequently to be seen in the west of the island. They hire themselves out to dance at feasts, and are ready to give their services at any time of the day or night. In their dress they ape the fashions of the *s'rimpi* dancers, but cotton takes the place of silk, and white metal and glass ornaments replace the jewels of the royal concubines In the dance the arms and fingers are sometimes bent backwards at unnatural angles, and one finger is occasionally made to quiver tremulously. To the European eye the dance is singularly unpleasing, though exceptions are met with. They accompany their dance with song, which is often composed on the spur of the moment, and abounds in references to topical interests, provoking loud applause from the spectators. Women are included in the travelling theatrical companies which are so popular in Java; they take the parts of mythical heroines and of the *widadari*, or heavenly nymphs, who were bestowed on the prince Arjuna by the gods Indra and Brahma as a reward for his conquest of the giants.

Photograph by O. Kurkdjian.

YOUNG BATAVIAN WOMAN, JAVA

Women as Agricultural Labourers.

Java is a country smiling with fertility, and the cultivation of rice has been brought to a very high pitch of perfection. In the west, square miles of land are terraced, and the terraces rising tier upon tier on the hillsides are fed by running streams of water, for the Javanese grow their rice in wet soil, not on dry soil as do most of the Borneans. The banking of the terraces, the cutting of channels for the irrigating streams, sowing, planting out the young plants, and harvesting involves an immensity of labour in which the women bear an equal share with the men. In the east of the island sugar-cane plantations, owned by Chinese and Dutch companies, largely take the place of the rice-fields of the west, and in these plantations as many women work as coolies as men.

General Position of Women in Java.

Women in Java, if they do not exert so powerful an influence in domestic and village affairs as in Borneo and Sumatra, nevertheless are far from occupying a menial position. The man in a Javanese household leaves much of the business of selling the produce of his land to his women-folk, and in the crowded market-places of the towns the majority of the stalls are kept by women;

and, as the writer can testify, a Javanese woman can drive a harder bargain than her good man. A feature of these market-places is the number of European sewing-machines all working at full speed. Many people buy at a stall cloth for a jacket or petticoat, and having bought what they want they get it made up into the required article on the spot. The sewing-machines are driven by men, not by women.

Manners and Attractions of Javanese Women.

The Javanese, in their works on manners and ethics, have laid down the qualities of a good wife. Here are two quotations:—"She must be well made and well mannered, gentle, industrious, rich, liberal, charming, of good birth, upright and humble. A stingy, curious, dirty, foul-mouthed, vulgar, false, intriguing, lazy and stupid woman is not only unfit for a housewife, but will never be beloved by a husband." "A woman who loves her husband so tenderly, that at his death she wishes to die with him, or surviving never marries again, but lives as if she were dead to the world, is valued above all others of her sex." *

Betrothal and Marriage.

Children of tender years are frequently betrothed, but they are not married until they have reached a suitable age. As elsewhere in Malaya, a Javanese marriage contract is the subject of much discussion between the parents and relations of the contracting parties. If the match is considered suitable, the bridegroom sends to his prospective bride a present, the value of which is dependent on his position in life; if the bridegroom subsequently repudiates his promised word, the disappointed girl is allowed to retain this present, but on the other hand it must be returned to the donor if the obstacles to the completion of the marriage originate with her. On the wedding day the bridegroom proceeds with his father and other male relatives to the mosque, and after informing the priest that he is willing to pay the necessary fees, the

* Raffles' "History of Java."

marriage is sanctified by the priest in words to the following effect:—"I join you X—— in marriage with Y—— with a pledge of two reals weight in gold or silver. You take Y—— to be your wife for this world. You are obliged to pay the pledge of your marriage or to remain debtor for the same. You are responsible for your wife in all things. If you should happen to be absent from her for the space of seven months on shore, or one year at sea, without giving her any subsistence, and are remiss in the performance of the duties which you owe to your sovereign, your marriage shall be dissolved, if your wife requires it, without any further form or process; and you will be, besides, subject to the punishment which the Mohammedan law dictates." *

The latter part of this injunction is the *talik*, to which reference has already been made (p. 164) as illustrating the less advantageous position occupied by Javanese women than by women in countries where the matriarchal state is upheld; in those countries the *talik* is omitted as unnecessary. After the ceremony the bridegroom and his party proceed to the bride's house with as much pomp as is compatible with their rank and station in life. In some districts the bride and bridegroom on first meeting simultaneously hurl at each other a bundle of *siri* leaves, one of the principal ingredients of the betel-nut quid; the one who succeeds in hitting the other in the face with the missile is regarded as likely to be the dominant partner in the married state. The bride then makes a low obeisance to the bridegroom in token of her wifely submission, and both enter the house, where, seated apart from the wedding guests, they share a meal and chew betel-nut and *siri* together. Ceremonial calls must be paid on following days on the bridegroom's parents and relatives before the young couple settle down in their own house, which may be situated in the bride's native village or in that of the bridegroom.

Amongst the Tenggerese, a people who have preserved their primitive customs, curiously intermixed with Hindu rites, the

* Raffles' "History of Java."

marriage ceremony is rather different from that described above. The bride and bridegroom are brought before one of the priests or *dukun* of the village, and bow, first to the south, then to the hearth, then to the earth, and then to the upper storey of the house where the implements of husbandry are stored. These obeisances completed, the *dukun* recites a prayer addressed to Brahma, while the bride washes the bridegroom's feet; presents are given to the newly-wed pair by their relatives, and in return betel-nut is accepted. The usual feasting follows, but the marriage is not actually consummated till the fifth day after the ceremony, a restriction that is observed occasionally in other districts of Java.

The much-despised Kalangs are one of the many savage tribes that regard the dog with great veneration, and they trace their descent from an unnatural alliance between a princess and a chief who had been transformed into a dog. When a young man of this tribe demands the hand of a girl in marriage he must prove his descent from a pure Kalang stock. On the wedding day, a buffalo's head covered with white, red, or black rice-powder is placed on the ground near the place on which the nuptial couch is laid; the wedding guests dance in pairs, at the end of each dance presenting the bride to the bridegroom, and making suitable offerings to them. The bridegroom, who is accompanied to the bride's house by his friends, must bring with him as a marriage portion a pair of buffaloes, a plough, harrow, hoe, whip, and a sheaf of rice. The bodies of the bride and bridegroom are rubbed with the ashes of a red dog's bones, and at sunset they both eat rice out of the same dish. On the following night they partake of the buffalo's head, which is previously laid by the place where they sleep. Ceremonial calls on neighbours and relations are paid on following days. There is much that is remarkable in these wedding festivities, and it is to be hoped that further information on the matter will one day be forthcoming. At one time it was supposed that the Kalangs were Negritoes, and hence one of the most

A Curious Tribe and its Wedding Customs.

Photograph by O. Kurkdjian.

JAVANESE WOMAN (KEDIRI PROVINCE).

Making pottery on a primitive wheel.

Photograph by O. Kurkdjian.

JAVANESE WOMEN MAKING *BATIK* SARONGS.

The background of the pattern is laid on with melted wax ; the cloth is then dyed and the wax is removed with boiling water, leaving the dark pattern against an undyed background. The process is repeated for every colour employed.

primitive tribes known to exist, but it is now certain that they are of Indonesian stock, and it is probable that they are the remnants of a race once spread throughout Java before the immigration of the Tenggerese, Sundanese, and Javanese proper.

BALI.

Balinese Beauties. A young Balinese woman is a physically perfect specimen of humanity, and by virtue of bearing loads on her head instead of on the back, acquires a carriage and deportment that would have delighted the heart of a Greek sculptor. This method of carrying loads, though common enough in Africa and India, is unusual in the Malay Archipelago, and it is interesting to notice that Bali is the only Malayan island in which the Hindu religion persists at the present day.

Dress in Bali. The only garment worn by a Balinese woman of the lower class is a long dark blue skirt ; the upper part of the body is uncovered, though occasionally a light scarf is thrown round the neck. In Lombok, where many Balinese are found, a dark blue jacket is worn in addition to the skirt. The ear-lobes are pierced, and in the enlarged hole a roll of palm-leaf is worn by the lower-class women, a gold or silver ear-plug by the wealthy.

Men carry off or elope with their brides, leaving behind them a compensation for the parents in the form of a money payment or in kind.

Sacrifice of Widows. Formerly it was customary for a widow to follow her husband's corpse to the funeral pyre, and to seek death in the flames that consumed her dear departed. The death of a rajah entailed the sacrifice not only of his widow, but of many of the women of his household. Crawford * relates that no fewer than seventy-four women voluntarily sacrificed themselves at the burning of the corpse of a rajah of Boeliling; they were borne to the funeral pyre in litters, were then stabbed, stripped naked, and cast into the flames. The female relatives of the rajah, on account of their high rank, could not be touched by the profane hands of the executioners, but climbed on to a

* "Journal of the Indian Archipelago."

scaffolding built over the fire, and leapt down into it.

A High Code of Honour.

Under Dutch rule these horrible sacrifices of life have been sternly forbidden, but a recent incident shows that the Balinese, under certain circumstances, regard their honour as of more account than death. The Dutch were engaged in the suppression of a rebellion in Bali, and readers of English newspapers must have been horrified to see one morning an account of an attack on a Bali stronghold, in which numbers of women and children were slain. The incident, however, was explained satisfactorily as a case of suicide, the men, women, and children in the fortress destroying themselves rather than surrender.

CELEBES.

Christianity and its Influence.

Much less is known of this island than of those that are collectively termed the Great and the Lesser Sunda Islands. Parts of it are still unexplored, and it is only from the more civilised districts that we have much information of the customs of the inhabitants. The Minahassa district in the north is perhaps the best known part of the island, just as it is certainly the most beautiful. The Dutch have been established there for some time, and Christianity has been introduced with conspicuous success amongst the natives.

Celebean Costume.

The women nowadays wear the costume affected by Dutch ladies during the heat of the day. It consists of a short white jacket or *kabaya*, fastened down the front by brooches or pins, and a coloured petticoat or *sarong* reaching to the ankles.

Betrothal and Marriage in Celebes.

In pre-Christian times descent was traced through the female line, and the husband lived with his wife's people, but now a married couple set up their own establishment. A mock marriage ceremony was often held with children of five to nine years old acting the leading parts of bride and bridegroom; a feast was held, the spirits were invoked to shower blessings on the twain, and food was offered to the dogs of the village. At the termination of the ceremony the children returned to their respective homes with their parents, and were not regarded as irrevocably betrothed to each other; in fact, as often as not on arriving at a marriageable age they were joined in wedlock to other contemporaries. A Minahassa maiden exercises much more freedom in the choice of a husband than is usually the case amongst the non-Malayan folk. The wooing generally begins in the evenings of a *mapalu* or calling together of neighbours to assist in reaping the rice-harvest. After the day's work is ended all repair to the house of the owner of the rice-field and are feasted; song and dance beguile the hours after the meal, and it is then that the Minahasser finds his opportunity. He steals from the festivities to the couch of his *inamorata*, and the two lovers converse till nearly daybreak, when the man leaves the house and goes forth to his labour. If the lovers decide to wed, then one morning the young man remains with the girl until all in the village are up and about, and it is then understood that the couple are betrothed. According to our ideas it seems curious that in order to become engaged to a girl it is necessary, first to compromise her seriously, and then to noise it abroad; but such is, or was, the custom in Minahassa.

The Importance of the Betel-nut.

When a youth first falls in love with a maiden he sends her a betel-nut prepared for chewing, and if his advances are regarded favourably the girl accepts the token, and sends the love-sick swain a similar offering. The betel-nut, which, as already shown, plays an important part in every ceremony connected with matrimony in Malaya, is frequently mentioned in Minahassan love-songs, *e.g.*, "Place half of the betel-nut you have cut in two in my mouth, and my feelings will be always well towards you." "If a man could fly like

Photograph by O. Kurkdjian.

TWO SUNDANESE LADIES (WEST JAVA), WITH CHILD.

The nurse is standing at the back. The man on the right is a Sundanese, the other two are from Solo, in Central Java.

the wind I would take this betel-nut out of my mouth and send it to my lover." * Before the wedding-day the bridegroom sends to his bride a preliminary present of nine betel-nuts, nine *siri* fruits, and some gold or silver ornaments, as a token of good faith; in ancient times the head of a foe was sent, but the Dutch have stamped out head-hunting for good and all, so that the grisly trophy is omitted now from the list of wedding gifts.

The price paid by the bridegroom formerly to the bride's parents was so much land, so many *saguier*-trees, and so many head of cattle, but nowadays it is paid in hard cash. The wedding ceremony takes place

* S. J. Hickson, "A Naturalist in North Celebes."

in the house of the bride's parents: food is served to the guests, and the *walian* or officiating priest chews some betel-nut and *siri*, and then hands the quid to the bridegroom, who finally hands it on to the bride for further mastication; the young couple partake of food from the same dish, and the ceremony is at an end. On the following morning there is another wedding feast, after which the *walian* takes the bride and bridegroom to the boundary line of the district, sticks a piece of bamboo in the ground, and says, "Here is a mouse: may your riches be as numerous as the hairs on the mouse."

The Price of a Bride.

Photograph by O. Kurkdjian.

JAVANESE LACE MAKER.

The lace pillow and bobbins are very like those used in Europe, and it is probable that the industry was introduced into Java by the Dutch. The lace is made of silver thread.

In Central Celebes there is a considerable variety of tribes, and the dress of the women is sometimes very striking. The Bada women for full dress wear on the head a sort of diadem, shaped like a "pork-pie" hat, and a simple pattern is worked in colours on it; yellow is the colour reserved for those of high rank, and the dye is obtained from the saffron-yellow cuticle of certain orchid-stems. The caps are further ornamented with plumes composed of fowl's feathers, to which are fastened with resin the scarlet breast feathers of a species of *Pitta* or ground-thrush. The jacket, of some dark coloured material, is short and ornamented in front with a lozenge-shaped breastplate, made of differently coloured materials and resembling a patchwork quilt; with the more wealthy the patchwork is replaced by an ornament of brass filigree. The long petticoat, reaching to the feet, is very wide, and when gathered in at the waist a large flounce of material is left above the cincture, and stands out all round, giving the figure a very bunchy appearance. Ear-plugs of buffalo-horn are worn in the distended orifices of the ear-lobes, and occasionally these ornaments are joined by long strings of beads. Necklaces of beads, fish-bones, seeds and other natural objects are worn, also armlets of white shell. The face is painted on festal occasions with streaks and spots of resin, and appears as if tattooed.

Dress in Central Celebes.

Many of these inland tribes have no knowledge of weaving, and their fabrics are obtained from the bark of a tree The bark is softened for a long time in water, and then beaten with wooden hammers into long strips of comparatively thin texture; the strips are cut to required lengths and stitched together. In Buol, North Celebes, the women are adepts at weaving, and make patterned silk *sarongs* which are much prized in all parts of Celebes; they are in various brilliant colours. In spite of the great dexterity of the weavers, the manufacture of a *sarong* is a painfully slow process even in a country where time is of small account.

Weaving in Celebes.

The Topebato women wear a broad girdle, or rather corset, of plaited fibre, dyed black and red. One woman will plait this girdle round the waist of another, and it is fitted so closely that it can only be taken off by the method employed by Alexander in solving the difficulty of the Gordian knot. These people wear necklaces of various natural objects that they consider decorative, such as the yellow beaks of a species of cuckoo, the metallic green wing-cases of certain beetles, and the heads of long-horned Dynastid beetles, decorated with pieces of tin-foil. The Kulawi women wear broad rings of wood or plaited fibre on the top of the head, and collars of sweet-smelling root-fibres with brightly coloured feathers worked in; they are fond of gaudy colours, and travelling traders find a great demand for cloth striped with the Dutch national colours—red, white and blue. Discolouring, filing, and even removing some of the front teeth is practised by many tribes, for it is considered unsightly to have regular white teeth "like a monkey."

Curious Ornaments.

Photograph by O. Kurkdjian.

JAVANESE WEAVER.

The loom is fastened to a frame, and the threads are kept taut by means of a band passing round the weaver's back. The man on the right is winding thread.

Photograph by T. J. McGregor.

HOUSES OF ABORIGINES NEAR LUBO' KLUBI, ULU LANGAT, SELANGOR.

THE MALAY PENINSULA

By W. W. SKEAT

Environment and Race—Food and Cookery—Dress in Malaya—The National Costume—Malayan Coiffures—Miscellaneous Fashions—Negrito and Sakai Dress—Home-life of Malay Women—The Work of Malay Women—Birth Superstitions and Ceremonies—The Moon and its Influences—Malayan Childhood—How the Malayan Girl "Comes Out"—Malayan Beauty—Malayan Marriage Ceremonies—Bride Hunting—Mohammedan Influence on Malay Women—West Coast Marriage Customs—The Bridal Costume—Bride and Bridegroom's Race for Supremacy—Funeral Ceremonies—Curious Types of Malayan Women

Environment and Race.

To obtain an idea of the present environment of woman in the Golden Chersonese (the old and more poetic name of the Malay Peninsula) we may think of what Great Britain must have been in very early days when the Roman power extended over the greater portion of the country more especially that part inhabited by the Anglo-Saxon and Norse immigrants of an earlier period, when the Britons were left still undisturbed in the fastnesses of their hills and fens and forests.

There are in the Malay Peninsula several distinct social strata, consisting of civilised aliens on the one hand, and the semi-civilised and savage inhabitants of the woods and hills on the other. The races of which we are to treat here are, firstly, the civilised Malays, and, secondly, the uncivilised representatives of the three jungle races of the Peninsula—the Negritos or Semang, the Sakai, and the jungle Malayans or Jakun. In the towns the Chinese greatly preponderate in numbers, and there are also, especially on the European estates, a considerable number of Tamils, whilst in the northern portion of the Peninsula the Siamese are dominant.

Among all the problems suggested by the study of man there are few more fascinating than to watch the effect of its surroundings upon the workings of the human mind and its gradual development in accordance therewith. Owing to the prevalence of wild and dangerous beasts, such as the tiger and the elephant, not only do many of the wild men make their huts in trees, and at times even form an entire encampment, or what may be called a "tree-village," but they also obtain from the jungle their only supplies of food, raiment, simples for the sick, and, indeed, the entire material of their life.

This dense virgin forest is by no means confined to the plains—which, in the more settled parts of the Peninsula, have been to a great extent denuded of trees—but extends up to the very sky-line of the savage and precipitous hills that form the backbone of the Peninsula. In the rock-shelters of these uplands the wild Semang make their lair, and thence descend the thousand rock-strewn torrents which in the wilder parts of the country serve as foot-tracks for the mountain-dwelling Sakai, and which even in their smooth broad lower reaches still form a high-road for the Malays, whose scattered population was, in the old days at least, for the most part riverain. And here and there, in lonely islands off the coast, or where sandy beaches take the place of the widely present mangrove, and where strange creatures of the deep, such as the black coral and the sea-pen (called by the Malays the "sea-demon's boat-pole"), may be seen as one walks across the hot, bright, smoking sands, we may yet meet small groups of the Malayan Sea Gpysies or Orang Laut, in ever-dwindling numbers, engaged in fishing for the small fry or collecting shellfish.

Photograph by T. J. McGregor.

GROUP OF ABORIGINES, SELANGOR (F.M.S.).

Women dressed in the "Kăbaya" (a kind of loose gown which they have borrowed from the neighbouring Malays), worn over the Malay *sarong*. The man on the right has a blowpipe.

The Jakun are a mixed group composed of the Negritos and the Sakai and a third race (of aboriginal Malayan type) which, with their round heads, lank and somewhat coarse blue-black hair, and reddish- or yellow-brown skin, are of Mongolian descent. The Malayan element is strong enough to ensure the preponderance of old Malayan culture, Malayan customs, and Malayan speech; they are therefore, perhaps, in some ways the most important of the three. Against this aboriginal foundation has broken wave after wave of aggressive or peaceful immigrants, of Siamese in the north and of Mohammedan Malays from Sumatra and all the neighbouring islands in the south. In some cases these were agricultural settlers who blended with the aboriginal population, as in the confederation of the small states called Negri Sembilan, north of Malacca. In other cases they were Malay freebooters who, with all the zealot fanaticism of recent converts, carried fire and the kris before them, and in the name of the Prophet committed acts of indescribable ferocity and treachery upon the innocent and helpless indigenous inhabitants.

The aboriginal races of the Peninsula are all pagan, and are thus easily to be distinguished from the Buddhist Siamese of the north and the Malays, who without exception profess (superficially at least) the tenets of Mohammedanism, though the great majority of them are animists and Shamanists at heart.

Food and Cookery.

Though rice is by far the most important, it is by no means (except, perhaps, in the case of the very poorest) the only food of the Malay peasant. He plants in the clearing, or *kampong*, that adjoins his house, a great variety of catch crops, maize, sugar-cane, sweet potatoes, yams, tapioca, bananas, and many others, all of which are carefully watched and tended by the women-folk and children. Not infrequently, too, the house is surrounded by a dense grove of coco-nut palms or fruit-trees. A small plot near the house is sometimes occupied by a few betel vines, supported on props that recall a Kentish hop-garden. Scratching about among the roots, or in the open ground near by, are the fowls—a not unimportant adjunct of many Malay households. Goats and the black Malay sheep are also occasionally kept; fish caught by means of weirs, weels, spring-rods, basket-traps, and a variety of other ingenious devices, or stupefied by the poisoning of the stream with *tuba* (a Malay form of poaching discountenanced by the British Government) are brought home from the neighbouring river—few Malays live far from a stream of some kind. Then there are wild fruits from the jungle, each in its season, birds of many kinds, and certain small animals, such as the mouse-deer and the porcupine, which are considered to be allowable as food by Mohammedan law; occasionally perchance even a haunch of venison.

This list will give some faint idea of the varied skill that the Malayan housewife may any day be called upon to exercise in cooking. This, however, represents but one side of her culinary powers, for to those who have seen her in the act of making, with the help of a few iron pots and pans, split sticks, bamboo tubes, moulds, and banana-leaves, a legion of small rice-cakes, sweets, pickles, and preserves of all sorts of materials, shapes, and sizes, described under strange names, some weird and some poetical, she is at least known to be an adept in her calling. Daintily-cooked rice (and rice properly cooked is to its opposite as Paradise is to Purgatory) she prides herself on, and twice a day she prepares it, with its adjuncts of scraps of buffalo-meat (if her lord is a man of substance), or goat, fowl, egg, palm-cabbage, fern or fish, and the tasteful condiments that go to make up the unrivalled glory of a real Malay curry. In the up-country districts many strange forms of food are to be met with, among them being fried toads, cockchafers, and wasp-grubs dipped in honey!

The food of the jungle tribes consists usually of vegetable food, wild roots and palm-shoots, millet, maize, sugar-cane, tapioca, yams, and rice, eked out (when vegetable food fails) with game of every imaginable description that can be shot with the bow or blow-pipe, or caught by some one of their marvellously ingenious traps by land or water. There is, indeed, very little in the jungle, however unpromising material it may appear, that the pagan housewife is unable to make a dish of; in fact, so clever is she at utilising all the resources of the neighbourhood to the utmost, that she can make even poisonous tubers edible by steeping and pressing them till the poison is extracted. (One wonders instinctively how such a discovery came to be made.) Even in the case of game killed by the blow-pipe, the tip of which is furnished with the poisonous sap of the far-famed upas tree, all that is done is to cut out the flesh round the wound (which acquires a bluish tinge) and roast it as usual.

The National Costume.

The *sarong*, which is the national Malay dress, is a picturesque cotton or silk skirt, its name implying "wrapper" or "envelope." It is of universal use, and is variously worn as dress either by day or night, for sleeping in, or as a hood or girdle. An old one is often kept for use while bathing. In technical dressmaking parlance, it might be described as a perfectly straight, unshaped skirt of the same "fulness" at top and bottom, and reaching down, as a rule, to the ankles, though in some parts of the Peninsula it is worn much shorter—occasionally, indeed, but little below the knee. It is fastened by holding out the slack part so as to form a broad pleat on one or both sides, folding the pleated part over the front, or over the left hip, and rolling the upper borders of the *sarong* down upon itself; sometimes the ends of the slack parts are twisted or crossed, and occasionally a belt is worn to keep the garment in position.

Except when in full dress the women wear either this or a second *sarong* (or, on the east coast, a sort of broad scarf-like cloth called *kain lĕpas*), crossed and folded over the breasts in front. Out of doors the Malay women frequently wear as a veil either a thin cloth or piece of chintz, or two *sarongs*, one fastened round the waist in the usual manner, and one drawn over the head hood-wise, and distended by means of the stretched arms, so as to leave nothing but a narrow slit in front of the eyes.

The *sarong* is woven from coloured threads in a great variety of patterns, generally striped or with a small check pattern, like the tartan of the Highlander or the now extinct Irish tartan. The *sarongs* of the richer sort are often most beautiful productions of the loom, and are either of a self colour or a rich check, or flowered, or richly embroidered, either in whole or in part, with gold thread in a maze of beautiful patterns, among which the chevron motive and varieties of flowers predominate. It is noteworthy that the patterns worn by respectable women are of a more refined and delicate character (usually a smaller check) than those worn by the men. In Kelantan and Trĕnggānu, the centres of the weaving industry of the Malay Peninsula, where almost every other house owns a loom, the colour-designs are striking and often most artistic.

To the *sarong* the wealthier add an inner garment of white cotton cloth covering the hips, and the *kăbaya*, a long and gracefully flowing outer garment or gown, reaching to the knees, fastened with brooches in front and clasped at the waist with gold or silver clasps of imposing magnitude, which are often very beautifully inlaid or chased.

The wedding-dress of the bride, like that of the Malay *danseuse*, is an apotheosis of the attire of a well-to-do Malay woman with certain additions—*e.g.*, with the addition of a special head-dress of great splendour and a heap of borrowed jewellery.

Malayan Coiffures.

The hair, which is the chief glory of a Malay woman, is straight, luxuriant, glossy, and of a bluish tinge of black, the hue of the raven's wing. It is cleansed with limes, and is drawn up, usually in a simple roll or "knot," tied at the back of the head, and fastened with a gold dagger in the hair or with silver hair-pins. The bright yellow or red blossoms of the *champaka*, in a setting of the Malay woman's night-black tresses, produce a brilliant and striking contrast, the effect of which is heightened by the seductive fragrance of the flower.

Miscellaneous Fashions.

Great hoods of palm-thatch, protecting the head and shoulders from rain or sun, are met with up country, and so, too, are strange palm-leaf umbrellas that open like huge fans. Malays have as a rule bare feet, but wooden sabots are sometimes worn, and shoes have of recent years been coming

Photograph by H. W. Thomson.

RESPECTABLE MARRIED WOMAN OF KELANTAN.

Wearing the broad sash (*kain lĕpas*) about the breasts and skirt consisting of a flowered *sarong* of Trĕnggānu make.

into fashion. In Patani and Singora, on the east coast, where Siamese influence is now paramount, the quaint but richly-coloured national garment of the Siamese, the *pannung*, is fairly generally worn, and almost any morning the yellow-robed Sami or Siamese priests may be seen going on their rounds to collect the alms of the pious.

Negrito and Sakai Dress.

The Negrito women, when they wear anything at all, put on wonderful fringed girdles cleverly woven from the intertwined black, shiny, root-like strings of a particular kind of fungus. Elsewhere among the Sakai and Jakun the loin-cloth of beaten tree-bark is worn almost universally by the men, and a kind of short bark-cloth apron by the women, except where the Malay *sarong* is found. On festal occasions they all deck themselves out like Jacks-in-the-green, with leaves and flowers and high fantastic head-dresses of woven leaf or bark. Back-combs with magical designs are worn in the hair, and porcupines' quills through the nose and sometimes through the ear-lobes (by the Sakai women), whilst metal-ring armlets, bracelets, and necklaces, consisting of many strings of animals' tails and tufts of fur, teeth, seeds, beads, coins, and small bones form part of the indispensable "rig-out" of a Sakai belle.

Photograph by H. W. Thomson.

RESPECTABLE MARRIED WOMAN OF KELANTAN.

Wearing *kain lĕpas* (a broad sash), draped about the breasts (*kain kĕmban*), over a flowered *sarong*, flowers in hair.

Home Life of Malay Women.

Among the civilised Malay peasantry the proper sphere of woman's influence is still considered to be the home, although in the Europeanised settlements and in some parts of the east coast, in spite of all fanaticism can do, a considerable amount of independence is allowed her; but even in those parts of the Peninsula woman seldom

Photograph by H. W. Thomson.

RESPECTABLE MARRIED WOMAN OF KELANTAN.

Dressed in a "flowered" *sarong* girt about the breasts with a broad sash (*kain lĕpas*, of a Kelantan check pattern.

plays quite so prominent a *rôle* as in Burma and Siam, where the women generally form the "business" portion of the community, and not infrequently support the men. The Malays being a riverain and coastal race, their habitations forms of construction even in the forest, and the Malays do not, as a rule, abandon their pile-dwellings on moving inland.

Among the agricultural Malays, the men perform the tasks that require their strength,

Photograph by H. W. Thomson.

WOMAN OF LOOSE CHARACTER OF KELANTAN AND HER CHILDREN.

The *sarongs,* except that of the big girl, are of local make.

take the form of pile-dwellings. The object of this form of structure is, in all probability, to allow the waters of the incoming tide to perform their "priest-like task of pure ablution" in respect of the ground underneath it, which not infrequently serves as a depository of rubbish. On the other hand, the plan of raising the house floor on high posts has distinct advantages over other and the women take the work for which their slighter and less sturdy build may seem to be adapted. The felling having been completed, they lop the boughs and prepare the fallen trees for the "burn," which takes place when many weeks of vertical sun-blaze have sufficiently dried the piled-up timber. In the plains the rice-

The Work of Malay Women.

crop (wet "padi") is usually grown on the irrigation system; that is to say, in great square but shallow paddocks, divided by narrow embankments, into which water is led by means of small channels, usually from some neighbouring stream. On the low hills dry padi is grown without embankments, and in either case the Malay woman takes her full share of the day's burden. The men, of course, do the harrowing, rolling, and ploughing of the ground, but the women very frequently do the sowing, planting out of the young padi in the squares between the embankments, the weeding, and the scaring of birds. The plucking (for it can hardly be called cutting) of the padi a few heads at a time, with the primitive Malay reaping-knife (*tuei*), the gathering, gleaning, threshing, winnowing, and husking all come into the work of the women.

When the morning meal is over, the Malay woman returns to her work in the clearing, if her man is an up-country Malay, or otherwise to her weaving, mat- and rice-bag making, plaiting of creels and many-coloured baskets from pandanus leaf, bamboo, or rattan—the Malacca basket is known in England even—or, it may be, to her sail-work, or to the shelter of her palm-thatch stall in the market-booths of Kota-Bharu or Trĕnggānu. On the east coast of the Peninsula she is the maker of the gorgeous produce of the looms of Kelantan and Patani. Indeed, cooking and embroidery (in which we might include weaving) are, as indicated in the marriage ritual, the Malay woman's two greatest acquirements.

Among the wild forest tribes it may be said that, as among the Malays, the men perform the essential minimum of all such work as requires brute force, and the women do the rest. Among the nomadic Semang the men do the hunting, while the women erect their slight palm-leaf shelters (which show a regular course of evolution from the merely flat or beehive-shaped weather-screen sheltering a single family, to the elongated oval shelter intended for a whole tribe), and perform the scanty apology for cooking that suffices the savage appetite of their lords and masters.

Contrary to what one might expect among a race leading the simplest of all possible lives, and one in which the most perfect equality might perhaps be anticipated, the Negrito women are compelled to feed on what the men have left them, and perhaps on occasion to dance for the men's amusement afterwards, the men accompanying them with songs and by beating time with sticks, or upon strange musical instruments such as the nose-flute and other weird bamboo instruments. When the agricultural stage is reached, the women do the lopping of branches, the tilling of the soil with a pointed stick, the sowing, reaping, and storing of the grain in miniature granaries on high posts built by the men. When the grain is once sown, the plantation takes care of itself. The women, having collected water in their long bamboo receptacles or gourds, fasten on the back-basket and enter the jungle to collect roots and fruits for the early meal. When the food has been eaten, they spend their time in light work in or near the house, either in the collecting of jungle produce, in angling, in plaiting of leaf-work bags, mats or baskets, or in nursing their children. One or more slight snacks, usually of some vegetable food, are provided in the course of the day should the men be at home, and in any case there is a late supper, which frequently takes place at midnight among the Sakai. For the rest they make the most beautiful leaf-work pouches, and are adepts at the plaiting of bags, mats, and baskets. In districts where tin occurs women may not unfrequently be seen turning an honest penny by washing out stream tin in primitive fashion by means of wooden pans and sluices. In the collecting of jungle produce the pagan women bear a large share, their men being mercilessly cheated by the Malays when they come to the actual bartering.

If we take a few of the customs accompanying those events which are of most importance in the lives of their women, we shall see that the broad line of distinction between the Malays and the indigenous races (their former victims) comes out with remarkable clearness. Among the pagan races, for instance, the ceremony that attends a birth is of the scantiest description, the attendant offices being performed in many cases by the husband himself, and exciting few apprehensions. From birth to the grave, but most especially at birth, the Malay woman, on the other hand, is believed to be in danger from the supernatural world, and to some extent to be a source of danger to others, from both of which catastrophes she is defended by a rampart of ceremonial. The blood-sucking vampire-spirits that harass the mother and her new-born babe may be numbered among the most frightful conceptions that ever plagued the conscience of mankind. If apparitions of the dead in our more matter-of-fact northern climes can be thought to unfold tales "whose lightest word would harrow up" our soul, what must be their effect upon an unsophisticated peasantry, in the midnight of a tropical jungle? We can hardly wonder if the weird and bodeful shriek of night-birds upon the roof should suggest to their terrified imaginations the passing of the *Langsuir*, the flying demon of the Malays; the *Pontianak*, the blood-sucking bird which is able to change its shape at will to that of other animals, and which, as an old writer states, is "more dreaded than the tyger"; or, ghastliest of all, the nocturnal onslaught of the *Pĕnanggalan*, the flying trunkless head, with its trailing blood-boltered sac, all of which are believed to sup by night on new-born infants' blood.

Birth Superstitions and Ceremonies.

As if these ghastly accompaniments of child-birth, not to mention others, were not enough to try the nerve of any Malay woman who had hopes of offspring, it is usual, in addition, for the patient to be placed upon a raised platform of wood or bamboo, called the roasting-place (*salei-an*), underneath which a fire is lighted, and thus "roasted" in a way that must not infrequently involve acute suffering. Upon this platform she is made to lie day and night, throughout the entire period of her confinement; indeed, the very wood required for the fire of this roasting-place often takes several weeks' work to get together. This remarkable institution was the invention of the *To'Bidan*, or professional wise-woman, and its result has been known in some cases to produce mental aberration lasting for some months afterwards, and must, in cases of any difficulty, have been frequently fatal.

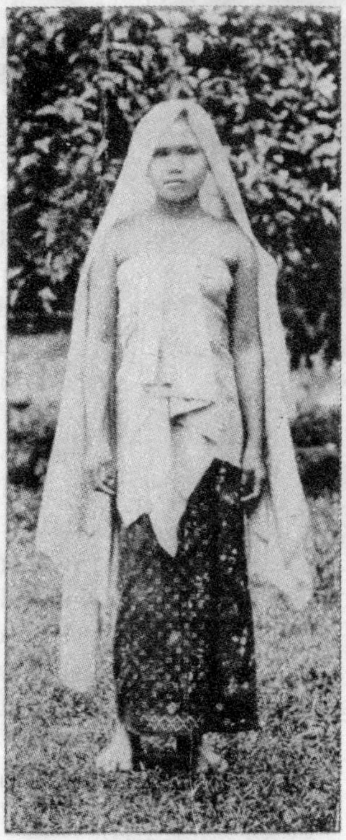

Photograph by H. W. Thomson.

RESPECTABLE MARRIED WOMAN OF KELANTAN.

Wearing a *sarong* of Kelantan pattern, surmounted by the typical broad sash (*kain lĕpas*), girt about the breasts.

Even apart from this, both the person of the patient and that of her husband were encompassed by an extraordinary body of petty restrictions and prohibitions, which it must certainly be exceedingly trying to have to observe under the severe conditions just described. Not only is she absolutely prohibited from reposing upon her own sleeping-mat throughout the day, but a large number of articles of common consumption are laid under ban, and even in her speech the victim could scarcely ever be sufficiently circumspect, for the uttering of a single word of reproach against any living creature—an exceedingly difficult thing for anyone so sorely tried to avoid—was bound to be followed (she would be told) by frightful and portentous consequences. Even her husband may not cut his hair or sit in his doorway (the latter a favourite

WOMAN AND CHILDREN OF PERAK.

observation-post among the Malays), or "divide the house" by passing straight in at one door and out at the other, or "make a single night of it" either in being a guest or entertaining one; or, finally, wound or kill any living thing during the whole of this period.

During an eclipse of the moon, should one happen at this juncture, some very strange precautions are taken which emphasise clearly the Malay belief in the influence of the moon over women. Should the child escape the actual as well as the imaginary perils that attend its birth, it is bathed, swaddled, and formally adopted by its father according to the rites of the Mohammedan law. In some parts of the country it is also passed through the smoke to protect it from evil spirits and convulsions, and in others its forehead is marked, in the case of a boy with a benchmark, and in the case of a girl with the sign of the cross. This last ceremony is by no means a compliment to Christianity. It is done in order that the Evil One may take it for a child of his own (his children being supposed to be similarly marked) and may on that account pass over it without doing it harm!

Malayan Childhood.

The Malay cradle takes the form of a sort of swinging cot or hammock of black cloth, usually a *sarong*, which is passed round one of the rafters of the hut-roof. Among the country-folk this hammock-cradle is often carefully protected, especially at first, by an arrangement of what can only be called "demon-traps," and whenever the child is taken out of it, a massive stone spice-block is laid in the cot, as the child's "substitute" (*ganti*), in order to deceive the spirits of evil. Soon after the little Malay girl begins to run about, and ceases to journey tied on to her mother's back or astride upon her hip, she has a heart-shaped ornament of silver (*chaping*) tied round her waist; but for the rest still continues to disport herself without any further garment but that of the unfettered grace and winsomeness of her little lithe brown body. At the age of a few months her ears are bored, preparatory to receiving the often beautifully decorated ear-studs (*subang*), which are the emblems of Malay maidenhood, and which are only discarded at marriage. At about five years old she will be induced to wear a tiny *sarong*, and at a slightly later age, when the at present experimental stage of female education has become permanent, she will be going to school in covered bullock-carts to learn cooking, embroidery, and the Koran.

How the Malayan Girl "Comes Out."

At a varying age, sometimes at her entrance upon womanhood, or, in some cases, just before marriage, she has to undergo some remarkable ceremonies, her teeth being sometimes filed, and the ends of the seven longest strands of her raven-black hair shorn off and dropped, together with rings of precious metal attached to them for the purpose, into the open bowl of a specially-prepared green coco-nut. No face-paint, scarification, or tattooing is practised by the Malay women, though all these forms of face-decoration were at one time practised by the pagans. Among the Sakai the face is either actually tattooed, the puncturation being performed by means of a thorn, or scarified in lines that converge on either cheek. Black and white, or coloured dots placed alternately, sometimes replace these lines, the design being completed by a pitchfork-like pattern being placed upon the chin, the result being to give the wearer a very smart and "fierce" appearance. Porcupines' quills, or short decorated sticks are worn through holes in the lobe of each ear and in the septum of the nose.

Malayan Beauty.

The Malay girl is not infrequently very pretty and winning, but she early loses her gracefulness, and frequently becomes, when middle-aged, plain, and even ugly, in spite of all the incantations with which she attempts to preserve her looks. If judged by a European standard she would not, perhaps, ever be considered really beautiful, though she is by no means destitute of good looks. Her often regular features are sometimes spoilt by the flatness of the nose and an excessive width of nostril, or by the distension of the mouth due to the over-frequent chewing of betel. Her eyes are usually of a deep rich brown or black, but have not, as a rule, much expression; her brown skin is often of great clearness and beauty; her teeth are often white to brilliancy and very perfect, but among the older women especially they are often encrusted with betel or ruined by "filing"; her head is round; her eyebrows are arched and distinct; her cheek-bones are prominent, after the manner found among all branches of the Mongolian race. Her greatest glory is her black and generally long hair, which is drawn up in a knot at the back. Short and sturdily built, rather than *svelte*, she is inclined to over-stoutness, and her build produces in middle age a tendency to become somewhat unpleasantly coarse and fat. Her feet and hands are small, but the latter are inclined to be somewhat too stumpy and flat underneath. Her joints are, as compared with those of Europeans, marvellously small and supple. On the other hand, it must be remembered that the Malay standard of a woman's comeliness is not ours; and it is at least interesting to see how well the Malay description of a beautiful woman emphasises the chief "points" of a typical specimen of the race.

Her brow, as we read in many Malay poems and romances, should be like the one-day-old moon, her eyebrows arched like the curved spur of the fighting-cock or like waved handwriting—anyone who is acquainted with the long and delicate curves of the Arabic caligraphy as employed by the Malays will appreciate the vividness of this comparison. Her cheek should resemble the soft, smooth side of the mango-

Photograph by H. W. Thomson.

MARRIED MALAY WOMAN OF TRĔNGGĀNU.

Dressed in a short jacket (*baju*) of Kelantan make, with two *sarongs* in place of skirts, one worn above the other.

fruit; her nose should be like an "opening jasmine-bud," or a freshly-sharpened reed-pen (the converse of the Shakespearian reading of "his nose was as sharp as a pen," which latter was hardly intended, perhaps, as a compliment). Her ear should be like a fading lotus or water-lily; her luxuriant raven-black hair like the "crisped" blossom-shoots of the areca-palm. Her neck should have a triple row of dimples; her breasts should be full and ripening, and her waist lissome as the stem of a flower. Her heel should be of a perfect oval, "like the egg of a bird"; her fingers should resemble the lance-like leaves of the lemon-grass, or taper at both ends like the quills of the porcupine. Her eyes should be as the splendour of the planet Venus, and her lips like the crimson fissure of a bursting pomegranate.

Malayan Marriage Ceremonies.

Before betrothal, some representatives of the youth's party have among the Malays the right to visit the girl in order to assure themselves that she is "without blemish and without spot." The preliminaries being over, a further messenger is sent to the girl's parents, who responds with the prescribed formulas to the polite depreciation of the girl by her parents, whose remark, "You desire to bespeak the hand of my daughter, who knows not how to cook nor how to sew," is waived aside, and the formal betrothal takes place before witnesses. After betrothal, presents are exchanged, the youth sending to his *fiancée* small offerings of betel-leaf folded up in richly-worked cloths like doyleys, or choice fruit or eggs contained in ingenious network receptacles; and the girl replying with special preparations of rice contained in beautifully-plaited receptacles of coloured leaf-work, shaped like peacocks or hornbills, which often assume highly decorative and artistic forms.

Marriage is undoubtedly the most important of all the ceremonies in the life of the Peninsula women, and it is interesting to trace the gradual development of the rite as we pass from the pagan races to the Mohammedan Malays.

In its simplest form, it appears to consist of a mere mutual acknowledgment of the parties before witnesses, usually the elders of the settlement. Commonly some form of the custom of eating together forms a second feature of the rite, a third being what is often a mere survival, representing what had originally been a definite act of purchase. The Semang, and indeed the great majority of the jungle tribes, are in the highest degree faithful to each other when once married, and are, as a rule, fairly strict monogamists.

Bride Hunting.

Among the Besisi a remarkable form of Mound Marriage occurred, the mound being moulded from clay thrown up for the purpose into the shape of a gigantic bell, round which the bridegroom had to chase the bride until he caught her. Among the Orang Laut or Sea Gypsies this hunting of the bride sometimes took the form of a canoe-race in which the bride was given a limited start.

Before the mound-ceremony was concluded, the bridegroom might have to submit to a curious catechism on the part of the bride's representative, who asked such searching and personal questions as "Are you clever with the blow-pipe?" "Are you clever at felling trees?" "Are you clever at climbing?" and "Can you smoke cigarettes?" The marriage settlements consisted of pots and pans, jungle-knives, hatchets, beads, and blow-pipes, the woman giving, as a rule, nothing in return. The marriage catechism concluded with the question, "Is all this true, so may a tree fall upon you?" the reply being, "Speak not of *Somebody's* daughter. Monkeys of all kinds do I search for and capture. And how much more then *Somebody's* daughter?" This reply being considered satisfactory (!), the chiefs of the tribe exclaimed that the marriage was "ratified," and the chase "round the mound and round again" commenced. A feast followed, at which the bride and bridegroom ate and drank from the same dish.

Among the Malayan tribes there was a regular season for marriage, namely, during the months of July and August, when fruit is plentiful. The price of a wife among some branches of the Orang Laut or Sea Gypsies was stated to be ten needles, three hanks of thread, sixteen cubits of cloth, and three Spanish dollars.

Passing to the Malays, two entirely distinct marriage systems prevail. In the southernmost division of the Federated Malay States, on the western seaboard (N. Sembilan), where matrilineal descent prevails, the family properly so-called is "Samandei," and really consists of the mother and her children. The mother's eldest brother is the head of the family, and the father belongs to his own mother's family, not to that of his wife and children. This peculiar organisation prevails in what is claimed to be the original home of the Malay race, the district of "Menangkabau" in Sumatra. Elsewhere the ordinary line of patrilineal descent prevailed, according to what may be called "Johor custom." It is possible that marriage among people of the Malay race was originally unceremonial, the ritual being a later development.

Mohammedan Influence on Malay Women.

Again, as concerns the women, marriage is so very general that an old unmarried woman is regarded as an eccentric. The re-marriage of a widow, on the other hand, is commonly a subject for jest, the ear-studs, already mentioned as the emblems of virginity among the Malays, being *tied* on to her ears in mockery of her status. The influence of Mohammedanism reappears in the jealousy with which the husband regards his wife, an idea which finds expression in Malay proverbs. Connected with this feeling of jealousy may be the punishment meted out to couples who have lapsed from virtue, who in days gone by were paraded together in a cart with their faces striped yellow, the striping being intended to represent that of the civet-cat.

The Malay woman, in spite of the seclusion enjoined by Mohammedan precepts, is yet not quite so jealously secluded as might be supposed, though whether this is not rather due to her capacity for getting her own way than to any special lack of jealousy on the part of her husband, may be doubted. At least the Malay proverb has it that whereas "a herd of buffaloes may be guarded, a single human being [a woman] cannot be so guarded," which looks as if they had had experience which had taught them to know *furens quid femina possit.* Moreover, another proverb attests the fact that henpecked husbands are not unknown, the expression being that the man is "steered from the bows." It should be remembered that it is in his mother-in-law's house that the Malay bridegroom first takes up his abode, often for a period of a year or more, and, judging from Malay proverbs touching on the subject, the Malay mother-in-law is not less of a butt than she generally is in Europe.

West Coast Marriage Customs.

The typical west-coast wedding, which differs in many respects from that of Kelantan and Patani, lasts several days, and takes place in the bride's house, decorated with broad vertically-striped rainbow hangings and ornamental ceiling-cloths. Two immense triple-branched candlesticks at the bride's door, and a magnificently decorated couch or divan, are erected, at one end of which is a double row of pillows, some of immense size (5 ft. by 2 ft. by 2½ ft.), white, and with richly-embroidered ends, and some smaller ones, red, purple, or orange in colour. The number of these "big pillows" signifies the rank of the parties, and daggers were freely drawn in olden days when the regulation number was exceeded.

Nowadays the evening concludes with the chanting of passages from the Koran, but in the more picturesque and unregenerate past the time was spent in watching a cock-fight, a wrestling or fencing match, or in listening to some old-world story of the fairy-tale kind, chanted by one of those interesting survivals of the ancient *régime,* the "soothers of care," which is the name given to the Malay professional story-tellers.

While these games were in progress the

Photograph lent by J. Brockerel, Italy.

SAKAI AT DINNER.

Note the bamboo utensils.

with delicate butterfly pendant. This band is made of gold-leaf among the wealthier class, and of tinsel among the poorer Malays; in either case it looks brave enough by torchlight. Her dress consists of a jacket with tight-fitting sleeves, sometimes gathered and extending down to the wrist, the material of the jacket being "flowered satin" among the rich: and madder-coloured cloth among the humbler classes. This wedding jacket fits tightly round the neck, has a gold border, is fastened with gold buttons, and, being close-fitting, sets off the figure of the wearer to the utmost advantage. Round her neck is hung a necklace or pair of crescent-shaped breast ornaments. The *sarong*, which takes the place of a skirt, is of as fine a silk and of as rich a pattern as may be obtainable. It should be girt with a waist-cord according to the older and stricter custom. A pair of silk trousers *à la turque* completes her attire.

bride and bridegroom at first separately at their own house, but later jointly, underwent the process of having their hands stained with henna. On the last day of the wedding takes place the procession of the bridegroom to the house of the bride's parents, where the ceremony of feeding them both together with the "presentation rice" is performed.

The Bridal Costume.

The bride, who has no veil, and is often a blaze of gems, not infrequently borrowed, has her hair done in a roll, surmounted with a head-dress of glittering artificial flowers, raised on fine wires, and trembling all over with the slightest motion of the head, whence its strange name of "Quake and tremble" is derived. Her forehead the hair of which is trimmed evenly in an oval, is bound with a fillet or band, wrought maybe into the semblance of two fighting dragons

Photograph lent by J. Brockerel, Italy.

FAMILY SCENE AMONG THE SAKAI

The bridegroom, no less gaily dressed, and armed with a *kris* specially selected for its magical virtue, is then escorted in procession to the house of the bride, and after the performance of the actual marriage ceremony by the priest, is led to the inner chamber, and seated on the divan, to the left of the bride, who sits with her feet tucked beneath her. The bride and bridegroom having each received a handful of what is called the "Presentation Rice," proceed to feed each other with it simultaneously, this part of the programme being a signal for a race, from which omens are drawn as to the future relationship of the pair when married. The bridegroom is then carried off to an outer chamber to pay his respects to his friends, the sweetmeats are handed around, and the wedding favours (*tĕlor joran*) distributed among the guests, each of whom is expected to bring a suitable gift. On the fourth day takes place the bathing ceremony, at which, the bride and bridegroom being seated on a bench, the entire company of young men present proceed to discharge what are called in Malay "waterbows" (really primitive bamboo syringes) until all are thoroughly wetted. The bride and bridegroom then take hold of a V-shaped slip-knot of young coco-nut leaves, and each pulls one end till it comes undone, this being called the "Freeing" or "Letting-go" ceremony (*lĕpas-lĕpas*). A girdle of thread is then passed seven times over the heads and under the feet of the couple (*lat-lat*), when the bridegroom snaps the thread, and all are free to return homewards. Seven days later the ceremony of discarding the ear-studs (*subang*, the emblems of virginity) is performed by the bride.

Bride and Bridegroom's Race for Supremacy.

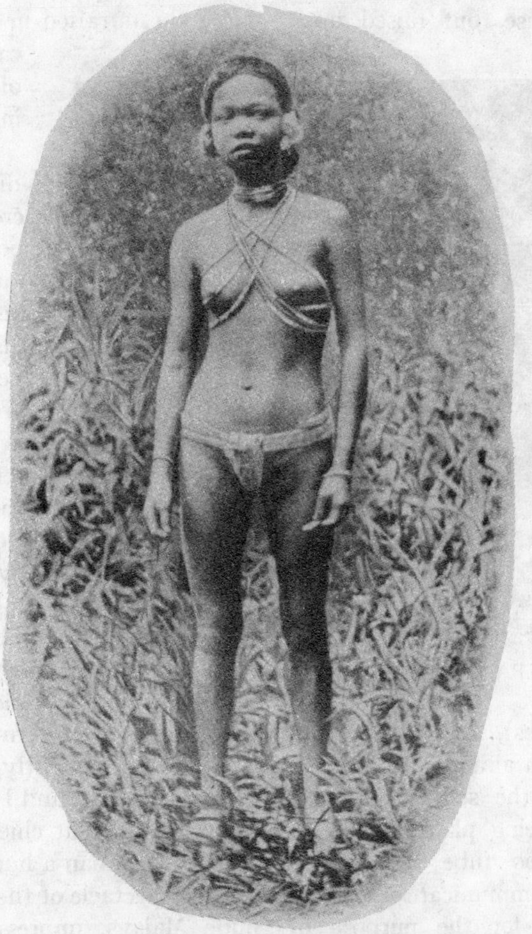

Photograph lent by J. Brockerel, Italy.

YOUNG SAKAI GIRL.

Outside the ordinary marriage rite, as described above, there is an exceedingly strange set of regulations governing cases of forcible seizure of the bride's person. This upon certain conditions is not discountenanced, the usual dower or marriage-portion furnished by the bridegroom, who acts at his own personal risk, being in such cases doubled. This strange institution appears to serve the purpose of a sort of safety-valve of the kind formerly supplied in our own country by Gretna Green.

Funeral Ceremonies.

Burial takes place, owing to the torrid heat of the climate, within twenty-four hours of dissolution. The Negritos practise a form of ordinary interment, but the genuine Sakai have so intense a terror of the ghost of the deceased that they will burn down the house, and even sometimes the village, in which a death has taken place, and never return to it, even their standing crops being deserted and left to rot upon the ground.

Platform burials and the depositing of the corpse in a tree are also practised, and in a case of ordinary interment there are buried with a woman (or laid upon the grave) her combs, necklaces, bracelets, and other articles of attire, together with various kinds of fruit and flowers.

Among the Jakun the spirit of a deceased woman whose burial was witnessed by the writer was provided with the model of a hut (like a doll's house, but raised upon sticks to resemble piles), and with provisions to feed upon. In almost all instances food is provided for the soul—even rice, yams, and bananas being planted, and in some places a bamboo tube is fixed in the grave so as to communicate with the mouth of the corpse for the purpose of feeding it.

Photograph lent by J. Brockerel, Italy.

SAKAI PREPARING POISONED DARTS.

As among the Malays, the grave of a Jakun man can be distinguished at a glance from that of a woman by the shape of the grave-posts. In the case of a man these are round and notched, but in that of a woman they are flat, and sometimes roughly shaped, so as to give the outline of a woman's figure.

Among the Siamese in the north cremation obtains, as in Siam proper, a wooden effigy being sometimes burnt as substitute, should the deceased have died overseas; but among the small settlements of the Phram or Brahmans met with in Ligor and Patalung on the eastern coast, burial took place in a sitting posture. In the same neighbourhood were still to be seen a few examples of the exposure of the corpse in a cigar-shaped wrapper, slung between two trees about 8 ft. from the ground, as well as examples of exposure of the dead in large chests raised upon posts, of a kind recalling similar instances of exposure of the dead in chests in Borneo.

When a Malay woman dies, just below her crossed hands are deposited a pair of betel-nut scissors intended to keep evil spirits at a distance (iron being universally regarded as a great safeguard against evil spirits). The nearest relatives, when giving the last kiss, must not "disturb the corpse" by letting their tears fall upon its features. The shroud is bound round in five places by means of the selvage of the shroud itself torn into tape-like strips. The bier is frequently, in the case of chiefs, of immense size, and I myself saw one at the funeral of a great chief's wife that took not many fewer than a hundred Malays to carry it; the spectacle of these serried files of half-nude Malays, impressed for the occasion, and struggling desperately with their load, forcibly recalling certain pictures of the days of the pyramid-builders. The body, when laid on the bier, usually in one of the Malay box-like substitutes for coffins, is covered with a pall of as good coloured cloth as may be obtainable. Across this are frequently thrown the blossoms of the betel-palm and the scented pandanus woven into exquisitely beautiful and fragrant floral strips, called by the strange name of "centipedes' feet," and varying with the rank of the deceased, and which correspond to our own floral crowns and crosses. On the seventh, the fourteenth, the fortieth, and the hundredth days feasts are held in memory of the dead, and the anniversary is also kept as a holiday.

These are some of the employments of the Malay women, but what of the women themselves, and what of the life that they lead? The character of the Malay woman naturally lacks some of the boldness of her men-folk, the women resorting to poison where a man would employ the *kris*. On the other hand, it was formerly the custom of Selangor women to wear small poniards (of the kind called *tumbok lada*) concealed in their hair, though happily under the strong arm of British law these and other similar traces of the originally savage Malay nature have gradually disappeared, and the chief point now to be emphasised is the difference between the lazy, pleasure-loving, gaily-dressed, and only too often profligate and rapacious Malay women, who are to be found in all the large towns and at the courts of most of the Malay rajas (and whose character is hit off in Malay four-line stanzas, of the kind called *pantun*), and the somewhat shy but sober-minded, cheery, hard-working, and invariably hospitable Malay women of the far interior.

Curious Malayan Women.

Self-revelations on the part of the fast-vanishing past grow rarer with every falling tide, and rarest of all, perhaps, are sights like that of the Homeric hamlet, whose women employed everyday pots and pans that had been hammered into shape from the metal as it cropped out of the ground in blocks. Or the lady with a familiar spirit (of the bottle-imp variety, fed daily with drops of blood pricked from her finger-tips), who, after being photographed, dreamt that a great white magician from oversea had stolen her soul, and whom nothing could propitiate but a present of gold-dust. Or the woman of the strange wild-looking troglodyte race (guardians of the Bird's-nest islands in the inland sea of Singora) whom we found living in limestone caves of the islands where bats flew and the "edible" swallows built. Or the peasant woman who came to feed at the breast a pair of tiger-cats (picked out of their nest in a hollow tree as we passed thereby in the morning) on the ground that she had once before performed the same kind office "for a bear-cub." Or the Malay wise-woman, who, at a great medicine-business in Patani, whirled her head round in the fury of the dance until indeed, as she boasted, she "made a cart-wheel of her hair." Or the woman of the West coast, who, singing weird chants the while, made the sheaf of areca-blossom or the "wasp-waisted" fish-trap dance in our presence as if possessed. Or she for whose sake Che Dris ran *amok*, slaying man, woman, and child in indiscriminating fury, until struck down. Or the East coast woman who, startled by the glimpse of a large snake that we were carrying, fell incontinently into weird imitation of the reptile's writhing, a victim to the strange hysterical affection of the nerves known to the Malays as *latah*, which compels those who suffer from it, while fully conscious of the absurdity of their acts, to imitate the actions or the movements of the object that caused their fright.

By permission of War Dept., Bureau of Insular Affairs, U.S.A.

TYPES OF VISAYAN GIRLS.

THE PHILIPPINE ISLANDS

By N. W. THOMAS

Origin of the Race—Negrito Aids to Beauty—Marriage Customs of the Aetas—Head-hunters—Women's Work—Igorot Music and Dancers—Ilongot Ghastly Bridal Presents—The Magindanao—Mandaya Women the Beauties of the Island—The Cuyonos—Curious Beauty Aids—Secret Marriages Customary—Plurality of Husbands and Wives—Strange Ornaments and Customs

THE inhabitants of the Philippine Islands are a very mixed lot. It is probably safe to say that the oldest element in the population is the Negrito, known under the name of Aeta (*i.e.*, black), and found in the interior of Luzon, in North Mindanao and elsewhere. Superposed on this is an older Malay stratum, and on this, again, a younger Malay stratum which shows strong traces of Hindu influence. The Spanish intermarried with the aborigines and brought Chinese with them, and there was a small early Japanese settlement on Luzon. Nearly 7,000,000, or 99 per cent., of the population are reckoned to the Malays in the American census, but this includes half-bloods, whose type is however indistinguishable from the pure bloods. Space fails even to enumerate the tribes of note ; suffice it to mention the Igorots, the Ilongots, and the Tagalos of Luzon, the Visaya, the Bagobo, and the Mandayas of

Origin of the Race.

Mindanao. There is a Mohammedan population known as Moros, with some Arabic blood in it, in Mindanao and elsewhere.

It is natural that in such a mixed population there should be a great diversity of appearance, culture, and manners. To take the wild and shy Negrito first; the women, on an average, are about four feet high, with a variation of some six inches; they are chocolate brown rather than black, with broad flat noses, dark brown eyes, and kinky hair, sometimes burned by the sun to a reddish brown. They beautify their persons by filing their teeth, and explain that it enables them to eat corn with greater ease; they also decorate the breast, shoulders, and back with scars. Necklaces of seeds are worn, and in the hair bamboo combs; the only clothing is a strip of cloth round the waist.

Negrito Aids to Beauty.

We know little about these Aetas, but their marriage ceremonies have been described, and it appears that a wife is so invaluable that the whole wealth of the young man and his family is expended on the purchase of one. Of course a dance and a feast are essential parts of the proceedings, but of actual marriage rite there is hardly a trace beyond the custom of exchanging food. The girls are often betrothed while very young to men old enough to be their fathers, and many tears are shed when the time for marriage is at hand. A resolute girl may resist for years, and in such cases it does not appear to be the custom to return the bride price. In one such case a Yankee intervened in favour of the bridegroom, and, by a gift of a few yards of cloth, a mirror, and a string of beads, quite reconciled the maiden to her fate. For was she not the best dowried wife in the village?

Marriage Customs of the Aetas.

In South Luzon the ceremony is quainter, for it consists in man and maid sitting on a platform and having their heads bumped together; after this follows the "home coming," at one period of which the bride puts on all her dresses. But before this stage is reached there is a critical point for the future husband; for there is a spot where the bride stops to see how many presents are coming to her. If they are not enough, she promptly returns to her mother.

The Igorot (mountain people) are mountain agriculturists, and were until recently

By permission of War Dept., Bureau of Insular Affairs, U.S.A.

YOUNG IGOROT WOMAN OF AMBUKLAO, BENGUET.

head-hunters. They are spread over a wide area, and the groups differ considerably. The women average four feet nine in height; they wear their hair long and load their ears with heavy copper earrings. In youth they are supple and well formed, but by the age of thirty they are already old women, flabby, wrinkled, and unsightly. As little girls they have few pleasures; dolls are unknown, and even puppies have no attraction for them; but they take charge of younger scions of the family at a preternaturally early age, and find full scope for their maternal instincts in minding the baby. Girls and boys never play together; the great game of the former is "catch your ankle," a kind of prisoner's base played

Igorot Marriage Customs.

nightly on the grass. The players line up in a state of nature, crouch on the heels, and jump towards their opponents, trying to catch one by the ankle and carry her off. A great feature of Igorot society is the *olag*, or spinsters' house, which though primarily the sleeping place of the unmarried girls, is in fact the mating place of young people of marrying age. Marriage takes place before the birth of a child, but not earlier, as a rule. The young man, however, is pointedly invited; a common form of invitation is to steal his pipe or even his breechcloth, and he seldom recovers it without visiting the *olag*. A girl is usually faithful to her temporary lover, and unchastity before puberty or after marriage is hardly known. In fact, when a man visits a maiden at the *olag*, he enters into a kind of trial marriage, which is so far recognised that the young couple take their meals at the house of the girl's parents, the young man giving his labours to the family. On a rest day courting goes on all day long, and the happy couples spend their time gossiping, each with an arm round the other: it is asserted that all enter into this trial marriage, cripples and idiots excepted.

It may be imagined that marriage is the ordinary state of the Igorot adult, and as he makes sure that he will be blessed with offspring before going through the ceremony, the man seldom divorces his wife; when he does so he leaves her the house, and builds a new one for himself. When one of the parties dies, it is the custom for the other to remain single for a year.

Women's Work.

A girl begins to work at the age of five. Women weave and spin, make pots and sell them, and produce the salt; the men are the basket-makers. Both sexes work at the plantations, but only women plant the rice and transplant the palay (seedlings); in digging the women use a six foot stick some two inches in diameter. The soil is moistened by irrigation, and crumbles into the water as the line of toilers push the tools before them, and as it falls away the women begin to sing. When a small square is ready, the women level the soil, trample it to discover the stones, and then in line abreast slowly tread backwards and forwards making the bed soft and smooth beneath the water.

The work of threshing and winnowing falls to the women and girls, but cooking is often allotted to the man unless there is a boy or girl not employed in the fields, and big enough for the work. When the man undertakes the task he is up by 4 a.m., and between 5 a.m. and 6 a.m. the girls are home from the *olag*, and the family sits down to breakfast. At 7 a.m. the workers leave for the fields, and remain away till 6.30 p.m., or later; then comes supper, and by 8 p.m. husband and wife turn in, and the young folks set out in quest of adventures.

The Igorot woman is strong, she carries as big a burden as a man, usually on her head, and as a protection wears a ring of grass. At sundown she may often be seen returning from the river, a child on her back, and a six-gallon jar of water on her head, but strong and joyful, though she has toiled all day in the field with bent back and eyes fixed on the earth.

Igorot Music and Dancers.

It is strange that the music of the Igorot is usually serious; mothers do not sing to their babes, nor a lover to his mistress. But they make up for their music by their dances, which they accompany upon the metal gong. A woman's toes often scarcely leave the earth, but a few of the older women have a high pawing movement which throws the dust and gravel behind them; the women dance immediately outside the circle of male dancers, and from them the infection spreads to the onlookers till a score of women are imitating them, and the little girls are imitating their mothers. Some of the women's dances show us the beginnings of the drama; with her two-foot long "camote" stick, her pestle or her spun thread, she simply reproduces her ordinary occupations, but it is the seed of dramatic art.

Like the Igorots, the Ilongots are an agricultural people. They are not a tall race; the skin is dark brown with a dash of yellow, and the pupil of the eye is said to be veiled with a curious bluish tint, which suggests incipient cataract. Both men and women file their teeth, and, like many other peoples of the Philippines, blacken them till the mouth resembles a miniature coal pit. They are perhaps more savage than the Igorots, and a bridegroom's present to his bride includes a human head, part of a breast or heart, as well as a finger or two, and without these no one can hope to wed. There is so little secrecy about the matter that the head of the victim—man, woman, or child—is put on a pole before the youth's house for all to see, and then after nine days interred under the house which the couple are to occupy.

Ilongot Ghastly Bridal Presents.

As a type of the civilised and Christianised dwellers in Luzon may be taken the Gaddons, whose features are refined and far from suggestive of former savagery.

The Magindanao.

The Magindanao, whom the Spaniards called Moros (*i.e.*, Moors) from their dark colour, are said to be by far the most faithful and intelligent people in the Archipelago. They are dark with a yellowish tinge like many of the other tribes, and the women have well-formed hands and feet. Out of doors they wear trousers like the men, very loose, but the jacket is cut so tightly as to show every line of the figure. Sometimes they use the *sarong* to screen their faces from strangers, but indoors both sexes remove much of their clothing. Mohammedan marriage is much the same everywhere; the middleman makes a pilgrimage to the bride's house with gifts, and according as they are accepted or rejected the suit goes on or comes to an untimely end.

The jealous Mohammedan wife disposes of her husband by means of poison which is said to be compounded of human hair, poisonous roots, and woman's blood, and the first constituent, which is cut fine, is said to work up after death, and show itself on the lips.

Mandaya Women the Beauties of the Islands.

Some of the Mohammedan tribes cause much trouble by stealing Mandaya women, who are particularly white-skinned, and therefore specially attractive; they have besides dark expressive eyes, and wear a profusion of ornaments, which are among the most beautiful things they make. Where the short red coat with blue

By permission of War Dept., Bureau of Insular Affairs, U.S.A.

BUKIDNON WOMAN IN CHARACTERISTIC DRESS, PROVINCE OF MESAMIO.

sleeves, which is the woman's dress, leaves a piece of the neck bare they hang a large silver disc with geometrical designs on it; their arms, from the wrist to the elbow, are covered with numerous metal and shell bracelets, and from a kind of sea vine heated over the fire they make armlets which have a sort of metallic sheen. On the left side they wear a bundle of bells, and in the ears huge wooden earrings inlaid with tinfoil and beads; on their chain belts are numerous charms—alligator teeth, shells, herbs, etc.—and these no other woman may touch, for

By permission of War Dept., Bureau of Insular Affairs, U.S.A.

DATO CHIEF AND HIS BRIDE.

that would bring bad luck. Their dress consists of a short skirt which falls as far as the knee, and a huge silver-mounted wooden comb adorns their hair. They twist their hair into a knot, and leave a long lock projecting behind, and one on each side of the face. Their skin is light brown in colour, and it is curious to find this associated with very prominent lips, which, according to one observer, project as far as the tip of the nose (which is, it must be remembered, very much flattened).

The Cuyonos.

In connection with the Moros it may be well to mention the Christian Cuyonos, the only islanders who can really be called workers. They are excellent navigators, and leave their women at home, so much so that the latter outnumber the male sex by seven or eight to one. In their love-making, however, they are not energetic; the swain leans against a bamboo pillar, and gazes with dreamy eyes at his sallow *inamorata*, who never opens her lips. The Cuyonos have a curious dance, taken over perhaps from a wilder folk. The *Suring* is graceful, and dignified; the point of the dance is that the girl must whirl rapidly round and keep her partner from dancing in front of her while he must use all his wiles to force his way before her; as the contest goes on the music quickens till the spectators too get excited.

Curious Beauty Aids.

One of the most noteworthy of the Mindanao tribes is the Bagobo, a handsome people whose beadwork possesses considerable artistic merit. They are fond of brass ornaments, which they make themselves, and wear enormous earrings of wood or ivory, if they can afford them, or, failing that, of coco-nut leaves. They usually file their teeth to a point, and blacken them. Below the knee they wear several strings of beads.

Also on Mindanao are the Tirurays, a small well-made folk, with yellow complexions and slanting eyes. The lips are

By permission of War Dept., Bureau of Insular Affairs, U.S.A.

GADDON YOUNG GIRL.

rather prominent, and women are given to adding to their charms by reddening them; their ears are pierced in seven holes which are kept open by the insertion of pieces of wire, and artificially elongated, greatly to their detriment. But their most extraordinary feature is the belt of brass wire, twelve or fifteen turns in length. In addition they have numerous tightly wound bracelets — brass coils with little bells at the end, large and heavy anklets of brass, and shell armlets on the left arm only. But perhaps the most typical female decoration is the neck ornament of strings of glass beads and shells, from which hangs a small case for *tarrau*. The women have a curious dance in which with a most doleful face they revolve the hand in a circle, keeping the fingers all the while quite straight.

Secret Marriages Customary.

Marriages are secretly arranged, and a curious custom demands that the intended spouse who accidentally hears of the prospective marriage must pretend to commit suicide. The wedding is short and simple, the youth tears from his bride's face the veil which conceals it, and runs away, imitating the call of the *uya-uya* bird. The mother of the bride chews some betel-nut and lime, her daughter continues the process, and finally the bridegroom receives it; then the pair touch each other on the head, and they are married.

By permission of War Dept., Bureau of Insular Affairs, U.S.A.

BAGOBO MAN, WOMAN, AND CHILD.

The long island of Palawan contains more than one interesting tribe. The Batacs are a retiring folk who never even fight among themselves, and if the men carry weapons it is for sporting purposes only. The marriage ceremony is as brief as it can be; after the bride price has been paid the girl gives the man three mouthfuls of rice in the presence of the elders, and he does the same to her. They practise polyandry—that is, a woman has more than one husband; but one imagines that it must need an ardent love to submit to the inconveniences entailed, for the second husband becomes the slave of the first.

Plurality of Husbands and Wives.

The Tagbanouas on the other hand practise plurality of wives, but not of husbands. Where there is more than one wife in a menage, the senior has the whip hand, but each wife receives her husband's preference in turn, and the others may not interfere—a golden rule strictly obeyed, if European observers can be trusted. The marriage ceremony is curious—the first finger of the bridegroom is smeared with coco-nut oil, the palm of the hand being held downwards; after the same ceremony has been performed for the bride comes the wedding feast; and here the viands are wild hog, honey, roots, sugar-cane, etc., while as liquor they have a rice brew, which four persons drink simultaneously from the cup by means of straws.

On the island of Mindoro live the Manguianes. They have flat noses, almond-shaped eyes, straight black hair, and a dark chocolate complexion. Both sexes file their teeth to the gums for some reason unknown. The women are said to be gentle and affectionate, and are noted for their beautiful figures. They are fond of ornament, and often wear a row of Chinese brass bells round the waist hanging on the right hip; their anklets are of brass or red beads, and they have large shell bracelets and bead necklaces, but their most characteristic feature is the rattan belt buttoned behind, and the band of the same material over the shoulder blades, and under the breasts.

Strange Ornaments and Customs.

On the Sulu islands there is a custom which should make them the Paradise of believers in women's rights; for it is the practice to accept a woman's evidence in preference to a man's where there is any conflict of evidence, and it speaks well for the truthfulness of the women that the stronger sex has permitted this privilege to subsist to this day.

By permission of War Dept., Bureau of Insular Affairs, U.S.A.

NATIVE STUDENTS AT THE INSULAR NORMAL SCHOOL, MANILA.

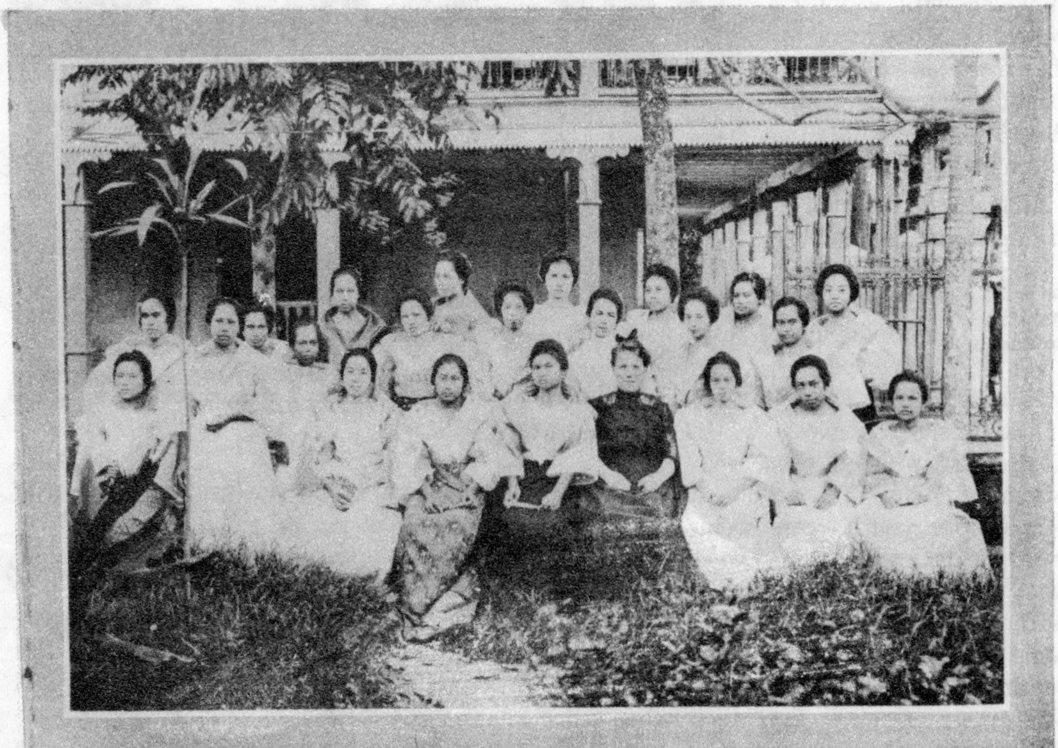

MADAGASCAR

By A. VAN GENNEP

Various Tribes—Physical Types—Woman's Work—Position of Women—Feminine Characteristics—How Women's Wrongs are Righted—A Curious Dance—The Artistic Sense of Malagasy Women—Women's Dress—Methods of Hair-Dressing—Music and Dancing—Birth and Childhood—Significance of Names—Polygamy—Marriage Ceremonies—Matrimonial Legends

YOUNG BETSILEO GIRL

Of the so-called Malayan type, with slight admixture of negro blood.

THE general scale of civilisation in Madagascar varies considerably according to the different tribes, such as the Hova or Antimerina, the Betsileo of the central plateau, the Sakalava of the Western coast, the Bezanozano of the virgin forests between the central plateau and the Eastern coast, the Betsimisaraka, the Antaimoro, etc., of the Eastern coast, the Mahafaly and Bara of the extreme South, and the Antankarana of the extreme North. The tribes of the plateau are the most civilised and the gentlest, and of these the details of everyday and social life are the most fully known. Thus the term Malagasy women is principally intended to refer to the Antimerina and Betsileo.

Various Tribes.

There is as much variety in the female type as there is in that of the male. The women of the central plateau—Antimerina and Hova—resemble the Polynesians, possess regular features, small hands and feet, a light yellow skin, and are of medium height. The women of the other tribes are of a deeper colour, and present all the gradations as far as the negro type (certain tribes, the Sakalava, Bara), or the negroids (Bezanozano). They are also taller and more thick-set. Although all the dialects of the island belong to the same Austronesian stock, from a physical point of view the tribes of Madagascar are far from being homogeneous.

Physical Types.

Throughout the island there is a clear division of labour between the sexes. The

A SAKALAVA WOMAN.

Negro type with curled hair, wearing *lamba*.

men occupy themselves mainly with warlike matters, hunting, fishing with heavy tackle, with the construction of the framework of their dwellings, with the breaking up of their rice grounds, and with the raising and care of their cattle (zebus). The women for their part busy themselves with the preparation of food, the covering in of newly erected dwellings with matting and other materials, with the lighter kind of fishing, with the cultivation of rice, and, of course, with the care of young children. It would not be correct to say that the husbands

Woman's Work.

A BETSIMISARAKA WOMAN.

Mixture of so-called Malayan and negro types; in semi-European costume.

leave the lightest tasks to their wives; on the contrary, the women's work is the hardest, so that, from our point of view, this division of labour is made on a basis in which trouble and fatigue are not taken into consideration.

Throughout the island also, excepting perhaps amongst the Bezanozano, woman is considered as a being equal to man. We do not find in Madagascar, as a general rule, that subjection of woman to the man which is so characteristic of the negro country, and even prevails among more civilised peoples, to wit, Mohammedan and Christian. Thus, marriage is not a mere formality of purchase by one of the parties of the other. The bride keeps the control of her belongings, and possesses the right, which is not merely theoretical, to the protection of her husband. Formerly, when polygamy was the universal custom, each wife lived in a separate dwelling surrounded by an enclosure which was allotted to her as her own property; moreover, before marriage a young girl was perfectly free to do as she liked, and if unhappily wedded could easily obtain a divorce.

Position of Women.

According to explorers and settlers who have been close observers of native habits, the Malagasy woman was regarded as quite the equal of the man. In this sense certain ideas and administrative measures introduced by the Europeans may be regarded as having put back her social and moral condition.

The important political part played by the women before the French Conquest is only one of the aspects of the situation. Among the Sakalava, as among the Antimerina and other tribes, are found unmistakable traces of a former matriarchate, a political economical system in which the man is subordinate to the woman. As the social life of the Malagasy has, as yet, been little studied it is difficult to ascertain how far the matriarchate prevailed amongst the various tribes. One fact, however, is certain, that the royal power could be transmitted to women, and that by preference. The history of the Sakalava, which has been pieced together by Commandant Guillain, and that of the dynasty of Tananarivo, remind us of numerous queens whose husbands were, in fact, only prime ministers.

Nevertheless, in many districts—for instance, at Majunga and at Ste. Marie—the position of woman is on a much lower scale, and this may be attributed to the influence of Mohammedanism. This may also be noticed in towns where Europeans have settled. The original independence of the Malagasy woman is disappearing owing to the manner in which it has been abused by white men, and to the new ideas which have been imposed by French laws, notwithstanding that, as a general rule, the French carry out the principle of leaving to subjugated aboriginals their own customary legislation.

Feminine Characteristics.

It is natural that, being accorded a recognised social status, the Malagasy woman should be animated by sentiments which assimilate her to our European women, such as a keen sense of her dignity and domestic responsibility. She is, moreover, sensitive to any friendship or love which may be shown her, as she attaches a great importance to these sentiments, and differs in this respect from so many other women of semi-civilised races. The Betsileo and Antimerina women are tender-hearted—a term which would scarcely apply to the negro population of the neighbouring African coast.

How Women's Wrongs are Righted.

In many tribes the women constitute a social group with its own peculiar customs. The most characteristic instance of this is that of the Zafisoro, a tribe of the south-east. If a man has been guilty of any grave offence towards a woman, complaint is made to the "head woman," who has been elected in order to defend feminine interests. This chieftainess summons a council of women, and, after the matter has been talked over, calls upon the king of the

A HOVA (ANTIMERINA) WOMAN.

A good example of the fair Malayan type. She is wearing an unembroidered *lamba.*

tribe to punish the culprit—a request invariably granted.

A Curious Dance.

Among ceremonies peculiar to women I would cite the dances and songs performed by the Antaimoro women during the absence of their husbands (when either hunting or fighting, etc.). These ceremonies are intended to endow their husbands with strength, courage, and good fortune. The women also carry amulets and talismans, intended to facilitate the troubles of child labour, of suckling, of field work, etc.

In the provinces the women wear the "simbo," a kind of sack open at both extremities, and the "akanjo," similar to the 'lamba" worn by the men, but smaller and closer round the chest. The ornamentation and the material of these garments differ according to the tribes; thus, among the Antanory in the southern part of the island the "akanjo" is made of widths of red and white spotted calico sewn together alternately. The "simbo" made of reed matting is held up round the waist by a broad ox-hide belt. In addition a broad band of plaited grass is worn round the chest and breasts, and held in position by strings of raphia behind the back.

Women's Dress.

The women of the tribes of the interior, moreover, possess a well-developed æsthetic taste, displayed chiefly in the manner in which they drape their garments, and also in the ornamental trimming with which they adorn them, more especially the silk "lambas," the embroidered patterns of which are usually geometrical, and finely and delicately executed; but what is more to be admired is the harmony with which the shades of colour are blended. Some embroideries are *en camaïeu* (white on white, etc.)—in fact, it was at Tananarivo during the period of native rule that this *industrie de luxe* was developed, especially as the "lamba" (a simple square of material which is wrapped round the body, one corner being thrown over the shoulder) is the traditional costume alike for men and women of the central plateau. Of late years European costume has begun to predominate, at least in Tananarivo and other large towns.

The Artistic Sense of Malagasy Women.

The æsthetic taste of the Malagasy women is further marked in their head-dresses, the construction of which requires many hours and the assistance of many hands. They begin by parting the hair down the centre; then they plait ten or twenty little tails on each side, commencing very tightly, and tying the ends in such a manner as to form a sort of crimp; finally, with the ends of these tresses they make round knots varying in size according to their tribe (*see* p. 209). Generally they plaster the whole edifice with clay or beef-fat, so that the hair need not be re-dressed more than once a month. In many tribes among the Bara both the male and female head-dresses are formed of knots coated with clay and grease. As under these conditions the scalp is always dirty, both men and women possess among their most necessary articles of toilette a comb, and a long copper or bone needle, with which they vigorously scratch their heads.

Methods of Hair-Dressing.

The Malagasy women are greatly devoted to music and dancing. The musical instruments played by the women are of an exceedingly simple type, being mere pieces of bamboo which are rhythmically struck, or bamboos from which strips of bark have been partly separated and stretched over a bridge. These strings are of different lengths, and give forth shrill notes. With regard to the dances, these consist of swaying movements and steps backwards and forwards. The dances are executed either individually or by a number together.

Music and Dancing.

A birth forms a subject of rejoicing for the whole of the family. Shortly before the expected arrival a small private room is constructed in the house by means of a partition of matting, and here a wood fire is lighted and carefully tended, even in summer, for the Malagasies consider that a high temperature facilitates the birth and hastens the convalescence of the mother. All the relations and friends, having been notified, come to pay a visit to the mother and bring her presents —as a rule, money, "intended for firewood." Old women fulfil the duties of midwives and nurses. The birth of a girl causes as much pleasure and delight as that of a boy.

Birth and Childhood.

The babies are suckled for a considerable time; as a rule, for two years, but sometimes for three or even four. The mothers carry their children, wrapped in the "lamba" or the "simbo," on the back and occasionally on the hip. Among the Imarina a special custom prevails with regard to this. When the children come to a mature age they offer their mother a piece of money, known as "perfume of the back," in grateful recognition of the trouble taken by their parent in thus carrying them during their infancy.

Significance of Names.

The names given to girls indicate their order of birth; for instance, "Rafaravavy," signifies the last child. Sometimes they are named after an animal, such as a mouse.

When a woman has children, she is merely styled the "mother of So-and-So." Women of a certain age are called indiscriminately "Ramatoa," a title of respect; and the old women, "Ineny," a homely term which means "mother."

BETSILEO WOMEN.

Showing the method of draping the *lamba*. They are good examples of the so-called Malayan type.

In the case of polygamy the first wife exercises a species of pre-eminence over the others, but this does not include any greater authority or any special privilege.

Polygamy.

Each wife maintains complete control over the whole of her possessions, both those which she has brought as a dowry and such as her husband may have given her. The position of the different wives of the same man is very similar among the Sakalava. It may be also mentioned that in Madagascar, as in many other countries, polygamy is only really practised by the rich, for, as each wife has her own private household, plurality of wives entails a very considerable expense.

Marriage Ceremonies.

When ethnographical researches were first instituted in Madagascar it was thought that the habits and customs among the various tribes were as uniform as the language. We know now that they differ widely. In connection with marriage ceremonies, however, there is one common feature—the part played by the intermediaries, who are either relations or friends. With most tribes the preliminary steps are taken by the relatives of the young man. On the other hand, with the Antaimoro the girls choose their husbands, an interesting parallel to the Hindoo custom of *Svayamvara.*

As a rule marriage is permanent, and can only be dissolved by legal measures, divorce being usually to the man's advantage. But in addition there is a form of union known as temporary marriage, which is equally celebrated by ceremonies (particularly on the Eastern coast). Among some tribes trial marriage exists, and with the Bezanozano may be said to prevail.

The marriage ceremonies follow a usual course—that is to say, the two families come to an agreement after discussing the matter. "When the bargain is concluded the youth comes to claim his bride; but before she is allowed to depart she has to exhibit her charms in competition with the other girls in the place, all of whom are dressed up for the occasion: this ceremony is called "being compared."

After the negotiations are completed the two families take part in a ceremonial feast. Among the Antimerina the bridal couple are enveloped in the same "lamba," and eat off the same dish. Among the Sakalava one of the young man's relatives or friends kills and cooks a fowl, and offers him the two feet; the bridegroom gives one to his bride, and eats the other, while the two families devour the rest of the bird. Among the Bara and a few other tribes an ox is killed ceremoniously, and eaten in common. (These ceremonies symbolise not only the union of the two individuals, but in a greater measure that of the two families.)

Matrimonial Legends.

As girls mature very early they are married while quite young—at the age of twelve or fourteen years. In the interior and among certain coast tribes marriage is arranged by the parents while the children are still quite little. Nevertheless love plays a very considerable part in connubial arrangements, as is manifested by numerous songs and legends such as the following, relating to the volcanic lake of Tritriva, which tells of a Malagasy Romeo and Juliet. In the West, at the foot of a mountain are two neighbouring villages. In one resided a young man famed for his strength and skill, and in the other dwelt a young girl celebrated for her beauty. These young people were betrothed, and had sworn eternal love to each other. Nevertheless, they could not marry; their families, divided by a violent feud, refused to consent to their union. In despair the young lovers climbed the mountain of Tritriva, and, binding themselves together in their silk "lambas," threw themselves into the bottomless lake. From that day, every time a young girl died in the village of the unhappy *fiancée*, half the waters of the lake turned red; and if in the village of the lover a young man died, the whole of the lake became the colour of blood. Andrianamjoinimerina, who reigned then at Tananarivo, recognised the hand of fate, and ordered his subjects not to run counter to the loves of their children, but to let them follow their own inclinations.

Photograph by Mr. C. Duncan Cross.

AN EGYPTIAN BRIDAL CAR.

In which the bride journeys to her new home.

NORTH AFRICA

By CLIVE HOLLAND

Egypt—A Mixed Race—The Fellahīn—Dress—Fellahīn Aids to Beauty—Home Life of the Fellahīn—How a Marriage is Arranged in Egypt—Egyptian Marriage Customs—Concerning Egyptian Children—The Copts—Coptic Dress—The Famous Dancing Girls—The Women of Algeria and Morocco—The Berber Race—Berber Dress—Position of Kabyle Women—The Arabs of Algeria and Morocco—Arab Love of Jewellery—Arab Marriage Customs—Arabs and Divorce—Moorish Women—Moorish Jewellery and Ornaments—Home Life of the Moors—Moorish Ideal of Beauty—Moorish Marriage Customs—The Bride Box—Position of Moorish Women

EGYPT

EGYPT is inhabited by what is commonly known as a "mixed" rather than by a "pure" race. Its geographical position is, indeed, such as to render this an unavoidable circumstance.

A Mixed Race.

Its history explains how the mixing of various races occurred.

Of the pure Egyptians, or the original inhabitants, there are two surviving types which at the present day form the more important basis of the population—the Fellahin and the Copts. They are the lineal descendants of the ancient Egyptians, in whose facial and other characteristics can still be traced resemblance to the types found depicted upon the mural decorations of ancient temples and tombs.

Of the two peoples we have mentioned the process of intermixture has been most strongly marked in the case of the

Fellahīn, who form the greater portion of the population in Lower Egypt and the rural districts of the Nile Delta. They are possessed of the distinguishing characteristics of a broad, flat forehead, large black eyes, a straight, well-formed nose and thick lips, and a rather high average height of about 5 feet 6 inches. But notwithstanding Arab inter-marriage, and influences in the Fellahin type, one can trace their ancient Egyptian ancestry.

The Fellahin.

Dress.

The dress of the men of the lower class is very elementary; those of the upper classes have adopted Turkish, Arab, or European garments.

The dress of the women of the lower class is very simple, and frequently consists of little more than a long garment of blue cotton stuff, like a dressing-gown, confined at the waist by a girdle. The costume of the better class women is not only more elaborate, but in some cases is rendered very handsome by a profusion of gold ornaments. The principal garment is usually a loose-fitting white robe, hanging from the shoulders to the feet and girdled at the waist. It is sleeveless, but has side openings reaching from the arm-holes to the knees. Underneath this outer robe, in summer time, is worn a chemise of gauze, and loose drawers of cotton or other material, reaching to just below the knees where they are confined. Sometimes these latter are replaced by loose trousers of similar material and of the well-known "Turkish" shape. In cool weather an additional chemise, or an under robe of the same type as the outer one is worn.

Fellahin Aids to Beauty.

Most of the women and girls of the upper class darken their eye-lids with antimony for the purpose of adding lustre to their eyes, and not a few ornament their bodies with tattooed designs and paint. Their hair, which is often very luxuriant, is plaited into thin "tails," some of which are dressed at the side of the head, and others are allowed to hang loosely down over the shoulders at the back. The many ornaments worn in the shape of pins, chains, bangles, etc., are generally of gold and, from their number and weight, are of considerable value. The hair itself is often adorned and retained in place by pins and combs of gold, and fringed with rows of coins of the same metal, tiny bells, and discs or shell-shaped pieces of the precious metal. The plaits of hair are secured at the ends with silken cords to which are attached gold coins and fringe.

Home Life of the Fellahin.

The women mix little, even nowadays, in the life of the villages or towns, but are supposed to find their chief interests in the care and rule of their households when married, or of their father's home when single, cooking, washing, and sewing making up their principal home duties. The first meal of the day is a light one, consisting generally of a cup of coffee, with, perhaps, some of the flat cakes of unleavened bread (something of the nature of griddle cakes) baked directly over the fire. Though on the whole less confined to the *harīm* than are Turkish women, the wives and daughters of Fellahīn of the better class do not have unrestricted freedom of movement in the outer world. They are permitted to pay calls upon other women in the morning, and whilst doing so pass their time mostly in idle gossip, smoking, telling stories, drinking coffee, and watching the professional dancing girls. Women of the lower class usually have more liberty than those of higher rank in life.

Of systematic education for women there is none, and comparatively few women possess any knowledge of things outside their own family circle or those of friends of their own sex.

The women of the better class are never or seldom seen, even though closely veiled, in the public market places, and only in the streets when so muffled up as to be quite unrecognisable. Only those of the courtesan class are met in the more frequented streets, but even they are at least partially veiled, and are only seen there at all because they have long ceased to value their reputations. Occasionally some poor

EGYPTIAN WOMAN.
Drawn by Norman H. Hardy.

Facing on page 216

old peasant women pass through the streets of a town unveiled, but these seem to have gained immunity from the universal cus-

earning a living and able to support a wife, without marrying is regarded as indicating that he is a ne'er-do-well and a libertine.

Photograph by Miss M. A. MacGregor.

WIFE AND MOTHER OF A DRAGOMAN.
A scene in Cairo.

tom by reason of their age and lack of physical charms.

As a general rule marriage in Egypt is undertaken earlier than in European countries; girls marry at any age from fourteen, and boys at sixteen or seventeen. Indeed for a man to attain any considerable age, provided he is capable of

How a Marriage is Arranged in Egypt.

Owing to the fact that there is practically no intercourse possible between young people of opposite sexes, when a young man wishes to marry he is compelled to employ a marriage broker, who is known by the name of a *khatbeh,* or betrother. This woman, who is in the way of her business acquainted with many families, visits those who at the particular time happen to possess daughters of suitable age and rank still unmarried. Frequently she combines with her profession of matrimonial agent that of a seller of cosmetics, ornaments, or dress stuffs. But whether she is one or the other matters little, she has seldom much difficulty in gaining an entrance into the family circle of a suitable household, who are not long left in ignorance of the main object of her visit. Marriage being esteemed the proper and ultimate goal of most girls, the mothers of eligible maidens do their best to make them in every way attractive so that the *khatbeh* may be favourably impressed with their qualifications and charms.

When the matrimonial agent has selected a candidate suitable to her employer she loses no time in communicating the fact to him. As he, of course, cannot himself see the lady whom it is proposed he should marry, his mother, sister, or other near female relative hastens to inspect her with a view to assuring themselves, on his behalf, that the *khatbeh's* report of her charms of person and suitability is not exaggerated. If they are satisfied, then the *khatbeh* pays another visit to the young lady's family and formally proposes on behalf of the young man for her hand in marriage. The young lady's parents are not long in coming to a decision, for, of course, from the first they have clearly understood what the *khatbeh* has been seeking, and would have early broken off negotiations had they been unfavourable to the marriage.

Photograph by Miss M. A. MacGregor.

A GROUP OF FELLAHĪN.

It will be noted that the women are partially veiled, merely their eyes and noses being visible.

As for the bride-to-be, although she has a traditional right of refusal it is seldom exercised. She has no reason for thinking the marriage unsuitable, for—unless the intended bridegroom is her cousin, and she may have known him when a small boy—she will probably never have seen him. The *khatbeh* is eloquent in her praises of him, and so the bride-to-be generally accepts the position without demur.

Of course amongst the lower and labouring classes whose daughters work in the fields, and cannot in consequence be always veiled and shut up in *harīms*, men who wish to marry select their own wives according to their own ideas and without any intermediary.

After the two families have arrived at a general agreement that the marriage arranged by the *khatbeh* is desirable the bargaining regarding the bride's dowry commences. The rule is for the bridegroom to promise a fixed sum to his wife-to-be, of which two-thirds are paid when the marriage is agreed upon, but the remainder is not paid except in the event of divorce. By a strange custom the bride's family usually pay her dowry out of the money thus received from her future husband! So that things in the end are frequently very much as they were in the beginning. On the settlement of this matter the contract is considered ratified, and a declaration is made before a magistrate or other legal authority to this effect.

Soon after this the bridegroom and a couple of his friends go to the house of the bride's mother or father, where they are formally received. Witnesses and a *Fikêe* or reader also attend, and friends of both parties are also usually present. After a recital of the first chapter of the Koran the bridegroom and bride's father kneel opposite one another on a carpet in the midst of the spectators, clasp each other by the right hand, and raising the thumbs press them closely together. The bridegroom has already mentioned the amount agreed as the bride's settlement. The *Fikêe* then delivers a short address, having first covered the clasped hands with a cloth, and afterwards pronounces the words of betrothal. Presents are made, the *Fikêe* receives his fee or tip, and the witnesses and others eat together.

Photograph by Miss M. A. MacGregor.

WANDERING BEDOUIN WOMAN DANCING.

There only now remains the actual marriage, preceded by the introduction of the bridegroom to the bride. Then follows a grand night festival to which all the friends of both and many neighbours are invited, and the newly wedded pair take up housekeeping.

One quaint wedding custom in connection with a bride of Lower Egypt is the visit paid by herself and friends to the bath. The progress to it partakes of the nature of a procession. Headed by Arab musicians (in the case of a bride of position) with tambourines, flutes, and other instruments it wends its way slowly through the streets to the bath house, over the door of which is hung a handkerchief to intimate that only women may enter. After the bride and her friends have bathed they abandon themselves to the enjoyment of an entertainment provided by the musicians, story-tellers, and singers who have come with them for the purpose.

Egyptian Marriage Customs.

When the time arrives to depart from the bath the bride takes a large piece of *henna* paste into which the various guests stick a gold coin of a value varying according to their means. Then the bride's finger-nails and toe-nails are reddened with the *henna*, and she says adieu to her friends, who afterwards divide the rest of the cosmetic amongst them.

The earlier part of next day is spent in those beautifying arts of the toilet which are known amongst Western nations as "make-up." Towards the middle of the afternoon the bride starts for her husband's home, accompanied by her nearest female relatives. The procession also includes camels or horses on which the bride's belongings, dowry, etc., are packed; Arab wrestlers, musicians, water carriers, and others who give entertainments in the streets at various points of the progress of the procession. On arrival at the bridegroom's residence there are feasting and amusements for the guests, and it is not until late that the latter depart. At last even the *bellaneh* (nurse) leaves, and the bride and bridegroom are left alone and at peace. Then, and not till then, is the latter permitted to lift his wife's veil, and catch a glimpse of her features, and decide whether or not she is as desirable as the eloquence of the *khatbeh* had represented.

The Fellahin children are kept in such rigid seclusion for seven days after birth that not even their own fathers are allowed to see them for fear of injury. On the seventh day, however, the infant is borne on a sieve or tray, and accompanied with lighted tapers through every part of the house, whilst the nurse seeks to propitiate the evil spirits by scattering salt and grain. The baby is afterwards shaken about in the sieve to give it confidence, and then held up to the sun so that it may have its eyes strengthened. If the baby is a girl the guests will be chiefly women invited by the mother; but in the case of a boy the father will also have invited his friends. The boy baby is ultimately carried to the men's apartments, where the father will see it for the first time.

Concerning Egyptian Children.

The usual method of christening will probably not appeal to Western peoples. It consists of the *kadi* sucking a piece of sugar-candy, and allowing the melted sugar to flow from his own mouth into that of the infant, after which sadly un-hygienic proceeding he gives the child its name.

Owing to the fact that the upper class women in Lower Egypt, more especially of the towns, lead such secluded lives there are few occupations of at all a public character open to or followed by women. The peasants do a considerable amount of agricultural work, but amongst the shopkeeping classes the women are conspicuous by their absence.

The Copts, the second great native division of the people, are nowadays chiefly the inhabitants of Upper Egypt. They are found more especially in the district near Assiût, and on the shores of, and in the vicinity of, Lake Birket-el-Kerun. Those found in Lower Egypt are mostly artisans, shopkeepers, and scribes. Owing to the fact that the Copts are not followers of Mohammed but are Christians, they have come into contact with the Arab divisions of the population to a lesser degree than the Fellahīn, and they remain much purer in race than the latter. But it should be noted that, whilst thus retaining many of their original racial characteristics and religious beliefs, their customs and ideas have altered considerably since ancient times. In many of their customs, indeed, and in attire, they have become little distinguishable from

The Copts.

Moslems, although in dress they prefer the darker colours.

Coptic Dress.

The costume of the women does not differ very materially from that of Fellahin of the better class. There is the same love of ornament, and much the same form of hairdressing. There is one merit, however, about their ornaments—they are never tawdry or sham. They are often purchased, or otherwise acquired, in times of prosperity either before or after marriage, and are handed down from generation to generation. It is only in cases of direst necessity that they are sold outright, although when hard times come women will frequently pawn them.

Photograph by Miss M. A. MacGregor.

WANDERING BEDOUIN WOMEN.

In addition to the garments we have already mentioned as being worn by Fellahin women, over the chemise Copt women often wear a narrow-sleeved, bodice-like garment which fits closely to the body, and is secured in front by a series of knots, commencing just below the breast line. Forming a part of this is a skirt which falls in straight folds from the hips to the ankles. During the hot summer months the tight-fitting undergarments are abandoned, sometimes even the trousers or drawers, and only the outer robe, generally of light blue cotton fabric, or a bright blue striped one, is considered

Photograph by Miss B. C. Reynolds.

MOORISH WOMEN OUT FOR A WALK.

necessary. Either there is nothing on the feet, or merely loose-fitting slippers are worn which in no wise destroy their natural beauty.

Out of doors, however, most women are careful to conceal both their faces and persons from the vulgar gaze.

The dress of young girls is very similar to that of their elders, but girls from four or five up to ten or twelve, however, are generally spared the outer robe, and wear only the chemise and loose drawers, although they very early commence to imitate their elder sisters and other women by drawing their head covering across their faces when a stranger approaches.

The women of the towns follow few public occupations, for they are chiefly concerned with the management of their homes. But in the rural districts they assist with agricultural work, and much of the milling of the flour is done by women of the lower orders.

Photograph by J. Geiser, Algiers.

WOMAN OF SOUTHERN ALGERIA.

The Famous Dancing Girls.

There is, however, one class of women in Egypt whose mission of public entertainers brings them in contact with the outer world, and whose profession dates from the times of the Pharaohs. They are found in almost every town of any size in Upper Egypt, and they claim to be lineally descended from Barmek the favourite of the famous Haroun el Raschid. Some authorities contend that they are genuine gipsies, but this is unlikely owing to the intermarriage which has undoubtedly taken place with all grades of the population. In most towns, although sometimes employed to entertain at feasts in private houses, these dancing girls are confined to one particular quarter, where morality and respectability count least. As a rule the women and girls of the better class are magnificently dressed in a more or less modified form of Turkish costume, with a wealth of bright coloured stuffs and many valuable ornaments. Indeed, numbers of these girls possess not only jewellery of immense value, but also cash in hand to large amounts.

In modern times their ranks have been largely recruited by handsome slave girls purchased by the heads of troupes, or by the proprietors of the houses where dancing entertainments are given.

ALGERIA AND MOROCCO

Although a glance at the map of North Africa shows that Algeria and Morocco are two distinct countries as regards political division, the inhabitants of each are practically identical, and may therefore in most matters be regarded together. The main part of the population of both countries is formed of Berbers, the less important divisions of the inhabitants being comprised of Arabs, Jews, and negroes.

The Berber Race.

The Berber race is essentially "white," though in past ages it has been modified locally by Arab influences. Consequently, and from the fact that they are Mohammedans and frequently speak Arabic, the Berbers have often erroneously been regarded as Arabs. There is one thing, however, both Berbers and Arabs have in common which has doubtless led to some additional confusion at times. This is the common "Caucasian" origin, and the fact that in physical characteristics they present some features of resemblance. There are, notwithstanding,

Photograph by J. Geiser, Algiers.

A WOMAN OF BOU SAÂDA, SOUTH ALGERIA.

Showin,, the method of carrying children.

some very important points of divergence. The Arabs have a longer, more oval face, and less fair skin than the Berbers, with a less broad and more aquiline nose, smaller mouth, less heavily modelled jaws, and darker hair and eyes. They are also less energetic and industrious, less inquisitive and more contemplative than practical. The Arab is very frequently a dreamer rather than a worker. The Arab mind is of a finer grade, and the Arab himself of a more self-controlled and stoical disposition.

The divisions or clans of the Berber race alone in Algeria are very numerous; some authorities state that there are at least twelve hundred. Doubtless this fact has earned for them the sobriquet of the "Scotch of North Africa." The tribes are divided into three principal groups. The coast tribes, or inhabitants of the North, are known as Kabyles, together with the Riff pirates whose depredations in the past caused them to be one of the scourges of the Mediterranean; the second comprises the Shullahs of the Atlas, and the Sus of the Mogador district; the third includes the Black Berbers or Haratins, who dwell chiefly on the Southern slopes of the Atlas Chain.

Berber Dress.

The costume of Berber women is simpler than that of the Arabs, and consists chiefly of a long tunic-like garment fastened with a girdle round the waist, and a coloured shawl or cloth worn over the shoulders. The women are permitted much greater freedom than among the Arabs, and the all-enveloping veil or *haik* is not worn. Their ornaments consist chiefly of necklaces, bracelets, chains of gold or beads, ear-rings, and sometimes nose-rings.

The Berber dwellings in towns and villages are sometimes of two storeys, built substantially of stone, but in the country districts, especially among the Tuareg in the South, many of the people live in tents or movable huts of straw, and follow the pursuits of agriculture or the more simple industries.

Position of Kabyle Women.

The Kabyle woman occupies a much superior position in the esteem of men than a Moorish or Arab woman. She is not compelled to veil herself nor is she prevented from mixing freely in the outer life of her people. She is treated more in the light of an equal and companion of her husband, and in most cases is the sole wife, although some few Kabyles are polygamous. Her dress is of a simple character, consisting chiefly of a loose-fitting robe of light colours, and a head-cloth, arranged somewhat in the fashion of a close-fitting turban, with a fold of the material hanging down over the head and neck behind.

The Arabs of Algeria

The Arabs who conquered Algeria and Morocco in the seventh and eleventh centuries are found to-day throughout those two countries, and, indeed, politically speaking, are still the dominant race in the latter country as they were in the former until its occupation by the French. The Arab element of Algeria is found chiefly in the Western portion, although it is in a measure scattered throughout the province. The dress of Arab women usually consists of a white striped shawl, called a *haik*, made of coarse or fine stuff according to the social position and wealth of the wearer, which is thrown over the head, and completely veils the user from head to feet. Underneath this *haik*, arranged across the lower part of the face so that it covers all but the eyes, the bridge of the nose, and a small portion of the forehead left uncovered by the *haik*, is worn a handkerchief of white linen known as an *adjar*, which is fastened securely across the face. Sometimes, more especially in the towns, the *adjar* is of so gossamer-like a material that it forms but the thinnest disguise to the wearer's features. The effect of this semi-transparent veil, and the uncovered eyes, which are generally beautiful, dark, and expressive, is rather coquettish than repellent as one would suppose was the intention.

The life of Arab women proper is of a freer character than that of many other Oriental races. In marriage this is decidedly the case, as women very frequently have a distinct voice in the matter of whom they shall marry, and after the event they enjoy much more personal liberty than most Eastern women. Honeymoons and wedding tours, however, are quite unknown, although as it is rather the custom — and considered luckier — for the bride-to-be to journey to her future husband than for him to come to her—a girl very frequently makes a considerable journey before her marriage. It is the practice with many wealthy Arabs living in the larger towns to send their sons to reside with tent-dwelling Bedouins, so that they may grow up hardy and full of those qualities of daring and skill with the matchlock and sword in which the Arab takes so great a pride. Thus it is that many young Arabs in after years, when they have returned to their fathers' houses, and seek a wife, find her amongst the girl playmates of their early desert days. When this is the case the girl is sent for, and in due course arrives, riding with a woman companion on a richly caparisoned camel and accompanied by attendants and a protecting guard.

Arab Marriage Customs.

On another camel or camels, according to the wealth of the bride, is carried the trousseau and dowry; and after the latter, even when the journey is a long one, often ride musicians beating drums and playing upon other instruments.

The marriage feasts of the Arabs are important ceremonies to which rich and poor are invited, but the marriage ceremony itself is extremely simple. In the towns it generally consists of a declaration made before the *Kadi;* whilst in the desert the only act necessary is the killing of a sheep in front of the tent of the bride's father, or other person standing in that relation to her.

Whilst polygamy is permitted, it is not usually practised, although, as divorce is very easy, an Arab may, in the course of a long life, marry a number of women in succession. It is by no means an uncommon thing for Arabs to exchange wives, and this is stated by some authorities frequently to be done with the utmost satisfaction to all concerned! It will, however, be easily understood that such practices cannot conduce to the stability of the family relationships, nor would one imagine to the best interests and happiness of the women.

Arab Divorce.

Should an Arab be dissatisfied with his wife he is at liberty to send her back to her father, but such act must be accompanied by the return in full of any dowry that he may have received with her. It is a very common thing for a brother to offer marriage to his brother's widow, a practice which is more followed amongst Eastern peoples, especially of the nomadic tribes, than is generally supposed. The Arab has also an absolute right to marry his girl cousin, who if she possesses several cousins is held to be at the disposal of the eldest, or oldest unmarried, of them. If divorce can be easily obtained by the man it can be procured with similar ease by the woman. A man is considered bound to provide for the necessities of himself and his women folk, and if she be so disposed a wife can obtain a divorce if her husband fails to do this on even a single occasion. In the event of an Arab woman earning money by any means she is at full liberty to dispose of it as she pleases. Usually it goes in the purchase of jewellery and toilet articles such as *henna* and *kohl.* With some tribes it is the custom for the men to pay the women for any special work they may perform.

The Arab women are almost without exception treated with a chivalry which is somewhat strange when one considers the freedom of marriage relationship as regards divorce. But be this as it may, an Arab woman guilty of an offence against morals is almost invariably sheltered and the scandal hushed up. The Arab's attitude is well

Position of Arab Women.

expressed by the saying, "We must give women greater indulgence, for they are weaker whilst equally tempted, and less able to stand temptation. So we must cover them with our cloaks."

Europeans understand the term, there is as yet practically none. Few women can read, and still fewer can write, save those belonging to the highest classes amongst the inhabitants of the towns.

Photograph by J. Geiser, Algiers.

GIRL OF BOU SAÂDA, SOUTHERN ALGERIA.

Marriage by capture is still practised by several of the Bedouin tribes. But notwithstanding this somewhat summary method of marriage, Arab wives are usually treated with consideration, and even tenderness, and on the whole marriage amongst the Arabs is happy.

Of education amongst the women, as

Moorish Women.

Although closely allied to the Arabs, the Moors, who are chiefly the inhabitants of the towns in Morocco, are fairer in complexion than the sons of the desert. This circumstance may be accounted for by the fact that many of them are undoubtedly the direct descendants of the Moriscos, who

WOMAN OF BOU SAÂDA, SOUTHERN ALGERIA.

over which is worn a jacket of coloured material elaborately embroidered in gold or silver. A pair of wide and beautifully worked trousers of green, blue, or red cashmere, girded in with a handsome silken sash at the waist, where they meet the short jacket, usually completes the costume. Some women, however, add other drapery, fastened in front, and allowed to fall down behind as a train. One leg is always left uncovered, on which is worn a heavy silver anklet, and the tips of the feet are thrust into tiny slippers of morocco leather.

Photographs by J. Geiser, Algiers.

ALGERIAN GIRL OF MIXED RACE.

were driven out of Spain at the commencement of the sixteenth century, but who by intermarriage had acquired a considerable strain of Spanish blood. Probably, also, to this is attributable the fact that they are of a more mercurial temperament than the Arabs proper, more gifted with humour and vivacity, and more cultured. Some of the Moorish women are of distinctly Spanish cast, possessing fine dark eyes, well-marked 'brows, and dark olive complexions.

The national colour in dress for both men and women is white. The men's costume is simple in character, but that of the women often very elaborate. As a general rule the latter consists of a white muslin chemise,

The Moorish women are inordinately fond of jewellery and ornaments. Half-a-dozen massive bracelets on each arm is the fewest number a well-to-do woman will wear, whilst the wealthy deck themselves to the fullest extent of their means with jewels, precious stones, and gold coins. Women who cannot afford gems deck themselves with numberless gold and silver coins of any country or period, made up into long necklaces, or sewn upon the dress material itself. The jingling noise made by these coins is much appreciated by the wearers.

Moorish Jewellery and Ornaments.

Moorish women are also devoted to the use of perfumes, dyes, and unguents, which are, indeed, so generally in favour with Eastern women. The darkest of dark eyebrows are the height of fashion, and the more nearly they meet in one continuous line the better is their owner pleased.

Home Life of the Moors.

Moorish homes are of much greater architectural merit than those of the Arabs. The most striking feature is the courtyard which is partially roofed over, and usually of large size, though frequently approached from the street by merely a narrow passage. The second storey rooms overhang this very considerably, and are supported by pillars. There is invariably a stream of running water in the courtyard, and in many are to be found pleasant fountains and foliage. The courtyard is surrounded by long, narrow rooms, which open into it, and are entered through high archways, closed by huge carved doors or gates in which are smaller doors like posterns. Tiles cover the floors of the rooms, on which are often spread handsome skins and rugs, and very frequently there is a dado of ornamental tiles running round the walls, which are otherwise whitewashed. The ceilings of the better class houses are ornamented with beautiful arabesques in gold and brilliant colours. The upper rooms are reached by narrow staircases varying in number according to the size of the house, and sometimes, so irregularly are the rooms arranged, these staircases and the passages leading to the different chambers are bewilderingly tortuous.

Another great and most important feature of most Moorish dwellings is the *stahr* or flat roof, on which the women are wont to sit, gossip, and enjoy the fresh air quite safe from intrusion, as this part of the building is held sacred to their use, and seldom or never visited by the men of the household.

The Moorish Ideal of Beauty.

Moorish women are not only generally stout, but as girls they are fattened for the marriage market, much as a poultry farmer treats his livestock. The principal articles of food, too, all conduce to fat-forming, consisting as they do of barley cakes made with buttermilk, porridge formed of flour rolled into small grain-like particles, sausages composed of minced meat, which is rolled round a short stick and roasted over the fire. The staple food of women, however, is bread, and it is chiefly with this that they are fattened. Long-shaped pellets of it are constantly forced down their throats for a period of about three weeks prior to their marriage. Although both wines and spirits are drunk by Moors, tea is the national beverage.

Moorish Marriage Customs.

By an inversion of the Western order of things, marriage almost invariably precedes wooing, as neither the wife nor husband see one another, as a general rule, until after the wedding; though occasionally the latter may see his future bride once after the marriage details have been finally settled. Sometimes this is done by stealth, when she comes to pay her future mother-in-law a visit of introduction; but of free intercourse socially between young people about to take each other "for better, for worse" there is none whatever in Morocco.

A bride is always borne to her husband's house at night, and when possible by moonlight. The wedding festivities of the Moors are elaborate, and it is because of their love of taking their amusements after sundown, in the cool of the day, that weddings are almost always evening festivals. In the case of a marriage between rich families a great interest is taken in the proceedings by

Photograph by J. Geiser, Algiers.

MOORISH WOMEN DANCING

all the street (and even further afield) in which the bride dwells. It is crowded for hours before the bridal procession is timed to leave the bride's old home, and slaves and servants push their way amongst the throng bearing refreshments, bags of money, and other presents. The refreshments are offered to all, and a piece of money or cloth is given to those who request it. But, although the beggars may usually be numbered by scores, no one—such is the unwritten law—asks for a gift twice, or as a general rule accepts both money and cloth.

The Bride Box.

A strange and, one would imagine, horrible ordeal awaits the bride. She has to be put into a badly made and ill-ventilated wooden cage, usually whitewashed, and in it taken in procession through the streets to the bridegroom's dwelling. The *cortège* is accompanied by musicians; a number of closely veiled maidens, friends of the bride; and the hangers-on of such ceremonies who are to be found in every clime. Often many shrines are visited ere the unfortunate prisoner's new home is reached, and at each of these a priest will pray and bless the bride. If the wedding is that of well-to-do people, neighbours, acquaintances, and the curious come to their doors (at least the men do) and shout congratulations and expressions of good will. The women lean over the parapets of the flat roofs and peer down into the street, and add theirs.

On arrival at the bridegroom's home the bride is released from the terrible confinement of the box, but not until it has been carefully carried into the house and placed in the wedding chamber. The bride is then placed upon a couch, and the bride box is decorated by the bride's attendant with flowers and jewellery, and the various articles of her trousseau. Then the bride herself is, so to speak, redecorated. Her cheeks are rouged afresh, her eyes darkened by *kohl*, and her nails re-stained with *henna*; whilst her garments, which have been crumpled by her confinement in the narrow box, are straightened out, and re-arranged where necessary. Then the attendant, locking the door of the room and taking the key with her, hies herself to the mother of the husband-to-be. The bridegroom eventually receives the key from his mother, after she has had a short interview with the bride, and then goes to seek his wife.

After a two days' honeymoon, the now discarded box is placed upon the roof of the house in a prominent position so that all may see it. This is an official intimation that the newly wedded pair are now ready to receive their friends.

The bride, of course, receives only women visitors and in her own apartments. Her reception lasts three or four days, and she is supposed to doze all the time, and not trouble herself at all about her guests!

The bridegroom's reception of his friends and acquaintances, which often lasts a week, is a very joyful and hilarious occasion, and usually takes place in the courtyard or garden of the house. He joins heartily in the amusements of his guests, and in the case of wealthy people the entertainment offered is of a lavish and even magnificent character.

Position of Moorish Women.

The position socially and morally of Moorish women has often been described and discussed. It presents many problems because of the vivid contrasts of which it is full. Passing her life from birth to death first within the walls of her father's house and then those of her husband's (if she be married), and strictly guarded as she is, yet her life presents more possibilities of variety than can be readily conceived. Although coming into contact with but one man (after marriage), with the exception of her sons, she still plays many parts. While nominally her husband's slave she still manages frequently to rule him. She possesses innate wisdom which makes it possible for her to be his adviser, comforter, and unrealised tyrant all in one. He invariably tells her his business, and his troubles; and, indeed, it is doubtful if the women of any other race share their husbands' lives so intimately. She works for him, and she entertains him; cooks for him;

and when he is sick acts as his untiring and devoted nurse. For this reason most Moorish women are happy wives, not so much because they pass their lives in ministering to their husband and children (although that in itself is no mean mission), but because owing to these ministrations they form so important a factor in the life of the household, and are objects of such keen interest and tender solicitude on the part of the men with whom destiny, or the fortune of marriage, has elected they shall live and pass their days.

Their lives are narrow to Western ideas. Granted. But living in almost windowless houses, and, if of good social position, immured, they must perforce gain their happiness from within and not seek it from without. It is certain that they do not regret the system in which they are brought up, and it is possible that they live all the happier for it.

Of education they possess very little. Most, indeed, are entirely ignorant of "book learning," and of "the other side of the wall," and the wider interests of life as understood by Western women. But in social arts they could teach many a Girtonian not a little!

Photograph by Miss B. C. Reynolds.

The street in which the Ouled Naïl dancing girls live at Biskra.

Photograph by permission of A. C. Hollis, Secretary East African Protectorate.

WIVES OF THE SULTAN OF LAMU DANCING.

EAST AFRICA

By Dr. R. W. FELKIN

I

Area described—Climate—Character of the People—A Beautiful Country—The Contamination of Civilisation—The Women of Uganda and Unyoro—The Aristocrats of the Race—Vitality of the Race—Feminine Characteristics—Dress in Uganda—How Bark Cloth is made—Tanning in Uganda—Waganda Ornaments—African Garden Cities—Waganda Houses and How they are Built—Domestic Arrangements—Position of Women in Uganda—A Woman's Day in Uganda—Birth Customs—Funeral Customs—Wedding Ceremonies—Education of Children—Waganda Fairy-Tales—Waganda Superstitions—Religion in Uganda—Wanyoro Women—Obesity *v.* Beauty—Character and Position of Wanyoro Women—Wanyoro Ornaments—Cannibalism—Wanyoro Medicine Women—Curious Traditions

Area described.

IT may be well at the outset to describe shortly the area occupied by the tribes treated in this chapter. It is an account of the anthropology of the women living in the area in Central and East Africa comprised in the British Protectorates, as well as those living south of latitude 10° N., which are under the Anglo-Egyptian rule. This area, then, is bounded upon the north by the water-shed between the Bahr-el-Ghazal, Darfûr, latitude 10° N., and Abyssinia; on the east by the Indian Ocean as far south as the frontier of the German Protectorate just south of Mombasa; on the south by the frontier between the German and British Protectorates; and on the west by the Congo Free State territories. It includes

EAST AFRICA

By Dr. R. W. FELKIN

an area of some half million square miles, the habitat of many tribes and sub-tribes.

The Island of Zanzibar is really, politically, within the East Africa Protectorate, but it is not dealt with in this division. One may say that the whole of the land inhabited by the people to be described are within the tropics—therefore the climate, which has always so great an influence on the physical and moral character of the people, needs a brief description.

Climate.

Apart from the great Nandi plateau, where we find a climate almost like that of England, it is hot, moist, and not suitable for Europeans. The mean annual temperature may be said to be about 70° F., the extremes being 50° F., as the minimum, which is very rare, and 90° F., as the maximum, save in some isolated spots, where the temperature may rise as high as 100° F., or more.

The annual rainfall is some sixty inches, and there are two periods of maximum rainfall—March, April, and May, and September, October, and November—varying slightly in different districts as they are nearer to or further from the equator. During the rainy season rain falls nearly every day, and thunderstorms are very frequent. In Uganda, for instance, there may be, for days together, a thunderstorm every afternoon, short but sharp. Some of the storms are very severe indeed, tropical rain accompanied by vivid lightning and deafening thunder. These storms occur with south or south-east winds. Sometimes hail may be seen. Emin Pasha noticed hailstones as large as horse-beans; so has the writer of these pages on many occasions. Local rains occur often, coming down in torrents in one place, while at hardly ten minutes' distance there is no rain at all.

It is not necessary to give details of the geological formation of the country, save to say that it has a volcanic or metamorphic rock formation. The upper stratum of land to a depth of two or three feet is a rich, black, alluvial soil, under which is a bed of red, sandy clay, perhaps thirty feet deep, and lower still in some parts a layer of tolerably pure porcelain earth. Much iron is found, but we need not refer to other metals or precious stones.

Photograph by permission of A. C. Hollis.

WIVES OF THE SULTAN OF LAMU.

It follows quite naturally from what has been said that the people living in such a country will not have a great fight for existence; that is to say, Nature is very lavish. There are often two crops in a year, which grow in great profusion and with little trouble. Naturally, therefore, the people are often happy-go-lucky and indolent.

Character of the People.

The only scourge of the country is epidemic disease of man or cattle, and there is the usual war against wild animals, of which there are great numbers — lions, elephants, buffaloes, leopards (it is a delusion to imagine that there are tigers in Africa). In the rivers and swamps live hippopotami, crocodiles, and many poisonous reptiles, pythons and scorpions; there are also the white and driver ants.

A Beautiful Country.

With regard to the scenery and vegetation, it may be said roughly that one meets with virgin forests, rolling plains, and park-like country. The forests are often very impressive. "We were completely surrounded by trees, whose mighty branches were so thickly interlaced that we could not see the crowns, which in many instances must have risen to a height of a hundred and twenty feet. The dense foliage completely shut out the rays of the sun, and even at mid-day we marched along in a dim, mysterious twilight. Bright-coloured creepers drooped in graceful festoons from the trees, forming bowers of ever-varying beauty; here and there we caught glimpses of shady avenues, through which darted the startled denizens of the forest. Now and then birds of lovely plumage flew overhead, uttering shrill, piercing cries; rainbow-hued butterflies fluttered hither and thither; while the hum of myriads of insects made the silence more intense. Sometimes we passed under lofty arches formed by the intermingling branches, the soft greensward underneath being a pleasant contrast to the tangled underwood through which we had often to force a passage. At times the path was obstructed by a gigantic tree, which, unable to resist the force of some fierce blast, had fallen, but, though fallen, was still beautiful, its soft covering of moss looking like velvet. Far above us the wind sighed in the branches, the rustling of innumerable leaves sounding like the murmur of the ocean on a sandy shore. The atmosphere, heavy with the overpowering scent of tropical vegetation, produced a feeling of oppression; and, though wondering and rejoicing at the marvellous beauty so lavishly displayed around us, we were glad when a welcome break in the forest allowed us to breathe a purer, cooler air." *

Sometimes we may see wide stretches of country which resemble a good old English park; or, again, the ground may be covered with tall grass growing to a height of ten or fifteen feet. At a distance it looks like a huge wheatfield. These grassy steppes are very difficult to march through; they are the haunts of many an animal. Once or twice a year the people set fire to them, either to drive out the game or to clear the ground in order to plant their grain.

When the traveller comes upon a homestead, it is usually in such a clearing in the forest, and is surrounded by banana groves and well-tilled fields.

With the exception of Uganda itself, where good roads are made and kept, they may be said not to exist; paths winding in and out, round boulders or fallen trees, are met, but as a rule they are mere tracks, sixteen to twenty inches broad. Often in marching it is needful, unless one has the sense of direction and locality which is so markedly possessed by the natives, to walk compass in hand, since any view is frequently impossible to obtain owing to the long grass or the overhanging trees.

The above is sufficient to give, in broad outline, a general idea of the country in which dwell the people who are the subject of this chapter. We may add, further, that there are some good streams, apart, of course, from the Great Nile and many swamps; there are several great lakes, the Victoria Nyanza being the largest fresh-water lake in the world.

Woman is always an interesting study, but a difficult one, owing to her many-sided-

* "Uganda and the Egyptian Sudan," by C. T. Wilson and R. W. Felkin.

ness. And what obtains in Europe obtains in Central Africa. In the space at my disposal it would be obviously impossible to give a detailed description of all the tribes inhabiting the vast area with which I am dealing, so the subject will be dealt with in four groups:

The Contamination of Civilisation.

First, the women living in Uganda and Unyoro; next the Masai; then the Eastern tribes; and lastly, those dwelling in the White Nile regions, such as the Madi, Bari, Dinka, and Shillûk.

One more introductory remark is needful. It is well known that native tribes are soon influenced by contact with European races. Missionaries, traders, soldiers, all speedily impress the native with ideas and customs far different from their original ones. The writer, who had the pleasure of visiting many of these tribes some years ago, is, he hopes, able to give an account of them before they were contaminated—at least by European civilisation! Arabs certainly had, in parts, exerted some influence, but not to any great extent. A fair idea, therefore, of the conditions, customs, folklore, and so forth could be obtained by a careful observer — one who had sympathy with the people, and who could look a little beyond the obvious, to the deeper thoughts and feelings which lay under possibly crude, or even repulsive, externals. This must be borne in mind in reading what follows. In certain cases due reference will be made to the work of more recent observers, and the influences which have been at work amongst the people will be pointed out. In the main, however, it will be sought to show how the women were born, lived, married, hated, loved, and died, as seen in the years before contact with Europeans had affected native institutions to any great degree.

The Women of Uganda and Unyoro.

As far as physical nature is in question, the description of the women of Uganda and Unyoro is identical; it is only when we come to deal with their habits and customs that we shall have to differentiate them.

On the whole, the women are divided into two classes: the bulk of the population on the one hand, and a small class belonging to the reigning race, the Wahuma. These latter came from the southern part of Abyssinia originally, and from this stock, no doubt, sprang the reigning families—in fact, the aristocracy of Uganda.

This migration from the south of Abyssinia took place some two or three hundred years ago; the people arrived near Mombasa, but they were driven back by the coast tribes, and finally crossed the Nile just north of Ripon Falls, and, dividing there into three parties, one conquered Uganda, one Karagwe, and one Unyoro.

The Aristocrats of the Race.

This migration probably gave rise to the Kintu myth (to which I refer later) which relates to the origin of the Uganda kings. These Wahuma women can at once be distinguished from the bulk of the population: they are taller, more aristocratic-looking, and possess a peculiar grace of their own. The Uganda women are of a dark chocolate colour; their eyes are brown, they are well proportioned and have very good features, and in their youth are very good-looking, with small, delicately formed hands and feet.

They differ widely from the surrounding tribes in so far as that they are never scarred; their teeth are very good, and are neither filed nor, as is so often seen elsewhere, are the front teeth extracted—in fact, all mutilations are absolutely forbidden by law.

Their facial expression is very animated, and they gesticulate freely in conversation and when telling stories; for, although they are not professional story-tellers, as one might dub many of the men, yet they are not far behind them, and it is a pleasant sight to watch them educating and amusing the children with long, elaborate stories. They dress their hair very neatly, but there are no elaborate coiffures such as may be seen in other parts of Africa; the hair is short and woolly, and grows uniformly over

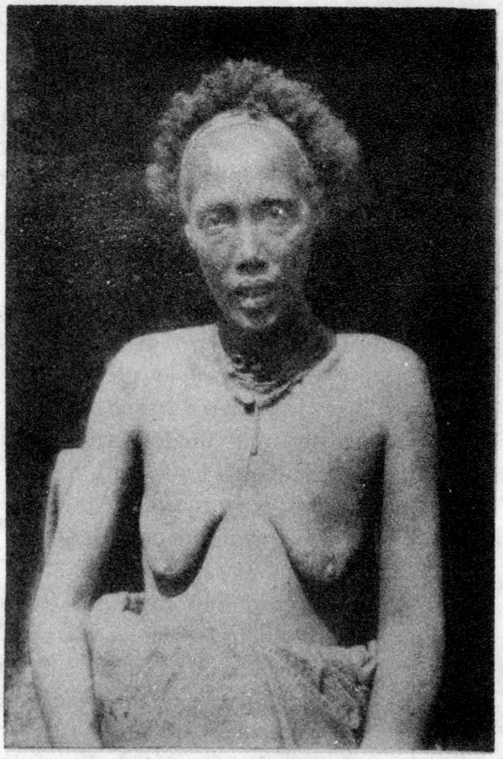

Photograph by Sir Harry H. Johnston, G.C.M.G., K.C.B.

A WOMAN OF THE BA HIMA: ANKOLE.

the skull. Most of the women, however, have their heads shorn; they act as their own barbers and use small sickle-shaped razors which are sharp on the convex side; they often use their own milk for lubrication.

The ears are small, unspoiled by ear-rings; the skin is velvety to the touch, and this feeling is due to the natural secretions, not to the application of grease; the voice is melodious and rather deep in tone.

Vitality of the Race.

The people do not mind the hot sun and, as a rule, do not wear any covering on the head, but they do not like cold, and have good fires in the huts on cold nights. They may be seen sitting round fires built in the open in the early morning hours. They are a hardy race, and can bear fatigue well. The inhabitants of Uganda, women as well as men, possess considerable vitality; they bear pain exceedingly well, and although when disease does occur it is frequently acute and severe, they recover wonderfully, while wounds, whether accidental or otherwise, heal readily. They do not seem to suffer pain so acutely as Europeans, but they are not such stoics as the Arabs.

It is impossible to say exactly what the usual span of life may be; puberty is attained early, and the women cease child-bearing at a comparatively early age. Grey hair is very rarely seen among either men or women.

Feminine Characteristics.

They all possess a national and distinctive odour; this is noticeable, but not so objectionable to Europeans as that exhaled by other tribes. It is certainly not due to dirty habits or to cosmetics; with one exception, which will be noted later, the people do not use any cosmetic application.

The women walk with a long, easy, swinging stride. The body is well balanced, the head slightly thrown back, the arms permitted to swing freely; the foot is well planted, the toes slightly turned out. When standing at ease, one foot is placed in advance of the other and the knees are slightly bent. All their attitudes are most graceful and unrestrained; in running and jumping their actions are easy and light. The joints of the hands and feet—which, as I have already mentioned, are small and well formed—are very supple, and care is taken to train the children from an early age to use fingers and toes, though the toes are not so useful as among some peoples.

The face of a woman in Uganda is most expressive—joy, sorrow, anger, disgust, betraying themselves on the features immediately. These women also possess the power of mimicry, though not to such a marked extent as the men. They are very strong, good walkers, and capable of lifting and carrying heavy weights; all their senses are very acute.

Deformity is very rarely observed. Sometimes an albino makes an appearance, but this is rare. Such are not liked, as they are irascible and treacherous; what causes them the people do not know. A dwarf may be seen now and then; but, when and wherever met, they are privileged nuisances.

The Waganda women (Waganda is plural for Muganda) are always clothed in a respectable manner when in the streets. The national dress is called *mbugu,* which consists of bark made from a species of fig. The women wear a loin-cloth and then the bark cloth, which is fastened round the chest just below the armpits. In King Mtesa's time the death penalty was attached to any neglect of proper clothing in the streets. In the harems, however, the younger women usually dispense with clothing altogether, or at most wear a simple string of beads round the waist.

Dress in Uganda.

It may be of interest here to explain how the bark cloth is made. The fig, which is used for this purpose, is abundant all through Uganda. The bark is taken from young trees: two incisions are made round the trunk, joined by a third which is vertical. The bark is then stripped off, and the outer surface removed with great care, and rapidly beaten with heavy wooden mallets in time to a low chant.

How Bark Cloth is made.

These mallets have circular grooved heads, which give a ribbed appearance to the *mbugu* somewhat resembling corduroy, and under the blows it very soon spreads out and becomes thin and flexible. When the proper texture has been obtained it is hung out to dry, and afterwards any holes that may have appeared during the beating are neatly patched with the trimmings from the edges and thread made from the bark or from the fibre of the plantain: a long thorn is used as a needle, and the sewing is wonderfully neat. When new, *mbugu* is a yellowish-brown, not unlike freshly tanned leather, though some of the finer qualities are a dull brick-red. The cloth varies very much in quality, the finer kinds being beautifully soft; the best is procured principally from the Sesse Islands. Its chief drawback is that it decays if it gets wet; sometimes it is dyed, generally black, or patterns in red, blue, and black are printed on it. The tree from which the bark is obtained does not die from its removal; the wound is bound up with plantain leaves, and new bark grows after a time.

Quite a number of people are employed in its manufacture; the women strip the bark from the trees and do the necessary repairing, while the men do the beating out. In 1878 Europeans had just introduced steel needles to the country, and a girl could be bought for six!

Skins are used to construct robes or mantles, and are often sewn together. The people also make very good sandals, usually out of buffalo hide; these are boat-shaped, with a thong over the instep and between the great and the second toes. They are very good tanners, and contrive to get their skins as soft as our fine kid; they are proud of their skill in this art, and laugh at those who attempt to compete with them. The

Tanning in Uganda.

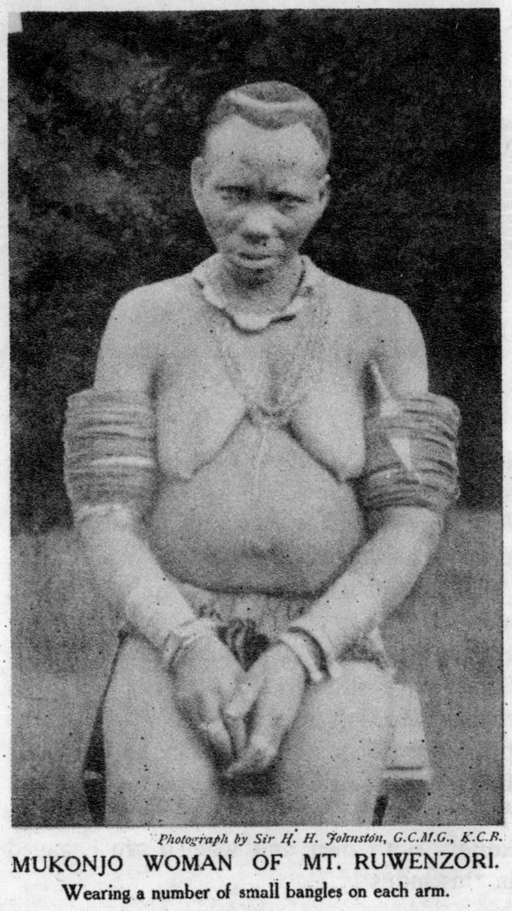

Photograph by Sir H. H. Johnston, G.C.M.G., K.C.B.

MUKONJO WOMAN OF MT. RUWENZORI.

Wearing a number of small bangles on each arm.

skins of lions, oxen, leopards, and different kinds of antelope are used for leather; in some cases the hair is removed, but for the most part it is left on. The skins are first dried in the sun, then stretched out on a frame, and the inner surface is carefully scraped with a knife. Next they are rubbed for a long time with flat stones till they are quite smooth and a fine grain is produced. After this, butter or oil is applied freely, and the skin is again exposed to the sun; this latter process is repeated several times. Some skins from which the hair has been removed are dyed; others have patterns printed on them; and the thick buffalo skins from which sandals are made have designs drawn on them with a red-hot nail or a knife. Both men and women are engaged in this industry.

The Waganda use five colours: black, green, orange-yellow, red, and blue. The black dye is obtained from the soot of a sweet-scented wood mixed with oil, the yellow from a gum exuded by a tree called *mulila*, not unlike the laurustinus. The article to be dyed is either immersed in the fluid, or else wooden stamps are smeared over and a pattern printed on with these; the common design is a lozenge-shape.

Photograph by Sir H. H. Johnston, G.C.M.G., K.C.B.

A PEASANT'S HUT, UGANDA.

Waganda Ornaments.

The Waganda women differ greatly from the men in the number of ornaments they wear; the men, as a rule, wear hardly any decorations, save perchance one or two small wire bracelets or a few little charms hung round the neck by a cord of plaited hairs from a giraffe's tail. The women, on the other hand, are very gaily decorated. They wear numerous necklaces, bracelets, anklets, and waistbands made of very fine beadwork. All these articles are extremely well made; the colours are arranged with great skill and artistic taste, and the forms are varied and unique. Some of the necklaces and bracelets are made of neatly carved wooden beads of home manufacture, and many of the women wear suspended over one shoulder or round the waist a cylindrical pocket, highly ornamented with beads; in these they carry their tobacco—for they are great smokers—coffee berries (which they chew), and various odds and ends. Some of the big chiefs' wives, as well as their lords and masters, have good, solid silver finger-rings, made from Maria Theresa dollars brought into the country by Arab traders.

African Garden Cities.

A word or two must now be said respecting the villages with their huts and compounds. The first glance at a Waganda village informs the traveller that he is in a district inhabited by a tribe very differen from any he has hitherto seen. If the place is of any considerable size he will at once notice broad, clean streets between the compounds. The groups of huts are surrounded by gardens —in fact, they are real Garden Cities! Enclosed in well-built, wickerwork walls, made from the tiger-grass or sugar-cane, supported at intervals by a species of fig-tree which throws out a large crown of branches affording a pleasant shade, may be seen the conical roofs of, probably, the largest huts in all Africa.

Even in smaller villages the streets, though narrow, are well kept, and it is rare indeed to find a hut without a courtyard in front of it. It is remarkable that the streets are straight, and that the fences, too, are straight instead of the usual circular structures seen almost everywhere else. It may be noted that the compounds occupied by the principal chiefs are very large indeed; there is only one gate, just inside of which is a small hut erected for the porter. The whole of the enclosure is divided by fences into gardens and courtyards, each yard containing one or more huts. About the centre of the compound stands the largest hut, which is occupied by the chief. The women belonging to his harem inhabit others beyond it, and separated from it by a strong hedge containing a door. The huts between

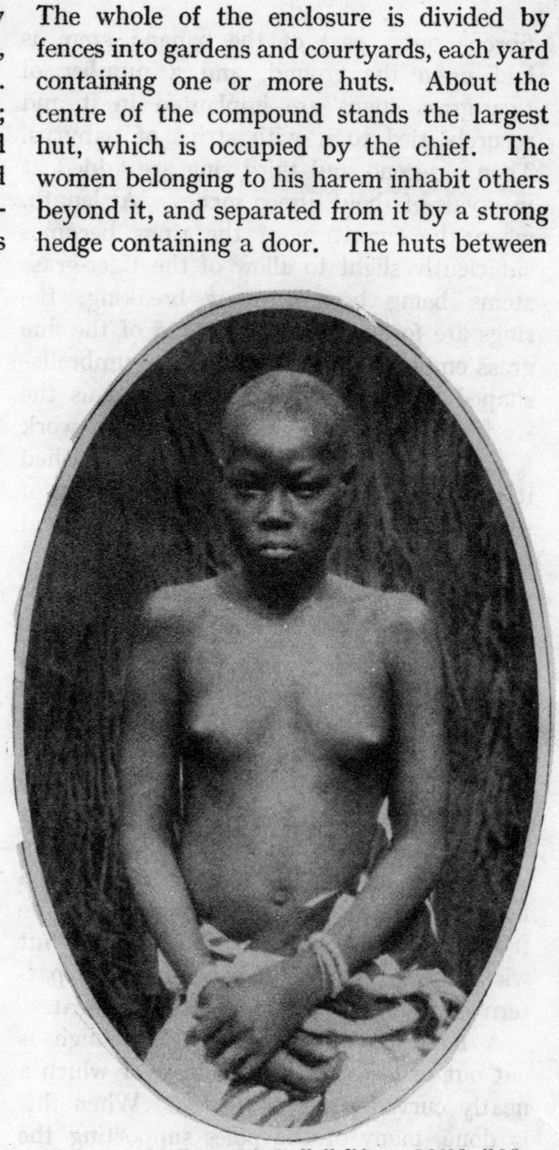

Photograph by Sir H. H. Johnston, G.C.M.G., K.C.B.

A MUGANDA WOMAN.

the chief's dwelling and the main entrance are allotted to the slaves, or are used as storehouses.

Waganda Houses, and how they are built.

The huts are dome-shaped, and, being thatched down to the ground, look like huge beehives. The materials used in erecting them are the stout stems of the tall tiger-grass, poles made from the fig-trees, and grass. They are constructed as follows: A fine ring of grass, closely enveloped with the fibrous outer part of the banana stem is laid upon the ground, and a number of tiger-grass stems are implanted in it and securely tied to it with strips of papyrus. Then a second and third ring are added at intervals of about fifteen inches. At length, when the curvature of the rings becomes sufficiently slight to allow of the tiger-grass stems being bent without breaking, the rings are formed of them instead of the fine grass employed at first, the whole umbrella-shaped frame being gradually raised as the work proceeds. This forms the framework for the top of the roof, and when it is finished it is turned over, and raised by means of poles to its requisite position. The ground to be occupied by the hut is then covered with poles in parallel lines, but decreasing in length from the centre outwards. These support the roof, and also form a scaffolding to enable the builders to complete the rafters of the roof and subsequently to thatch it. Long bundles of grass are now tied to the ribs to form the thatch, beginning from the bottom; and finally a peak, formed of a large sheaf of grass very tightly bound together, is added. The free edge of each layer of thatch is carefully trimmed to give it a regular appearance; inside the hut wickerwork walls are constructed, the pattern in many cases being extremely neat.

A large door eight or ten feet high is cut out of the side of the hut, over which a neatly curved porch is erected. When this is done, many of the poles supporting the roof are removed, and the interior of the hut is divided by numerous partitions of tiger-grass into compartments, in the innermost of which the owner's bed is constructed. The floor of the hut is level and beaten firm with clubs; the door is wicker-work, made to slide backwards and forwards, and fastened behind by a bar and pins; handles are placed in the middle of it, both inside and out, to move it with. No aperture is left for the smoke to escape.

Outside the hut a bank of earth is placed all round, consolidated by wetting and stamping, in order to prevent the water soaking into the house during the heavy rains. The floors of the huts are carefully covered with fine soft grass; first, a small bundle of even lengths is placed on the ground, another at right angles to it and partially overlapping it, and then a third at right angles to this, and so on. The wickerwork is often composed of varied-coloured grasses, and the patterns woven are various and clever. The chiefs pride themselves very much on their houses, and should they find the slightest mistake after they are finished they have them pulled down and rebuilt. The builders in such case get no compensation.

Here and there huts may be seen with gable roofs and vertical walls, but they have probably been copied from foreigners and do not need description, save that the walls are composed of three layers, the inner and outer being of wickerwork, and the middle one of grass some two feet thick.

Domestic Arrangements.

In the larger establishments huts are provided for different purposes. There is first a reception-hall, where the owner receives his guests; next his private hut, where he sleeps, has his meals, and keeps his greatest treasures. Then there are store-houses; one for dried plantains, another for *semsem* seed, which is kept in large wickerwork baskets, or pots; another serves the purpose of a cellar, and in it may be seen innumerable large bottle-gourds filled with the native drink, plantain wine, neatly corked with banana leaves. Another hut serves as a kitchen, and in it are several fireplaces constructed of three stones. People who only possess one hut use its various compartments for the purposes described. From the poles which support the roof, baskets of various descriptions are hung, suspended by ropes tied to the poles by a complicated clove-hitch. The beds are made of wickerwork, and raised a foot or two from the ground; they are covered with hides and *mbugu* cloth. In many of the huts the walls are hung with *mbugu* cloth, which is often dyed in various patterns. The huts are remarkably clean, and, on account of their large size, one is not so much oppressed by the smoke from the fire as is often the case in African dwellings. The only drawback to comfort is the grass carpet, which harbours an army of fleas. All stores of tobacco, coffee, etc., are neatly packed in banana leaves and tied with string. Remarkable order obtains in the huts, a place for everything and everything in its place being the universal practice.

Position of Women in Uganda.

As is only to be expected where polygamy prevails, women are more or less obliged to play second fiddle, especially in a place where the female population would appear to be somewhat largely in excess of the male. The numerical superiority of the women was, at the time we are considering, due to definite causes—firstly, the number of men killed in the constant tribal wars; and secondly, the numerous women taken captive in their raids.

The chiefs had many wives, and even the common men had two or three. Now, of course, since Christianity has made such headway amongst the people, matters are very considerably altered.

In 1878, however, the women were certainly considered to be inferior to men, although the principal wife or wives had a good deal of influence with their lords and masters, and all women had a rather higher status then in many African tribes.

This position is illustrated by the customs at meals and in salutation. When a woman meets a man she bends very low before him, or, if he be of high rank, will even kneel before him. Three meals are partaken of in the day; breakfast at about 7 A.M., dinner at noon, and supper soon after sunset. Each household provides its own food and eats separately. The arrangement of meals differs somewhat according to the rank of the family. In the upper classes, as a rule, the master and a few of his wives eat together, the head slaves form a different group, while the remaining wives and the children and slaves eat in their own huts. In smaller establishments the men and the women and children eat in two separate groups, whilst among the peasants men, women, and children all mess together.

All wash before meals, either with water, or with the circular napkins cut out of the succulent stem of the banana, which, containing as it does so much sap, renders water unnecessary.

Photograph by permission of C. W. Hobley, C.M.G.

A BANTU KAVIRONDO CHIEF AND HIS WIFE (STANDING).

A Woman's Day in Uganda.

About 5.30 A.M. the first signs of dawn appear; dogs bark, cocks crow, and in the huts the people begin to yawn and stretch themselves preliminary to rising. First one and then another dim form is to be seen moving about; this one unbars the door and opens it, another stirs the fire which occupies the centre of the hut into a blaze, and adds more wood. In a few minutes all is action—the men go out wrapped in their *mbugu* cloaks, and light their morning pipes; the children run hither and thither, fetching water or wood; the women place pots on the fire and set about preparing the food. Green bananas are brought, quickly peeled, one or two big leaves held over the fire to render them supple, and the bananas are then wrapped neatly up in them, and placed on sticks laid in the pots to keep them out of the water so that the fruit is steamed. When cooked they are placed on well-woven grass mats and taken to the various groups outside. This is usually all the morning meal.

After breakfast the hut is tidied up, the children are washed or made to wash themselves, then the mother may either shave the children's heads or plait their hair. Soon after breakfast the various daily occupations are commenced. The women are the real workers in the community; they clean the banana plantations, sow the sweet potatoes and other vegetables, weed the tobacco, plait, make baskets and pots. Beadwork, too, they do neatly and even artistically.

Photograph by permission of C. W. Hobley, C.M.G.

GIRL OF THE AWA WANGA TRIBE.

With head ornamentally shaven.

The women do not smoke at their work, but they do so a good deal at intervals of relaxation. After working for a few hours they prepare dinner, at the end of which they eat coffee berries, smoke, and then, perhaps, go off to "a naming of a child."

A birth is celebrated with great rejoicings, especially so should twins be born. The whole village assembles on the fifth or sixth day at the fortunate mother's hut. It is considered a very lucky event for the whole village, and the general congratulations are hearty and prolonged.

Birth Customs. The women and girls deck themselves with flowers, tie banana-leaves round their waists, and dance round drums, singing meanwhile a song adapted to the occasion. The rest of the company sit in groups, watching the dancers, drinking beer, and smoking. The father makes the round of the groups to receive the congratulations of his friends, the mother sitting in the meantime with her child at the door of the hut, where, one by one, the guests congratulate her. During a pause in the dancing the people assemble in a semicircle round the happy mother, and the eldest grandfather takes the child, and holding it up cries, "Its name is So-and-So," *e.g.*, Mwenda or Kataruba. This is greeted with shouts of "Mwenda, may he be happy, may he be brave, may he have many wives, may he become great!" and such-like good wishes for the child's future. A Waganda child receives only one name, but the variety of names among them is very great. The names of gods, animals, or insects are often given.

Or it may be that they go to a funeral, though women are buried without any ceremony whatever. When a man dies

Photograph by Sir H. H. Johnston, G.C.M.G., K.C.B.

A MARRIED COUPLE: BANTU KAVIRONDO.

a messenger is sent round to his friends to summon them to the funeral, which always takes place within twelve hours of his decease. The body is not embalmed, but simply wrapped in *mbugu* cloth, during which process his friends sing funeral dirges, and a minstrel is often engaged to sing an extempore eulogy on the man's life. The body is then carried into a jungle, where it is buried in a deep grave. Nothing is buried with the body. The friends then generally return to the dead man's hut, where a cow is killed, and a funeral feast takes place.

Funeral Customs.

Again, a wedding may be attended. These ceremonies are of a very primitive character. After a bargain has been settled for the price of a bride—in the lower classes three or four oxen—the young husband simply erects a hut and, having paid the dowry, takes his wife home with him. A little higher in the social scale a dinner is provided by the bride's father, and the afternoon and evening are spent in dancing, singing, and drinking, after which the bride and bridegroom are conducted by their friends to the new house, the door is shut, and the friends carouse outside most of the night. The next day the newly-married couple are congratulated by their friends, and a feast may take place. The songs on these occasions celebrate the joys of marriage, and detail the duties of husbands and wives.

Wedding Ceremonies.

If no such feasts occupy the afternoons the women pay attention to their children, who, from the earliest age, are well brought up. They are taught to follow their parents' occupation, strict obedience to and respect for their elders are also inculcated; but the children are happy, merry little creatures. They do not have purposeless games. Instead of the British "mud pies" they make miniature villages, copies of mountains, and rough models of men and animals in clay. They are most courteous to strangers, sitting silent in their presence, but ever ready to run on errands or anticipate the visitor's wants. They are taught physical exercises, the girls to dance and sing, the boys to fight, wrestle, and kick—but in the latter no sandals are permitted.

Education of Children.

Stories are told to the youngsters, sometimes simple jingles like "Five little pigs went to market," thus:—"*Mkasi, nyumba, mulongo, toki, mwengi*," illustrating the five chief wants of a Waganda, that is, "A woman, a hut, twins, bananas, and beer." Others again are more elaborate, sometimes a fairy-tale, sometimes a bit of folklore. Of these I will give some examples:—

A chief once had a favourite wife, to whom he committed the care of all he had. Even his other wives, and they were very numerous, were under her control. He returned home from hunting one day and called his wife, but she had disappeared mysteriously, and was nowhere to be found. This loss was a great grief to him; his household was disordered, and his other wives quarrelled. He was in despair, when one day, as he was walking in the forest and thinking of his lost wife, he cried aloud, "Oh! my treasure, could I but find you!" A honeybird flew to him, and said, "Your wife is in the sky." For a moment he was overjoyed, but then became more sorrowful than ever, for, although he might seek throughout the forest, he could not climb the clouds. A rat then came to his aid, telling him of a tree that grew very quickly, and offering to show it to him. He followed the rat through the forest until he came to a tree which was visibly growing, and the top of which had passed almost out of sight. At the rat's bidding he climbed the tree, and the honeybird kept him company and encouraged him. As he climbed higher, so the tree grew, till at length, far above the clouds, he landed in the spirit world. The spirits asked him what he wanted, and he begged for his wife, who was given to him as a reward for his perseverance, and they descended the tree together. Then he rewarded the rat and the honeybird. Some time afterwards he went to look for the tree, but it had vanished.

Waganda Fairy-Tales.

Two men once had a dispute as to which

was the most successful liar. The one proposed they should each tell lies, and that the one who told the best should be acknowledged by the other as the cleverer. His friend agreed, and asked him to begin. So he told a number of outrageous lies, and then said to his friend, " Now, how do you propose to beat me ? " " Easily," said he; " everything you have said is true—now that is the biggest lie." Then they both burst out laughing.

Some driver ants once invaded a man's hut. He was so angry that he killed a great number by setting the grass on fire. The ants went away, but held a council of war, and their leader addressed them, saying : " A man, because of his great size, injures us, for he thinks we are small ; he is cruel, so we must punish him." Messengers were then sent by the ants far and wide, and at the appointed time, the next new moon, they assembled in great numbers, so great that they could not be counted. Several leaders were then appointed, and they attacked their enemy's hut, which was soon all eaten up. Even the man, with his wives and children, were not spared. The big should not ill-treat the little.

Innumerable such stories might be given, but these will suffice to show the style of those in which they delight.

Waganda Superstitions.

The women of Uganda are very superstitious, and lay great stress on the significance of dreams, imagining that they depict and foretell future events, also that impending evil may be avoided by attention to nocturnal warnings, and that the names and faces of those who would do them harm are revealed with unerring accuracy in the night-watches.

Their daily life is thus influenced by their dreams. Evil may, they opine, accrue to them from the sprites which inhabit the trees or bask on the banks of the streams, or from the incomprehensible denizens of the sun, moon, and stars. They fancy that some demons are able to spirit away children and even grown-up men and women.

Animals, too, are in some cases supposed to have an evil character, while others possess virtues to guard and direct men. Thunder and lightning may be said to be

Photograph by permission of C. W. Hobley, C.M.G.

MARRIED WOMAN OF THE KETOSH TRIBE.

Showing scar-tattooing.

worshipped, and most diseases are referred to some deity or demon. If going on a journey, or even for a walk, it is thought unlucky to turn back, and they will always, if possible, return by a different road from the one used in going to a place. A stumble in walking is unlucky; the evil eye is believed in; charms for all sorts of purposes are used, some made of roots or stones, others of more complicated construction, such as ointments which women often use to retain their husband's love or to attract a lover. They also use charms to protect their dwellings from fire, their possessions from thieves, to ward off sickness or to cure disease. All charms are manufactured with due mystery and secrecy, in some remote forest glade, at dead of night, or on the appearance of the new moon or when it is at the full. Some charms are made of claws, teeth, or horns of animals, often blended into fantastic ornaments with highly decorated beadwork. Others consist of cunningly devised powders containing numerous ingredients such as burned roots, bark, leaves, hair, dead men's nails, and sometimes human teeth. Such powders are usually placed in horns closed by python skin, or else they are packed in neatly made boxes covered with skin.

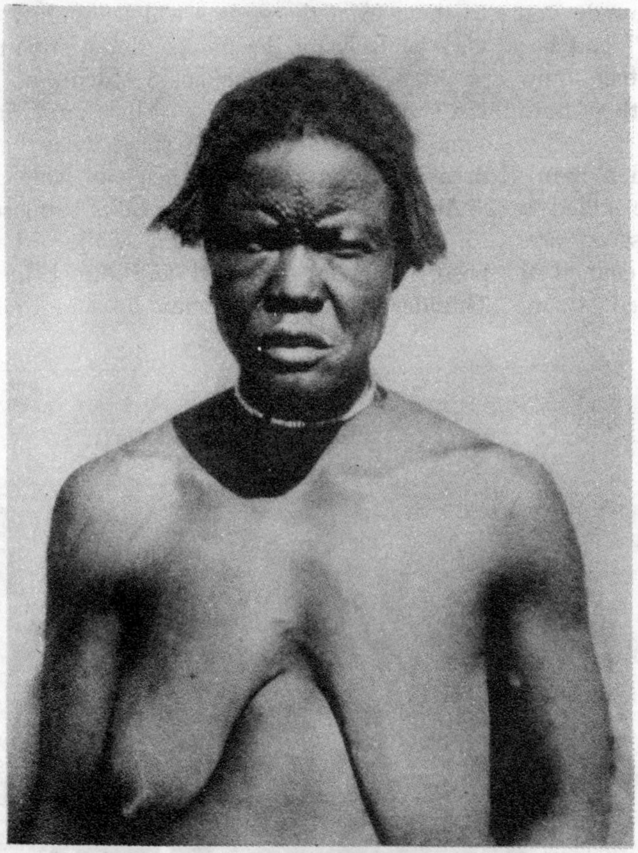

Photograph by Sir H. H. Johnston. G.C.M.G., K.C.B.

LENDU WOMAN.

Showing scar-tattooing on the forehead.

Charms are hung round the neck or waist, suspended to the rafters of the hut or over the doorway, or they may be hung on the branch of some mighty forest tree supposed to be inhabited by a demon or deity; others again are cast into a stream or lake to propitiate an offended river-deity.

Religion in Uganda.

With regard to religion, it may be taken that the people believe in a supreme deity who has created the world, and having done so, and found that his creation was good, has left it in charge of various lesser deities. The people do not in any sense worship idols. They do indeed make offerings to the god of the lake (Victoria Nyanza) and to the gods of war, thunder and lightning, but these are to be thought of as emanations of the deity. True it is that a certain "influence" envelops the trees and some localities, and to these constant votive offerings are made, but idolaters the Waganda are *not*.

If one can at all penetrate into their ideas, one must admit a natural religion higher in conception than that of many of the surrounding tribes, but not on a par with the great religions of the world. Superficial observers will think the religion colourless; those going deeper into the matter will admit that there is a great and solid substratum of truth in it; and the remarkable progress of Christianity in the past twenty years would seem to prove that the Waganda possess an innate religious consciousness.

The Waganda traditions and legends deal with the origin of the tribe and colonisation of the country, so the Kintu myth—which says that the origin of the Uganda nation was due to a man and his wife who, with a cow, a dog, and a banana-tree, set forth in search of a home and settled in Uganda—may be held as true, a myth real in fact, though doubtful in interpretation.

We must now pass on to consider briefly the Wanyoro women living just to the north of Uganda.

Photograph by Sir H. H. Johnston, G.C.M.G., K.C.B.

WOMAN OF THE BOSIA TRIBE NEAR MOUNT ELGON.

Wanyoro Women.

It will not take us long to see how they differ from their sisters a little further south. They are rather lower in the scale of progress. Generally speaking, their surroundings are less neat and tidy than those of the Waganda women, nor are their huts and persons so clean. Also they are more down-trodden and are treated more as slaves than is the case in Uganda. The people altogether are not of so markedly superior a type. The traveller will speedily observe that their faces are much less expressive.

One very curious custom obtains here—the fattening of wives. The king and some of his chiefs consider that obesity is beauty, and their wives are therefore compelled to subject themselves to a certain process of fattening to increase their charms. They are obliged to drink an immense quantity of milk, and so fat do they become that they can only crawl about on their hands and knees. Casati says: "In the centre of a column was a palankin made of ox-hide fixed on two poles, upon which one of the royal wives sat wrapt in a bright-coloured mantle of peculiar pattern. . . A cry of astonishment was uttered by everyone as a woman, almost a shapeless mass of flesh, with immense limbs and small eyes, sitting on a sort of sedan chair, and supported by stout poles, was carried across the royal threshold by four men. The accumulation of fat proceeds gradually so as to render the person unable to stand up. They are compelled to walk on their hands and knees, and even move with great difficulty."

Obesity *v.* Beauty.

These women are only allowed a handful of salt occasionally, and salt porridge made with broth twice a week.

The Wanyoro are very indolent; intelligent, however, and cleanly save for the use of unguents made of a mixture of fat and red ochre.

Character and Position of Wanyoro Women.

Another matter which exerted a great influence on the status of women in Unyoro was the fact that the king maintained a very large harem, the members of which, except about a hundred who were always on duty in rotation, were at liberty to go about the country. If they took a fancy to a man they could go and stay with him for a month at a time, taking precedence of all his wives, and on leaving might demand from him a considerable largess which they professed to take to the king. No one dare refuse either to house or to give them what they required. This custom bore very heavily on the people, and the ordinary women greatly resented it.

Wanyoro Ornaments.

The birth, death, and marriage ceremonies are much the same as those in Uganda; and the dances, music, and songs are identical or closely akin. The Wanyoro women affect ornaments to a greater extent than do the Waganda. These are made of lead, iron, and copper, and women often wear a series of anklets extending over two-thirds of the leg, while the arms may be covered with bracelets from wrist to elbow. Sometimes the rings are passed over a thin leather strap to keep them in position, and collar supports, much like those now used in this country, are used in connection with the necklaces. So does modern woman copy her primitive sister in her personal adornment! The chignon is frequently seen, but it is worn by man to increase his charms, and once fixed on it cannot be removed. These chignons are made by women.

The necklaces, bracelets, and cinctures are very tastefully made, and ornaments constructed out of finely plaited grass, to which are suspended numerous bosses covered with fine beadwork, show considerable manipulative skill in their manufacture, and taste in the arrangement of their colours. Some of the people, however, do not indulge in ornaments at all. The writer once gave a princess some European earrings and necklaces, which she refused to wear, saying that she did not need to add to her charms.

Cannibalism.

There are one or two peculiarities to be noticed before closing this brief notice of the Wanyoro. Hereditary cannibalism is known, but girls from a family so tainted will rarely find a man willing to marry them. "Earth-eating" is practised, sometimes as a cure for disease, more often to gratify a craving; it is said to result in discoloration of the skin and hair, emaciation and death.

Wanyoro Medicine Women.

The Wanyoro have a great belief in dreams foretelling coming events. Many women are like gypsies, they roam about the country, wearing a fairly distinctive dress of beadwork, feathers, skin, and innumerable charms: they drive away disease and evil spirits by means of incantations, dances, and the use of herbs and roots, cautery and cupping. The following story heard at a camp fire in Unyoro, will illustrate a few points here:—

Many years ago two men rose up before it was light, as they wished to go on a journey. They had to pass by the hut of a noted medicine woman, and were rather shy of so doing. Just as they reached the glade in which the witch lived they saw a hyena run into the hut; at that moment the sun rose, and the beast changed into the witch; the men rushed forward and caught her, and when they told their neighbours what had happened the woman was condemned to death. Before she died she said that she had eaten many folk, and she threatened the people with much ill: her threats availed nothing, and she was clubbed to death.

Women in Unyoro have the monopoly of a certain power of charming which consists in bewitching vegetable or animal food with their eyes; the person who eats the bewitched substance is immediately seized with violent pains in the stomach, which continue till the culprit is found and made to spit three times on the body of the sufferer.

Many women anoint their head with a mixture of red ochre and fat. Sometimes the whole body is rubbed with scented oil. The finger-nails are cut to a point in the middle, and the parings are carefully preserved and buried in the jungle secretly.

Curious Traditions.

If children cut the upper teeth before the lower it is a sign of evil import, and a magician is summoned to perform a dance for the child's protection.

According to Unyoro tradition the elephant and chimpanzee were once men, and the dog was gifted with speech, which, however, he used only in addressing his master.

The following Unyoro stories in this connection are interesting :—

An honest man had an only daughter, and she was wooed by a neighbour for his son who had turned out badly. The young couple lived happily for a short time, but when the young wife absented herself occasionally from the house to visit her parents her husband reproached her with availing herself of this excuse to go after other men. Each day he treated her worse, so she fled and returned to her father, to whom she related her misfortune, and he, angry at the stain which had fallen on his own and his daughter's honour, killed himself. At this moment the son-in-law arrived, and was transformed by the "Great Magician" into a chimpanzee. But the wife, who would not desert him in spite of all that had happened, followed him, and from them sprang the chimpanzees, who still talk among themselves like men, and have a fondness for women.

The leopard entrusted her three little cubs to the custody of the dog, assuring him that he should have as his recompense plenty of meat, on condition that he never gnawed the bones. The arrangement went on very well for a time, but one day the dog, yielding to temptation, gnawed a bone; a splinter flew from it and, striking a cub on the head, killed it. He found it easy to deceive the mother on her return by bringing the two survivors up to her to be fed one after the other, the first one twice. Soon the same fate befell a second cub; then the dog, seeing that his fault must be found out, fled and sought shelter with a man, who promised to protect and defend him on condition that he did not leave the house. The dog promised, but a few days later, seeing a heap of bones at a little distance, he broke his word and went out. The leopard, who had been in search of him to avenge the death of her cubs, sprang upon him, killed and devoured him; and from that day the leopard has not ceased to wage war upon dogs and to eat their flesh.

II

The Madi Women—Dress and Decoration—Eating and Drinking Customs—Women's Work among the Madi—Medical Superstitions—A Test for Insanity—Madi Religion—Curious Ceremonies—Women as Fighters—Women Workers—Position of Madi Women—Madi Marriage Customs—Polygamy—Madi Childhood—Madi Legends—The Dinka—Cattle of More Value than Women—Dinka Women's Duties—Curious Marriage Customs—Religion and Magic—Golo Witchcraft and Superstition—Tribes of the East African Protectorate—The Kikuyu Women—A "Move" among the Kikuyu—Feasting Customs—Kikuyu Religion—The Akamba—Akamba Marriage Customs—The Masai—Racial Characteristics of the Masai—Domestic Life of the Masai—Masai Marriage Customs—Masai Girls—Masai Superstitions—Attitude to Strangers

WE will now pass on to the women of the tribes of the White Nile area. As an example of these tribes we may take the Madi, who live partly on th east of the Nile, partly on the west. Broadly speaking, they represent the Shillook, Jûr (Djour), Bongo, Shuli, Makraka, Golo, Bari, Luri, and Umiro. A few words on the Dinka will be said later on; the Niam-Niam or Makraka, a cannibal tribe, must also be noticed.

The Madi Women.

The Madi are apparently pressing from east to west. There is a very gradual

Photograph by Sir H. H. Johnston, G.C.M.G., K.C.B.

MADI WOMEN ENGAGED IN HAIR-DRESSING.

Note the curious spiral growth of the hair.

movement of all African tribes in that direction, and this is why many of the habits and customs now met with on the West coast probably originated on the East or North North-East.

The Madi (sometimes called Moru) live in a large district about 50° N. lat. Their chief town was, at the period of which I am writing, called Bengue. Their women are of medium height, well formed and nourished; they do not tattoo themselves, nor do they dye the hair, which is abundant, growing in spiral tufts; when it is eight or ten inches long it is shorn, but a small ring of hair is left on the crown. The women alone act as barbers. The features are good, but the custom of extracting the four upper and lower incisors does not improve the personal appearance, and also renders the speech somewhat indistinct. Until recent times no clothes at all were worn, but a string was tied round the waist from which a small bunch of leaves hung down in front and behind. Notwithstanding that frequent ablutions are practised, these people have a strong and very distinctive aroma.

Dress and Decoration.

There is only one point which is noteworthy in regard to their cooking: they practise a custom of sprinkling some white ashes on their cooking-pots before filling them, at the same time uttering a few words, with the object of rendering the food more appetising and satisfying when cooked.

Eating and Drinking Customs.

Another of their peculiarities is that they set apart a hut in which to drink beer. This is made in large quantities from millet-seed by the women. The brew is kept in large jars and regarded as common property. No one pays for it, but none drink it elsewhere, only in the special huts, and never at meals. The people often eat in companies, the women bringing a basket, tray, or bowl containing their contribution to the common meal. The women do not wait upon the men, but the children may fetch extra supplies if required.

Women's Work among the Madi.

In this district the men do the heavy hoeing; the women's work is confined to weeding, reaping the corn, winnowing and threshing in harvest. They also extract salt from ashes. Every married woman carries a curved knife stuck in the string round her waist, the handle usually being ornamented; a common form is that of a tortoise.

Women are the chief medical practitioners; the men, who are never paid, deal only with wounds, accidents, and snake-bites. The women may receive one cow, two sheep, or a bundle of arrows in return for their services. They do not possess many medicines, and use much magic. When called to a patient the lady-doctor takes with her a basket containing what may be called her magic wand. This wand is a double tube about twelve inches long and four inches in diameter; one tube is partly filled with small stones, the other is empty so that the doctor's hand may enter it and perform certain manipulations within. The wand is painted red and oiled. On reaching the patient the woman rattles the wand and mutters incantations for some time; she then feels the patient all over, afterwards drawing the wand over him or her; when the wand comes to the painful part it is held upright over and touching it. The woman puts her hand into the empty tube, and after some manœuvring professes to draw out something which she says is the disease, but which she is careful not to display to the bystanders. Cupping is also practised. Medicine made from roots and leaves is used sometimes, especially for fever.

If the patient is a child other ceremonies take place. It is thought by the Madi that elves live underground who are called "Odi," and whose help is invoked to cure sick children. The "lady-

Photograph by permission of C. W. Hobley, C.M.G.

GROUP OF JA-LUO WOMEN.

doctor" goes to a forest glade at some little distance; there she builds a miniature hut of twigs and leaves; the child's mother then carries food and a fowl to the hut. The Odi, being then invoked, appear to the doctor, or they may say that they are busy and will come next day—they are visible only to the doctor! Usually a male and a female appear. Food is offered to them, the magic wand is shaken, and they are asked to cure the child. They reply and vanish, and the doctor falls down over the little hut, destroying it: she apparently goes into a fit or trance, and is unconscious for a short time. Before the fit comes on, however, she directs the child's mother to run home quickly, and to shut the door of the hut where the sick child lies. The doctor always provides an assistant who, after the fit passes off, raises her up, gives her water, and then assists her back to the hut; arrived there, some formula is gone through, after which she enters the hut and sees if the child will recover or not. The prognosis is usually very correct. The child's father then escorts the doctor home, taking the fee with him.

Medical Superstition.

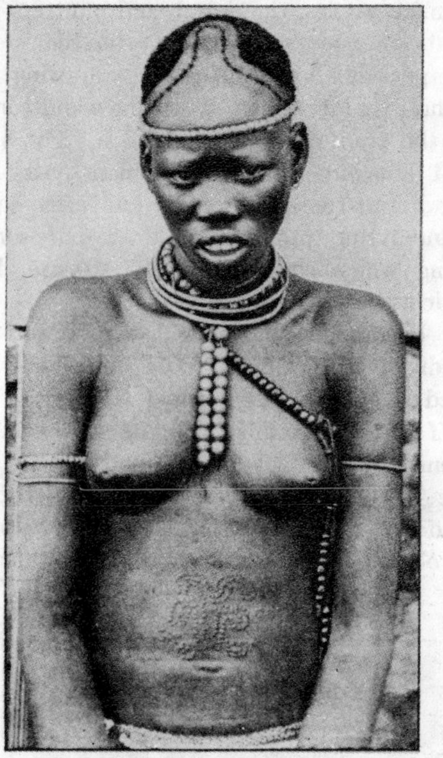

Photograph by permission of C. W. Hobley, C.M.G., and the Council of the Royal Anthropological Institute.

JA-LUO GIRL

With head ornamentally shaven and scar-tattooing.

A Test for Insanity.

It may be mentioned in passing that if the people think a person mad they hang the unfortunate being. If the birds eat the flesh, insanity is confirmed; if not, why, a judicial murder has been committed. Small consolation for the relatives or the sufferer!

Madi Religion.

The Madi have some religion—what it is, is not easy to say. They have a vague belief in a Great Being who made the world and man, also in "isa"—the soul or thinking part of man which is supposed to perish with the body. Yet they think that their departed friends can at times speak to them, but when they look for them they only see smoke. When this happens the people feel sad, and they kill a lamb and sprinkle themselves with its blood.

They are rather superstitious and believe in

Photograph by permission of C. W. Hobley, C.M.G.

MARRIED WOMAN OF THE JA-LUO TRIBE

Wearing the decorated goat-skin which is a sign of wedlock.

omens. They have two ceremonies which must be very briefly described; the first is that of "killing a lamb."

Curious Ceremonies.

About once a year, as far as can be ascertained, the whole tribe gets depressed; a great gathering takes place, and they all sit down round a circle of stones erected near a road. A lamb is then led round all the people three times by a young boy. As it passes they pluck off bits of fleece, which they place in the hair, or somewhere about their bodies. The lamb is then led to the circle of stones and killed by a man who seems to have some priestly office. He takes the blood and sprinkles the people with it four times; on the children he makes a small circle of blood over the lower part of the breastbone. The women and girls are anointed over the breast, and the men on the shoulders. The priest then gives an address somewhat as follows:—

"You who are rich, deny not a cow or a sheep to a poor man who asks for one. When you eat, do not seem unaware of a passer-by, but invite the stranger to share your meat. Children, when you see a stranger, run to your mother and ask her for water to offer to him; should you see an old woman fall, laugh not, but assist her," and so forth.

When the address, which is often very long, is over, the audience rises, and each places a leaf on, or by, the circle of stones, after which they depart in joy.

A similar ceremony on a smaller scale is held at other times—if, for instance, a family is in great trouble, to avert further evil, or at the grave of a departed relative or friend; sometimes also on a joyful occasion, such as the return of a relative from a long journey.

The "harvest home" ceremony is also of some interest. This is a feast held in the open space which is usually found in the centre of each village. The

Photograph by permission of C. W. Hobley, C.M.G.

DAUGHTERS OF A KISUMU CHIEF.

villagers may attend their own festivals only. After the feast, at which one man presides, speeches are made, and both men and women address the assembly. The old are listened to with great respect as they give good advice to the young people. The village belle makes the final oration, after which the assembly disperses. The clapping of hands expresses approval; the face is covered with the hands if a person is rude enough to show disapproval of any sentiment uttered.

When a group of villages have celebrated the "harvest home" they combine together for the first dance of the season. A band composed of drums, horns, and rattles is in the centre; around it the performers dance, the old people sitting in a wide circle. A young woman opens the ball by a *pas seul;* she then dances up to a young man, and he takes up the dance; he next invites a girl to take the floor, and so on; but in this district men and women do not dance together. The women put on their war-paint, viz., necklaces, bracelets, and anklets, and flowers in their hair.

Women as Fighters.

Women sometimes fight duels, and a fierce fight it is, for before setting-to the combatants put on iron bracelets with straight and curved spikes. After a few minutes' encounter the duellists are covered with blood, and one or both may faint from loss of it. The women are very dexterous in avoiding arrows and spears, and they teach even young children to do the same.

Women Workers.

Madi women are very skilful at weaving baskets from *dhurra* stalks; the pulp is removed, the stalk opened out flat and cut into the requisite lengths. The bottom of the basket is first made, and then the sides are worked up from it, closely woven; so close is the mesh, in fact, that these baskets will hold milk. Sometimes coloured stalks are used, and patterns formed with them. Young palm-leaves are often used for making smaller baskets. Pots are also covered with loose wickerwork, either for carrying them about or for hanging them up in the huts.

Pottery is made by women. After preparing the grey clay it is left for a day; no wheel is used, but having formed the bottom

Photograph by permission of C. W. Hobley, C.M.G

JA-LUO WOMEN, KAVIRONDO.

of the jar on a board, the women work up the sides with their hands. Some shapes are very graceful; the clay is ornamented with the fishbone pattern, and the pots are painted either black, or red, or black and red. They are then placed in a hut for a day or two, next in the sun, and finally fired. A good trade in pottery is done by the women, and they keep a store of it to sell to neighbouring tribes.

The women also make fine twine and small nets, but the making of rope and fishing-nets is men's work.

Position of Madi Women.

Madi women have a very good time on the whole; they are respected and well treated by the men; if ill, they are tenderly cared for, and at no time are they the beasts of burden that some of their sisters are.

Any insult to a woman meets with a speedy retribution. The greatest insult that can be offered to a man is to revile his mother—only by blood can such an offence be atoned for. Women are buried in this district, and the mourning lasts for a month. Very different this from some tribes among whom, though a man's body is buried, a woman's is simply thrown into the bush! A man when dying is surrounded by his family, and he always exhorts his eldest son to take good care of his mother.

Madi Marriage Customs.

Just a few of the marriage customs may be mentioned. The Madi may not marry amongst their own friends, but usually get a wife from a neighbouring village. When a young man is ready for marriage, his father makes a tour throughout the neighbourhood to find a suitable bride for the lad. Having made his choice, he ties a twig of a certain tree round the girl's wrist, usually the left, and then asks her father's permission for her to marry his son. If the price in cows and sheep can be amicably settled, little further difficulty is likely to arise. Or, if in his travels a young man sees a girl who takes his fancy, he may, if she be willing, tie the twig round her wrist, and she will then go home and tell her mother, who tells her father; he settles the price, which is then communicated to the young man's father, and if he agrees the match is made. If the parents do not consent the marriage is broken off, as the young people obey their parents and run-away matches are unknown. Before the marriage the engaged couple can meet as often as they like. The young man works hard to get together as much property as he can, and the girl's father builds her a new hut, into which she goes a few days before the marriage takes place. Wedding presents are as great a tax there as here, and all friends are expected to help the couple in providing household stores.

On the morning of the wedding-day a number of boys take the cattle which form the bride price, each boy leading one cow or sheep by a string, the animals being decked with flowers. A group of girls accompanies them, but the bridegroom remains behind. A cow is killed by the brothers of the bridegroom, if he has any; if he has no brother, then his nearest friend takes his place, and a feast is held, lasting for two days. During this time the bride must not leave her hut. She is not, however, quite alone, as her future brothers- and sisters-in-law keep her company, and tell her what a good husband she will have. They bring her food, but it is not the correct thing for her to be seen eating. On the third day another cow is killed, and dancing follows the feast. The bride now appears, accompanied by her brothers-in-law, who walk behind her to the centre of the dancing-ground, around which the company is collected. The bride is left alone, and she then dances the wedding dance accompanied by special music. The longer she can dance, the more she is applauded and the prouder she is; word is sent to the bridegroom as to how she has acquitted herself. Next day she rests, and the day following the bridegroom arrives with his unmarried friends, enters the hut, and claims his bride. The newly-married couple spend a week or ten days in the bride's village, during which time the bridegroom's father builds a new hut. When the bride

IN THE MARKET AT KISUMU.

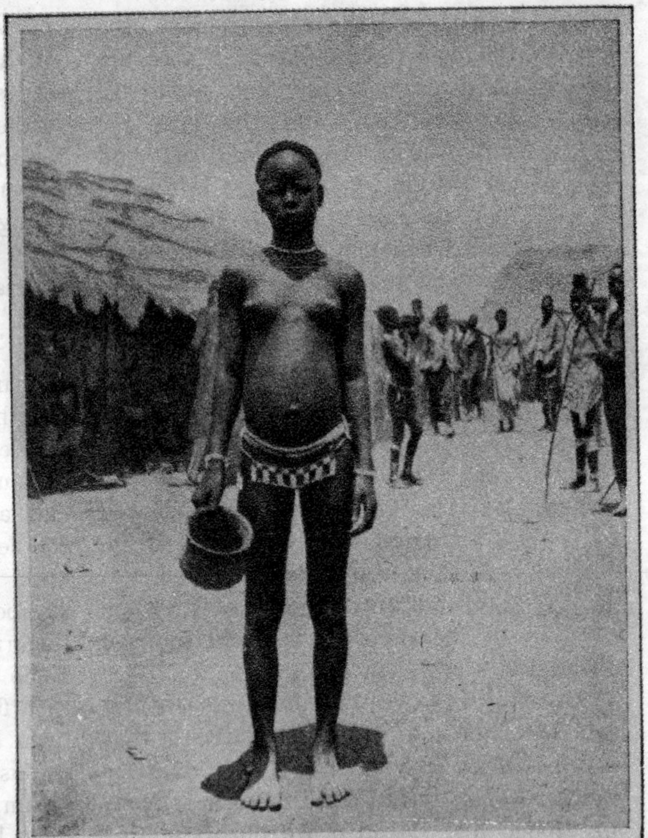

Photographs by permission of A. C. Hollis.

NATIVE GIRL IN KISUMU MARKET.

and groom arrive a sheep is killed before the hut, and they enter over the body of the dead animal.

Polygamy. Polygamy is permitted, but this and divorce are both rare. The greatest number of wives allowed is four, and usually an interval of two years must elapse before a new wife is taken. Each wife has a separate hut, and the husband must apportion his time equally between his wives; if he does so the ladies generally keep on very good terms with each other. The Madi women make capital wives, and married life is apparently a very happy state among them.

About a week after a child is born an assembly of friends is called together; a fowl is killed, some of its blood is applied to the child, and it is given a name, often the name of the season, *e.g.*, Krauobi, famine; Kradaru, hunting season; a child may be named after a deceased relative, rarely after a living one.

Madi Childhood. Family names are not used, but a son takes his father's name as well as his own.

The babies are carried slung in a skin which has been well tanned and is very soft; the child's body is under the mother's arm, the head behind—it is often covered with a gourd to protect it from the sun.

Considerable care is taken in the training of the children. They are taught to eat properly, not to put their hands into the dishes until their elders have begun to eat, to rise as soon as finished, wash their hands and mouths, and retire to a little distance. They are taught to be silent when their elders are speaking, to salute their superiors, and to show kindness to the aged and the sick.

The girls are trained in cookery, and

various domestic and matrimonial duties; they are taught to dance, to elude arrows, to carry water and collect firewood, to show hospitality to strangers, and in due course to take care of infants. The education of both boys and girls is considered incomplete until they have travelled. When about ten years old, both boys and girls are sent to visit friends in the surrounding villages.

The Madi women may be said to illustrate the well-known fact that the fewer clothes a woman wears the more modest and moral she is, for the Madi are a great contrast in this respect to the well-clothed and most immoral Waganda and Wanyoro.

Madi Legends.

The Madi have many legends about animals, of which the following is a short example:—"A monster lion is said to have shaken the earth by his roars. The shock was so great that all the people fell to the ground, and the lion proceeded to eat them. One man, however, entreated the Being who had created both man and beast to make the lion a little smaller, as he was too great and powerful for man; his request was granted, and the lion was at once reduced in size to his present dimensions."

The Dinka.

The Dinka are subdivided into about four groups—the Kesh, Atwot, Gok, and Agar—and occupy the district on the west bank of the White Nile, about 7°30′ to 8°30′.

The people are tall, very tall, sometimes lanky—"stalk-like," Schweinfurth called them. The women wear a belt round the waist, from which is suspended a short apron in front and a longer one behind them, for all the world like a swallow-tailed coat! They adorn themselves with numerous bracelets, anklets, and necklaces, and a series

Photograph by permission of C. W. Hobley, C.M.G.

WOMEN OF THE NANDI TRIBE.
Showing wire armlets and other ornaments.

of small earrings in each ear. They always shave their heads, but do not smear themselves with oil and ashes as the men do; oil alone is considered sufficient.

In some parts of this district huts built upon piles are to be seen; the ground around the huts is beaten into a hard plaster, on which the women grind the corn, do their cooking, etc. The huts have very small doors and no windows.

Photograph by permission of C. W. Hobley, C.M.G.

WOMEN OF THE SÛK TRIBE NEAR LAKE BARINGO.

Showing wire armlets and other ornaments.

The position held by Dinka women is not so satisfactory as that of the Madi. Polygamy prevails, and a man will have as many wives as he can contrive to purchase. They pay for them with cattle, and the Dinka are the greatest cattle-breeders on the White Nile.

Cattle of more Value than Women.

Photograph by permission of C. W. Hobley, C.M.G., and the Council of the Royal Anthropological Institute.

LUMBWA WOMAN AND YOUNG GIRL.

Showing ear-plugs and distorted lobes.

It has been well said that cattle occupy all their thoughts, and doubtless it is the greed for cattle which causes the frequent feuds, not only among the various divisions of the tribe, but also with neighbouring tribes—feuds arising from "cattle-lifting," and resembling those which used to be carried on between the lowlands of Scotland and the northern counties of England.

The sheep are of a peculiar breed, with a mane-like covering on the head and shoulders, the rest of the body to the meagre tail being clothed with short hair. As Schweinfurth remarked, this tribe seem to hold their cattle in reverence, for they never slaughter them, but tend them carefully when sick, and use them for food only if they die. If the cattle are captured in war, the Dinka will willingly redeem them with their wives and daughters, so great is their attachment to the beasts. Schweinfurth estimated that there were three head of cattle to one of the human population, but the population has greatly altered since then.

The women are not employed in tending the cattle in any way, but they are very good housekeepers, and used to be in great request as domestic slaves, notwithstanding that they were very troublesome and much less docile than the women of other tribes. It is not, therefore, surprising to find that they keep the houses exceedingly clean. They are first-rate cooks and clean eaters; the food is passed round in pots or platters, and the people eat one after the other, all having washed before commencing the meal.

Dinka Women's Duties.

In this tribe only the four lower incisors are removed at puberty.

Marriage is conducted on the same lines as in the Madi district, but there may be said to be two distinct classes of wives—those paid for in cattle and hoe-blades, and those obtained by capture. The former hold the superior place in the household, though the children of both are equal in status.

Curious Marriage Customs.

When a man dies, his wives are inherited by his son; if children are born to the son they are reckoned to be his brothers or sisters.

It is a recognised custom that old men should marry young wives, who are, in fact, married to their sons, but whose children are looked upon as the old man's offspring, and counted as the brothers and sisters of their real fathers. The women nurse their children till they are old enough to fetch water for their fathers to drink.

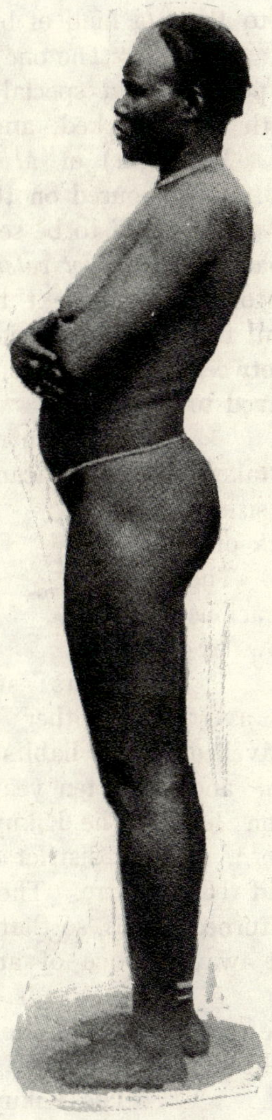

Photograph by Sir H. H. Johnston, G.C.M.G., K.C.B.

A KARAMOJO WOMAN.

A Great Spirit is believed to have made heaven and earth, and once upon a time there was a roadway or ladder between the two and communication was easy. A small hut was built in each village, and sacrifices and offerings were made before war or in times of distress. Should it rain during a sacrifice before a journey it is postponed. A devil, or evil spirit, is recognised, who was once a friend of the Great Spirit, but they quarrelled.

Religion and Magic.

The Dinka believe that the spirits of the departed have the power to revisit the earth; their appearance is of evil import. They believe in white and black magic, and black magicians are often killed.

They have a very strong feeling that neighbouring tribes possess collective magic, especially the Jûr. Cattle disease may therefore, they think, be caused by some tribe living upon their borders, and not infrequently fights take place on this supposition.

The women as a rule do not take part in the fighting, but hide in the bush with the children. Nevertheless they can give a very good account of themselves if they should be compelled to fight.

The writer did not come into close contact with the Golo, and he therefore gives an extract from Captain S. L. Cummins' article on them. (*See* "*Anthropological Journal,*" vol. xxxiv. p. 164 *et seq.*) :—

Golo Witchcraft and Superstition.

"Witchcraft is widely believed in, and all misfortunes are attributed to it. The evil eye is greatly feared. The charming of roots and stones into the body of an enemy is as widely attempted, and as firmly believed in, as among the Dinka; and the method of cure (the root being sucked out by a wise man) is identical.

"Ghosts are believed in, but are supposed to be very rare. When seen they are always the harbingers of death or disaster to the beholder.

"The shadows (Vu-vu) of things and people are regarded as important. At death the shadow departs to the place of God. The word 'Vu-vu' is used in the sense of soul when speaking of the departed.

"The Golo theory of dreams is that the shadows of things and people enter into the dreamer's mind during sleep. From this it would appear that the connection between the shadow and the substance is believed to be severed during sleep.

"When on the march the Golo will take a stone, or a small ant-heap (about the size of a man's head), and place it in the fork of a tree, to retard the setting of the sun. The fact that this is believed to be efficacious shows that the Golo does not allow experience to shatter illusions.

"Various charms are worn to avert evil. For instance, a man, who travelled to the country of the Niam-Niam and back with a letter, showed me, on his return, a grass-seed that he had worn, of a kind locally called *Magar*. He said that lions, meeting him on the road, turned their faces from the charm, and crept away into the bushes.

"The Golo's God is named Umvile (pronounced Umveeley). He is the father of mankind by his wife Barachi.

"Umvile lives above the earth, in a place called Van-do-Bah. The word in this connection means heaven, but ordinarily means a house and its surroundings. Bah means a house.

"The souls (Vu-vu) of the virtuous after death go to heaven, but a Satan named 'Hah' employs himself, at God's command, in burning the souls of the wicked.

"It is interesting that the Golo believe Satan to be the servant of God.

"Prayers are not offered to God, but in times of sickness and trouble He is propitiated with sacrifices.

"The sacrifice is carried out as follows: A feast is made; about twenty chickens are killed, and the first of these is kept for Umvile. The remainder are cooked, and eaten with *Marisa* (native beer) and *Kissra* (a kind of bread).

"The one chicken kept for Umvile is placed in a special hut, without being cooked or plucked, and next it is placed a *Bourma* (jar) of *Marisa*. Possibly the *Marisa* is poured on the ground. If the offerings are still to be seen next day, they are removed, but *not eaten*. A little house is said to be built next their own houses by the Golo for sacrificial purposes. I have not seen such houses. There are no priests."

Tribes of the East Africa Protectorate.

We turn now to the tribes inhabiting the East African Protectorate between Uganda and the Indian Ocean. Until recently very little has been known of them: those living near the coast have been under Arab influence for hundreds of years: still the Masai, Kikuyu, Kamba and other tribes have not much altered their habits and customs until within the last ten years.

The Kikuyu, to take an example, live in the district of which Mount Kenia forms a centre. Their villages are built upon hilltops, so that their watchmen may give early notice of any threatened raid upon their homesteads. We are indebted to Mr. H. R. Tate for the greater part of what follows.

The Kikuyu Women.

The Kikuyu people are a hardy, prolific, well-built race, dark reddish-brown in complexion; living as they do amongst the hills, their legs are much better than those of other tribes—the legs being the weak part of most African races. They are hard-working, thrifty, and moral. Agriculture in this district is very well conducted, the field work being done by the women. The people, owing to Masai raids, are distrustful and treacherous until real friendship has been established.

Photograph by H. Binks, B.E.A

KIKUYU GIRLS POUNDING GRAIN.
Showing the curious methods of ear distortion.

As the women do most of the manual labour they age early. Comparatively few cattle are kept, and even those few are never used for food, so that the women must work hard to keep the household well fed. They have a larger variety of food than some of the tribes, as they cultivate sweet potatoes, yams, *sem-sem*, bananas, and sugar-cane. The only use made of the cattle is to buy wives or to settle fines with them, or to pay blood-money in case a man has committed murder or some great crime. The women marry very young; they are very clean and tidy, and shave their heads with the exception of a circular crown of hair at the back.

A triangular notch is filed in the two upper incisors, while the two lower ones are frequently extracted.

For clothes, the women wear three garments made of skin; the married ones wear a poncho which reaches below the knees, with no sleeves, and open in front; a small apron is worn, and a half-petticoat is suspended round the waist. Before marriage they adorn themselves with innumerable bracelets, anklets, earrings; the ears are stretched and pierced to admit large discs of wood, which greatly disfigure them. After the birth of the first child most of these ornaments are discarded.

Photograph by permission of A. C. Hollis.

KIKUYU GIRL WASHING CLOTHES.

The eyebrows are shaved off and the ears laden with ornaments.

Curiously enough, the women in this tribe do not make their own clothes, this duty falling to the lot of mere man. The latter, however, are adepts at the work, and turn out very passable garments, in spite of the fact that they have to sew with eyeless needles! Both men and women are tattooed, the latter being the operators.

Married women have each a hut to themselves; the unmarried girls occupy a hut apart.

When the people move to a new site, to build either a single hut or a village, the owner pours some porridge upon the ground,

Photograph by permission of A. C. Hollis.

KIKUYU WOMAN.

Carrying gourd vessel.

A "Move" among the Kikuyu.

as does his chief wife. Then a prayer is offered to *Ngai*, asking that a prosperous home may rise upon the site, and that property, wives, and fruitful fields may be his while he lives. Building is then begun, and at its conclusion a sheep is killed. Wine is made, and drunk by the men and married women, and a little is spilt on each new hut. Before moving from the old site the man sends a goat to a neighbour to take care of until the building is completed, when the animal is taken to the new house, and to ensure good luck the head wife of the chief sucks a little blood from a wound in the neck of the animal; her husband must sleep in her hut the first night of occupation, or she will be grievously offended.

Feasting Customs.

When the women return from work in the fields at night they bring in firewood and cook the supper, and also food for the next morning, as all the people eat before going to work. The women and children eat together, the men apart.

The oldest woman in a village plays the chief part in the sacrifice of sheep and goats to *Ngai* every three months.

The animals being killed and cooked, the men eat a goat, the women a sheep; after all are satisfied, the oldest woman takes a piece of fat from the entrails, stands in the centre of a group of the people, holds it

Photograph by permission of C. W. Hobley, C.M.G.

N'DITO, OR YOUNG UNMARRIED GIRL OF THE LUAS'NGISHU MASAI.

Showing the enormous ear-plug used as an ornament.

aloft, and then prays to *Ngai* for prosperity to the village, to the men, women, and children, husbands for the women, and health for the flocks and herds. She promises good conduct on the part of members of the village, and finally places the fat on the embers.

The next day is a feast day, and the older people get drunk, but the younger are only allowed to drink sufficient to produce a certain amount of exhilaration. For eight days after this, men and women remain apart, to insure fertility in their flocks.

Kikuyu Religion.

All disease is thought to be produced by the "bad deity"; they do not think a demon enters into a sick person.

They believe in a God of Fire, seen at times in a camp fire, not in the huts; a man may be carried into the air by this power, and told how to propitiate *Ngai*. Should this happen, a feast is held next day; a sheep and a she-goat are sacrificed beneath a spreading sacred tree, and the elders eat the flesh; the skin is cut into strips and given to the women for luck, and they wear it as a necklace. Men, women, and children drink blood, or blood mixed with milk.

Tate says:—"The Akikuyu make small images of clay which represent men and women. They are not idols, but seem more in the nature of dolls; the children play with them, and in a dance between unmarried men and girls the former carry the dolls, both male and female, in the palms of their hands. These images seem to be part of a game concerning which the Akikuyu are unwilling to say much. It is also stated that they are used in certain ceremonies, such as the praying for rain, and the celebration of the gathering in of crops."

When people sacrifice to *Ngai*, the meal is placed in the sacred tree, the worshippers crossing their lips with a piece of meat before sacrificing. As this tribe regards spiritual powers much as do the Masai, nothing more need here be said concerning them.

The marriage customs do not vary from those mentioned elsewhere.

Of the Akamba tribe in the East Africa Protectorate, Mr. Tate says:—"The people are moderately well built, of a medium height, their brown skin being a shade darker than the Akikuyu's. The young girls shave their heads two or three times a year, but do not keep the head as closely shorn as do the married women. The front teeth are filed to a point for ornamental purposes. The young women are fairly good-looking, but hard work and family cares soon render them dull and ugly.

The Akamba.

The young unmarried girls wear two garments—an apron, a cloth, some six inches deep and fourteen long, and a flap slightly larger behind—both being secured round the waist by a beadwork belt. The married women dress similarly, but with more ample material.

Until the children can walk they are carried slung in a leather sling on their mothers' backs, their legs being around the mothers' loins. Girls wear an apron from the time they can walk.

After the birth of the first child the women discard the ornaments they had previously worn to attract lovers; these consist of strings of blue and white bead necklaces, the waist and ankles being bound round with strings of small white beads. The aprons are embroidered with cowries or beads as well as the belts. Sometimes a leather cape decorated with beadwork is worn at dances; this cape falls as low as the mid-arm.

Akamba Marriage Customs.

After a marriage has been arranged by the payment of three or four cows, the bride runs away and pretends to hide. The bridegroom and a small party of friends start out to hunt for her, and when caught she is carried to the bridegroom's hut, accompanied by a merry crowd of women and girls. She is taken into the hut, and, after some horseplay, is left for three days with her husband. At the end of that time she is escorted back in procession to her father's hut for a feast, and then begins the usual round of domestic duties at her new home. Polygamy prevails; a man may have five or six wives, and he is not at all averse to lending one or more to a friend who may happen to be childless.

MASAI WOMAN : BRITISH EAST AFRICA.
Drawn by Norman H. Hardy.

Facing on page 266

The Akamba cannot be said to be a very moral race, and open flirtation is far from unknown. Even married women may be seen carrying on flirtations under their husbands' very eyes. The lover is expected to pay the husband for the wife's fancies, however!

The Masai.

The first and best description of the Masai, the great warlike tribe of East Central Africa, was published in 1885 by Joseph Thomson. It is to his account and to the works of Sir H. H. Johnston and Mr. A. C. Hollis that one chiefly turns for information as to this interesting people, now woefully diminished by war, disease, and famine.

There are many divisions of the tribe, some of less pure breed than others, and war frequently broke out between them—war by declaration, not the sudden, treacherous raiding which so often obtains among savage tribes, and which the Masai themselves were wont to practise before the "*Pax Britannica*" put a limit to such excesses.

The Masai are not Bantu, and they hold a position distinctly superior to that of other Central African tribes.

Racial Characteristics of the Masai.

In facial configuration they are not unlike Europeans, for the nose is less depressed, and the lips are thinner than those of other tribes. The head is broader than in Bantu races, and the face has almost a Mongolian look, with slanting eyes, pointed chin, and rather prominent cheek-bones. The nose is "often beautifully shaped, with high bridge, and delicately curved nostrils, which obey sensitively the passing feelings of the owner, quivering and dilating with pride and rage, or widening and relaxing with good humour." The hair is longer and wavier than with the true Negro.

Naturally large, the ears of the Masai are distorted and rendered more noteworthy by the ornaments they affect. Even small children pierce holes through the lobes of the ears and place twigs in them, till at last the lobe can contain a disc of wood some five or six inches in diameter, the lobe of the ear being replaced, as it were, by a loop of tough, cartilaginous skin. At times a wooden stretcher with a groove on each side is used to extend the ear. Iron chains, changed after marriage to copper-wire discs, are also suspended from the ear. The hairs of the eyebrows are pulled out, and beards are scanty or absent. The teeth are bad (this is unusual in Africa), and the mouth when open displays hideous, discoloured fangs. The notch filed between the two upper incisors is used for spitting through—for to spit at a person is a mark of great respect and friendship, and it is reckoned an insult to wipe off the saliva!

The Masai arms are long in proportion to the body, and the fingers as a rule reach to the knee when the arms are pendent.

Domestic Life of the Masai.

Boys and girls are called *en-gesa* (a kind of sheep) till they are about three; then the boys are called *en-aiok* until puberty, after which they are termed *el-barnode;* and, finally, when they go to war they receive the name *el-moran*. The various tribes of Masai are easily distinguished by the distinct heraldic devices clearly depicted on the warriors' shields in black, white, red, or yellow.

The girls continue to be called *en-gesa* until puberty, and afterwards *en-doya*. Clothing usually is conspicuous by its absence.

The Masai huts are not beautiful erections; they are merely oblong boxes, three and a half feet high, nine feet long, and five broad, made of bent and woven boughs, giving a flat roof with rounded ends, and coated with cows' dung and hides to keep out the wind and rain. These huts are placed in a rough circle forming the enclosure for the cattle, and all are surrounded by a thick thorn hedge to protect the dwellers from the attacks of man or beast. Here dirt reigns supreme!

Girls are at a disadvantage in this tribe; boys are welcomed, girls are not. Nevertheless there is an excess of women owing to the fights which used to be of such constant occurrence.

Photograph by Sir H. H. Johnston, G.C.M.G., K.C.B.

WOMEN OF THE PASTORAL MASAI IN FRONT OF THEIR PECULIAR FORM OF HOUSE.

Masai Marriage Customs.

The men marry somewhat late in life, after their fighting days are done. Then, having bought a bride, a betrothal takes place, but the marriage is deferred till the following calving season, as a great deal of milk is considered essential to the honeymoon. During the period of "engagement" the girl lets her hair grow, and wears round her head a band covered with cowries, from which hang a number of strings forming a bridal veil. The marriage ceremony itself consists in discarding the chain earrings and substituting the copper-wire discs, shaving the head, and for the first time donning real clothes. These garments are an apron in front, and a skin suspended from the shoulders behind. The husband wears his bride's discarded apron for a month!

The Masai usually have two or more wives, for they are very anxious to have a goodly number of children.

The women design and frequently build the huts; they likewise do the cooking, so their occupations do not lack variety. The pots and household utensils are made by a sub-tribe, the Andorobbo, who also make the warriors' shields; the spears, swords, and knives are made by the Elkonono, a tribe of slaves.

Thomson describes the Masai girls who live with the *el-moran* as follows:—

Masai Girls.

"Happily facts support the verdict of gallantry when I say that they are really the best-looking girls I have ever met in Africa. They are distinctly ladylike in both manner and physique. Their figures are slender and well formed without the abnormal development about the hips characteristic of the Negro. They share, like the men, the dark gums and the bad sets of teeth. The hair is shaved off totally, leaving a shiny scalp. As to dress, they are very decent, and almost classical, if a stinking, greasy hide can have anything to do with things classical. They wear a dressed bullock-hide from which the hair has been scraped. This is tied over the left shoulder, passing under the right arm. A beaded belt confines it round the waist, leaving only one limb exposed. Frequently it is slipped off the shoulder, and depends entirely from the waist, leaving the bosom exposed. Their ornaments are of a very remarkable nature. Round the legs from the ankles to the knees telegraph wire is coiled closely in spiral fashion. So awkward is this ornament that the wearer cannot walk properly, she cannot sit down or rise up like any other human being, and she cannot run. Round the arms she has wire similarly coiled both above and below the elbow. Round the neck more wire is coiled—in this case, however, horizontally—till the head seems to sit on an inverted iron salver. When these ornaments are once on they must remain till finally taken off, as it requires many days of painful work to fit them into their places. They chafe the ankles excessively, and evidently give much pain. As they are put on when very young, the calf is not allowed to develop, and the consequence is that when grown up the legs remain at a uniform thickness from ankle to knee—mere animated stilts, in fact. The weight of this armour varies according to the wealth of the parties, up to thirty pounds. Besides the iron wire, great quantities of beads and iron chains are disposed in various ways round the neck."

It is strange that, after leading a free and easy life in the camps with the warriors,

Photograph by permission of A. C. Hollis.

WOMEN OF THE PASTORAL MASAI IN FRONT OF A HOUSE.

Showing the coils of telegraph wire used as ornaments.

the women should ever settle down to sober married life, yet they do so, although their morals are not of the highest.

The Masai have peculiar views with regard to milk, which is held to be a sacred

Photograph by Sir H. H. Johnston, G.C.M.G., K.C.B.

WOMAN OF THE PASTORAL MASAI.

fluid. It is never given or sold to strangers, by the men at least; the women are not quite so strict, and may be bribed to provide the traveller with it on the sly. But woe betide the luckless wight who boils the milk!—he will find himself in a very awkward position, since this is regarded as a deadly insult to the cows, who retaliate by refusing to give any more.

Masai Superstitions.

The Masai, unlike the Bantu, do not believe in ghosts, nor do they pay any attention to dreams as do the other tribes we have mentioned. They do understand that there is a God, but their ideas about him are vague, although they pray to him constantly—in fact, nothing can be undertaken without hours of prayer. They also believe in a sort of earth spirit called Neiterkob. They have faith in witchcraft, though the powers of the medicine-man lie not in any innate attributes of his own, but in his power of intercession with their god *Ngai*, who works through him and imparts magical virtues to various objects. *Ngai* is thought to dwell amongst the snows of Kilimanjaro.

Grass is their most sacred object; held in the hand it is a sign of peace and welcome, thrown on any person or place it is an invocation for a blessing on that person or place.

One word in conclusion must be said on the attitude of East African women to strangers. In whatever district it may be one's lot to wander, these African women show themselves kindly, courteous, and willing to please. As an illustration of their ready gratitude for kindness the following little story is given of an incident which befell the writer:—

Attitude to Strangers.

I was marching with a small party of Waganda towards the Egyptian frontier. The soldiers, as was the custom when on the king's business, robbed the poor people in the villages we passed through, while I could do little to prevent such behaviour, as I had only one faithful boy with me. One morning the inhabitants of a village were incensed by the men drinking up all their banana wine, stealing their poultry, and generally misbehaving themselves. The leader of the escort was rather frightened at the angry voices and gestures of the people his men had raided, and gave orders for a speedy retreat. He had with him his wife and two servant-girls, one of them a pretty Wahuma maid. The path we followed was very rough and thorny, and a few hours after starting I noticed this girl sitting at the side of the path, vainly endeavouring to extract a thorn which had pierced her foot. Her master was angry at the delay and struck her, telling her roughly to get up and move on, but, seeing the girl's pain, I stopped, and to her great relief soon extracted the thorn.

On and on we marched while the sun beat down on us, hotter and hotter as the day advanced, so that we were all glad when about noon a halt was called, and we were told we could rest for an hour or two in a forest glade. After eating a few bananas and drinking a cup of coffee I leant against a fallen tree and fell sound asleep. I must have slept for some time when I was awakened by a cool hand placed on my forehead, and on opening my eyes I saw the Wahuma girl holding my revolver with the butt-end towards me as she cried, "Wake! we are attacked." I hardly needed her words to inform me of this fact, for spears were flying over us, and as I sprang up, one passed through my sleeve and buried itself in the tree on which I had been resting. I emptied my revolver over the attacking natives' heads, and they at once halted, not understanding how I could fire six shots without reloading. Afterwards they told me they thought I must be the devil to be able to fire more than two shots!

Photograph by Sir H. H. Johnston, G.C.M.G., K.C.B.

WOMAN OF THE NAIVASHA MASAI.

Showing the distorted ear-lobe in which ornaments are strung.

What had happened was this. Whilst I slept, some of the men had again been stealing at a village near our halting-place, and the natives in revenge had attacked and driven off their tormentors. The girl, hearing the noise of the fight, had wished to save me out of gratitude for the help I had rendered her that morning. The commonsense she displayed greatly pleased me, and this incident shows, I think, both the quick wit and the good feeling of the African native.

ZULU GIRLS AFTER BATHING.

Photograph by B. W. Caney, Durban.

SOUTH AND SOUTH-WEST AFRICA

By ALICE WERNER

The Great Bantu Race—General Position of Women in South Africa—A Missionary's Evidence—Polygamy no Hindrance to Happiness—Misconceptions of African Life—The Brighter Side of African Life—Tribal Wars and Witchcraft—The Zulu—Zulu Girl Life—The Old Zulu Marriage Law—How Zulu Marriages are now Arranged—Zulu Marriage Ceremonies—The Hair and its Ornamentation—Celibacy a Reproach—Restrictions upon Zulu Women—A Zulu Lady Godiva—Women as Food-finders—Women as Brewers—Zulu Tailor-made Costumes—Skin Cradles—Women as House Builders—Zulu Cookery—Zulu Basket-work—Doctors and Witches—Treatment of Widows

The Great Bantu Race.

SOUTH AFRICA—indeed, all Africa as far north as the Equator, and a considerable area beyond it—is mainly peopled by the Bantu race; so that we shall have to deal chiefly with Bantu tribes in the following pages. The few exceptions will be noted as they occur. As might be expected in the case of a people extending over so many degrees of latitude and living under such diverse conditions, the various tribes differ greatly in physique, customs, and institutions; but all of them have a great deal in common, as is shown (to take one point only) by the close affinity between their languages; and it is evident that the groundwork of their social organisation, where this has not been broken up by outside influences, is everywhere much the same. We may, therefore, before proceeding to deal with the women of each tribe separately, consider very briefly the position of women among the Bantu in general.

General Position of Women in South Africa.

There are several misconceptions current on this subject. It is popularly supposed that the African woman is a poor, degraded, down-trodden being, with no rights and no morals, subjected to constant ill-treatment, and (it is added, in some cases) deserving little better. Mistaken views like this—arising, in the first instance, from imperfect or careless observation—are repeated by one writer after another till they come to be accepted articles of belief, which it seems almost impertinent to call in question. Usually they are based on accounts of some custom taken by itself, and not in connection with the national life of which it forms a part, or of some incident quite misunderstood by the European who witnessed it; and such accounts, even if quite accurate as far as they go, may be woefully misleading. It is true enough that the Bantu are polygamists, and that their wives do a large share, if not all, of the field-work; yet the women are not slaves. It is also true that marriages are usually arranged by parents and guardians, and that the bridegroom has to make a certain payment; yet it is untrue to say that he buys his wife.

When native customs are taken as a whole, and looked at in their true light, it will be seen that the position of women is by no means unfavourable. The law makes no distinction between the sexes—except that, in some cases, a wrong done to a woman is more severely punished than one done to a man. Many religious ceremonies can only be performed by women, as we shall notice more in detail when speaking of the Hereros and the Anyanja. Among the Balolo (on the Congo) women take part in the public councils of the tribe; and though this is not common elsewhere, their influence unofficially counts for much. The mother of a

Photograph by B. W. Caney, Durban.

NATAL NATIVE WOMEN GATHERING PUMPKINS

Which grow half wild in the fringe of the bush bordering the cultivated ground.

chief is nearly always, and his sister very frequently, a person of great importance.

That agriculture should chiefly fall to the lot of women is the natural consequence of a primitive state of things, in which men are usually occupied with war or hunting. In fact, it has recently been suggested as probable that women were really the inventors of agriculture. Women also do the field-work where the men are in the habit of going away on long trading journeys, or engaging themselves to work for Europeans at a distance; but the system is only completely carried out in the case of warlike and pastoral peoples like the Zulus. Among agricultural tribes, such as the Bechuana and Anyanja, the men and women cultivate the fields together.

A Missionary's Evidence.

Perhaps I can hardly do better than quote the words of a German missionary, Dr. Merensky, well qualified to speak by many years' experience in Africa :—

" It is said that girls in Africa are sold in marriage. But this is only a European way of putting it. The black man is indignant at such a suggestion. The gift in cattle, or other things, which the would-be bridegroom has to hand over, is an essential part of the legal marriage ceremony. No African speaks of ' buying ' in this connection—he ' marries the girl by means of cattle.' Hard cases arise, indeed, when parents pledge their daughter before she is old enough to have a will of her own; and, when the time comes for the husband to take her home, she is frequently compelled, perhaps by cruel treatment, to follow him, whether she likes it or not, since she is legally bound to him. But all this is not the rule."

The writer might have added that similar hard cases are not unknown among ourselves. We need not go very far back in our history to find parents denying in theory (whatever they may have done in practice) that a daughter had any right to a voice in the disposal of her hand. The idea survives in a convention on which half our popular fiction is built up.

" In some tribes the girl's right to a voice in the selection of her husband is expressly recognised; and it is a very general and laudable practice which forbids the bride being taken home before she is of full age. . . . Only those quite unacquainted with native life can assert that love—even of the higher kind—between husband and wife is unknown. They have been misled by the natural disinclination of the blacks to reveal their deepest feelings to strangers, and by what seems to a casual eye the dull apathy with which they endure the greatest suffering."

He goes on to point out that, though women's work is heavy according to our ideas, it is not so through the oppression of individual men, but because the woman's sphere—within which, it must be remembered, she is supreme—has been strictly defined by custom and tradition; and the most selfish husband cannot at his pleasure add to his wife's burden. If she has the labour of hoeing, weeding, and reaping, she also has the control of the resulting food-supplies; he cannot help himself from her stores, or sell the grain without her permission, though it is her part to provide him and his guests with food, and to brew the tribute-beer for the chief. In other ways, too, married women can hold property independently to an extent which, within the memory of persons now living, was not recognised by English law.

Polygamy no Hindrance to Happiness.

Even polygamy—that is, where the Arabs have not introduced their degrading harem-slavery—cannot be said to make the lot of African women intolerable. Each wife has her recognised position, and, as a rule, their relations to each other, and of each to the children of the rest, are friendly, and even affectionate. Quarrels and jealousies, of course, do occur, sometimes with tragic results. In the case of a great chief's family they become as famous as other " scandals in high life," and lead, perhaps, to inferences as unjust. Though to our notions such an institution may seem incompatible with any true home life, this is by no means the case. Everyone who has been behind the scenes knows that, while perfection cannot be expected of poor human nature, its groundwork, in white and black, is everywhere much the same, and that love between husbands and wives, parents and children, brothers and sisters may be, and often is, very real and very devoted. Children are never unwelcome—the more the merrier. Even granting the advantage to parents of having sons to work for them and add to the importance of the village and the tribe, and daughters to bring in property when they marry, we need not reduce all care and kindness to calculation. In any case, surely, this is a better state of things than for the little ones to come unwanted into wretched homes, where the struggle for life is so sharp, and the pressure of discomfort and misery so keen, that there is no love to spare.

Misconceptions of African Life.

The most shocking stories have sometimes been told about the Bushmen — of their cruelty to their children, and utter lack of natural affection. But, hunted and persecuted as these unfortunate people were, it is no wonder if they became somewhat callous: the surprising thing is that there should be any human feeling left among them or other tribes who have constantly suffered from wars and slave-raids. Yet Moffat, after retailing assertions of this sort seemingly from hearsay, when he comes to his own observation, tells of hungry mothers sharing the food given to them among their children, without keeping a mouthful for themselves. Or we might refer to the touching account, in Dr. Stow's "Native Races of South Africa," of 'Korinna and 'Kouke, the old couple who had lost everything—children, kinsfolk, and home—but still clung to each other with undying affection.

Again, it is difficult for those who have grown up in the conventions of a European civilisation to believe that people who go about with little or no clothing, as we understand it, can have any sense of modesty or decorum. Yet, undoubtedly, they have; and, what is very sad, only too often, as the clothing increases, the modesty diminishes. There may be various reasons for this. One, we cannot doubt, is the loss of self-respect engendered when superior beings tell you how very shocking it is to do what your mother and grandmother and you and all your friends have always thought quite right and proper. Be that as it may, it will be found that, while ideas may differ as to what constitutes the indispensable minimum of clothing, a respectable African woman is quite as particular about that minimum as an English lady would be about hers. The feeling may show itself in what we think grotesque ways; a Herero matron will think it improper to be seen without her leather hat, or a Zulu bride to cross the path to the cattle-kraals; and, so believing, no consideration on earth would induce them to commit the acts in question. The light in which such things are regarded is illustrated by the story, told later on, of Zwide's mother, who is honoured to this day for having saved her son from a wicked and ruinous war by doing such outrageous violence to her own feelings that it was supposed she could only be acting by supernatural inspiration.

The Brighter Side of African Life.

It may be thought that the necessarily slight and imperfect account of African life given in the following pages does not sufficiently dwell on the darker side. But it seems to me that the darker side is quite sufficiently emphasised already, and we need to be reminded that there is another. Besides, many, if not most, books on Africa make one see things in a false perspective. One would almost think that there was a witchcraft trial every day and a cannibal feast once a week, and that all the various horrors which have happened at different times and in different places are going on everywhere all the time. But it is a trite reflection that these things get chronicled, but not the uneventful years when people go on quietly marrying, and building huts, and bringing up children, and hoeing their gardens.

There is a common notion that the negro —I use the word loosely for the dark African in general—is ferociously cruel and bloodthirsty, besides being possessed by an irrational hatred for all white men. There could not be a greater mistake. I do not know how the idea grew up unless it be that Europeans have so often seen him in a state of violent exasperation, without knowing what provoked it. But if we ever hear of "unprovoked aggression" on white people, we may be sure there is some dark story behind it—perhaps so old that those responsible have forgotten all about it. There are plenty of stories to prove it—only this is not the place to narrate them.

Photograph by G. T. Ferneyhough.

NATAL NATIVE GRANDMOTHER GRINDING MEALIES

On a stone beside the hut door. Note the basket (*iqoma*) containing mealies.

But the tribal wars? you will say. And the witchcraft trials?

Tribal Wars and Witchcraft.

Well, the first seem to be an experience nations have to go through in their early stages. We ourselves fought each other pretty constantly in these islands when we first settled here. To consider this fully would lead us into a historical disquisition which is likewise out of place. I will only add that the most disastrous tribal wars are those in which civilised nations have interfered, for their own advantage, on one side or the other.

As for witchcraft, I have not said much about it—not because I wish to minimise the tragedies that spring from the belief, but because they are more than sufficiently described elsewhere, and because the killing of persons under such circumstances does not necessarily prove men and women to be fiends. The history of our own witch trials shows what even good people may do under the influence of such ideas.

Callous the Africans may be—sometimes, as children are, from want of thought; and if so, the remedy is the same. Deliberately cruel I have never found them, and I do not believe they ever are, unless deliberately brutalised.

Coming now to a detailed survey of South Africa, we will begin with the eastern part, where the natives chiefly belong to the great Zulu race. These

Photograph by B. W. Caney, Durban.

NATAL NATIVE WOMEN WORKING IN THE FIELDS.

They are breaking up ground for a new garden. Note the baby on the back of the central one, who is wearing a handkerchief on her head instead of having her hair dressed in a cone as described in the text.

are to be found, not only in the country called Zululand, which lies north of Natal and south of St. Lucia Bay, but in the south and east of what is now the Transvaal, and through the greater part of Natal itself. The people usually known as "Cape Kafirs" (properly Amaxosa) are very closely related to the Zulus; so probably are the Amampondo (Pondos), Abatembu (Tambookies), Pondomisi, Amabaca, and others, though some of these have a considerable proportion of Bushman blood, having intermarried with the earlier inhabitants when they first settled in the country, between two and three hundred years ago. Many individuals in these mixed tribes are distinguished by smaller stature and a different facial type, with high cheek-bones and somewhat oblique eyes. The genuine Bantu, especially the Zulu, are tall and well-made, both men and women. The colour of their skins is brown, varying a good deal in shade—some families, or even individuals in the same family, being darker than others; but none are quite black. Sometimes a person is seen of quite a light yellowish-brown complexion; this (if there is no probability of European descent) is no doubt the result of Hottentot or Bushman blood. The sooty shade often noticed in Africans who come to this country is not natural to them—it is the result of new conditions and, in particular, a disturbed circulation. When ill, or badly frightened, a native turns a dull, slatey-grey, and the appearance of the skin when neglected and unwashed is often lighter than the real colour, because dust shows white instead of black against it.

The Zulu.

No one looks well or feels comfortable who does not regularly anoint his or her skin—probably because so much of it is exposed to the air—with oil, or some sort of grease. No doubt there are some who do this instead of washing, but (in my experience) the better sort—like the ancient Greeks—do both.

The illustrations will give a better idea of Zulu women's faces and figures than pages of description.

Zulu Girl Life.

The old custom was for girls, in their own homes, to wear little except beads till their marriage. This, however, is less usual now, and I doubt whether it is to be seen in Natal, unless in remote kraals. They are most carefully looked after by their mothers and grandmothers, and never go any distance alone. If they go to town—perhaps with mealies or *imfe* for sale on market-day—a dozen or more will start together, accompanied by two or three matrons, and perhaps escorted by a brother or two. On such journeys they usually wear a blanket or a piece of dark-coloured calico, passing under one arm and knotted over the opposite shoulder, and reaching to the knees. Various kinds of skin petticoats, fringed and ornamented with beads, etc., are shown in the illustrations. One kind (called *umbodiya*) is trimmed with brass ornaments round the lower edge.

Little girls are expected to make themselves useful to some extent—they have to mind the baby, or help their mothers at the weeding, or sometimes to stay out by themselves, or with one or two companions, in the mealie garden to scare the birds when the crops are ripening. It cannot be said that they are over-burdened or unkindly treated; but they have their duties and responsibilities till they are about sixteen or seventeen. Then, and for the next two or three years, till they are married, everyone seems to combine to make much of them and give them a good time.

The careful supervision already referred to does not prevent them receiving the attentions of young men, or forming attachments which, as often as not, end in marriage; for the arrangement between the fathers is frequently only the formal sanction of an understanding already reached by the young people themselves. As we have said, hard cases sometimes occur, when selfish and grasping parents force a girl against her will to become the wife of some wealthy or influential old man, just as fashionable mothers have been known to do nearer home, with or without a *bonâ fide* anxiety for their daughter's good.

The Old Zulu Marriage Laws.

The old Zulu marriage-laws (which Cetshwayo wished to abrogate, as he probably would have done but for the disasters which overtook him and his people) pressed hardly on the girls; but they are no longer in force. They arose from an institution found among many Bantu tribes, which was modified by the Zulu kings in the interests of their military organisation. All boys born in the same year or period of two or three years form a class, called in Zulu an *ibuto* or "regiment," and known by some collective name. (Where initiation ceremonies are practised, the "class" includes all those initiated the same year.) Girls are classified in the same way. The regiments of young men, when they reached a sufficient age, were called out by the king, either for war, or (as is still done by chiefs in Natal) to do his work in hoeing, weeding, hut-building, etc. Tshaka introduced a law forbidding them to marry till they had received permission. This was granted by the king to each regiment, as he thought fit, assigning at the same time a junior regiment of girls from which they were to be allowed to choose their wives. It was then a capital crime for any of these girls to marry outside the regiment in question. The object of the law seems to have been to secure a healthy population by allowing neither sex to marry too early, and, no doubt, also, to stimulate the energies of the men by making them win their spurs, so to speak, before they could found a family.

Photograph by G. T. Ferneyhough.

NATAL NATIVE WOMAN GRINDING MEALIES.

A mat is spread in front of the stone to catch the meal.

How Zulu Marriages are now Arranged.

This custom, of course, is a thing of the past, and native law, as at present administered in Natal, requires that the chief, before whom marriages are celebrated, should ask the woman formally whether she is entering into the contract by her own choice.

When negotiations for a marriage (under native custom) have been settled, the next thing is to decide the amount of *lobola* to be paid to the girl's father. This is not so much a price paid for the bride as a guarantee that the husband is able to maintain her, and a settlement for the benefit of her children. It is usually paid in cattle, which are held in trust by her father or other guardian. Should she misbehave and be divorced, or should she die without children, the cattle are returned to the husband; but if he illtreats her and she returns home, he forfeits them. They are not always paid over at the wedding, and may be claimed (with all their increase) years afterwards, or even in the next generation; there are endless complications and lawsuits arising from debts that have thus stood over.

Zulu Marriage Ceremonies.

a good deal locally, so that it would be impossible to give a full account within the limits of our space. We may just glance at a few of the more interesting points. It is quite a recognised thing, though in these days rather the exception than the

Photograph by B. W. Caney, Durban

A ZULU BRIDE HAVING HER HAIR DRESSED BY TWO COMPANIONS.

Skewers are used for pushing the string in and out between the strands. The woman on the right is married and wears a short skin petticoat ornamented with beads, while the unmarried girl on the left (who wears her hair short) has only a bead girdle. The skirt (*umbodiya*) is often longer than this.

Native women do not feel that they are bought and sold; on the contrary, they would feel slighted if no payment were made at their marriage, as if they had no value in the eyes of parents or husband. The payment of the *lobola* is usually considered the decisive point of the transaction, which may extend over many days, or even weeks. Some, however, say that the knot is really tied by the killing of an ox after the amount of the *lobola* is settled, the meat of which is sent to the bride's escort.

The usages at weddings have been described by several writers, and they vary rule, for the first overtures to come not merely from the bride's family, but from the girl herself. She goes with one or two companions, but without the knowledge of her relatives, to the man's kraal, where, if his family approve of the alliance, the women raise the shrill cry called *umkosi*. She sits down outside the fence til an ox is driven out and presented to her, the idea being that she is too weak to enter till refreshed with meat; this ceremony is gone through a second and a third time before she enters the hut and consents to eat. After a visit of a week or so, she is escorted home by her lover and his friends, with an instalment

Photograph by B. W. Caney, Durban

ZULU GIRLS.

The style of hair-dressing differs from the ordinary married women's coiffures, and may be merely a fancy style. The one on the right wears a necklace composed of bits of a sweet-scented wood, strung alternately with large beads. The brass studs on the thongs round the waist of the left-hand girl are a favourite adornment; the *umbodíya* is often edged with them.

of the *lobola* cattle. When she gets home she sets to work brewing beer, and gets together some girls to help her carry it to the bridegroom's kraal. I knew a young woman in Natal who had revived this almost obsolete custom for her own benefit and that of the man on whom she had set her affections. Her father, who had opposed their marriage, no longer withheld his consent when she had taken this decisive step.

Mr. Dudley Kidd, who gives a somewhat different account of the above custom, tells us what happens under the embarrassing circumstances of the girl not being wanted. They convey the truth to her delicately by giving her a burning brand, "to show her, symbolically, that there is no fire at the kraal for her to warm herself at."

One account of a custom observed at the actual marriage ceremony is as follows: "The bride is taken by force by the young man from her father's house, where all the girls of the kraal support her, and other young men seize and hold them or keep them back, while she is carried off to her husband's hut. Then, if strong, she will hold out still, perhaps, for two or three days, not yielding without a struggle. If so, the contest is at last brought to a close by some girl of her husband's family managing to strike her slily on the ankle with a rod, when she submits to her fate."

The Hair and its Ornamentation.

Before marriage girls usually wear their woolly hair short, or plait it into small tails. It is seldom seen plaited as Zatshuke's daughter has it in the illustration on p. 292, unless by those who have been partly Europeanised. The commonest ornament is a little chaplet of beads, like the one in the illustration on p. 280, but sometimes beads, brass rings, etc., are strung on the hair, or plaited into it. The head is frequently shaved for coolness and cleanliness, which is the reason why the hair does not grow long. Pondo girls, however, let it grow, and plait or twist it (with a liberal stiffening of some greasy mixture) into long strands, which recall the *coiffure* of the women in ancient Egyptian paintings.

When a girl is going to be married she lets her hair grow, in preparation for the elaborate structure shown in the photograph (p. 280), which marks her new status. String is woven in and out of the hair, to make a kind of basket-work crown, and, when finished, the whole is plastered over with red ochre. As the hair grows, the whole thing has to be undone and reconstructed from time to time, and gradually assumes the shape of the long spike which enables one to recognise a married woman a mile off. The women of the Amabaca (a tribe living both in Natal and the eastern part of Cape Colony), instead of this, have the front part of the hair twisted into stiffened ringlets, so as to form a thick "fringe."

Celibacy a Reproach.

Each wife has her own hut, in which her children sleep with her as long as they are small. There are separate huts assigned to the boys and girls respectively, as they grow older, which they occupy till they marry and depart to homes of their own. An unmarried woman of mature years is almost unknown and old bachelors are not common. Want of means may delay a man's marriage, but seldom proves a permanent obstacle; if his father or uncle cannot furnish the necessary cattle, and no friend will oblige with a loan, he can always go to service or work in the mines till he has earned them. If a man, not blind, lame, or conspicuously deformed, reaches the age of sixty, or so, without finding a wife, the presumption is that he was in his youth too unpleasant and unamiable for any girl to accept him. To escape such a fate young, and even elderly, men in doubt about their own attractions will take great pains to secure adventitious ones; they have a great belief in "medicines for making the girls like them," and will often ask for them in chemists' shops. Among the plants reputed most efficacious for this purpose is a species of smilax called *ibuta*, whose delicate, light green leaves have a silvery sheen; if you meet a man with sprays of it wreathed in his hair, you may be sure he is on his way to the kraal where he is paying his attentions. He is probably

PONDO GIRL : SOUTH AFRICA.
DRAWN BY NORMAN H. HARDY.

Facing on page 282

wearing, in addition, all he can afford in the way of bead ornaments, and bangles of brass, copper and iron wire on his arms and legs—perhaps also a set of brass rings fastened to his front hair and jingling across his forehead. But, though some giddy girls may be impressed by these adornments, they are not generally regarded with much favour; there is an idea that a man who beautifies himself to excess is likely to take to drink later on and prove a bad husband.

Restrictions upon Zulu Women.

The round huts—"beehive huts" the books call them, but they never struck me as like beehives, being flatter in shape—are ranged round a circle, in the middle of which is the cattle-kraal—that sacred place forbidden to all women. They may not even, as a rule, cross the path by which the cattle leave the enclosure. No woman is supposed to have anything to do with the cattle; the milking is always done by men and boys, and even the milk-sack, which forms part of the household utensils, must not be touched by any woman unless related by blood to the owner of the kraal.

The various prohibitions which have to be observed by women (and sometimes also by men), and designated by the term *hlonipa*, are a very interesting subject of study. Here I have only space to mention one or two besides the above. A man must never meet his mother-in-law face to face; consequently, if he comes upon her by accident, he holds up his shield before his face, or otherwise ostentatiously ignores her presence (*see* p. 284). No woman is supposed to mention the name of her father, her husband, or the head of her husband's family; and, in the case of a great chief, men too have to observe this restriction. If the name means anything, or resembles a word in common use, that word must be avoided as well. Thus the women of a family whose ancestor was named Mtimkulu, "The Great Tree," could not use the ordinary words meaning "tree" and "great," but had to find or invent others.

A Zulu Lady Godiva.

It is this prohibition about the cattle-kraal which gives its point to a remarkable tradition related by the Angoni—a Zulu tribe now settled in Central Africa—a story reminding one of the legend of Lady Godiva. It must have happened about the time of the battle of Waterloo. A chief named Zwide, then living in Zululand, had a quarrel with Zwangendaba (father of the Angoni chief, Mombera, who only died a few years back), attacked him, and was taken prisoner; but Zwangendaba treated him generously, released him, and sent him home with a gift of cattle. But his proud spirit could not endure the humiliation, and he determined on revenge. His mother was grieved at this; in the words of a native narrator, "she reasoned with him, saying, 'My child, shall the Ngoni perish? Did they not send you back, giving you many fat cattle with you? Is it right to go out to war against them?'" But he would not listen, and began mustering his army. Unable to bear the thought that her son could be guilty of such baseness, and dreading the disaster that it was likely to bring on the tribe, she took a desperate step, seemingly with the idea that an outrageous violation of decency would arrest him in his ruinous career, though he would not listen to reason. She went into the cattle-kraal, and, slipping off her skirt, stood there unclothed before all the people. "The soldiers, seeing her thus, wondered greatly, and Zwide also wondered. The soldiers declared it was an omen, that perhaps an ancestral spirit had prompted her to do thus, and they, being afraid to go out, were disbanded forthwith. So Lowawa, Zwide's mother, prevailed." The story is told by Dr. Elmslie in "Among the Wild Ngoni," published some years ago.

Women as Food-Finders.

Zulu women, one might say, come near to carrying out Ruskin's ideal, in that it is their principal business to provide food for their families. Towards the end of the dry season (about September) they begin breaking up the ground (as shown in the illustration on p. 277) in order to plant "mealies" (maize)

Photograph by G. T. Fernyhough.

THE CUSTOM OF *"HLONIPA."*

The Natal Zulu in the picture, coming unexpectedly upon his mother-in-law (a Baca or Pondo woman by the arrangement of her hair), seated by her hut door, hides his face with his shield till he has passed her.

and "Kafir-corn" or *amabele* (sorghum). Now that ploughs have come into use in many parts of Natal, this heaviest part of the work is often taken off their hands by their husbands, but the hoe is not altogether out of fashion as yet. In December the corn is already fairly high, and everyone's energies are tasked to keep the weeds under—hoeing between the rows every fine day. In this season of the summer rains there is often a forenoon of perfect beauty, with clear sunshine and a wonderful freshness—you can almost see and hear things growing. In the afternoon comes a thunderstorm, and rain for the rest of the day and on into the night. Sometimes it goes on raining for three or four days together, and then, perhaps, by way of compensation, will come a day that is entirely fine. By February, if not earlier, the maize is ripe; the cobs are broken off by hand, piled up in great round baskets, and carried off on the women's heads, to be stored, either in pits underground, or in huge baskets which are kept inside the hut; or, sometimes, in bins like small huts raised on platforms.

The cobs are sometimes boiled or roasted green; but most are allowed to get ripe, and then ground into the meal (*impupu*) which is made into porridge. This and curdled milk (*amasi*) form the chief food of the people. Meat is reserved for somewhat special occasions, though at a chief's kraal it would be cooked every day, and, on the whole, the Zulu eat much more meat than the agricultural tribes farther north. Fresh milk is given only to small children, and not always to them, for babies appear to be weaned on *amasi*, even if not introduced to it at a still earlier period.

Baking is an unknown art in most parts of Bantu Africa; porridge takes the place of bread where cereals are grown; where manioc is the staple food, it is often made into a kind of cake, and roasted in the ashes; and the same thing is done on the Zambesi with bananas. The Natal natives also make a kind of bread (*isinkwa*) out of green mealies. Meat is either roasted (usually in the ashes) or boiled—formerly in a home-made earthen pot, nowadays very often in the three-legged iron ones bought at the "Kafir stores," or even in an ordinary saucepan like the one in which the woman in the illustration is bringing the pig his supper of chopped pumpkin (p. 286). Pigs are, comparatively speaking, an innovation, and a man advanced enough to keep them would see nothing out of the way in his wife's feeding them, though he would not dream of letting her attend to the cows. The fowls, of which there are any number scratching about between the huts, and, as likely as not, roosting in them at night, belong more particularly to the women. They are kept in order to kill one occasionally for the pot, or for sale—not for the eggs, which natives seldom eat: they are considered especially bad for young people.

Women as Brewers.

Though the women do not bake, they brew, and that pretty extensively. There are several kinds, or rather degrees, of beer, for it is all made from *amabele*, and only varies in strength. It is usually more like gruel than what we understand by beer; in fact, it is very nutritious, and the people say of it that "it is both food and drink." The best kind is of a pinky terra-cotta colour and slightly effervescent; it has (when one is used to it) a not unpleasant acid taste, and is very refreshing, but (like the Mexican *pulque*) one needs educating up to it. The inferior quality is grey, and looks much like soapy water. The difference, no doubt, arises from the greater or less degree of care and cleanliness with which it is made and strained through a long funnel of neatly-woven grass; certain herbs are also sometimes added, to improve the flavour or assist the fermentation. It is kept in earthen jars, or calabashes, or in baskets so closely woven as to hold liquid quite as well as jars, which they resemble in shape. Great quantities of beer are consumed at weddings, when it too often happens that the latter end of a feast is the beginning of a fray. It is only right to say, however, that comparatively little harm would be done by *utshwala*, were it not that it is nowadays frequently adulterated with spirits, etc.

When a girl has visited her future husband's kraal, in accordance with the custom previously referred to, she sends on some of her companions, a few days after returning home, with pots of *utshwala*. Such a party (only

Photograph by F. E. Colenso.

A NATAL WOMAN WITH BABY.

The saucepan contains chopped pumpkin—food for the pig. Notice the baby's hair, with beads strung on some of the tufts; also an unfinished hut in the background. The photograph was taken near Bishopstowe.

in this case consisting of matrons) is shown in the photograph on the opposite page.

Two of these women present a somewhat grotesque appearance in white men's coats, a popular article of dress in the cold weather, irrespective of sex — policemen's cast-off tunics or old military great-coats being valued, when procurable, for their warmth and durability. The second and third in the procession, on the other hand, are wearing the native cloak made from a cow-hide, scraped and rubbed till it is as soft as a glove. Under this is worn the characteristic skin petticoat of the married women, reaching from the armpits to the knees. A man makes this garment for his wife; it is a work of time and patience to prepare the skin. This is about the utmost that is done in the way of tailoring or dressmaking, except by women who have learnt to sew at the Mission School and taken to the wearing of print dresses.

Zulu Tailor-made Costumes.

Sometimes the master of the house is seen devoting his energies to a goat-skin pegged out on the ground before him, which he will spend some weeks in scraping and rubbing and anointing with fat. This is to make the *imbeleko*, or cradle, if we may call it so, in which a baby is carried about on its mother's back, so as to leave her hands free for work. The skin is that of the goat killed for the doctor, whom the father consults on the important occasion of an increase in his family. The baby soon learns to hold on when necessary; but its attitudes seem very casual sometimes —especially when it is supported, not by the skin, but in the looser folds of its mother's blanket.

Skin Cradles.

It is part of women's work to fetch water and firewood; they will walk miles with their little axes to bring home a bundle of the latter, and sometimes they will cut down and trim a suitable sapling to make a post for the hut. But the building of the hut is chiefly men's work. They dig the holes and set up the posts, fix the arched wattles in the ground, plant a second set crossing the first so as to make a lattice-work, and then tie all the intersections with bark-string. Then the women come and do the thatching, and nothing could be neater or prettier than a newly-finished hut, with the thatch accurately and smoothly fixed, and netted over with plaited grass ropes. The door is so low that you have to go down on hands and knees to enter; there are no windows and no chimney; the smoke has to find its way out through the thatch. This, however, is less dreadful

Women as House-builders.

than it sounds, for (at least in my experience) the smoke does not trouble you if you do in Rome as the Romans do—*viz.*, sit on the floor. The latter is of beaten earth, very hard and smooth, and kept cool and clean (extraordinary as this may sound to any-one who has never seen it) by being fre-quently smeared with a mixture of cow dung and water, which leaves a light greenish deposit. The smearing (called *ukusinda*) is done in a sort of pattern—as Scottish housewives ornament their stone floors, after scrubbing, with "cam" or whiting, in scrolls and volutes.

The fireplace is a round depression in the middle of the floor, with the earth banked up in a ledge round it. The furniture con-sists chiefly of mats for sleeping or sitting on, pots and pans, baskets of all sorts, wooden bowls and dishes, milk and beer vessels, and such like. Sometimes you may see a pot on the fire; but, as a rule, the cooking, except in wet weather, is done out of doors. The hut is really only a place to sleep in, and take shelter from the rain.

Most huts have a little semi-circular court-yard in front, formed by a high reed fence which screens the door from the prevailing wind and shelters the cooking-fire. The entrance is close to the hut on the less windy side. The hut can be closed with a wooden door at night, or when the inmates are away. It is the custom for anyone who calls in the owner's absence to make some sort of mark (like the Gypsy *patteran*) to show that he has been there, and the word for this kind of mark (*incwadi*) is that now used for a message, letter or book.

Photograph by B. W. Caney, Durban.

WOMEN TAKING CALABASHES OF BEER TO A WEDDING.

The beer is made by the bride, and sent as a present to her future husband.

Of course, many natives now live in square houses after the European pattern, and sometimes very good ones; but they are usually wattle and daub erections, of a very transitional character, and on a par with the frightful second-hand clothes which render many otherwise decent and worthy persons such distressing spectacles. Women, how-ever, look well in simple, tolerably well-made print dresses, and the soft silk handkerchiefs which they are fond of wearing on their heads: their choice of colours, as a rule, shows a strikingly good taste.

The cooking done at a native kraal is not of a very elaborate character. We have already spoken of the meat and beer; sour milk (*amasi*) is produced by pouring the day's milk into a vessel (among the Pondos and Xosas, a skin bag) kept for the purpose, which has a little of the old milk left in it—or milking into a pail with a little whey at the bottom. Porridge is made in the most elementary fashion by bringing a pot of water to the boil and stirring in the meal till it thickens, carefully crushing all lumps with the "spurtle" against the side of the pot; it is then considered ready. It is turned out into a wooden dish, and eaten with the fingers; or sometimes a number of people sit round the pot and eat out of it with spoons—iron ones, which are fairly common now, and can be bought at all the traders' stores. Native spoons are made of wood, and often very neatly carved; they are used for eating *amasi*.

Zulu Cookery.

Meat is brought in on a wooden dish and portions handed round on grass mats, which serve as plates; they are very neatly and strongly woven out of the stalks of the *cyperus* rush. Gourds are used as dippers or ladles for water or beer, and small ones as drinking-cups.

Men and women never eat together; the latter, after setting a meal before the men, either wait and eat what is left, or cook for themselves and the smaller children at some other time. It should have been mentioned, by the bye, when speaking of *hlonipa*, that the *right* side of the hut, as you enter, is the men's side, the left the women's. A man's sister is allowed to cross to the right side, but not his wife—at any rate, not during the first years of her marriage. When she is the mother of a grown-up family the restriction no longer holds. This is only one out of many rules which have to be observed by young married women; but the subject is too wide a one to discuss here.

Among the incidental occupations of women is the making of mats and baskets, in which some of them show great skill. Some tribes north of the Zambesi, as we shall see, consider this exclusively men's work, while pottery is entirely the women's affair, as is the case almost everywhere among the Bantu, except in some places where the men smoke pipes with clay bowls, which they model and bake themselves.

Zulu Basket-work.

There are many different kinds of baskets—some shown in the illustrations—of the most various shapes and uses. Large round ones, worked in coils of grass (something after the manner of our old-fashioned straw beehives), are used for bringing home the maize at harvest time. Some are almost globular, with a cover, and woven so closely that they will hold liquids. These are sometimes used for carrying beer. Others, fitted with lids, are used for storing food—or valuables. Each kind has its own name, but there is not, as far as I can make out, any word which means a basket in general. The English word "basket" is used (in the form *ubaskidi*), but it means "any basket not of native make," and in particular a basket with a handle, which native ones never have—they are always carried on the head, or else on the flat of the hand.

The late Queen Victoria, in a conversation with Cetshwayo (during his visit to England in 1882) expressed her interest in this industry of the Zulu women. On his return to his own country, he told his family that "the Queen desired to see a specimen of every kind of basket made by the Zulus"—for so he had understood her remark as interpreted to him. His mother and his wives at once set to work, using their best skill; but the King was prevented by the Colonial authorities from sending envoys to England, as he wished to do, and the greater part of the baskets themselves perished in the burnings of kraals which were all too frequent in the next few sorely troubled years. Some, however, were saved, and preserved with religious care, even after Cetshwayo's death, by the royal women, in the hope that they might yet find opportunity to make their offering to "the Great Inkosikazi, our Mother." Finally, in 1890, when Miss Colenso came to England, to plead the cause of the exiled Zulu chiefs, the pathetic little gift was entrusted to her, and, an opportunity having been found of explaining the matter to the Queen, it was presented and accepted.

Treatment of Widows.

Widows may either marry the late husband's brother—in which case any children born are counted as belonging to the deceased—or they return to their father's house, or live with one of their sons. The latter must often happen, judging by the number of kraals where there is a grandmother—generally a useful and cheerful person, who helps to grind the corn and nurse the babies, and, according to the immemorial wont of grandmothers, neutralises the efforts of the parents to bring up their children with wholesome severity. It must be from a very partial view of the case that one writer asserts the lot of old women in South Africa to be so miserable as to leave them no refuge but suicide. It certainly is not the rule in Natal, and on the Zambesi and Shiré, where I was assured that "the Kafirs" were in the habit of poisoning off the aged, I never found this statement borne out by any lack of grey heads in the villages. I do not know what foundation there may ever have been for this persistent tradition; but I can safely say it has none among the people I know.

Professional women are not unknown among the Zulu. The prophetess (*isanusi*) is a person of great consideration, and the herb-doctor (*inyanga yemiti*) may be either a man or a woman. These practitioners often have a really useful knowledge of medicinal

Photograph by Ravenscroft.

KAFIR WOMAN BAKING BREAD.

Her dress and the mud buildings roofed with corrugated iron are typical of a town location.

herbs, handed down in their families. But they are not now allowed to practise without a licence.

Doctors and Witches.

The ordinary diviner, or witch-doctor, is not the same as the prophet or prophetess, though sometimes, I believe, the two callings may be united in the same person. The diviner discovers lost property, and finds out the cause of illness by "throwing the bones" (casting lots), or by various methods of "smelling out," which chiefly reduce them-

Photograph by T. Lindsay Fairclough.

A ZULU LADY DOCTOR OF SOME RENOWN, PRACTISING IN BASUTOLAND.

selves to a habit of observation and a faculty of putting two and two together. While, no doubt, there is a great deal of trickery in the practice of these diviners, they are frequently (as the Rev. Duff Macdonald noticed in the case of the Yaos) shrewd and well-informed men, who give sound advice according to their lights, and are listened to with respect; whereas their opinion, if given on its own merits, and unassisted by hocus-pocus, would count for little or nothing. At the same time, it is probable that many of them possess a certain hypnotic power, and are subject to trances. The circumstance that a man or woman often develops the gift of prophecy after a serious illness points in the same direction.

The "doctor" in the illustration is a Zulu woman, said to be of considerable standing among the Basuto,* in whose country she practices. She is wearing a large collection of charms, and also, probably, though these are not conspicuous, a number of small bags containing real medicines. The string of bead-like objects hanging below the rest on her right side, which looks something like a rosary, are the "bones" used for divining. They consist of the knuckle-bones of goats and sheep, and some other animals, with other objects, each of which has a certain meaning assigned to it; and when they are shaken up and thrown down, their rela-

* People usually say "a Basuto," but this is much as if we should say "an English." The singular is *Mosuto*, but it is best, when using tribal names in English, to drop the prefix, and say "a Zulu," "a Yao," etc.

Photograph by B. W. Caney, Durban.

ZULU WOMAN, WITH GOURD.

Notice the longer skin petticoat, with many rows of beads.

tive position one to another is interpreted according to the rules which have to be learnt by every one initiated into the profession. If the doctor can make nothing of the dice as they have fallen, there is nothing for it but to throw them again. The wire bangles visible among the doctor's outfit have probably been received as fees from patients—that is, if the Suto practice coincides with that in vogue about Delagoa Bay—though not directly by the present wearer. There (among the Baronga) the young man still in the medical-student stage, who has begun to practise, but not yet, so to say, taken his degree, is not allowed to receive fees in money, but only these bangles, which he fastens to the basket containing his dice, and hands over to his instructor on passing the final examination. This lady received most of her fees in cattle.

The objects on the "doctor's" head are the gall-bladders of goats which have been killed for her in the course of consultation. This ceremony is a necessary part of medical treatment for all who can afford it, and the meat is the physician's perquisite. The more bladders the latter has in his hair the greater his reputation, for it is not likely that a family will call in a man for whom one or more animals will have to be slaughtered unless they feel some confidence in his ability.

"In olden times," says Mr. H. E. Mabille,* "the doctor received no payment unless his patient got better. But now things have greatly altered, and the doctor is paid even for 'opening his bag' of drugs—that is, before he has done anything."

* "Journal of the African Society," No. xx., p. 353.

II

The Basuto—Women Agriculturists—Basuto Huts—Basuto "Schools" for Girls—Basuto Marriage Customs—A Basuto National Heroine—The Hottentots—The Bushmen—Nama Women and their Duties—Nama Marriage Customs—The Hill Damaras—The Herero—Herero Costume and Ornaments—The Sacred Fire of the Herero—Herero Marriage Customs—Herero Birth Customs—Childhood among the Herero—Agricultural Tribes—The Barotse—A Barotse Legend—Women Chiefs—The Matabele—Anyanja—"Calicoes"—Maize and its Uses—Anyanja Ornaments—Yao Women

The Basuto.

THE Basuto are a branch of the Bechuana, which name includes a vast number of tribes, extending from the Drakensberg and the Orange River more or less to the Zambesi. Most of these tribes are rather agricultural than pastoral. "The intense love of agricultural pursuits," says the late Dr. Stow, "formed such a striking trait in the occupations of the Bachoana and Basuto tribes that the early travellers were filled with admiration and astonishment at the wonderful proofs of industry which the extent of the cultivated land surrounding their great towns exhibited. Some of the latter contained . . . eight to ten thousand inhabitants. . . . At the time of Mr. Campbell's visit to Lithako, the great place of the Batlapin, he remarks that on approaching the town they passed through extensive cornfields spreading out on both sides of the road. Even the Hottentots who accompanied him were amazed at the extent of land under cultivation, never having seen so much before in one place." *

In tribes like these, as has already been mentioned, the cultivation of the ground is not entirely left to the women. This does not appear from Moffat's account of the Batlapin tribe of Bechuana, among whom he lived at Kuruman; but at the time of which he speaks—about 1821—it would seem as if the tribes had been unsettled by recent wars and migrations, and it comes out

* "Native Races of South Africa," p. 417.

incidentally that the men were often engaged in war and hunting. Game was then so abundant—though now almost extinct in that part of the country—that hunting was really a serious contribution to the support of a man's family.

Basutoland proper, it may not be out of place to remind the reader, lies west of Natal and north of the eastern districts of Cape Colony, and is enclosed between the Drakensberg Mountains, the Orange River, and the Caledon. The Basuto in some respects occupy a middle position between the Zulu and the northern tribes; they keep more cattle than the latter, and grow more corn than the former. They raise for their own food *amabele* and maize, chiefly the first, and wheat, which the missionaries have taught them to grow, for sale to traders.

Photograph by F. E. Colenso.

A NATAL FAMILY GROUP TAKEN AT A KRAAL NEAR BISHOPSTOWE.

The father, seen on the right, is Zatshuke, a son of the late Hlubi chief Langalibalele.

Canon Widdicombe says: "The field-work was formerly almost entirely performed by the women, but since the introduction of Christianity into the country the men have gradually learnt to take their share in it; and at the present time both men and women work hard in the fields during the ploughing and harvest seasons." He adds that ploughs are coming more and more into use, and that it is a common thing for a girl to refuse a man because he has no plough. The wheat harvest is at midsummer (January); the maize and millet are reaped in June and July. The same writer describes the women's work at harvest time.

Women Agriculturists.

"A woman will leave her home a few minutes after dawn, carrying her infant on her back, and a large *seruto*, a basin-shaped basket,* on her head. She will trudge along bravely and patiently until she reaches her corn patch, at perhaps four or five, or even seven or eight, miles distance. . . . She will work with scarcely an interval of rest until the long, slanting rays of the declining sun warn her to return home. Then she piles her basket to the brim with maize cobs or bunches of millet, and with her little one still at her back, cooing out in the prettiest and most engaging way its baby accents, she will plod diligently homeward. Ar

* Similar to the one in the illustration on p. 276.

Photograph by Ravenscroft

RED KAFIRS, KING WILLIAM'S TOWN.

"Red" is a common Colonial designation for the "raw" or "kraal" natives, from the red ochre with which (mixed with grease) they anoint their skins and hair.

rived at her cabin, she will at once commence the preparation of the family meal, having herself partaken of nothing but a cup of *leting* (light beer) before starting for the harvest field, and a mouthful or two of *bogobe* (porridge) during the whole day."

Probably the woman so described would be surprised to find herself an object of compassion. For her it is all in the day's work, and it must be remembered that her indoor duties, apart from the cooking, are by no means heavy. There might be two opinions as to the desirability of providing her with a house which will take all her time and strength to keep clean, and rigidly confining her within it.

Basuto Huts.

The Suto huts are constructed on a different plan from the Zulu ones—at least, some of them; for here, too, we have a transition state of things. The northern Bechuana tribes, like most of those beyond the Zambesi, build a circular enclosure of upright posts, filling in the spaces between them with grass, and cover it with a conical thatched roof. Some huts of this description—only that the walls are here constructed of sods—are found in Basutoland; others are of the Zulu pattern already described.

Basuto "Schools" for Girls.

The Basuto, as well as most Bantu tribes of Cape Colony, have the institution of the *bale* (or *boyale*) called by the Colonists "school," for girls entering on womanhood. All those of the same age in the neighbourhood are "isolated for one month in a hut set apart for the purpose and only the instructresses and the old women in the village are allowed access to them. At the end of the month they are daubed with white clay from head to foot, and dressed in aprons of goatskin, with a coil of grass rope round the waist." The old women are supposed to drill them in all the duties of married life. After the first month they are allowed to go about accompanied by one of the old women, and wearing a kind of veil made of bits of reed. Anyone whom they meet is bound to give them anything they may ask for. The period of seclusion lasts five or six months. The Zulus do not observe this custom, but celebrate the "coming out" of a girl as a family affair.

Basuto Marriage Customs.

The marriage customs, including the *lobola* (here called *bohali*), are much the same as among the Zulu, though the details differ, and some of them are very curious. Thus, when a young man wishes to marry, he signifies the same, not by wearing smilax in his hair, but by getting up early and driving the cows out of the kraal, letting the calves suck them, instead of keeping them separate as usual. His parents (if, as is probably the case, they have, like Irish peasants, arranged the match long ago), seeing this, send off a messenger with a cow to the girl's father. He signifies his errand —not, indeed, in dumb show, but in symbolic language, saying he is come to ask for a calabash of water. If both father and mother consent—for it is always recognised that either party may have had reason to change their minds—the messenger is anointed with mutton-fat. If he does not meet with this attention, no further explanations are needed; he goes home and reports that "the incident is closed."

The usual amount paid by the bridegroom is twenty head of cattle, perhaps ten sheep or goats, and a horse. At the time of the marriage, he and his friends drive the animals over to the bride's village, and, before they come in sight of it, two bullocks are sent on in advance, one for each of her parents. These furnish the occasion for the romping which, all the world over, and even to this day in the less sophisticated parts of Europe, seems to be considered an essential part of wedding festivities. Here it takes the form of a contest between the women of the village and the men who have brought the cattle, the former, armed with long sticks, trying to prevent the animals from entering the cattle-kraal, while the men do their best to drive them in. The bride's relations, by the bye, so far from trying to outshine their guests in the splendour of their apparel, "are dressed in rags, which means that the other party must enrich them"; and the other party, as they arrive, walk in front of the cattle to frustrate premature attempts at counting them. The haggling that goes on before everything is satisfactorily concluded is a sort of "signing the settlements" carried out in a more primitive way. A full description of the proceedings is given by Mr. Mabille in the paper already quoted.

A Basuto National Heroine.

Suto traditions mention at least one remarkable woman—the chieftainess Mokwatsi, commonly called Mantatisi. She was the wife of the Batlokwa chief Mokotyo, who died in 1819 or 1820, when his eldest son was still a child. It was the time of what the Basuto call the *Difakane*—not so much an ordinary war as a series of migrations, in which each tribe, displaced by another pressing on it from behind, is forced to overrun its neighbours in front. Moffat, in his "Missionary Labours and Scenes in Southern Africa" gives an appalling account of the miseries of this time, and the terror spread by the invading hosts—as they were supposed to be, though they suffered as much as the invaded. But Mantatisi somehow piloted her people through the worst of their troubles, and left her son, Sikonyela, safely established in the chieftainship. She seems to have died about 1830. "When she was first brought to Mokotyo she was a tall, slim girl with an exceptionally fair skin, and very handsome. . . . It is estimated that she was about forty years old when Mokotyo died, and the weight of chieftainship fell upon her. She was then a large, strong woman, inclined to stoutness, as is usual with healthy native women of middle age. She used to sit in court with the men, on the biggest stone in the circle, hear cases, and discuss politics; and the policy of the tribe during her regency was conducted by her alone. She did not lead the fighting men to battle, but while the tactics were those of the commander, the strategy was hers. She was affable and sociable, and very popular with all her people."

On one occasion, during a war with Pakadita's tribe of Zulu, she had sent the fighting men to a distance for supplies of grain. While they were gone she saw the enemy approaching, and quickly collected the cattle on the top of a steep rise, making the women and taller children stand in front of them. The Zulu, thinking, as they espied them in the distance, that it was the warriors, on whose absence they were reckoning, drawn up in battle array to receive them, retreated, and the Batlokwa were safe.*

Another Suto woman of whom one would like to know more was Maliepollo, widow of Mohlomi, a son of the Kwena chief Monyane. This Mohlomi must have been a truly remarkable man. He was a great doctor, cared nothing for the chieftainship, and hated war. He spent much of his life in travelling about to seek knowledge, and, wherever he went, he tried to induce people to live in peace. Moshesh, the great chief of the Basuto, who was related to him, owed much to his teaching and advice. He died in or about 1816. Maliepollo, his youngest and favourite wife, came, in the course of years, to Grahamstown, where she listened to the missionaries and became a Christian in her old age. The Basuto say that she sent a message to Moshesh to advise him to ask the "teachers" to settle in his country.

The Hottentots.

The Bantu are not the aboriginal inhabitants of South Africa; they seem only to have reached the eastern part of what is now Cape Colony towards the end of the seventeenth century. When Van Riebeek and the first Dutch settlers landed at the Cape in 1652, they found the country occupied by yellow-skinned people, with high cheekbones, oblique eyes, and woolly hair growing in separate tufts on the scalp; who wandered about with immense herds of cattle, and lived in huts made of rush mats, which could easily be taken down and put up again. The name of "Hottentots," which the

* "Basuto Traditions, Compiled from Native Sources," by J. C. Macgregor, Assistant Commissioner, Leribe.

Dutch gave to these natives was derived from the uncouth sounds of their language, which it was declared impossible for a white man to learn—" it was nothing but *Hot* and *Tot*." Those still living at the Cape have quite forgotten the tongue of their forefathers, and speak Dutch, or rather that form of it known as " Taal " or " Afrikaans." The Griquas, who at one time occupied what is now the Kimberley district, are Dutch and Hottentot half-castes, or at least descended from such. The Mohammedan Malays of Cape Town are the descendants of slaves brought from Batavia by the Netherlands East India Company. They know no language but Cape Dutch, and sometimes English ; but they keep up the observances of their religion, and even make the pilgrimage to Mecca. Other slaves were imported from Ceylon, Mozambique, and the Guinea Coast. From all these different elements is compounded that large population known to-day as " the coloured people."

Further up country we find two genuine and tolerably unmixed " Hottentot " tribes—the Kora (Korannas), and the Nama or Namaqua. The Nama have given their name to the tracts of more or less desert country known as Great and Little Namaqualand—the former lying beyond the Orange River in the German Colony. Their languages, which are of a totally different character from the Bantu, are very much alike, so that Nama and Kora can readily understand one another. The Nama in old times extended much further south than they are now to be found, as they were neighbours to the Grigriqua and Cochoqua tribes, with whom Van Riebeek first came in contact. All these tribes seem to have had much the same character, manners and customs, though the Dutch thought the Nama were far bigger than those nearer the Cape.

A NAMA GIRL.
A convert of the Rhenish (German Lutheran) Mission.

The Bushmen.

The Hottentots, however, were at that time comparatively recent arrivals in the country. The real aborigines were the Bushmen, who have now almost disappeared from the Colony, though there are still some to be found in Bechuanaland and the Kalahari. The common idea of the Bushmen, as a miserable and degraded people, without government, social organisation, or even family ties, is an erroneous one, derived from the fact that they only became known to Europeans as the scattered and persecuted remnants of a once flourishing people. There were several large tribes under powerful chiefs, each of whom lived in or near the " Great Cave," with the tribal token painted on its walls, where the people assembled on important occasions. They lived by hunting, and had no need to do anything else, as the country swarmed with game ; the nearest they ever got to agriculture was collecting the seeds of wild grasses, which the women pounded in mortars hollowed out of the rock. These are still to be found in some parts of the Orange Colony. They must have cost years of labour to make, as they were gradually chipped out with a hard piece of stone. The late Dr. Stow also saw the pegs which the Bushmen had driven into the face of a steep cliff, to enable them to climb up and take the wild bees' nests. Other traces which have been in existence since the European occupation, if not now remaining, are the cairns they piled up on graves, and the ruins of stone fences (sometimes miles in length) intended for driving the game into pitfalls.

Though the Bushmen, as such, have disappeared from the country, some of them became incorporated with the Bechuana and "Kafir" tribes, so that many of their descendants still remain. It even seems probable that there is, in some parts, a considerable Bushman substratum in the Bantu population, as in the western districts of British Central Africa.

HILL DAMARA GIRLS, AT A RHENISH MISSION STATION.

The Hottentots, as a whole, are a pastoral people, but those within the Colony were deprived of their cattle, and passed through a period of serfage, and at the present day most of them work for other people—the men usually as herdsmen or waggon-drivers. They are famous for their power of managing animals, and the "boy" who knows his work drives his team of oxen chiefly by conversing with them.

Nama Women and their Duties.

The Nama, in their original state (for many have embraced Christianity and settled at the stations of the German missionaries) live probably in much the same way as the Cape Hottentots did in the seventeenth century. They are nomads, moving from place to place with their cattle, sheep, and goats, encamping wherever they can find grass and water, and moving on when these are exhausted. It must be confessed, however, that for many years, at any rate, the greater number of the Nama cattle were those they "lifted" from the Herero, with whom they were continually at war. This is now at an end, and they have also lost most of their possessions, legitimate or otherwise. They are not a strong people, nor fitted for continuous hard work, and it does not seem clear, at the moment, what will become of them.

Another of their occupations is making the rush mats of which their portable huts are constructed. This is always going on, more or less, for a thrifty housewife likes to have spare mats in stock—either to replace any which may be worn out, or for sale to white traders. If a daughter is going to be married, extra production is necessitated, and the whole household sets to work. First, the rushes have to be collected, which may take some weeks; then they are soaked, cut into lengths, and strung together by means of an iron needle about half a yard long. When finished, each mat is about three or four yards long by one yard wide. The string with which they are sewn is made from the inner bark of the acacia, which yields our gum-arabic. The collection of this material is a combination of duty and pleasure, for the bark, which contains a sweet juice, is prepared for use by chewing. When it has sufficiently yielded up its sweetness, the fibre is teased out and twisted into string.

An ordinary house requires from fifteen to twenty mats. The men collect about a dozen long, slender wands of a particular kind of tough wood, sharpen them at one end, and bend them by drying one side over the fire. After tracing a circle on the ground, they make as many holes as they need, insert the pointed ends of the sticks, and tie the others together at the top. The framework is now ready, and the women can come and tie on the mats.

Such a hut may be four yards across and six or seven feet high. If more air is needed, it is easy to roll up the mats at the bottom. If it rains (not a common occurrence in Namaqualand) the rushes swell and become water-tight, and a trench is dug round the hut to let the wet run away. The front door faces the east, and is provided with a curtain of tanned cowhide, and the floor is covered with skins. There is a smaller entrance at the back of the hut, used chiefly by the servants, if any. The fire is in the front, between the centre and the entrance. At the back of the hut is a stage of poles, with several shelves, on which various household goods are kept—mats, skins, bundles of rushes, saddles, calabashes, milk-pails, pots, and—nowadays—the kettle for making coffee. There is also, probably, a green-painted wooden box, containing the more precious possessions of the family.

Most Nama now wear more or less of European clothing, some of it bought ready-made from traders, and some made by the women at home. They are also very clever in sewing *karosses* (skin rugs), either for their own use or for sale.

Nama Marriage Customs.

When a Nama marries he makes no payment to the bride's family as the Bantu do, but it is considered very mean if his relations do not supply several cows to be killed for the wedding feast. The bride brings with her a dowry consisting of cattle, and the mat-hut aforesaid, which her mother has had erected in time for the couple to occupy on the wedding-day. At the same time, she gives her daughter a handmaid—a Hill Damara girl, or perhaps a Nama orphan, who is thus provided with a home. The marriage ceremony is performed by the chief, who is said to address the bridegroom to the following effect: "You may consider ——— ——— as your wife, but take good care of her. If she will not obey you, you must not strike her so as to disfigure her; if you can do nothing with her, just bring her back, but don't beat her." Our informant adds, however, that this admonition is in most cases a dead letter. In that case it is difficult to understand the assertion of another writer that the Nama woman is much better off than the Zulu, whose family have in the *lobola* cattle a guarantee against ill-usage of her. He points out, however, that she is the owner of the house, which ought to give her some advantage; though we do not learn that she is in the habit of pulling it down and moving on with it when the husband proves refractory.

The Hill Damara.

The Hill Damara just mentioned are a curious people, of whom not very much is known. They are supposed to number about 30,000, and live scattered in the mountainous parts of Hereroland. A small proportion of them have been collected together and induced to settle near the Okombahe mission station; but till recently they have led a miserable life, enslaved and oppressed by Nama and Herero, and sometimes also by white settlers. They speak the same language as the Nama, but are certainly of a different race, and are also distinct from both the Herero and the Bushmen. They are black, or nearly so, though, according to a German missionary, Herr Irle, they appear, as a rule, of an ashy grey, for want of either washing in water or anointing themselves with fat. They live chiefly on what the Boers call *veldkost*—*i.e.*, anything that may be picked up on the veldt or in the bush—wild bulbs, roots of grass, honey, locusts, mice, lizards, caterpillars, the gum of trees, etc. In good years they dig up huge quantities of the edible bulbs (*uintjes*, or "little onions," in Dutch) and sell them to the Herero for sheep and goatskins. They make pots in a very primitive way, which is found among some other African tribes as well, though the art is more advanced among most of the Bantu. They pinch the clay into a long, thin roll, like a rope, and coil it round till the pot is finished. They also make some attempt at cultivating the ground, which neither Nama nor Herero do. "Wherever a secure spot offers suitable soil and water for a small garden, they take advantage of the situation and plant tobacco, *dacha* (hemp), pumpkins, and melons." *

The Herero.

The Herero are a finer race than either of the two last mentioned, and have many points in common with the Zulu, though, again, many of their ideas and customs differ widely. They are called by the Colonists "Damara," but their name for themselves is Ova-herero; the prefix *ova* corresponding to *aba*, *ba*, *wa*, or *a* in the names of other tribes—*e.g.*, Abatembu, Basutu, Wayao, Anyanja. Not much has been heard of them in England, except for the war carried on with them for some years by the Germans. Into the rights and wrongs of that war I cannot enter here. Suffice it to say that the Germans have not, as a rule, been fortunate in their Colonial undertakings, and that the Herero have suffered terribly—quite out of proportion to their original offence—whatever that may have been.

Photograph supplied by the Barmen Mission.

A HERERO MATRON

Wearing the three-pointed hat described in the text.

Herero Costume and Ornaments.

Physically, they are a tall, finely-built race, who often have oval faces and almost European features. They chip out a Λ-shaped gap between the two upper front teeth. Women and girls shave their heads except for a tuft in the middle of the scalp, to which they fasten little strings adorned with iron beads (a favourite form of jewellery with this tribe) and similar ornaments. The rest of their costume is somewhat elaborate. Young unmarried girls only wear a belt, from which thirty or forty leather thongs, ornamented with beads, hang to the ground. Married women wear a skin apron reaching from the waist to below the knee; a skin cloak, more or less ornamented, which reaches the ground behind; and a kind of belt or corselet (*omutombe*) covering the upper part of the breast, and made of ostrich-eggshell beads.† In addition to this, they have the characteristic head-dress assumed at their wedding: a sort of mitre or tiara of skin, of which the illustrations give a better idea than any amount of description. The construction of such a hat is a work of time and patience: the three flaps are cut out of carefully-prepared calf-skin, stitched in patterns, and ornamented with iron beads. No married woman is ever seen without this hat—to leave it off would be as great a breach of modesty as for a Moslem woman to go out unveiled. A sort of veil—a goatskin, tanned so as to be very soft and pliable—is fastened to the hat in front, but is usually worn rolled up out of the way; while a number of thongs, strung with iron beads, are attached behind. If we add the bracelets and anklets

* Stow, "Native Races of South Africa," p. 259.

† These beads seem originally to have been made by the Bushmen, and were sometimes bought from them by other tribes, before the introduction of European beads. They are still made and bartered for grain, knives, iron arrow-heads, etc., by the Bushmen of the Central Kalahari. "The shell, which is naturally very hard, had first to be boiled and softened in cold water, then cut into small pieces through which a hole was pierced with a little flint or agate drill, then rubbed into small rings like beads, and polished" (Dr. Stow). The same authority says, "No other race except that of the Bushmen had either the skill or the patience to manufacture these beads," but it would seem that the Herero women have learned the art. The task of stringing them together to make the *omutombe* is also a very long and tedious one.

(either single rings or coils of iron wire), the former sometimes reaching to the elbow and the latter nearly to the knee, it will be seen that a well-to-do Herero woman carries a considerable weight of iron about with her. In sewing skins the women use a needle, or rather awl, made of a sharp thorn; their thread is made from sinews of animals.

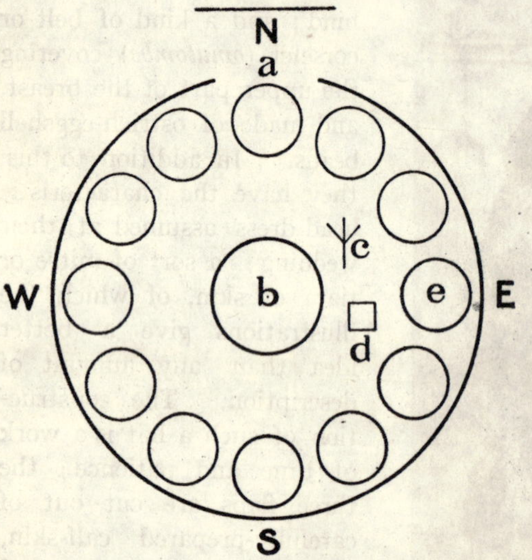

PLAN OF A HERERO KRAAL.

The site of the sacred fire (*okuruo*) is marked *d*. The huts are arranged in a circle round the cattle-kraal (*b*).

The Sacred Fire of the Herero.

Many points in the customs of these people are exceedingly interesting, but we cannot here do more than indicate a few of the most remarkable. The women milk the cows, which, so far as I know, is the case with no other Bantu tribe. It is also a woman—the chief's eldest unmarried daughter—who is the guardian of the sacred fire. This she always keeps burning in the "great wife's" hut, and from it every morning she kindles the fire on the *okuruo*, or "altar," the position of which in the kraal is shown by the accompanying diagram. The cattle kraal (*b*) is in the middle, all the huts being ranged round it in a circle with their doors facing inward. The whole is surrounded by a thorn fence, with its gateway (*a*) facing north. The "great wife's" hut (*e*) is on the east of the cattle kraal, and between them is the "altar" (*d*). A little to the north of the latter is the sacred tree (*c*). This is either an *omumborombonga* (botanically, *Combretum primigenium*), the tree from which, as the Herero believe, the human race originated,* or a dry branch of the *omuvapu* shrub (called by Colonists the "raisin-bush"), which is supposed to represent it, and is also held sacred. All round the *okuruo* are the skulls and horns of the oxen sacrificed on solemn occasions, and these serve as seats for the old men when they come to discuss affairs of public importance with the chief.

No strange fire may be kindled on the *okuruo*, and no stranger is allowed to take from it a coal to light his pipe. In the evening the chief's daughter carries the embers back into her mother's hut, and keeps them smouldering all night. If by any chance the fire should go out, it may only be re-lit by rubbing certain sacred sticks. If the kraal is removed, the family carry the fire with them. The huts are built much on the same plan as those of the Zulu already described, but somewhat narrower and higher in proportion, because the wattles are bound together at the top, instead of being planted in a series of arches, and they are also plastered with clay outside, instead of being thatched.

Herero Coming of Age Celebrations.

Herero children, both boys and girls, have the two lower front teeth knocked out at about eight or ten years of age, and the upper ones chipped or filed into the triangular gap already described. The ceremony observed when girls grow up is called *efundula*; they are not secluded, but a great dance is held at the chief's place, to which all the girls within reach come, attended by their mothers. The young men assemble to see them, and, no doubt, make their choice; but no special steps are taken at this time for entering on engagements. After the dance, the girls are rubbed all over with ashes, put on a peculiar kind of cap, and march about the country in procession, carrying long sticks in their hands and chanting as they go.

* The original tree is supposed to be somewhere in the Kaoko country, in the north-west of Hereroland towards the Portuguese border.

At every kraal they come to they are entertained with the best the place affords, and all men and youths are expected to keep out of their way. Anyone failing to do so is soundly beaten by the girls. After a month of this travelling about, they return home, and are now supposed to be marriageable.

Herero Marriage Customs.

Marriages are usually arranged by the parents, though this statement must be understood with the reservations previously indicated. The young people are betrothed between the ages of fifteen and seventeen or so, when the youth gives the girl an iron bead, and she knots it on one of the strings of her apron. After this they are not supposed to meet till their marriage, and it is considered very improper of him to show his face at her home. It sometimes happens, though not often, that the girl refuses to accept the token, and, if the parents are not exceptionally hard-hearted, this puts an end to the negotiations. The actual marriage ceremony presents more curious details. When the bridegroom arrives at the bride's house, she takes hold of a strap which he wears hanging down his back, and marches after him all round the kraal, followed by a long procession of friends in single file, all shouting the young man's clan name (*eanda*) *—*e.g.*, "Child of the sun," "of the rain," etc. A sheep is killed for the feast; the bride and bridegroom do not eat of it, but they breathe on the meat before it is passed round to the guests. The bride's girl friends take out part of the inside (the caul, to be precise) of this same sheep, and put it over her head, and she wears this extraordinary decoration till the end of the festivities (lasting, perhaps, for several days), when her mother takes it off and puts on the cap or mitre already described.

Some of these ceremonies are gone through

From a photograph supplied by the Barmen Mission.

A HERERO FAMILY.

again at the bridegroom's kraal when he has taken the bride home; but, this time, during the processional march, she carries in one hand a wooden bowl, into which the inmates of each hut in turn, as the couple come to a halt there, put sweet-scented herbs. During this march, which concludes the ceremonies, the bride wears her veil down.

Herero Birth Customs.

When a child is born the nurse announces the event by calling out "*Okauta*—a little bow!" if it is a boy; if a girl, she says "*Okazeu*—a little onion!"—or rather one of the edible bulbs which it is part of a girl's business to dig up. In the former

* The *omaanda* (sing. *eanda*) are clans or castes, to one or other of which every Herero belongs, and each of which is distinguished by some badge or token—the sun, the rain, etc. The subject is too technical and complicated for further discussion in a work like this.

case, the father goes about shouting "*Okauta*," which is echoed by all the men in the place—in the latter, he covers his face and hides himself—not because the event is a mournful one, for, after all, a girl represents an increase in the family property—but probably as a sort of conventional demonstration of modesty. The head of the kraal keeps a leather thong in which a knot is made at the birth of every child—a kind of family register.

The birth of twins, which is by many savage tribes considered a terrible misfortune, is, for the Herero, an occasion of great rejoicing. The customs observed are too numerous to describe; it is enough to say that a special sacredness attaches to the twins and their father for life.

Children are always welcomed and treated with affection; the Herero, like most Africans, in normal circumstances, are of opinion that "happy is the man that hath his quiver full of them." A mother carries her baby on her back in a goatskin (as the Zulu women do), and, when she wants to feed it, simply shifts it round till it rests on her hip. An old man is sometimes seen walking about the kraal, or sitting in the sun, with a little grandchild in his arms.

Childhood among the Herero.

From a photograph supplied by the Barmen Mission.

AN AANDONGA (OVAMBO) MARRIED COUPLE.

It is very common, when weaning children, to make a nanny-goat act as nurse; the baby very soon learns to catch her by the hind legs, and milk her into its mouth. As elsewhere in Africa, children are seldom weaned before they are old enough to run about.

Boys begin to herd the cattle at five (of course in company with their elder brothers and other companions), and this forms their chief occupation for the next fifteen years or so. Less is expected of little girls; they dig up bulbs, collect gum or berries, and help to fetch wood and water, but they are not overburdened with work. There are few, if any, English books giving a detailed account of this interesting people. Sir Francis Galton came in contact with them in 1850, but his account is not very flattering. If we consider it fairly, however, we find that he saw very little of them, that the only man of any standing he met (the chief Kahityine) made a very favourable impression on him; and that, for the rest, the case might be paralleled by an Indian traveller landing in London for a week or so, and forming his opinion of our nation from a few of the boatmen, longshore loafers and lodging-house keepers in the neighbourhood of the Custom House. A more just notion may be obtained from some German works, among which we may mention those of Dr. Schinz, the Rev. J. Irle (who lived and worked in the country over thirty years), and the late Dr. Brincker.

The Ovakwanyama and Aandonga (together called by the Herero, Ovambo) live in the fertile flat country to the north-east of the Herero, near the Kunene River. They are an agricultural people, differing from the Herero in language and in many of their customs; their costume, for one thing, is much scantier, as may be noticed in the illustrations. The villages, instead of having huts arranged in circles, either quite open or surrounded by a simple round fence, are embedded in a complex labyrinth of passages enclosed between high palisades, through which it is impossible for a stranger to find his way without a guide.

Agricultural Tribes.

From a photograph supplied by the Barmen Mission.

THE CHIEF COUNCILLOR OF UEYULU (CHIEF OF THE OVAKWANYAMA), WITH HIS WIVES.

The country of the "Ovambo" reaches up to the Okavango River, beyond which the Barotse country begins. This country really includes other tribes besides the Barotse, who are the ruling caste. Their king, Lewanika, who asked some years ago for permission to place his people under British protection, has had his sons educated in England, and himself came to London for the Coronation. As might be expected, the customs of the people are rapidly changing, even where they have not actually been converted to Christianity by the devoted labours of the French missionaries, and it is probable that many of their traditions will before long be entirely lost. Like other Bantu of Central Africa, they reckon relationship in the female line, and a man's next heir is not his own, but his sister's son, while children belong to their mother's tribe, not to their father's. The Zulu do not follow this system, though there are indications that they may once have done so, and the Herero do so partially, though for some purposes they count descent on the father's side. It is in accordance with this system that the Rotse king's sister is a person of great importance—much more so than any of his wives. She "has the right of veto on all his actions and decisions," which is shared by only one other person—the king's maternal uncle, officially called the *Natamoyo*, or "minister of mercy."

The Barotse.

The late M. Coillard tells a pleasant story, related to him by the natives, of the first Rotse king, Mboho, who was not much of a warrior, but, being hard pressed by

Photograph by the late M. Coillard; by permission of the Secretary of the Barotseland Mission.

THE MOKWAE (QUEEN) OF NALOLO (KING LEWANIKA'S SISTER) IN HER STATE CANOE.

his enemies, prepared a certain powerful "medicine," and directed his people to scatter it over the path by which the foe might approach.

A Barotse Legend.

"Everyone refused, seized with terror, not because of the enemy, but because of the medicine itself. 'For,' they said, 'if it has the power of annihilating our enemies, why should it not kill us, too?' Only one person, a woman, had the courage to come forward. She took the formidable medicine, and went bravely towards the enemy's camp, scattered it all over the paths, and cast the remainder to the wind in the direction of the Mankoya, to such good purpose that the next day they were all dead and the Barotse delivered. The king then said to this woman, 'To-day you are a man; you shall sit in the *lekhothla* (the place of assembly) as a man, and among your descendants there shall always be a woman-chief to take your place.'"

This legend may have been invented by the Makololo—a Suto tribe who came from the south and conquered the Barotse about 1830—to account for the existence of an institution new to them.

Women Chiefs.

For we find that women chiefs are not at all uncommon among the tribes north and east of the Barotse. Livingstone mentions several whom he saw, or heard of, in his travels. We may remember the Londa chieftainess Manenko, who, with her husband and suite, escorted him, when on his way from Linyanti to Loanda, to the town of her uncle Shinte. There was also Nyango, who seems to have been at one time lady paramount of the tribes on the Upper Shiré; and the chief near Lake Mweru, who goes by the hereditary name of Kazembe, is also a woman. At Shinte's village, Livingstone says: "This was the first town I had ever seen females present in a public assembly. In the south the women are not permitted to enter the *kotla*, and even when invited to come to a religious service they would not enter until ordered to do so by the chief; but here they expressed approbation by clapping

Photograph by the late M. Coillard; by permission of the Secretary of the Barotseland Mission.

BAROTSE BASKET-MAKERS.

their hands, and laughing, to different speakers; and Shinte frequently turned round and spoke to them."

East of the Barotse, the Babemba and Bawisa tribes need not detain us at present. South of these, along the course of the Zambezi, come the Batonga (Batoka) and Basenga, and, on the other side of the river, the Mashona. These are part of a people who, under different names, and interrupted by settlements of other tribes who have invaded and broken them up, extend as far as the north end of Lake Nyasa, and down the Shiré and Zambezi to the east coast. They are called—on the Lake, Anyanja; on the Shiré, Mang'anja; and elsewhere Chipetas or Maravi. They, like the Ovakwanyama and Barotse, cultivate the soil, and build round huts with conical roofs.

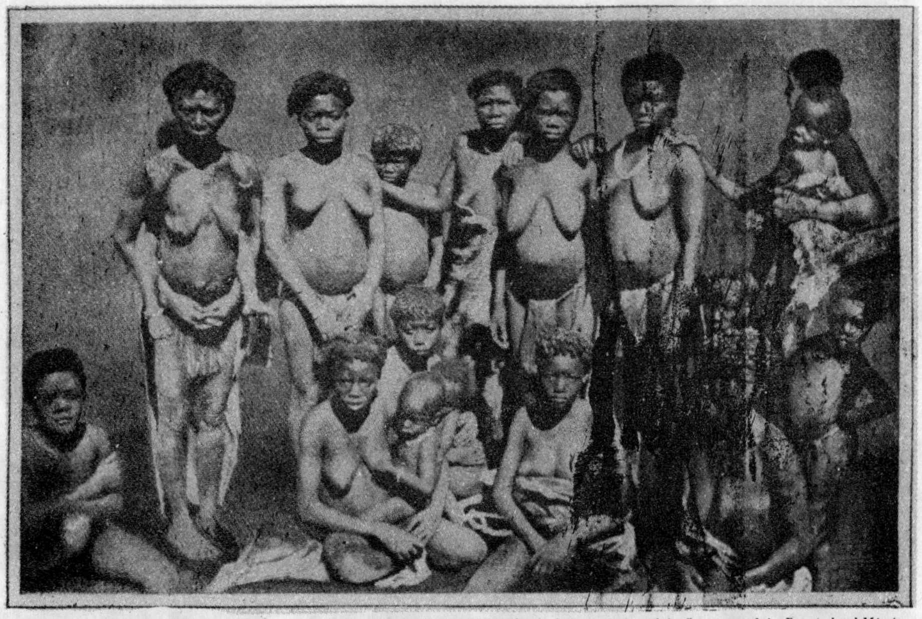

Photograph by the late M. Coillard: by permission of the Secretary of the Barotseland Mission.

MAMBOE WOMEN (UPPER BAROTSE VALLEY).

Prisoners taken by Lewanika in a punitive raid on the tribe for having failed to pay the tribute due to him.

The Matabele.

South of the Mashona, and in some parts scattered among them, live the Matabele (Amandebele), originally a clan of Zulu, whose head (Umziligazi, better known as Moselekatse, and called by the Boers "Salkats"), quarrelled with King Tshaka, and, flying for his life, founded a kingdom of his own in the north. Another detachment of Zulu left their country about the same time, and for a similar reason, under Zwangendaba the same whom Zwide wished to attack, as already related, and was dissuaded by his mother. They crossed the Zambezi in 1825, and their descendants are the "Angoni" of West Nyasaland.

The Anyanja.

Some of these Angoni still speak Zulu, but only the chiefs and a few other families are really of Zulu descent, and those, probably, not unmixed. The name was indiscriminately applied to all the different tribes whom they conquered and incorporated with themselves; and in British Central Africa—at any rate in the southern part—"Angoni" virtually means "Anyanja." A good many of these Anyanja, especially those west of the Shiré, are small, wiry people, cheerful, kindly, and hard working, with several characteristics which suggest that their Bantu ancestors may have intermarried freely with the aborigines of the country—

probably the Bushmen, or some allied race.

Other Anyanja, as those of the Shiré River, usually called Mang'anja, are tall and largely made; but on the whole, they, including the Mashona, are of slighter and less muscular build than the Zulu and Matabele. They live chiefly on maize or millet porridge and other vegetable food, instead of meat and milk; they do not keep cattle, only a few goats and sheep; and, as already stated, both men and women hoe the gardens. They are more skilled in arts and industries than the Zulu. Their iron-work and wood-carving attain a higher level, and they spin and weave excellent cotton cloth, though this art has fallen somewhat into disuse since it has become easy to procure cheap English or American calico. The spinning and weaving is done by the men, who also sew—nowadays with English steel needles—formerly with implements made out of a splinter of bamboo.

Photograph supplied by the British South Africa Company.

MASHONA WOMEN,

Wearing leather skirts, bead girdles, and brass bangles. The two middle ones have discs of white shell (brought from the coast and much valued as ornaments and possibly charms) round their necks. Those worn by the girl on the right may, however, be made of ostrich egg-shell. The single disc of the left-hand figure is that called *mpande* in Nyanja; it is cut from the top of the *conus* shell.

"Calicoes."

Calico is almost the universal wear—the cheap unbleached kind that costs $1\frac{1}{4}$d. or $2\frac{3}{4}$d. a yard in this country. A man wears his cloth round his waist, reaching to his knees or his ankles, according to circumstances, viz., his means, or the nature of his occupation. Women's calicoes begin higher up, being usually wrapped round under the arms, sometimes merely secured by tucking in a fold, sometimes supported by a piece of stuff tied round the waist. Better-dressed women have two cloths, the lower coming down to their feet like a skirt, and the most complete costume includes a little short-sleeved cotton jacket just big enough to cover all that the upper calico would leave exposed, and a sash of Turkey-red twill, or something similar, tied in front with the ends hanging down. All these garments are sewn, if at all (a "calico" for ordinary wear may be just a raw-edged piece of cloth, but careful people have theirs hemmed at the ends), by the husband, whose duty it is to supply his wife with clothes, as it is hers to provide him with food.

Photograph by J. G. Kunje.

A MAKOLOLO WOMAN AND CHILDREN.

Newly-husked *maere* is spread out on the goatskin. The Makololo on the Shiré are people descended from some of Livingstone's followers who came from Sebituano's country on the Zambezi.

Maize and its Uses.

The method of pounding maize in the wooden mortar (cut out of the trunk of a tree) is well shown in the photograph on p. 308. The grinding on stones, which in Natal is the whole process, here comes afterwards, when the coarse meal has been taken out of the mortar and separated from the husk by shaking and winnowing in flat baskets. At the end of the grinding it is a fine white flour. The grain of the sorghum, here called *mapira*, a slightly different species from that grown in Natal, is used for making beer—in Nyanja *moa*. There is a third kind of grain (*Eleusine*), known as *maere*—a small kind of millet, like bird-seed, not specially grown, but springing up of itself in and near the gardens, and gathered in bad years for food. It is so troublesome to husk and prepare that it is not regarded at ordinary times; the porridge made from it is dark in colour, and requires a good deal of hunger-sauce to make it appetising. A quantity of this *maere*, just husked, is seen spread out on a goatskin in the illustration on this page. When the *mapira* is gathered, the heads are laid on a mat and beaten out with a long thin stick. Maize is stored in granaries like huge round baskets mounted on platforms, and covered with a conical roof. One of these is seen behind the old woman in the second photograph on p. 308, but it is not in very good repair.

Maize porridge (*nsima*) is eaten off little flat, round baskets or wooden platters. Some relish (boiled in a small pot put on beside the big one for the porridge) is eaten with it—it may be green vegetables, or

Photograph by J. G. Kunje

AN ANGONI GIRL WINNOWING MAIZE.

She is kneeling on a mat of split *bango* reeds—behind her on the left is an earthen pot containing the gourd used for drawing water.

Photograph by J. G. Kunje.

AN ANGONI GIRL POUNDING MAIZE.

The mortar is formed from a tree-trunk. Note the reed fence surrounding the little yard and the growing maize behind it.

seen with their shaven scalps glistening with castor-oil. Many of them are marked on the face and body with cuts into which something has been rubbed, either to make the flesh heal in a raised scar, or to darken the skin. They often have their ears bored for the insertion of ornaments, and some of the old women wear an ivory ring, the size of a napkin-ring in the upper lip. This fashion passed from the Anyanja to the Yao, and seems to be now going out, even among them, but is in full vigour among the Anguru (West of Lake Chilwa), who sometimes wear—not a ring, but a little metal cup. The Yao women wear a metal stud (like a drawing-pin) in one side of the nose; this fashion has probably been borrowed from the Indian women on the coast. Beads and brass rings are as popular as in most other places. The former are often worn round the neck in ropes made by sewing them on to thin rolls of calico. Wealthy

beans, or fish, or perhaps a fowl. It is the height of bad manners to eat alone, and not share the food with others. Cooking is only done once, or at most twice a day, the principal meal being taken about sunset. A native story tells how a husband and wife, each unknown to the other, abstracted a leg of the partridge which was cooking, and retired, separately, into the dark interior of the hut to eat it, where they came violently into collision, and had an explanation, each promising to say nothing about the matter if the other would only keep the story quiet. African natives are as sensitive to ridicule as most other people—perhaps even a little more so.

Anyanja Ornaments.

The Anyanja women have no special way of dressing their hair, though some shave it in patterns, and occasionally one is seen with red beads threaded on strands of it. They never let it grow more than an inch or two, and are often

Photograph by J. G. Kunje.

AN OLD CHIPETA WOMAN

Seated on the rocky hill-side with a basket of meal before her; a granary and garden in the background. The mortar is on her left—on her right is one of the large baskets (*mtanga*) used for carrying maize, etc.

Photograph by permission of the British South Africa Company.

MASHONA BRASS-WORKER PUTTING ON A GIRL'S ANKLETS.

men's wives sometimes have so many brass anklets that they can scarcely walk. These are sometimes solid brass rings; sometimes a coil of brass wire is worn which requires a brass-worker to put on. When a craftsman of this sort is known to be passing through a village the women flock from far and wide—

Photograph by J. G. Kunje.

A YAO MOHAMMEDAN WOMAN AND CHILDREN

Seated on a *bango* mat. Note the nose-stud worn by the mother.

they may have been waiting months for the chance of wearing their jewellery. When the coil of wire has at last been coaxed on to the leg it is necessary for some time to pad the lower round with rags, in order to keep the brass from chafing the foot.

Yao Women.

The Yao live chiefly on the eastern side of the Shiré—in some districts a good deal mixed up with the Anyanja. Their old home is in the north, by the eastern side of Lake Nyasa. Yao women have a tribe-mark consisting of two rows of small cuts on the temple, but I fancy this is no longer rigidly kept up. They are a race of sturdy mountaineers—somewhat "dour," and very touchy, but lovable withal, and very faithful when their hearts are won. Many of the men, especially those who have been down to the coast—for they are great travellers and traders—call themselves Mohammedans, and have Arab names. This influence is probably undermining the old matriarchal constitution of society. A Yao not only counts his descent through his mother, but he goes to live in his wife's village when he marries, and hoes a garden for her parents. I have heard that it is generally the Yao woman who proposes marriage, and it is possible that this may be so, for it would be quite in accordance with a system where the man is not the sole bread-winner.

The religious institutions of the Yao are described very minutely and graphically in the Rev. Duff Macdonald's "Africana." Women have a certain prominence in these, in the persons of the prophetess and the *Mabisalila*, or witch-detective, who dances herself into a frenzy, and then gives the name of the witch or the whereabouts of the property she has been asked to trace. The Rev. Henry Rowley gives a very impressive account of a Nyanja ceremony in which the chief's sister took the principal part, for the purpose of praying for rain. The religion both of the Yao and the Anyanja is chiefly ancestor-worship, with some vague acknowledgment of a supreme spirit called *Mulungu*, *Leza*, *Mpambe* or *Chiuta*, who appears—sometimes, at least—to be a personification of the sky, lightning or thunder. Huts are erected for the accommodation of the ancestral spirits, and offerings of meal or beer laid at the foot of a tree for them. But the subject is too wide a one to be treated in passing—even to show in how many ways it bears on the life of women.

THE CONGO FREE STATE

By E. TORDAY

The Congo State—The People of the Congo—The Pygmies—The Negro Population—The Slave Trade—Women under the Slave-traders—Birth and Infancy—Congo Love and Courtship—Personal Adornment—Congolese Dress—Ornaments—Congolese Coiffures—Marriage Customs—Child Marriage—Congolese Wedding Dance—Conjugal Infidelity—Social Conditions on the Congo—Death and Burial—Widow Sacrifice—Cannibalism—Physical Attractions of Congolese Women—Negroes—Cleanliness—Preparation of Food—Religion—Home Life

By permission of the Ethnographical Museum, Tervueren.

YOUNG BAKUBA GIRL.

The Congo State.

THE mouth of the River Congo was discovered by the Portuguese navigator Diego Cão in the fifteenth century, but no part of the upper river was known until Livingstone first reached it at Nyangwe, when, however, he believed it to be the Nile. It was first explored by Sir H. M. Stanley, who called it the Livingstone, a name which has passed into oblivion. The actual Congo State was founded by the King of the Belgians, and extends over an area of about 800,000 square miles, with a population which has been estimated variously between eight millions and forty millions, the correct figure being probably about twelve millions.

The population is continually decreasing, in consequence of an epidemic of sleeping-sickness, which ravages Central Africa from the West to the East coast. A great part of the State was under the domination of the Arabs until the year 1892, when they were driven out by an army composed of native troops commanded by Belgian and Scandinavian officers. It is now actually governed by a central administration in Brussels, represented by a Governor-general at Boma. The government is absolute, but it seems likely that the country will become a Belgian colony under the control of the Belgian parliament.

The People of the Congo.

The inhabitants of the Congo form many tribes, which differ greatly in their customs. It cannot be of interest to the general reader to enumerate them; so I shall endeavour to arrange them in groups, each group containing those which show the greatest similarity. In this attempt I shall not classify them according to their origin in remote times; for, contrary to general belief, the negro is not very conservative and easily assimilates himself to the people with whom he has been brought in contact in his wanderings. And indeed, as far as their origin is concerned, all is conjecture. A people without writing or historical monuments, which forgets even its traditions in less than a century, can give us no clue, and the ethnographer alone can arrive at a more or less satisfactory conclusion.

It must, nevertheless, be mentioned that the original inhabitants of the country were probably the Pygmies, of whom some specimens were recently seen in London. Few of these interesting little people are now left, and these are spread in diminutive colonies in all parts of the country. They are very simple in their habits, and have, for the most part, not yet risen above that stage of civilisation when agriculture is still unknown, and when man still lives only on the products of the chase, and the roots and wild fruits provided by the forest. Only a few condescend to barter their superfluous game for the agricultural produce of their more civilised neighbours.

The Pygmies.

Pygmies cannot be called fine specimens of humanity; their physique is slight, their height varying from four feet to four feet six inches. Their heads are rather big in proportion to their bodies. Their skin varies from a dirty yellow to a brown tint, their hair is short and scanty. In consequence of the active life they are obliged to live they are very thin, to such an extent that their bones may be easily seen through the skin. A most offensive odour attaches to them, but this is probably due to the want of cleanliness so common to people of the forest.

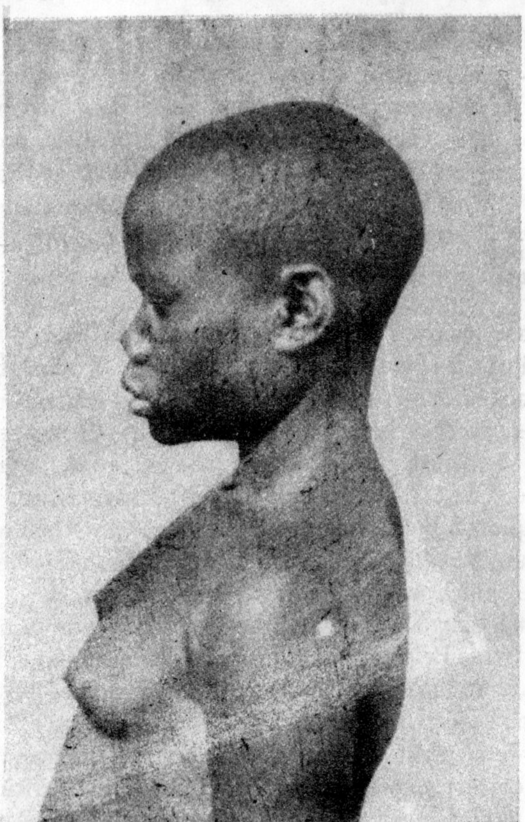

Photograph by Sir H. H. Johnston, G.C.M.G., K.C.B.

A PYGMY WOMAN.

The Pygmy women are purchased as wives for three or four arrows!

Some "savants" believe them to be related to the bushmen; but a multitude of physical and social differences throws great doubt on this subject.

All other inhabitants of the Congo are invaders. Their physical characteristics divide them into two groups, the Northern, who show similarity to the real Negroes, and the Southern, much more refined in features, who exhibit traces of "Hamitic" blood.

The Negro Population.

In a general study like this it will perhaps be best to divide the population into two groups, the Negroes as they naturally are, and the Negroes who have been influenced by foreign invaders, such as the Arabs or the Portuguese.

Although they have derived much profit from the Eastern civilisation brought to them by the Arabs, and some little from the Occidental imported by the Portuguese, their patriarchal habits have been greatly changed for the worse where they have been in contact with these foreign dealers in human cattle. The slave trade has destroyed the ties of relationship, and has brought the head of the family to consider its members as mere merchandise.

The Slave Trade.

Slavery has always existed amongst the Congolese, but, where they have been left to themselves, the slaves are considered as the children of their owners, are treated as a rule with great kindness, and are many times better off than the European "slaves" in mines and factories. Where the natives have been brought into contact with Portuguese or Arabs they have been taught to consider their wives and children as a source of wealth, easily exchanged for articles of comfort and luxury.

It has been the good fortune of the author to be in contact with both kinds of inhabitants, and he has found that the cannibal of the interior is by far the wiser and better man of the two.

Only a short sketch of a woman's life in those parts of the country where the slave trade flourished will be given, and then I shall pass to the more cheerful picture of life where patriarchal habits still persist. Happily it is true that the latter prevail over the greater part of the country, in fact the whole of the interior.

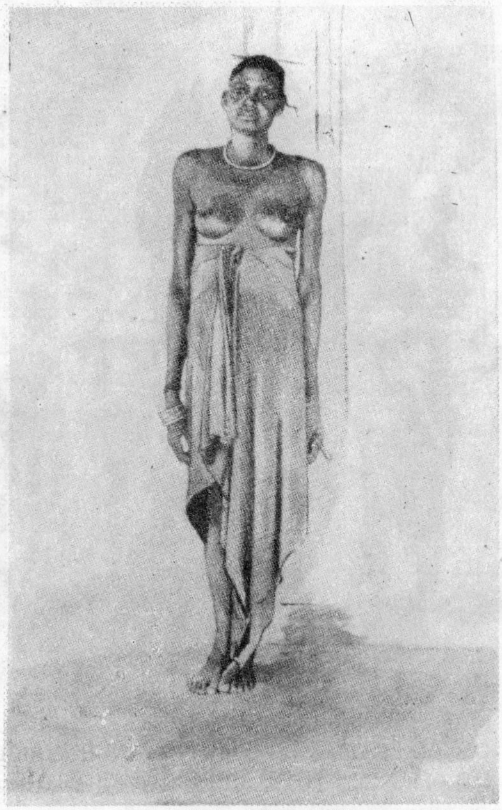

Drawn by Sir Harry Johnston, G.C.M.G., K.C.B.

GALITZIA—A BATÉKÉ WOMAN.

Women under the Slave Trade.

The parts of the Congo which for centuries have been the great slave-providing districts are situated in the East, where Arab and Wanyamwesi raiders have carried on their operations, and in the South and South-West, where the Portuguese have been at work. It is painful to have to admit that the Portuguese were by far the worst offenders. It is true that the Arabs in their expeditions did not consider human life, and showed the greatest cruelty, but as soon as they were settled they certainly improved the welfare of the people by teaching them order, agriculture, cattle-raising, and many useful crafts. Their Draconian laws against theft, adultery and murder, although inhuman in our eyes, would not have been considered so in the England of a century ago, when people were hanged for petty theft, and they have certainly bettered the moral standard of the aborigines. The great drawback to their domination did not lie in the fact that they kept slaves, but in the manner in which these were seized and in the fact that they were exported. It is evident that family ties were by this means destroyed, and that the position of women, the most coveted form of merchandise, was degraded. And this is still felt, for, in spite of the expulsion of the Arabs, much of the evil still exists, and a man will still barter his women relatives for the necessaries of life.

The Arab invaders were warrior merchants, cruel indeed; but we cannot help admiring their courage and the spirit of chivalry which they displayed. A few bold adventurers, without any assistance from a mother country, they were able by their own pluck to conquer and keep for a long time a territory larger than England, and inhabited by a dense population of cannibal warriors. No such mitigating qualities can be found among the Portuguese traders, the majority of whom were convicts, who had left their country for their country's good, and who had formed the scum of its population. The Arabs conquered with the sword, the Portuguese with gin. The natives could fight the one, but were powerless against the insidious attacks of the other, and what good qualities the "curse of Africa"—alcohol—left to them were destroyed by the vicious example of the white man. That part of the country which had been under Arab domination is slowly returning to a better state of things, but no such happy prospect can be expected in the other territory.

arms; this entitles the mother to a little present, which is bestowed gladly in proportion to the donor's means. If the young mother is a slave, her owner will continually bring her dainties, whilst his wives will nurse her. In choosing the child's name,

By permission of the Ethnographical Museum, Tervueren.

CONGO BABIES FROM THE LORI TRIBE.

Their mothers have their lips pierced and distended by an ivory disc.

Let us consider now the Congo woman's life, where the savages are only guided by their natural good instincts.

Birth and Infancy.

When a child is born the greatest interest is taken in the event by all the inhabitants of the village. Old and young women bustle round the mother; men stand outside the hut and discuss gravely with the father. Everybody compliments him, and declares that never has such a strong and fat child been seen before. Just as in Europe, family resemblances are discovered over a glass of "*malafu*" (palm wine), which the proud father offers freely to his guests. And then the people of the neighbouring villages flock in to see the new-born infant; the poor simply look at it, whilst the wealthy, who can afford it, take the baby into their

that of some important man is often selected; and this is a very great compliment which is repaid by considerable presents.

One or two days after the child's birth the mother leaves her hut. This is the time of life when the Congo woman looks most beautiful. I always found that maternity greatly increases her beauty, an atmosphere of happiness seems to surround her, and she simply shines with it.

From this moment the baby does not leave its mother any more; carried in a kind of bag on her back, or later, on her hip, it clings to "mammy" and follows her to the fields, joining in the chase for crickets and locusts. But sometimes the child is taken by the father, who, as fathers always will, spoils it by indulgence. Among some tribes, the Bayaka for example, it is the father's privilege to carry the child; and to show that all his care is bestowed on the baby, he abstains from washing as long as the infant is unable to walk, though under ordinary circumstances the Bayaka are an extremely cleanly people. If we consider the great importance these people attach to personal ornament, it is a proof of great love to find that women with infants in arms do not ornament or paint themselves for such time as the baby is unable to walk by itself.

When the child is about a year old, her brothers, sisters, and cousins claim the right of looking after her, and, in fact, she takes the place of a doll. A doll is the substitute for a natural object of the affection inborn in mankind, and is especially strong in little girls; but the baby has no cause for complaint, except perhaps by reason of an excess of caresses.

"*Ne frappez pas un enfant, même avec une fleur,*" is a rule amongst these people; children are never punished, and seldom scolded. It would be easier to obtain pardon for murder than for a harsh word spoken to a child.

Thus it may be imagined what anguish a mother must feel in the Baluba tribe, where the child is liable to be claimed by the "*N'Ganga*" (witch-doctor) for religious sacrifice until it has cut its first tooth. But after this event has taken place this claim cannot be made, and the mother rejoices and feasts are often given in honour of the occasion.

Deformed children are hardly ever seen; the Spartan law of suppression at birth is in full force among most of the tribes. The Bayaka form an exception; no deformity could persuade these people to destroy a child.

How far fathers take an interest in children may be shown by a very curious habit (now tending to disappear) which prevails among the Bangala, and consists in the fact that when a child is to be born its father goes to bed, and is nursed in just the same manner as the mother!

Small children of any nationality are very beautiful, and the Congo children do not form an exception. I do not think that any child has eyes so beautiful as a baby from this country; they are big and shaded by long eyelashes. It is unnecessary to mention their teeth, which justify their great reputation.

Congolese children are very playful, and it may be new to the reader to know that games are found here similar to those in England. Blind-man's-buff is in great vogue, and a form of snap-dragon is much in favour. Any round fruit will serve as a ball, and the "*gombe*" game is not unlike lawn-tennis.

On Lake Tanganika the favourite game is "*bao,*" a game of intelligence, highly interesting, which the author has many a time played with little boys and girls, and, he confesses it with a blush, in which he, as a rule, got the worst of it. For negro children are *very* intelligent, probably more so than European children of the same age.

It has been said by many travellers that the Congolese do not know gratitude, and are not really affectionate. How untrue this is! I shall never forget how, when I left a certain region, the little children were sobbing and two little girls, Marisaka and Djimbu, to whom I had shown some kindness, were clinging to me and imploring me not to go away! And this happened in a country where cannibalism is openly practised!

Between games and instruction in her future duties the little girl grows up, to be, at the early age of twelve or thirteen, on the point of changing into a woman, and now the question of love becomes important.

Congo Love and Courtship.

Capello and Ivens say on this subject:* "Let us consider for a moment whether the negress does or can love in the lofty sense of that word. If she loved, if she had the consciousness of that sublime sentiment which opens to us on earth the gates of heaven, she would manifest it in her actions, and by its aid attain to some belief, some religious faith, inasmuch as her very felicity would help her to comprehend

* "From Benguella to the Territory of Yacca."

that there must be something better and purer above this material mundane life. But who is capable of inspiring her with such a feeling in the brutalised state of slavery in

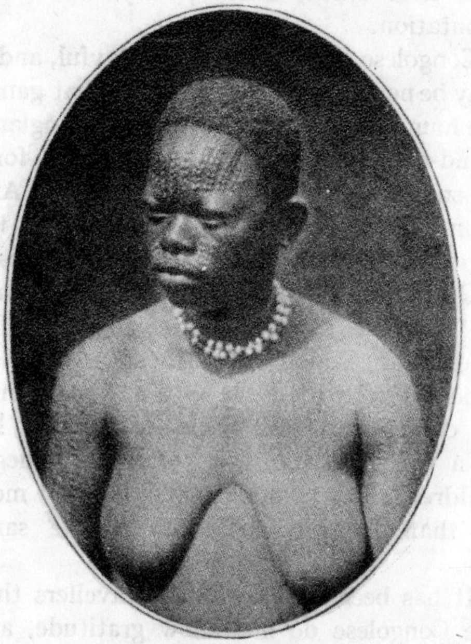

A BAZOKO WOMAN.
With typical scar tattooing.

which she lives? Her husband? Most certainly not. He simply encircles her with an iron girdle of obligations and despicable labour, compels her to live in the dirt, like his dog, and toil and travail for his pleasure; she in her part dares not touch or even look at him without permission, she may not eat at the same table, far less from the same dish as he, and must not accept liquor from his hand."

Some years ago, I should have subscribed in all sincerity to this statement, and certainly shared the Portuguese explorers' opinion. But since I have lived amongst natives uncorrupted by the slave trade, I have formed a very different opinion. It is all true concerning the women described in the early part of this article, but not a word of it can be applied to the Congolese women, whose tribe has remained uncorrupted by slave trade and *aguardiente* (gin). I feel competent to speak with perfect knowledge on the subject, having watched with Pickwickian benevolence many a love intrigue, and often contributed my modest mite to its happy conclusion.

When arriving in a village it often struck me that a few of the girls were more carefully dressed, oiled and painted than the others. On inquiring the reason of this from some old woman, I invariably got the reply: "She is in love, the dear child, and of course wants to be beautiful." And is it not a proof of love, that the heart of the Congo girl often runs away with her head and that important chiefs' daughters wed poor slaves?

Many a time has a father complained to me that his daughter has refused the husband chosen by him for political reasons, because, as she declared, she loved another man, and in countries, where human sacrifice is practised, the wife freely descends into the grave of her deceased husband, to be with him in death. Moreover the Bayeke woman, when her husband has been killed in war, charges like a fury on the enemy,

BANGALA WOMAN.
Showing the ornamental scars on forehead.

be his number ever so superior, in an attempt to revenge the death of her beloved.

Human hearts are the same whatever be the colour of the skin, and the

BAMBALA WOMAN : KWILU RIVER, CONGO FREE STATE.
(Painted with red earth.)
DRAWN BY NORMAN H. HARDY.

Facing on page 316

Congolese girl loves her "*Bakala*" as much as Miss Smith loves her young man.

Now how does the Congolese woman, who wants to please her lover, try to increase her beauty?

The most important form of ornamentation consists in cicatrisation, which is performed by making cuts in the skin.

Personal Adornment.

The wounds are prevented from healing for a time, sometimes by inserting some irritant substance, and the resultant scars form a more or less artistic design. Of course this process is most painful; but once finished, it lasts for a lifetime. Cicatrisation differs greatly from tribe to tribe, and I shall give a short description of the most characteristic forms.

The Batéké make parallel longitudinal cuts in their cheeks, descending in a column from the temples to the mouth; the Bayansi ornament the forehead with a single or double row of crosses, and a similar design is worked on the breasts. Several incisions of varying forms run from the throat to the abdomen, passing on each side of the breasts.

The Bazoko cicatrise the face only, which is covered with big incisions; the Bapoto do the same, but the incisions are much smaller and much more numerous.

The Wangata have a straight column formed of parallel incisions running from the top of the forehead to the nose, and a design representing a palm leaf on each temple; the Bangala have the same marking only more pronounced, the central line being carried from the nose to the summit of the head. Their marks stand out in high relief, and form a kind of crest. The Sango and Sakara ladies pinch up knots of skin on their foreheads, tying them round until they become permanent. They have about five

Photograph by Neville P. Edwards, Littlehampton.

BAPOTO WOMEN.

Showing the process of scar tattooing; the implement used is a short knife.

of these skin "beads" arranged in a perpendicular line between the nose and the forehead (*see* p. 324).

Most of the women have their backs elaborately scarred.

Painting is practised nearly everywhere; the favourite pigment, a bright red, is obtained from a tree, and is called *tukula*, but other vegetable and mineral pigments are equally used. Mourning is, as a rule, indicated by white paint, but an exception is formed by the Ubangi women, who on these occasions blacken their faces, while the Bambala women paint theirs brown.

By permission of the Ethnographical Museum, Tervueren.

BAPOTO WOMEN ORNAMENTED FOR A RELIGIOUS CEREMONY.

The figure in the centre is the Fetish Priest.

Congolese Dress.

The money spent by a Congo lady on her dressmaker would certainly not ruin her parents, and I have never heard of any of them resorting to cheating at bridge in order to satisfy the pressing demands of the milliner. Thus among the Budja, Bapoto, and some other tribes no dress whatever is worn, the tattooed decoration being all that is considered necessary, and when one comes from a sojourn among them into the country of the Bazoko, where a costume of *one bead* fastened round the waist is found, nay where even elderly women wear a small piece of pleated cloth nearly as big as one's hand, or to the Sango, who find a hair from an elephant's tail all they desire, one feels already again in the civilised world. And one must incline with respect before the rich costume of a Banza lady which consists usually of a few leaves or a bunch of grass; but it must be mentioned that *décolletage* is not unknown amongst them, since on festive occasions, these ladies remove their everyday costume and wear a dress consisting of a feather stuck into the hair.

Clothes made of native or imported cloth differ considerably; the size of the garment varies from a scrap of cloth four inches square to a piece extending from the armpits to the ankles; married Bakongo women even have a dress composed of three pieces; one in front, one behind, and one over the breasts.

The Bangala women wear a kind of short ballet dancer's skirt, as shown in the illustration on p. 320, which is made by hanging quantities of dried palm leaves round the hips. O vanity of vanities! The prettier a girl, the shorter the dress! The Bokele women wear similar dresses, but only behind.

The inhabitants of the Kwilu wear a piece of native cloth round their loins; but it is essential that no part above the legs should be covered behind.

Ornaments.

But if these daughters of Eve are satisfied with little dress, they are by no means averse to ornaments. It is wonderful to see the ingenuity they display in adding to their personal adornment. Amongst the most eccentric must be mentioned the Ubangi ladies, who have holes made in their ears in which they hang heavy weights, with the result that their ear-lobes frequently become lengthened to eight or ten inches. Some pass a stick through the septum of the nose; the Bakumu and Banziri pierce their upper lips, and wear in the hole a disc of wood or ivory of the size of a crown or even bigger. The latter make several holes in the lower lip as well, while others pierce the upper part of the ear in several places and hang string tassels from them. The Baluba women have the four front incisors knocked out, and most of the women have their teeth filed.

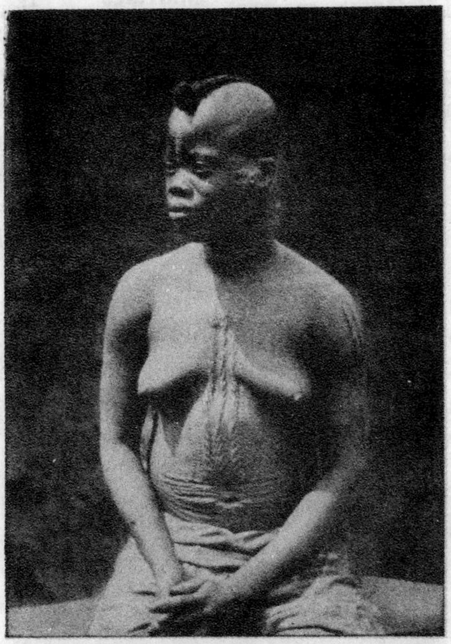

A WANGATA WOMAN.
With shaven head and scar tattooing.

It may be considered the rule, that the less dress a woman wears the more ornament she requires; of course I only mean Congolese women. Thus the Budja, who wear no clothes, have, around their necks, collars of forged brass often weighing as much as thirty pounds, and anklets nearly as heavy on their feet.

Bracelets are worn nearly everywhere; those of the Kasai, made of iron, are especially beautiful. The legs are also ornamented with brass circlets, which often reach from the ankles to the knees; in many tribes brass wire is wrapped round the legs and arms in spirals to the knees and elbows. Rings of iron, brass or ivory, are worn on all fingers, and often on the big toe, and the Banza women wear a ring in the nose. Many women of the "Province Orientale" have one side of the nose pierced and wear a button of iron or silver in the hole; whilst the Bubu in the Ubangi carry in their upper lip a piece of crystal two inches in length; if they cannot afford crystal, they use copal gum.

Necklaces are made of most varied material; all kinds of teeth (human included), beads, feathers, iron trinkets, wood and ivory carvings, seeds and shells, etc. These necklaces are not always very comfortable, such, for instance, as that shown in the illustrations on pp. 322 and 325, which are made of brass, are forged on to the neck, and sometimes weigh as much as thirty pounds.

Fans are almost unknown; in one tribe only, the Bakumu, women use a very primitive kind made of palm leaves.

As amongst all primitive people, hairdressing is naturally a great feature among the Congo people. In some parts the first process in the toilet is to extract the eyebrows and eyelashes, no hair being allowed to remain except on the head.

Congolese Coiffures.

In the lower Congo, the hair is cut short, greased with palm oil, and powdered red. The upper country head-dress varies from tribe to tribe. The Bangala shave the hair in front and behind the ears, but let it remain on the occiput, and on the side. The Sango women have very long locks, but they make them longer still by adding to them quantities of hair from the dead or from prisoners, or by twining them with palm fibres painted black (*see* p. 323). The Sakara form their *coiffure* of plaits literally covered with beads; these plaits are parted on the nape of the neck, and are brought to the front to form a kind of cap, which resembles the bonnets of the Dutch women (*see* p. 324); or they are sometimes built up like mitres. The more complicated *coiffures* take many weeks to complete, but once brushed they last for a long time. Some, the Manyema for instance, wear a circular wooden ring at the back of the head over which they draw the hair; others, like the Southern Baluba, weave their hair with the aid of basket-work into a kind of halo, decked with beads and cowries by way of jewellery. Nearly every lady wears in her hair a long pin of wood or ivory, which she finds very handy to scratch with at times. It is a fact worth mentioning that in some Azandé tribes women shave their heads while their husbands allow their hair to grow.

After having enumerated the means by which maidens try to please, let us pass to the result of all these preparations, and mention the different customs relating to marriage.

Marriage Customs.

There are so many of these customs in the Congo that it is not possible to generalise; it may only be stated that polygamy is nearly universal, and often practised to the furthest limit; thus certain chiefs provide themselves with several hundred wives. One honourable exception are the Banza, who never take more than a single wife, and pride themselves on their conjugal fidelity.

The Musserongo have a complicated nuptial ceremony. Three months before the date fixed the bride retires to a hut outside the village, where she is painted red with *tukula* wood. Then the bridegroom pays to the father-in-law the price of his betrothed wife, but it must not be thought that, in virtue of this purchase, she becomes his slave; the money only represents the expenses of the parents, and in case of divorce, or premature death, must be returned. The father, after having received the price of his daughter, goes to the "*Ganga*" or fetish man, who, by

TYPICAL BANGALA BEAUTIES.
Showing palm-leaf petticoats and scar tattooing.

making offerings to the "Bingu" spirit obtains fecundity for the new couple. On the day of the marriage the bride, accompanied by all the young girls of the village, dancing and singing, is led to her husband's house. The next day a great feast is given by the young husband, to which all friends are invited.

By permission of the Ethnographical Museum, Tervueren.

WOMEN OF THE WELLE DISTRICT.

Notice the nose ornaments and elaborate girdles.

Amongst the Bakongo the engagement lasts for a long time, as young girls are often engaged at the tender age of four, and cannot marry before eleven or twelve years of age. This involves great expense to the bridegroom, for whenever he visits his bride he must bring considerable presents to her parents.

The Azandé deserve to be specially mentioned. Here the chief allots wives to his people without consulting their taste; this tribe is an instance in favour of the *Mariage de raison*, as the Azandé are peculiarly fond of their wives, and the couples brought together by the caprice of the chief are generally extremely happy, and some of the ladies show remarkable fidelity to their husbands. The husbands, too, show themselves most affectionate towards their wives, but are exceedingly jealous, and object to strangers even looking at their spouses. In consequence the women are very shy. Not so the Mangbettu, their neighbours, where husbands are only too often hen-pecked, and where women have great influence in the assemblies deciding the destinies of the tribe. Their right to take part in such decisions has greatly influenced their minds, and has given them a spirit of independence and authority rarely found amongst the women of the Congo. There are some women-chiefs found in this tribe who govern with great justice and prudence.

The Momfu are perhaps the only tribe where it is the men's duty to do the agricultural work; they clear the forest, plant and gather the crops, while their wives only attend to the work of the house, such as cooking, the care of the children, etc. In this tribe wives and husbands eat from the dish together with the children, and this people considers woman as the equal of man: in consequence of this they are despised by their neighbours.

The pygmy ladies are bought by their husbands for three or four arrows!

The Mogwandi are nearly always monogamous because of the scarcity of women: and in order not to be left unprovided with a mate they are wise enough, if they come across a little girl of three or four years, who promises to become pretty, to arrange to marry her on paying the price to her father. As they, too, must bring a present every time they visit their bride, it may be imagined that the possession of a daughter forms a real source of wealth to the head of the family. But it is always understood that if later the bride bears no children to her husband, a part of the presents must be refunded.

WANGATA WOMEN.

One of whom wears the brass neck ornament—weighing upwards of 25 lbs. —which is characteristic among the women of the Upper Congo.

Child Marriage.

The inhabitants of the Kwilu are familiar with child marriage; any little boy may declare a little girl his future wife, and then, when she is of age, he may marry her. If she does not like him, she may refuse him, and this often happens; but in this case the man to whom she gives her preference must pay to the jilted lover, as it were, damages for breach of promise. In this country a man is not allowed to look at his mother-in-law; if he should see her coming he must run into the bush to avoid her.

A curious kind of child marriage exists amongst the Batetela. When a female infant is born, a man may drop an iron bracelet into the water in which she has been washed for the first time, and present the mother with a fowl—he thereby has a right to consider the child his betrothed wife; in case of twins, both girls marry the same man.

Amongst the Bayanzi, nobody but the husband and the brother may call a married woman by her name; all others must mention her as the wife of So-and-so.

Urua Wedding Dance.

In Urua, when the bride is related to the chief, the marriage is celebrated with great festivities. Everybody dances, shouts, and sings in the village, and drink flows in abundance. In the afternoon the bridegroom arrives, and, surrounded by his friends, executes a dance of an hour's duration; then the bride is brought in on the back of some strong matron; the crowd surrounds her, and her human steed executes a wild dance without putting her down; during this dance the bride lets her body and arms hang down and swing about. When the woman who carries her can do no more, the new husband approaches, and presents the bride with beads, tobacco, and other trifles. These are thrown by her amongst the crowd, who shout and fight to obtain part of the plunder, as it is considered to bring great luck. Then the bride is put on the ground and executes with her husband a *pas de deux* which cannot be described. Suddenly the husband lifts her in his arms, and runs off with her to his hut.

Conjugal infidelity is severely punished. In the Kwilu the co-respondent becomes a slave of the betrayed husband, whilst the wife receives a good thrashing. Amongst the Bangala the faulty wife has her ears cut and her calves pierced with red hot lances. The Azandé kill the faithless wife, and the rival has his hands and ears cut off. In the Ubangi the unfaithful woman is killed. The Mogwandi are very severe with a woman who leaves the conjugal home. She is put in the middle of the village, devoid of all dress or ornaments, and the inhabitants defile before her, insulting her and reproaching her with her bad behaviour. Some strike her and spit at her; this done, she is driven by the screaming crowd back to her husband's home.

Conjugal Infidelity.

Marriage for a limited time, as recently advocated in England, exists amongst the Basutanda. Here the young girl is stolen by her sweetheart, who hides with her in the forest till a child is born, when they return triumphantly to the man's village. But there the romance ends; for the wife returns to her parents as soon as the child can be separated from her, and she is only entitled to a part of the game obtained by her husband as long as she is not "stolen" by another man. Amongst the Mogwandi, where, as already mentioned, women are scarce, it often happens that a husband lets his wife to another man for a term of ten months. If during that time a child is born it belongs to the "lessee"; the lease may be prolonged by a supplementary payment.

The Bakuba, who have been in contact with the Arabs, not only often ill-treat their wives, but if tired of them they exchange them with a friend. Nevertheless, these people expect conjugal fidelity from their wives. If a chief's wife betrays her husband, she is bound to a tree and flogged, and then sent to the co-respondent, who may keep her, but must pay an enormous fine; in the case of an ordinary woman, both she and her lover are killed.

As a rule the social condition of women is not bad; they have to do the agricultural work, and manage their household; but field work is light in this country, where

By permission of the Ethnographical Museum, Tervueren.

SANGO GIRLS.

Showing the method of hair-dressing peculiar to this tribe. The natural locks are lengthened by adding to them hair taken from prisoners or dead women, or by twining them with palm fibres painted black.

the soil is of very great fertility. An intelligent woman can easily attain to honours; and women chiefs are not uncommon. Amongst the Balunda there were always two chiefs; the King "Muata Yamvo," and the King's mother "Lukokesha," who was almost of greater importance than the King himself. The actual Balunda empire was founded by a woman.

Social Conditions on the Congo.

As far back as the fifteenth century a great queen was known to travellers in the Congo; this was Zinga, or, as she was later called, Donna Anna Zinga de Souza, who governed an important country with great ability. A contemporary traveller says "that a certain chief Kambolo left an important state to his successors, who would still enjoy its possession if a woman, gifted with courage much above her sex, called *Zinga*, had not taken to arms, and having gathered the dissatisfied has dethroned Kambolo, on whom she gained great victories that put her in possession of a whole kingdom."

By permission of the Ethnographical Museum, Tervueren.

SAKARA GIRLS.

Their hair is braided with beads. Two of these girls have the curious knots of skin down the forehead—a form of personal adornment affected by this tribe.

The Baboma are at the present time governed by a female chief, and the great Mokanda Bantu ben Msiri, King of Garenganza, is absolutely under the guidance of his wife, to whom is due the peaceful condition of the Katanga, and the great friendliness shown by the inhabitants to Europeans.

Mungo Park, in his travels, always found that native women were of great help to him in evading difficulties with the savage tribes which he visited, and any explorer who succeeds in obtaining the favour of this sex may rely upon being unmolested, for, even in tribes where they have nominally no authority at all, women always succeed in the end in making the representatives of the stronger sex do as they wish.

Women are so closely connected with funeral ceremonies that I shall be obliged to describe many of them, irrespectively of whether the person to be buried be a man or a woman. In all cases it is the women's duty to lament the dead, and as a rule the ladies of surrounding villages come to join in the chorus.

Death and Burial.

In the lower Congo, when a person has died, the body is put on a kind of scaffold under a shed and smoked over a fire of green wood. When the corpse is sufficiently dried, it is wrapped in cloth; the richer the deceased, the more cloth is used; thus a wealthy person when prepared for burial looks like an enormous bale of cloth. The body is then exposed in a hut for a period which may extend to several months. On the day of the funeral all the people of the

A MARRIED BANGALA COUPLE.
Notice the woman's shaven head, and the scar tattooing on the forehead and scalp.

country gather in the village of the deceased, and, to the sound of drums, tom-toms, whistles, and the howling of the women, the corpse is carried to the grave, where all who have guns fire them off. Then eating and drinking begins, finishing up with a general dance which does not terminate until morning. The tomb is decorated with the deceased's belongings, such as pots, empty bottles, household articles, which are "killed" by breaking them, that their spirits may follow their owner to the other world.

In the Kwilu diminutive huts are erected in memory of the dead, in which offerings are placed by relations and friends, consisting of food and palm-wine: it is, perhaps, thought that the soul returns to partake of them. Great importance is attached to the faithful discharge of this duty; for, if neglected, it is believed that the deceased is sure to visit the culprits in their dreams and cause them the most terrible nightmares.

When an Abarambo woman dies her husband disappears into the forest and lives there, sometimes for months, lamenting his deceased wife. A widow does the same; when she returns to the village it is considered that she has forgotten her husband, and is prepared to try another union.

Widows' Sacrifice.

The Banza have a most disgusting ceremonial; the corpse is put on a chair-like scaffold, and a fire is lit under it; the grease, dropping from the corpse, is carefully collected by the mourners, who smear it on their hands and bodies, believing that they thus inherit the virtues of the deceased.

But it is difficult to speak of the Sakara burial ceremonies without shocking the reader.

On a bed, in an immense round grave, his head reposing in his favourite wife's arms, the deceased lies dressed in his richest costume; round him in a circle lie the strangled corpses of his other wives, who have refused to survive their husband. The grave is surrounded by a circle of slain slaves, whose bodies, after the grave has been closed, will serve as a dish to the invited guests.

The Barua have a somewhat similar custom; a deep hole is dug, and the chief wife, supported on her elbows and knees, crouches there, serving as a seat to the corpse; the second wife serves as a footstool, and the other wives sit round the body; all are buried alive!

The wives of the Bena Kanioka do not submit voluntarily to this treatment, so their legs and arms are broken, to prevent their escape from the grave.

One month after the death of a Baluba chief some of his wives are sent to join him in the next world; they are buried alive round the husband's grave.

Amongst some tribes in the Lado district the widows, together with a number of slaves, are clubbed by a shouting, enthusiastic crowd. When they fall, men and women rush up to them and drive their knives in the still quivering bodies; then the victims are thrown into the grave.

A dying chief of the Bakundi himself names the wives he wishes to be sacrificed after his death.

The inhabitants of the Bomu river are specially cruel in their sacrifices. If a chief happens to be ill he retires into the forest with the fetish man and a few faithful followers. His wives anxiously await the news of his recovery, for on that their lives depend. If he dies his followers spread the news that he has recovered, that his wives may not take the alarm and escape. Great preparations are made for his reception, and the women, full of joy, prepare a great feast, and adorn themselves with their choicest ornaments. Suddenly warriors surround them and inform them of their terrible destiny. Some show despair, but most of them take the awful news with resignation, having always known that it would be their fate; some even seem quite happy to follow their husbands to the other world.

The day after the decease all wives who have not borne children, and one mother of a male child, are shut up in a strong hut, together with numerous slaves who formerly belonged to the deceased. The people begin to lament the dead, and when the noise has risen to its highest pitch, fire is put to the hut in which are the victims. If they try to escape, they are caught by the warriors and thrown back into the flames.

Cannibalism.

A large proportion of the inhabitants of the Congo are cannibals; it is true that this statement, as a rule, applies only to men, for the women are usually debarred from taking any part in the banquet; but as they often provide

By permission of the Ethnographical Museum, Tervueren.

A CHIEFTAINESS OF THE WELLE DISTRICT WITH HER ATTENDANTS.

But some wives have been reserved. These are now brought, and, except the two prettiest, are slain above the corpse. The two former, after having their arms and legs broken, enjoy the "privilege" of being buried alive with their husbands. By a refinement of cruelty, holes are left in the grave to allow the air to pass in, and thus prolong for a while the agonies of these two miserable women.

Touching, compared with these customs, is the practice found amongst the Banza; if they have lost some one dear to them, they have his image carved in wood by a skilled artist; this figure is kept in the hut of the mourner, and is an object of great care and veneration.

the most appreciated part of the feast, it is impossible not to enter into some detail with regard to this horrible custom.

Cannibalism may arise from several causes; in some parts, where game is rare, it has resulted from a craving for animal food; in others, it has been caused by the belief that by eating the body of the slain enemy his virtues are transferred to the person who eats him; whilst in others (as some countries in the Aruwimi) a man considers himself a kind of family vault, thinking that no fitter tomb can be found for the dead than the interiors of his relations; moreover in this country the eating of the corpse is regarded as a religious duty to the deceased.

Nowadays, of course, cannibalism is only practised in secret; but when the first explorers came into the country, not only was it practised openly, but the Europeans, being alone amongst an unsubjugated population, were obliged to tolerate it, and sometimes forced to be among the spectators. One of the earliest white men to visit the Bangala, M. Coquilhat, thus describes a "Feast of man eating":

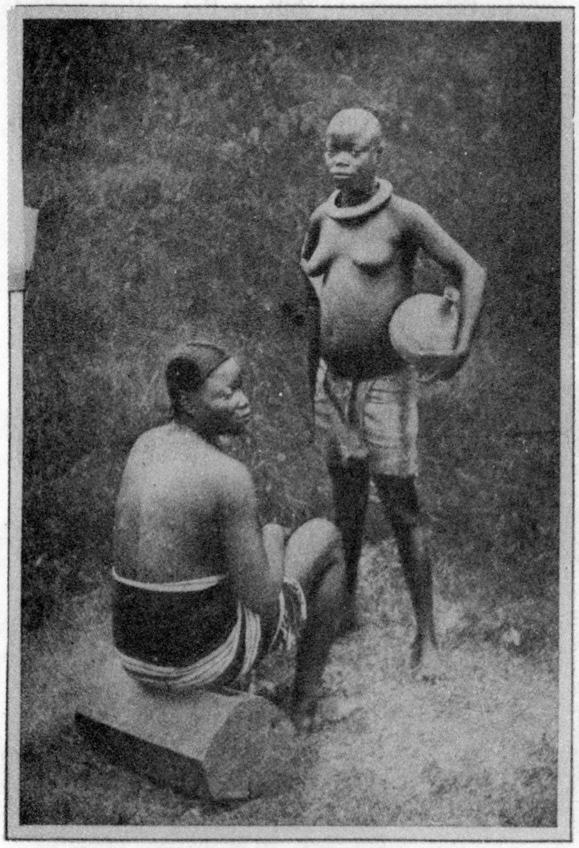

WANGATA WOMEN.
Showing method of shaving the head and scar tattooing.

"After a quarter of an hour's walk through the outskirts of the village, we turned a corner and stood before the whole scene. On the left is the band of wooden drums, iron gongs, and ivory trumpets, and the varied sounds of these instruments unite in terrible din; on the right, trembling with excitement, stand the spectators line upon line, in their best dresses, ornamented with feathers, caps, and skins, and paint. The musicians and the crowd form a circle round the place of sacrifice, and a grove of palm and banana trees surround the whole with a picturesque screen. In the middle of the circle, alone, sits the unhappy victim on a small chair; he is completely naked and blackened with soot. He seems to be twenty years of age, in good health. Not being bound, he contemplates the audience with interest, and it may be seen by the movement of his chest that his breath is perfectly regular and calm.

"The preparations are long, and whilst these are made by a few men with methodical coolness, the crowd joins in a furious dance, and the musicians beat their instruments madly. A stake, reaching to his shoulders, is placed behind the victim, and his body and his arms are tied to it. The hands, extended behind his body, are fixed to small sticks driven into the ground. A second stake is fixed into the ground before his chest, and his feet are fixed in the same manner as his hands. Then, about four yards in front of him, a long and very flexible pole, about twelve feet high, is driven vertically into the ground. A man jumps and seizes the top and hanging to it by his hands in such a manner as to draw it down, near to the victim's head, which is put in a roughly made net attached by a string to the end of the pole.

"The innocent victim follows, without emotion, the details of these preparations. Sometimes one of the dancers leaves the crowd and leaps about in front of him. The executioner runs round the assembly, brandishing his enormous Bangala knife, the curved blade of which seems to be shaped to the human neck. Many times he goes near the victim and feigns to try the knife on him. Finally a white line is traced on the spot at the back of the neck destined to receive the final blow. The victim remains unmoved. The executioner says a few words to one of his assistants the fatal moment approaches. The victim

By permission of the Ethnographical Museum, Tervueren.

BAKUBA WOMEN.

Showing the wire armlets and anklets.

is blind-folded and his body powdered with white paint.

"The vassals and slaves of the chief file past several times, attired in their war ornaments, brandishing their lances, shields, and knives; then follows a group of dancing women. At last the executioner advances, gloriously attired in blue and scarlet, with a magnificent cap of black feathers on his head, preceded by his wife and surrounded by a great number of people of both sexes. They all proceed round the victim in a kind of dance.

"All people retire from the circle; the executioner takes off his cloth and bends back, so as to touch the ground with one hand on the left side of the condemned; a little white clay is put on his cheeks; he now makes a movement as if to measure his blow, and suddenly strikes. The head describes a circle in the air as the bent pole is released, and falls to the earth at some distance."

The Bangala and Bapoto are great man-eaters, but as a rule they do not eat women, considering them much too expensive; whilst the Sango show a great preference for women and children.

When the first Europeans came to the Congo, a traveller once met a man walking freely about the market place. His body was marked with red and white lines, and it was said that he was a slave who was to be eaten. As nobody could purchase the whole man, he was sold in pieces, the lines on the body being marks of the purchasers, the red lines being the marks of one tribe, the white those of another. This slave seemed to be perfectly indifferent to his fate; he walked quietly up and down and stopped when some buyer wanted to mark the piece purchased and listened with interest to the discussion of the price!

By permission of the Ethnographical Museum, Tervueren.

BALUBA WOMAN.

The hair is elaborately dressed, but the clothing is singularly scanty.

The Bayanzi do not despise human flesh in a state of complete putrefaction; they even, like hyænas, exhume corpses for consumption.

Much more could be written on this subject, but a return must be made to matters more intimately connected with the central figure of this chapter—woman.

Physical Attractions of Congolese Women.

Are the women of the Congo beautiful? This is a very difficult question to answer, for the beautiful is what pleases, and certainly the negro women are far removed from our standard of beauty. It must be kept clearly in mind that the European, when first he arrives in the dark continent, can scarcely distinguish a man from a woman, and all natives seem to him to have the same features. But the more he lives amongst them the easier he finds it to distinguish sexes and individuals; and later on he is able to deal with the question of good looks.

The Congo women are slenderly built. During a stay of several years in the country I did not come across ten women who could really boast of *embonpoint*. They are not tall, but very well proportioned, and, as far as their figures are concerned, classical beauty is far more frequent among them than among their white sisters. Their back has a graceful "fall," their ankles and wrists are neat; their feet and hands are in proportion; most ladies' gloves made in Europe would be too large for them, and Cinderella's shoe alone might fit their tiny feet. Less pleasing are the racial characteristics exhibited by the head and features. The scalp is covered with woolly hair, which, as a rule, is abundant. The chin is weak, but no more beautiful eyes exist than those of a negro girl—great, bright, almond-shaped eyes shaded by marvellously long eye-lashes. In contradistinction to the pure negro, the Congo inhabitants often have normal lips; their noses are frequently slender and not uncommonly aquiline in shape. Their teeth are like so many pearls, but, unhappily, they are often deformed by filing. Their language is soft, melodious, and very picturesque. They like to speak in metaphors, and give great emphasis by intonation to what they say. They are very fond of a friendly chat, and are naturally inquisitive. When all other means failed to get on friendly terms with the inhabitants of a village, I used to take out some illustrated magazines and look carelessly over the pictures. The people for a time would keep at a distance, but slowly the women would begin to separate from the group and approach to have a peep. More and more would come, the "Eh," and "Oh," and "Ah," increased in strength, and at last one would take courage and request me to tell them what all these pictures meant, and of course I was quite disposed to do so. They seemed very curious to know all about Europe, especially about women. What long hair they had! How white they were! And a man never had more than one woman! As a rule they greatly approved of European beauty, and, when told about the social condition of their sisters "far, far beyond the seas," much envied them.

It is a popular belief that all women are open to flattery. In the Congo, at any rate, the occasion of paying compliments to ladies must never be let slip; they are highly pleased by it. But they are vindictive too; an affront to a tribe is resented more by the women than by men, and they are always ready to incite the latter to take a bloody revenge.

They are very kind-hearted, and in countries where food is scarce, and where men may refuse to sell provisions, a woman will never refuse the traveller the necessaries for his maintenance. Amongst the Balunda it was formerly the custom, if a foreigner came to a village, for some woman of the locality to undertake to provide his food during his stay; no compensation was required for this; if the traveller could afford it, he gave her a present at parting.

Women of tribes near the rivers are very cleanly, and bathe several times a day; the "negro smell" attributed to them becomes imperceptible after a prolonged stay amongst them, In the same way, we do not smell the "European smell" although it exists, and is not much appreciated by the negroes. At any rate, it seems a proof that their odour is less penetrating than ours if we consider that it is far less offensive to game. It is a fact that traps laid by negroes in the same manner as by Europeans are more successful than those laid by the latter.

Negroes and Cleanliness.

Among tribes of the forest, often living at a great distance from the water, women scarcely ever wash. The toilet consists of spreading over their bodies a mixture of red wood stain, called "*tukula*"; or "*n'gula*" and palm-oil, which is scraped off about once a month with a piece of bone or wood, and then renewed.

All women possess a piece of fibrous wood with which they continually brush their teeth.

Preparation of Food.

When it comes to the preparation of food, a duty which devolves on the women, the greatest cleanliness is found everywhere. The chief food is a kind of paste made of manioc flour boiled in water. This is stirred with a wooden spoon, and the housewife never touches it with her hand in preparing it, and in dishing it up. The preparation of this flour, which is pounded in big mortars, is one of the most important occupations of women; and the preparation of palm-oil is also part of their work. All women work; but in some tribes the favourite wife may be an exception for a short time. The food is the same as for man; but in some tribes certain dishes are not permitted to women. The Bambala women are not allowed to eat goats or game; the Bayaka women are forbidden to eat fowls or eggs, and it is supposed that if a woman breaks this restriction she becomes mad, tears off her clothes and runs away into the bush. When found she is caught and fastened to a log with a fork at one end in which her neck is fixed; thus secured she is brought to the magician. He knocks on the log three times, and the woman faints; he then pours water on her face, and the spell is broken.

On the other hand Bahuana women are allowed to eat frogs, whilst the men may not do so, and among the Marungu women alone are permitted to eat mulberries.

The principal food is manioc bread; but the dainties appreciated by Congo people are of a nature to make a European epicure shiver. Locusts, crickets, all kinds of caterpillars, and white ants are some of them.

Religion.

As for religion, very few of the inhabitants of the Congo country have an idea of a benevolent divinity, but the belief in an evil spirit is general. The so-called idols brought from the Congo are not believed by the natives to possess any supernatural power by themselves, it is only the "*Kissi*" or magic force that the fetish man smears on them that is powerful. No prayers are addressed to these 'idols"; their duty is to prevent mischief from happening to their owners, and, if they do not fulfil it, big nails or knives are driven into them to remind them of their obligation.

Home Life.

The habitation of the Congo woman is a hut, quadrangular, rectangular or round, according to the tribe, and, as a rule, made of straw or leaf. Each married woman possesses her own house, and the husband lives with his wives alternately; the wife with whom he stays provides him with food.

There is an unwritten law in accordance with which pottery-making and the selling of provisions is reserved for women.

Woman's greatest pleasure lies in singing and dancing, and the time of new moon is considered the right season for these amusements. The Congo woman's voice resembles that of a child and has no great compass. Many women smoke tobacco and take snuff; in the Bakuba and Basongo-Meno tribes they smoke hemp, the effects of which are very intoxicating, and highly injurious to the health; but the process forms a part of the religious ceremonies of these tribes.

Among many tribes, geophagists or earth-eaters are found, who devour a kind of kaolin earth, pretending that it frees them from pains in the stomach.

And now if one should want to know which is the most accomplished, the best, the most beautiful and most desirable woman of the Congo, go and ask the first young warrior to be met there. The invariable reply will be: "Why, it's the girl I love," so it is evident that opinions differ widely on this subject.

BAZOKO WOMEN MAKING POTS.

THE WEST COAST OF AFRICA

By NORTHCOTE W. THOMAS

I

Woman and Dress—A Sherbro Island Belle—The Question of Ornament—Beauties of the "Backlands"—The Charm of Native Dress—Variety of West African Types—Clothed and Unclothed Classes—Varieties of Colour and Looks—Styles of Hairdressing—Skin Decoration—Dress—Woman's Work—The Event of Initiation—A Secret Society for Women—The Bundu Devil—A Strange Funeral Ceremony—How Women become Members of the Men's Secret Society—Marriage Ceremonies—Official Lovers—Polygamy—Birth Customs—How Twins are Treated—Children's Food—Mourning Customs—The Position of Widows—How Widowers have to Pay Compensation

Woman and Dress.

THE impious male has been known to declare that woman does not always look her best tricked out in the latest fashions; independent bachelor minds, to whom milliners' bills are not, or should not be, a standing menace, have, greatly daring, put forward the proposition that woman unadorned is the loveliest of Eve's daughters. Whether the dictum is true of the European wife or maid we need not here venture to inquire; we are concerned with the dusky beauty of Africa, and there are no two views as to the impropriety of her bedizening herself with what were, a few years previously, the latest creations of Paris fashionable milliners. If the negress does not look her best absolutely unadorned, the simple black garb which nature gave her is at any rate preferable to balloon sleeves or whatever the receding tide of fashion in Europe may have cast up as treasure trove at her feet. There are many stages between the unsophisticated native belle of the interior, with barbaric silver chains standing out in brilliant relief from her glossy, well-oiled skin, and the Europeanised woman of the coast, say at Sherbro Island.

A Sherbro Island Belle.

Mr. Alldridge, in "Sherbro and the Hinterland," has described the progress of one of the latter, culminating in the acquisition of patent leather boots, which transforms her gait from the splendidly free and graceful walk born of the uncabined human foot and the bearing of burdens on her head, into the miserable hobble of the tortured votary of fashion.

The Question of Ornament.

The ornaments of the lower races may be barbaric, and even hideous, yet they are seldom incongruous; but it is a singular thing that when these races seek to leave the traditional path, and put on European garb, they often commit some glaring solecism, or fail to realise that there is such a thing as harmonising the colours of their attire. The lady described by Mr. Alldridge completed her costume—a Princess robe, with patent leather boots—by putting upon her head a brightly coloured, not to say gaudy, Madras handkerchief, with the two ends tied in orthodox fashion so as to stand up from her forehead like two horns.

As a contrast to the too receptive woman of the coast, let us look upon another picture. In the backlands, where chiefs are powerful, and happy in the possession of many wives, young and old, the proud husband comes to a palaver attended by a dozen or so of his junior spouses; each carries some article for his use, one his sword, another his snuff-box, and so on; and they vie with one another in paying him attention (*O si sic omnes*). Ornaments apart, their attire would not fetch in the pawnshop the price of a bottle of ginger beer; but they make up for it by the satiny sheen of their comely black limbs, polished perhaps with oil, and delightfully cool and velvety to the sight and touch. Unadorned, however, they certainly are not; barbaric silver chains and heavy plaques of the same metal hang loosely on them and give forth a metallic clang as they walk; five or six leopards' teeth strung on a cord press tightly on their ebony necks; and from wrist to elbow their arms are covered in the well-known African style, with massive silver armlets.

Beauties of the "Back-lands."

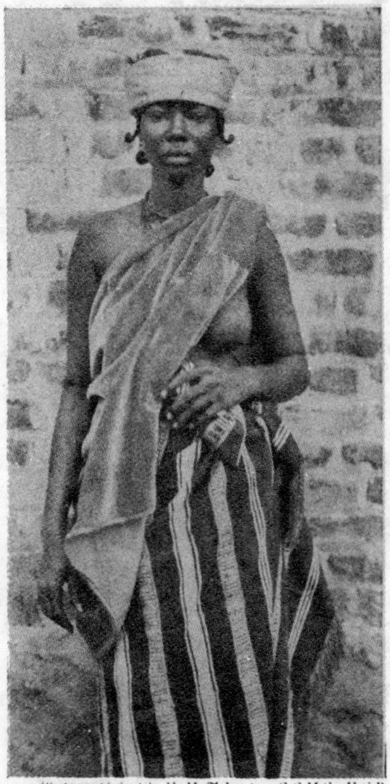

Photograph by Sir H. H. Johnston, G.C.M.G., K.C.B.

SANGE: A MANDINGO WOMAN.

Note the corkscrew curl above the ear.

But it would be unfair to suggest that the African woman only looks well, or looks her best, when she is, according to European ideas, unclothed. Clad in the products of native looms, especially if she belongs to the better classes, the black woman may be very charming, as Mr. Norman Hardy's picture of "A Kabinda Lady" shows, and for those who are inured or indifferent to the colour of her skin may rival or surpass her fairer sister. Mr. Alldridge was by no means indifferent to the charming picture presented by a small native girl, clothed though she was. One of the pictures that recurred to his imagination most vividly was that of a fruit-seller, a dot of a girl in a loose blouse and white muslin garment with coral earrings in her ears; she was the prettiest little creature imaginable.

The Charm of Native Dress.

To depict or describe any considerable proportion of the swarming peoples of the Western coast of Africa would be a gigantic task, and when it was accomplished the reader would profit little by the effort, unless his preference in literature is for works of the dimensions and dulness of an encyclopædia. As well might one take the British Isles county by county and attempt to produce a readable account of woman's life in each. There are diversities in the bodily appearance of African women—Sir H. H. Johnston classifies the peoples of the continent into long and short-legged—no less than in their headdress, ornaments and mode of life; woman's lot is not everywhere the same, and the customs of, and regarding, women are even more diversified; but a survey of woman's life at half a dozen different points will be more generally intelligible than the most conscientious Bluebookery work.

Variety of West African Types.

If we start from St. Louis in Senegal, at the mouth of the river of that name, and proceed along the coast we find first the Wolof, who extend to below Cap Verde, then a number of tribes, Bullom, Bissago, Felup, Serer, Timni, to beyond Sherbro Island; then for a short distance on the coast Mandingo, whose territory in the backland stretches six hundred miles east and west, and three

Clothed and Unclothed Classes.

KABINDA LADY : WEST AFRICA.
DRAWN BY NORMAN H. HARDY.

Facing on page 334

hundred north and south; there, too, are the Mendi, the Gora, and the Vai, and other Mohammedanised peoples, who are characterised by ample clothing; beyond them are the Kru, famous as the boatmen of West Africa, and, like sailors elsewhere, in the past if not in the present, lovers of strong drink; with the Grebo and other of their neighbours they are characterised by an almost complete absence of clothing, and the costume of a Kru maiden is often no more than a string of beads with a tiny beadwork square of leather or cloth in front. Between the Kru and the Mandingo of the backlands come the Kpwesi, of whom little is known; and intermingled with the Mandingo are the important Fula people, also Mohammedan, a cross perhaps between the negro and Libyan invaders in the dim prehistoric period, and themselves giving birth, it may be, by further crossing, to the already mentioned Mandingo.

Varieties of Colour and Looks.

As regards looks, a question which naturally claims the first place when we are dealing with women, the Mandingo, perhaps, take the first place among the tribes just enumerated; but good looks are found sporadically in most tribes, and the charms of the Vai, both in manner and person, have been sung by many writers.

The colour of the skin varies very widely; it may be golden yellow in some Mandingo, Kpwesi and Vai, and at the other extreme we find the deep black of some of the Kru; the Gora and others tend to be deep brown in colour. The hair is usually abundant, and Susu women, belonging to the Mandingo stock in east Sierra Leone, have a shock which is quite Papuan in character.

The Kru women, a short-legged people on the whole, are less good looking; they may have comely figures, but, whatever native beaux may think of them, more often present a misshapen appearance to European eyes, owing to a too luxuriant development; even where this is absent, they often appear very broad in the pelvic region, and across the back of the thighs.

The Gora women have rather a Soudanese type of face with broad cheek bones and rather prominent jaw, which makes them less good looking than the men; but the Kpwesi are described as well proportioned, even graceful. A singular feature about this tribe is that the women seem to be taller on an average than the men. The Vai woman of high degree is fascinating and altogether a picturesque and pleasing object.

Styles of Hairdressing.

The styles of hairdressing are countless; often a handkerchief is worn, and then, of course, the hair is short; it may be adorned, as with the Vai, by silver bangles. The Susu woman combs out her hair to full length; and the Grandi woman has a cone of hair, bound near the base. In the Sherbro district, where the coiffure, once made up, has to last for some time, the help of a friend is secured; the patient lies with her head in the operator's lap and a strong wood comb is applied; when the hair is at full length other pieces of wool elaborately plaited are made fast to it, till the erection is complete. In its finished form the hair runs in ridges from back to front upon a foundation of soft material; a silver or cane skewer is often passed through the mass, which as time goes on is called into more and more frequent use.

Skin Decoration.

In the way of personal adornment we find both cicatrices and tattoo proper in vogue. The Vai women have raised scars on their backs—made when they pass the bush school—and so do the Gora; the men abstain. The Kpwesi women, on the other hand, are less given to the practice than the men.

Tattoo is produced by introducing colouring matter under the skin, and the Kru, both men and women, have a broad blue band down the forehead; Gibi women have slanting blue lines down the neck and arms.

Another favourite form of personal adornment is to daub the body with white or coloured clay mixed with animal fat, or with stripes of indigo. A Kru woman in putting on her gala costume will not fail to smear her face with brown clay, and draw a circle of white kaolin round each eye. In the Sherbro district the marks are renewed each morning, and the paint is taken from its shell cup, and applied by means of the index finger.

Dress.

In the matter of clothing proper we find that the Mandingo women are usually naked to the waist—the amplitude of clothing in Mohammedan tribes is characteristic of the men—but from this point cloths of great length and breadth are wound several times round the body; a string may be added as a girdle, and additional folds thrown over it, to hang down more loosely. The Kru women, as we have seen, are not overburdened in their youth; but the coast women are tending more and more to add to their dress. Calico is wound round from the waist to the knees, and mothers often wind broad pieces of cloth from the waist downwards, forming a nest in which the child finds a comfortable resting place.

Woman's Work.

Weaving is generally looked upon as women's work, but, African fashion, it falls to the lot of the men among the Mandingo, though the carding and spinning are done by women. The seeds are picked out by hand in Western Liberia, and carded with a tense bowstring. Then swathes of cotton wool are wound round a stick, and this spool is held high in the left hand; the right hand draws the thread with a twisting motion, and it is wound off on another spool, weighted with baked clay. The Mendi woman sits down with the cotton before her, free of seed; in her hand she holds a piece of cane as spool, on one end of which she inserts a cone of steatite; this piece of cane she revolves in a shell, and, continually twirling, draws out the flaky cotton. Here, too, the cotton must be re-wound before use, but this work falls to the lot of the weaver, who may be seen walking round the town, spool in hand, engaged in re-winding the thread for his use.

The manufacture of pottery, too, is almost always the work of women, and some of the palm-wine jars will hold several gallons. The implements are simple, for the wheel is unknown. In the Sherbro district the woman seats herself before a wet slab of wood on which she puts a lump of clay; her tools are her hands, supplemented by a couple of palm

Photograph by Sir H. H. Johnston, G.C.M.G., K.C.B.

GORA WOMEN.

The prominent jaw and broad face are characteristic of this tribe.

canes and a supply of water; but a few minutes suffice for her to turn out the finished bowl.

The Rite of Initiation.

The most important event in a woman's life is in most tribes her initiation. Before that time she has little to do, save perhaps to look after the younger children; but as she goes to the "bush school" at the age of eight or nine this is hardly surprising. If she has already been betrothed—a matter of money payment, £3 or so among the Mendi—her *fiancé* bears the cost of her education till she is of marriageable age, otherwise the girl's own family is responsible. Let no one imagine that the school is anything like what we know by the name; true, some rude cooking may be taught, but of other women's duties hardly a trace—even the care of infants does not enter into the curriculum. The principal course of instruction is one in the *ars amoris*, and according to well-informed observers the girls emerge from their training with minds like cesspools.

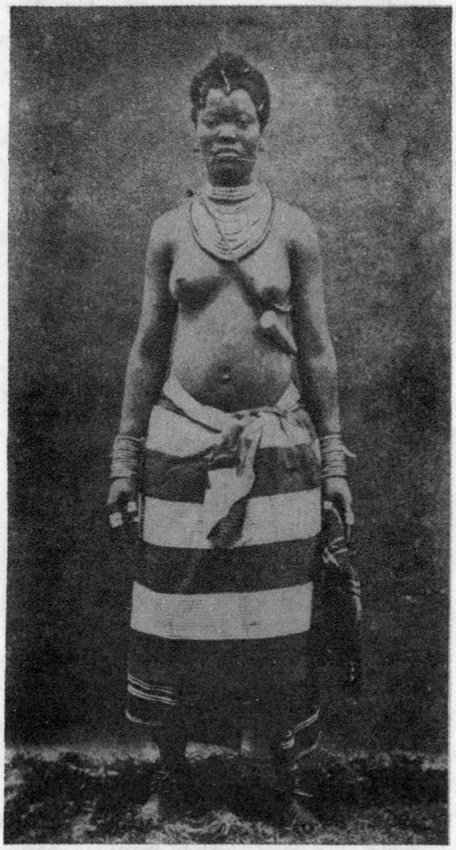

Photograph by Sir H. H. Johnston, G.C.M.G., K.C.B.

A KRU WOMAN.

Showing heavy finger-rings and other ornaments.

A Secret Society for Women.

As an example of the customs connected with these schools we may take the practices of the Mendi, with whom the training serves as an introduction to the *Bundu*, or women's secret society. The girls are under the control of elderly women; as a rule their costume is far more scanty than is shown in the illustration on p. 340, for it is composed of ropes of bugle beads—*Piso*—made of cane; on the top of their high *coiffure* they wear seeds as large as grapes; a leopard's tooth indicates that they are freeborn, not slaves, and in the way of ornament they have the usual massive silver armlets. For the decoration of the body they use the aforementioned scars, and the face is whitened with kaolin or some similar matter. They wander freely about under the guardianship of their duennas, for few men care to incur the wrath of the *Bundu* society. When they meet anyone they greet them by raising their hands at full length above their heads, accompanying the process by a weird, long-drawn-out note; then they bend forward till their hands touch the ground and return to the normal position. Often the wailing cry is the first intimation that they are near.

Their dancing costume consists of a net covering the body, short knickers of cotton cloth, and bunches of palm fibre hanging from armlets of the same material. To their dress are attached fragments of iron, and as they move these give out a melodious sound. The music of the dance is provided by the *sehgura*, a woman's instrument (*see* p. 341). It is a gourd covered with a loosely fitting cotton net strung with hard split seeds; the long loose ends of the cotton are gathered over the bulbous end of the gourd, and held in the left hand; the right hand holds the narrow neck. To produce the sound the gourd is shaken, and the cords alternately loosened and drawn taut, so that the seeds strike the shell.

When the time comes for girls to leave the school, they are first washed; for this purpose they are marched down to the water, and no man may grace the ceremony by his presence; he is not, however, forbidden to make observations from a coign of vantage in the window of a neighbouring house. After the washing, the girl is then probably smeared with a pomade of animal fat and palm oil mixed, and led to the house of her *fiancé*.

Photograph by Sir H. H. Johnston, G.C.M.G., K.C.B.

A BUNDU WOMAN, BOPASS, WESTERN LIBERIA.

The top of the *coiffure* is decorated with seeds.

The Bundu Devil.

But before we come to marriage and allied questions, mention must be made of the *Bundu* devil—a woman magician, whose function it is amongst other things to see that no man interferes with the *Bundu* girls. Everyone has heard of Mumbo Jumbo, the masked figure of the men's society upon whom no woman may look and live; the *Bundu* devil is his female counterpart, though the sight of her is not fatal to the fortunate male. She is a strange figure; no part of her body is visible; cloth covers her arms and legs, and the ends are sewn up, lest haply a finger tip should be seen. In each hand she holds, of course through the cloth, a bunch of twigs which plays an important part when a malefactor has to be sought out. Her dress is of long shaggy fibre, dyed black, and over her face is a mask, grotesquely carved. She dances occasionally, but in the warm climate her close fitting attire forbids much indulgence in such exertion. In fact her attendant, known as a *Digba*, carries a roll of cloth which she at times unfolds to act as an undressing room for her superior, when the latter gets too warm and finds fresh air a necessity. At other times the roll of cloth is carried by the *Digba* between herself and her superior, for the latter is charged with dangerous power which may do her subordinate an injury if she does not take care to insulate herself as much as possible.

If a man has been so rash as to put himself within reach of *Bundu* law, this strange figure sets forth, accompanied by several *Digbas*, and points at the man, when she has found him, with her twigs; he dare not refuse to follow, and when he appears before the chief will have to pay a heavy fine. In former days failure to find the money would have meant slavery. Often, however, a prudent man will come to terms with the head woman of the *Bundu* society, and avoid the unpleasantness of being sought out in this public way for his transgressions.

A Strange Funeral Ceremony.

Before we leave the subject of *Bundu*, allusion may be made to another society of women, the *Yassi*, all members of which must belong to the *Bundu*. Strange ceremonies follow the death of a *Yassi* woman; her body is laid upon a cloth and borne round the house in which she lived by women of the order, dancing and singing without a stitch of clothing on them. A decoction is sprinkled to keep off her spirit, and *Porro* men (members of the men's secret society) proceed to hold a *post-mortem*, in order to discover if the deceased was a witch or not. During this trial all have to leave the village, the jury alone excepted; they take out the dead woman's liver and try whether it will float or not, and according as the test falls out, she is pronounced innocent or guilty.

How Women become Members of the Men's Secret Society.

More curious still is the custom which makes certain women members of the men's secret society. It is the law that no woman may look on a dead man of the *Tasso* grade; should one hide and peep—and woman was ever curious—illness comes upon her, and when she confesses fines are imposed, and she is called upon to undergo initiation. Thenceforth she is called *Mabori*, and is reckoned as both man and woman; not the least of her privileges is that she is not liable to be called to account for conjugal misdemeanours.

Marriage Ceremonies.

When the bride, well oiled, makes her way to her future husband's village at her departure from the *Bundu* school, she probably finds great preparations for a feast; palm wine at least is there in plenty, and a bridegroom of any position will have a store of rum or brandy. Music, more or less melodious, will grace the feast—near a Mandingo settlement the little harps of the professional musicians discourse music which even a white man may appreciate—and at the height of the festivity the bride's mother leads her to the husband's hut. Other women, friends of the bride, surround the hut and keep up a loud singing to celebrate the happy event and permit the newly-married couple to exchange confidences, sure of not being overheard.

Official Lovers.

Among some tribes of the Kru stock feminine freedom takes a remarkable form. A girl who has been pledged from early childhood, says Sir H. H. Johnston, is nevertheless allowed to have an official lover, when she wishes, between twelve and fourteen. Some time later she is taken over by her husband; but, before he can enter upon his rights, his wife must not only have given birth to a child, but also have weaned it; so that by the time all these formalities have been observed the bride is sixteen or seventeen, for the negro mother suckles her child for at least eighteen months, and among the Mandingo custom demands that husband and wife shall remain continent for three years after the birth of a girl, or four after the birth of a boy.

Polygamy.

One result of this regulation is that polygamy is the natural state of things, though, of course, not all men among the common people can afford two legitimate wives; for, as we have already seen, a wife is purchased, and an ordinary bride price is a cow, a couple of slaves, or their equivalent in goods, and twenty pieces of kola nut. But a big chief may have a hundred wives or even two hundred, especially if he is the head of the tribe. However, the ordinary man who has only one wife does not really suffer much hardship at the present day, for infidelity after marriage is not regarded in a serious light; in fact, society is on the side of the young wife who relegates her old husband to the second place, if not the third, and the old men are beginning to look on the misdemeanours of their wives as a part of the natural order of things.

Secret misdemeanours are forbidden by the Kru laws, and the husband who catches his wife *in flagrante delicto*, either in his own or the woman's hut, may fall upon the male culprit and inflict a severe beating, while the wife does not get off scot free. But before doing so the husband must politely bow the male offender over the threshold, for hospitality is a law that knows no exceptions; and the adulterer, so long as he is on the premises, is the guest of the husband, who may do him no hurt; once outside there is no protection. Nowadays, however, the matter is generally put right by a present of a few dollars, and it is only the habitual adulterer who has to face a severer penalty; he may be haled before the chief and compelled to pay heavy damages, or in default be sold into slavery.

By the courtesy of T. J. Alldridge, I.S.O.

GROUP OF BUNDU GIRLS, YANDAHU (see p. 337)

During the initiation ceremonies.

to the same rule. Among other tribes the mother does not do more than rub her child with palm oil, but everywhere great care is taken to keep the children clean and healthy, though, of course, infant mortality is very high. There is a certain amount of infanticide, chiefly to dispose of the maimed or defective, and weaklings usually succumb owing to natural causes; but the net result of the death rate is to produce human beings of splendid physique.

Birth Customs.

The birth customs are usually simple, and up to the day of the little stranger's appearance the woman goes about her accustomed tasks. In some tribes a woman goes into the bush to be delivered, and in this case is frequently unattended; in others she goes into another house in the same or an adjoining village. Among the Kru she is confined in her own home, and the same is true of the Mandingo. Of course no man may be present, and in most cases the woman is invisible to the male sex for some days after the event. The Mandingo women remain at home seven days, and on the eighth go abroad, and the father provides a feast. As soon as a birth takes place the woman attendant goes out and announces to the village the happy event, and the sex of the newcomer. At the feast the baby's head is shaved, and it is clothed and washed in full view of the people, but it may not leave the village for forty days, and the mother is subject

How Twins are Treated.

There is a curious difference of opinion in Africa on the subject of twins; some tribes hold them to be extraordinarily auspicious, and render the mother all sorts of honours; others kill the children and ostracise the mother. In the tribes with which we are dealing the rule is less drastic, but they are regarded with suspicion. Girls are on the whole more valuable than boys, and so when the twins are of different sexes, and this, according to Sir H. H. Johnston, is the rule in Liberia, where the girl is kept alive. Twins seem to be by no means uncommon, and in 1905 a woman of the Gold Coast distinguished herself by giving birth to six children, all living; but in such cases the whole brood is probably put away, for the natives regard the event as a horrible reversion to beast customs, much as twins are regarded in other parts.

Three months after birth the children receive as part of their food pellets of pounded banana or mashed manioc, and at the end of twelve months they are feeding themselves on rice and other food prepared for their parents; but probably they do not cease to enjoy their natural nourishment for some months more. Children are rarely ill-treated, says Sir Harry Johnston, and both fathers and mothers have a great affection for them.

Children's Food.

When a woman dies her body is often painted with indigo or a dark green dye; or variety may be added by grey wood-ashes or white kaolin. Sometimes the hair is allowed to grow as a sign of mourning, sometimes it is shaved off; and rings of dried grass or palm bark are a frequent sign of mourning. In the Mendi country women and girls who are mourning for a chief put on their heads small circlets made of finely twisted grass cord, black, yellow, brown, or some combination of these colours; they may also be replaced by narrow strips of cotton fibre. As a further mark of mourning they shave a furrow one inch wide round the head.

Mourning Customs.

The widows of the chief live for six months in a barri or court-house, and are then free to marry again, but as a rule they pass to the eldest brother of the deceased; on his death they go on to the next brother, and so on till the family is finished. Then they become "free women," which means that they are at liberty to dispose of their favours, for a consideration, where they will. So far from being despised they are the leaders of society, and when a married man is successful in securing the goodwill of one of them, and inducing her to quit her former flame, his wives celebrate the occasion, and he gives vent to his joy by firing guns; for such a mark of preference means that the recipient becomes a more important man in the estimation of his neighbours.

The Position of Widows.

By the courtesy of T. J. Alldridge, I.S.O.

MENDI WOMEN PLAYING *SEHGURA*, OR GOURD-RATTLES (*see* p. 337).

It appears that among the Vai any male relative may propose, and his love letter takes the form of a strip of the bark of the *raphia* palm. The woman is free to accept or reject the proposal by retaining or returning the bark strip.

Divorce in these lands is a very simple matter; in fact, it consists in sending the wife home to her own people and then wrangling with them as to the return of the bride price. It is far more troublesome to become a widower. In the interior of the Kru country, if a man's wife, a stranger to his village, dies suddenly, her parents may make a claim for compensation, which has to be met by the chief or by the husband. If the demand is not complied with, the woman's parents are apparently allowed by custom to raid the hen-roosts of the place where the woman died, and may even go so far as to burn down the town.

How Widowers have to pay Compensation.

Among the Vai the custom takes another form: the widower sends a sum of money to the grandparents as a ransom for the children whom he has had by the deceased woman; if it is not paid, they will go to their mother's relatives. Compliance with the custom has the additional attraction of providing a fresh wife, for, if there is another daughter, she comes into her deceased sister's place.

II

Tribes of the Ivory and Gold Coasts—A Woman's Day in Ashanti—Woman is Man's Equal—Women as Traders—Wongave Dress—"Fetish" Dresses worth £200 each—Curious Wedding Custom—Women Officials of Dahomey—The Famous Amazons—"Water Women"—A Race of Trading Women—Bini Women—Houses in West Africa—Hausa Women—Cross River Women—Cross River Betrothal and Marriage

WHEN we leave the Mandingo tribes, among whom in the broadest sense the Kru may be included, we come to the populations of the Ivory and Gold Coasts, Ashanti, Togo, and Dahomey, to the Yoruba, Bini, and other Nigerians, and to the peoples of the Cross River. Then we pass into German territory in Kamerun, where a Bantu population prevails, speaking languages allied to those of the whole of South Africa, Bushmen and Hottentots excepted; and in French Congo and further south we find allied tribes. The mere enumeration of all the teeming tribes of this area and its backlands, not to speak of the central group round Lake Chad, would occupy pages; even a cursory survey of representative tribes of the main groups is a large task, and only salient points can here be selected for notice.

Tribes of the Ivory and Gold Coasts.

The Tshi-speaking peoples of Ashanti and the Gold Coast are forest-dwellers and cultivators. Before six in the morning the woman is on her way, water-pot poised on her head, to fetch water from the river, in which, if time permits, she takes a morning bath; and about nine she has the morning meal of bananas and yams ready for her husband and family. But before this she has brushed out the house and the courtyard, a duty which no self-respecting negress will neglect, though she may let a girl act in her stead.

A Woman's Day in Ashanti.

Perhaps, however, her husband has announced his intention of spending the day on the plantation, of which each family has, as a rule, two, one near the village, the other more remote. Then she sets out, one child on her back, another clinging to her hand, and on her head is a large basket. Her husband, of course, stalks along in manly dignity behind her, with his gun or matchet in his hand; unless perchance he is a Christian with only one wife, in which case he must perforce aid her, for polygamy is not allowed. In the ordinary native family it is the presence of more than one woman which makes it possible for the day's work to be done in twenty-four hours.

Between two and three she is on her homeward way, for the chief meal of the day must be got ready; her burden of sixty or eighty pounds is no joke in this climate, and her first thought when she reaches the hut is to take a bath, after which she anoints herself with oil; for without this her skin turns a dirty grey, and cracks in times of drought. Then comes the dressing of her hair, and if she has time she summons a neighbour to construct one of the erections shown in some of the illustrations; or if there is no one handy she may sit down before her mirror and perform the operation herself. More often these details of her toilette are postponed till the evening when she has more time.

By the courtesy of T. J. Alldridge, I.S.O.

A PRINCESS OF THE DAMA COUNTRY.

Note the leopard's-teeth necklace.

Woman is Man's Equal.

Hard-worked, however, as she is, the Ashanti woman is not a mere slave. Bonnat says that she is regarded as man's equal; a chief's wife acts as his representative in his absence. The queen mother is the regent during her son's minority, and in after-life remains one of his chief counsellors. She is the guardian of the royal treasure left by the preceding sovereign, and only gives up the charge of it when the new king has sufficiently proved his wisdom.

Women as Traders.

The woman of the Gold Coast is often a trader; in Soku market she sits on a little stool or a mat; her goods are in large baskets or small grass sacks, and they consist of shea butter; baobab seeds for soup, rice, maize, pancakes, etc.; nor must we forget to mention the salt crystals which represent the sweets of the little black youngsters, and are sucked with avidity.

Wongave Dress.

The Wongave women who frequent this market wear large cloths as dresses, made of wild cotton, strong and soft, and dyed with indigo. Their hair is dressed in three globular masses, one on the top of the head, and one on each temple; there are two stiff locks, one in front of each ear, with strings of bright beads at the ends; and their ears are pierced and decorated with beads.

"Fetish" Dresses worth £200 each.

The young women of the Gold Coast have, of course, to undergo various initiation ceremonies. The illustration on p. 345 represents their full dress at Krobo, and is known as the dress of the "fetish" Otufo. At the age of puberty they perambulate the country in this costume, dancing and receiving presents. It is a preparation for marriage, after which they do not appear in this semi-nude condition. Some years ago the Governor attempted to abolish the custom, but failed, except as regards some of the towns. The caps and other ornaments worn by the women in the illustration consist of Gold Coast silver and valuable beads; it is said that the market value of the dress of each girl is at least £200.

On the other side of the Volta River live the Ga-speaking peoples, but their customs need not detain us. The Mamprusi of the Gambaga country have a unique wedding custom. Unmarried girls wear little or nothing in the street, and perhaps it is just as well, for when they get married an important part of the ceremony is to bathe them in public. On the eve of the wedding,

Curious Wedding Custom.

By the courtesy of Mr. R. E. Dennett.

AN ACCRA WOMAN.

The hair is ornamented with shells, etc.

in two pots, six gallons of water are boiled with herbs, and during the process drums are beaten, and continuous watch is kept. At noon on the auspicious day a bath is made ready in a public place, with the water, which has been kept boiling; cold water and native perfumes are added, and the bride is bathed for five hours or more, while Kola nut and cowries are distributed to the guests and musicians. Then the bride is covered all over with perforated native cloth, and conducted home, to be led at midnight to the house of her husband, who has also undergone ablutions—though not in public. Unmarried girls may not cover the head, and it is a sign of the estate of marriage when a woman wears a cloth upon her head falling down over her back.

Beyond the Ga-speaking peoples come the Ewe-speaking peoples, whose district embraces the old kingdom of Dahomey, where, contrary to the usual practice, the king's eldest son was his heir; for the ordinary rule of succession is that a man is succeeded by his sister's son. Strangely enough this exceptional practice was associated with an extensive system of women officials and warriors; for while the officers of the kingdom were male, those of the palace were female, and within their own domain took precedence of the men, perhaps because they were, in name, the king's wives. By a quaint turn of phrase the female officials were the "mothers" of the male officials, and there was an "English mother" for the benefit of English visitors.

Women Officials of Dahomey.

These palace women had another function; they were the king's spies, and he had no difficulty in introducing them into the family of a chief or other suspected person, for all he had to do was to make a present of one or more of the women: this was regarded as an honour, and could not be declined, though it was common knowledge that they were sent to serve the king's interests.

But the most characteristic feature of Dahomey in the not very far distant days of the old *régime* was the corps of Amazons, also known by the titles of the "king's wives," and "our mothers." Their origin did not go back to a very remote period, for they seem to have been enrolled for the first time in 1729, and for nearly a century consisted mainly of criminals, that is women detected in adultery, together with termagants and scolds. Early in the nineteenth century the force was put on a new footing, every head of a family being ordered to send his daughters for inspection. The negro woman is inured to labour, and in Dahomey especially was, and perhaps is, physically superior to the male sex; for Burton tells us that the women were generally tall, muscular and broad, while the men were smooth, full-breasted, round limbed and effeminate looking.

The Famous Amazons.

The Amazons were sworn to celibacy, though the king had the privilege of taking

Photograph by A. Holm, Lagos.

THE "OTUFO" DRESS IN CROBO, GOLD COAST.

Girls are thus dressed during the period of their initiation ceremonies. The ornaments are chiefly of silver.

any of them to wife ; but though they were supposed to meet the male sex only on the field of battle, human nature is frail, and when Burton was at Agbomi, no fewer than one hundred and fifty of the women were put to death for misconduct, the results of which were only too evident. In peace time one of their duties was to escort the king's wives when they went to fetch water, and a bell was rung before them as a signal for all men to leave the road.

In war they are said to have displayed the most ferocious courage, disregarding danger, wounds, and death itself, and one of their chief aims was to carry off trophies in the shape of heads and jawbones.

"Water Women."

In many parts of West Africa tribes may be classified into people of the land and people of the water. In Nigeria, the home of the Yoruba-speaking peoples, we may take the Jekri and Ijo as representative of the latter, the Yoruba proper and Bini as examples of the former. The Jekri woman is a "water-dog"; she goes up river in her canoe, paddling on alternate sides when she is alone, to bring food down to the settlements, for she does not plant. She is clean and comely, she wears a shoulder cloth of red, blue, or yellow European stuff with bracelets of silver or brass.

Her house is on the water-side, and she helps to build it of wattles; among her other occupations is the making of rough mats. She decorates her cheeks and back with a series of round dots.

The Ijo women are like the Jekri; their husbands make for them the canoes which they need for their trade in smoked fish, captured with hook and line, traps, or spears. As becomes a people who live by the water their huts are built on piles. The tribal mark of this people is a deep scar down the forehead and nose.

The Yoruba women on the other hand are "land-rats." They, too, are great traders; they do no planting, but travel daily from town to market, starting at five a.m. Bargaining goes on till about eleven, and then they make their own purchases and set out on their homeward way, often with sixty pounds of load and the indispensable baby. The Yoruba woman is of slender build, she has good taste in dress, and wears mainly dark-hued raiment and a dark turban. So ingrained is her love of trading that even the wives of civilised natives cannot resist the temptation of it, just as the Englishwoman falls a victim to the delights of shopping, even when she has neither money nor credit with which to make purchases.

A Race of Trading Women.

Bini Women.

The Bini woman wears fewer clothes as a rule, often only a loin cloth; when she has more, they are in the Jekri fashion. Her chief ornament is coral, but the chiefs' wives wear brass anklets and bracelets. Common women wear the hair just brushed up and cut short, but the king's wives have elaborate *coiffures*—three great knobs of hair surmounted by coral beads.

Bini women do not go to big riverside markets like the Yoruba, they visit places some two or three miles from the water, and here they meet the Jekri. Their towns are chiefly on the hills, and they have to go down a mile or more to fetch water. Here, as elsewhere, the women are the potters; and their material is kaolin got from the river beds. The products are not so elegant in shape as in some parts, but they are large—a cooking pot will hold ten gallons.

Unlike the women of the west, the fair sex in Benin undertake the weaving as well as the carding; the cotton is spun with the aid of a stick, round which it is wound as it is finished. They also dye their goods with indigo and other colouring stuffs. Indigo they make from three kinds of plants—two creepers and a shrub; magenta is imported; for brown they use a weak solution of black.

Infant betrothal is the cause of the lack of fidelity of Bini women to their husbands. Many women arriving at the age of puberty

Photograph by A. Holm, Lagos.

A QUETTAH WOMAN.

side. In the passage are cooking utensils, the beds are raised platforms of dried mud, seven to eight feet long, allowing for the fire at the foot of the sleeper. The whole interior is black with smoke, and attached to the rafters are calabashes, mats, hoes, cooking utensils, and *jujus* (charms). In many cases a kind of oven is made under the bed, and heated; this is only used in very cold weather, but fires are kept going all the year round.

Houses in West Africa.

Bini women usually wear native loin-cloths, which sometimes serve as a pad on their heads when they have loads

North of the Yoruba and Bini peoples live the Hausa, extending over three hundred miles from north to south, and the same distance from east to west. The population numbers at least 15,000,000, and of these the majority are

Hausa Women.

Photograph by A. Holm, Lagos.

POPO WOMEN.

The coast tribes are becoming Europeanised in dress.

are handed over to comparatively old men as third or fourth wives, and find themselves with the duties of a slave. Many chiefs have over 200 wives, not all living in the same village or town, but scattered over the country. In many cases the husband, on visiting one of the outsiders, finds she has been living with another man, and has children by him. Formerly it was the custom for the husband to sue the adulterer and thus make a handsome income.

Infant Betrothal and its Evils.

On the death of the husband, all those wives who have not borne children to him pass to the eldest son. Often a wife will not declare the parentage of her child till the death of her husband.

Yoruba and Bini live in far more substantial houses. If you enter the women's quarter of the house, at the left hand of the building, you find yourself in a roofless passage with the rooms of the wives on one

Photograph by A. Holm, Lagos.

OLD AND YOUNG "FETISH" WOMEN, BADAGRY.

Many West African tribes have women as "priestesses."

slaves; in Kano, the chief town, the highest price is paid for a girl of fourteen—from £7 to £10. In this connection it may be noted that a free man may not marry a slave, and, if he has a child by his own female slave, he may not afterwards sell her. If two slaves marry with their masters' consent, the children belong to the latter alternately.

As regards the position of women in general, they are better off than in most Mohammedan countries. They are not secluded, unless they are royal, and as a rule they have freedom of choice, in respect of marriage. Not only so, but they have a married woman's property law, which enacts that after marriage the woman retains her own property.

Some of the Cross River women are, according to Mr. Partridge, more than passably good looking. They have well-shaped heads, small ears lying close, good foreheads, short, straight noses, curved lips not too thick, beautiful teeth, and finely curved eyelashes. Their eyes are pleasant when they smile, but to a European the absence of the soft changing lights makes them monotonous. Some women are shapely, too, and their dark brown skin is smooth and unblemished. It is curious to learn that the native standard of beauty demands a coal-black skin and a long neck.

Cross River Women.

As so often happens dress among some of these peoples is ornamental, at least in their eyes, rather than useful. The women of the Igbo-Amaban towns wear no clothing in front, but adorn themselves with a tail; the Ikwe women go somewhat further, but in their case superstition steps in to limit the amount of clothing, for they hold that if they have more than a small piece of cloth it will be detrimental to child-bearing.

Photograph by A. Holm, Lagos.

EGBA GIRLS SELLING FOOD.

Trade in which is confined to the women, who are also in the main the producers.

Photograph by Sir H. H. Johnston, G.C.M.G., K.C.B.

JEBU WOMEN, LAGOS.

They live much upon the water and paddle their canoes to market. Note the styles of hair-dressing.

A woman's pride is in her hair, and the people of this district spend many hours in hair-dressing; palm oil and grease are applied, and wonderful structures are built up which remain untouched for months. Horn-like protuberances seem to be the prevailing fashion; there may be a single horn on the top with the tip over the forehead, or two on the side, and one on the back, or four horns along the crown, the intervening spaces bridged with knitting needles of porcupine quills; there may be a single horn planted on a mound, or a coronet of small horns, or horns all over. Furrows from side to side take the fancy of others; and some adorn their hair with tassels, coloured red with cam-wood. A few score safety pins in the hair are held to be a neat decoration.

Cross River Betrothal and Marriage.

Betrothal is early in these tribes, and till they get married girls are put under the protection of a fetish named Nimm; his duty consists, however, not in looking after their morals, for everything is permitted save only the bringing of a lover into their father's compound, but in seeing that no one poisons them. Nimm's shrine is just outside the entrance, a small stockade, two and a half feet high, with a mushroom-shaped ant-hill in the centre, smeared with paint, and tied with a wisp of grass in which is a wooden knife.

Before marriage the bride is fattened, being painted white all over, and on festive occasion with geometrical patterns in black paint into the bargain. When she is of age to be married her betrothed paints her red all over, and henceforth she must remain faithful to him. After marriage the husband has his own hut among the Ikwe; the stockade of branches, three or four feet high, is set up by the woman, for her own or her husband's hut, but the thatching is the work of the man. Husband and wife work jointly on the farm, too, but for trading purposes they have separate property. Cooking is the woman's task, and, as many hands make light work, the head wife encourages her husband to marry again. Pottery, too, is made by the women; it is built up on a base, dried in the sun, and hardened in the smoke of a fire.

If a wife runs away she cannot be forced to return, but of course all expenses of courtship must be repaid to the husband, and a jury sits to determine how much he has spent. As a rule the children go to the father in such a case. Twins are here abhorred, and in the Efik countries the mother is driven away, and the children put to death; elsewhere a free woman may keep one of them; one twin child of a slave will be killed, and the other given to some other woman.

III

Decoration in Kamerun—Field Work—Women as Councillors—The Mucilongo Women—Women's Work among the Mucilongo—Mucilongo Dyes—Mucilongo Costumes—Birth Customs—How Children are Trained—Child Marriages and Conjugal Fidelity—Women as Doctors—Funeral Customs—Position of Mucilongo Women—The Kabenda and Kakongo Women—Wife Burial—Kakongo Conjugal Fidelity—Women's Work—Kabenda Dress and Ornaments—Angola Women—Loando Market and its Women Traders—How Farîna is Made—Angola Marriages.

IN Kamerun the distinction is not so much between water and land people as between the dwellers in the forest, and in the grass country. In this area dress is mainly decorative, the women of some tribes wear nothing till the first child is born, or only a thin string of beads; then a four-inch grass apron is donned before and behind, with a fanlike extension of bamboo like a peacock's tail.

Decoration in Kamerun.

At the present day, however, empty cartridge cases and sardine tins are in great demand as articles of female adornment.

The hair is as usual dressed in many fantastic styles, the Bakundu and Batom shave it or let it grow long; the Banyang cut it into arabesques, rings, squares, etc.,

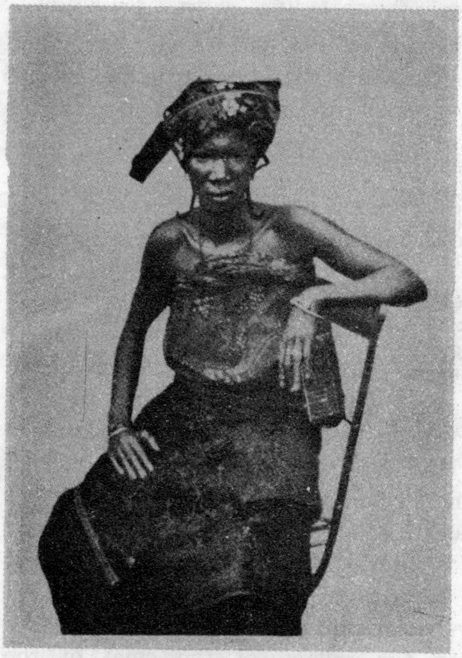

Photograph by A. Holm, Lagos.

A HAUSA WOMAN.

The Hausa are Mohammedan, and wear more clothes than "pagan" tribes.

as the individual fancy dictates; some tribes work cowries into the *coiffure*, as many as two hundred being needed. Some of the forest tribes wear long fur caps of monkey skin and rub the body with red wood, and both body scars and filed teeth are among their personal adornments. A curious form of decoration, found also on the Nile, is the wearing of an object in the lower lip; a European thermometer is held to be a highly effective ornament in this situation.

Field Work.

The field work, as usual, falls to the lot of the women, and after an early meal women and slaves set out for the farms, the children astride the mother's hips, hanging to her arm or supported on a band passed round her forehead. Sometimes the husband goes too when the clearing is distant, for in Kamerun they tell how the chimpanzee is enamoured of womenkind, and carries them off to be his wives. Sometimes the husband on these occasions will carry the child home himself, his spear in the other hand, and an umbrella as a protection if it is raining.

Women as Councillors.

In the grass country woman occupies a high position. The mother of the chief is a member of his council, and he has a great respect for her; his chief wife may also aid in its deliberations. The husband is, however, the head of the house. Polygamy exists in practice if not in name—a man gets his wife by agreement, by betrothal, or by purchase; but with her he has a number of concubines, who enjoy no rights, from the slave caste.

Patience seems to be practised in these regions. A traveller has recorded that he once saw a woman sitting in a courtyard eating. She was hailed by another woman well within earshot, but did not feel called upon to put herself out, and calmly went on with her meal; at last, her appetite satisfied,

Photograph by A. Holm, Lagos.

AN EGBA MOTHER CARRYING HER TWIN BABES.

As a rule one or both of twin children are killed, but in some tribes they are regarded as auspicious.

she did rouse herself so far as to reply "woi" (I am here), but before this happened the summons to her had been repeated one hundred and seven times.

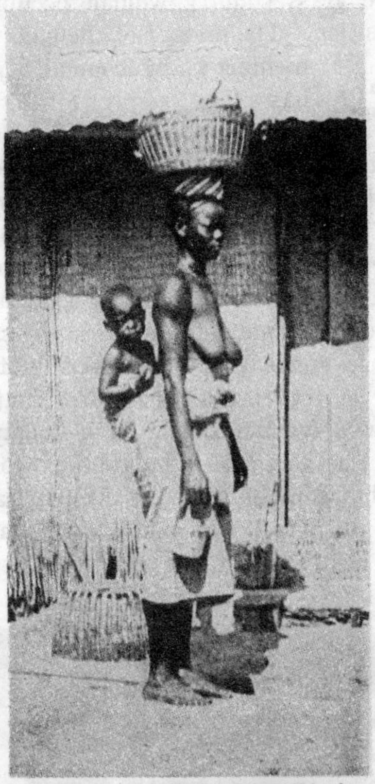

Photograph by A. Holm, Lagos.

WOMAN GOING TO MARKET.

Wherever she goes the African mother carries her child—even when she is at work in the field or laden with market produce.

As already stated, in many parts of Africa it is possible to divide the tribes into water and land people. On both sides of the mouth of the Congo there is a tribe known as the Mucilongo or Musserongo; they are the water people of the district, while the Kabinda, Kakongo and Loango people are the land folk. The Mucilongo live in rectangular huts, constructed by the men, and each wife has her own dwelling, separated in some cases from the others by a kind of enclosure. The hut is perhaps ten feet by six, built of bamboo with a door of the same material; the roof is of mats made of bamboo leaves which are laid on the top of the walls, fastened on with string. The furniture is inexpensive, a bamboo bed stands in one corner, chairs and tables there are none; on the walls are hung boxes, cooking pots, and other utensils. A wooden box, large or small according to the wealth of the owner, serves as a wardrobe, but a favourite method of keeping cloth is to bury it in the ground well wrapped up in leaves, mats, or the like.

The Mucilongo Women.

Women's Work among the Mucilongo.

The Mucilongo women are expert laundresses; in their dug-out canoes from ten to forty feet long, they carry their produce to market, singing their boat songs as they paddle along, or steal silently up a creek to set their fish traps.

A woman rises with the sun, say 5.30 a.m., and sets to work to cook for herself and her family, and, if it is her turn, for her husband too, for the wives take a supply of food to him turn and turn about, unless there happens to have been a quarrel.

My friend, Mr. R. E. Dennett, was once visiting the village of the chief of the Mucilongo, when his attention was attracted by groans and howls proceeding from the hut of the chief, which was better furnished than the ordinary dwelling, as became the residence of the king. His majesty was discovered reclining on his couch in a very distressed condition, which he explained by the remark: "Dem women, he fit for kill me; my belly be too hungry." Further inquiry showed that owing to some dispute his wives found it impossible to give him any food, for no single one dared face the wrath of her fellows by approaching her lord and master. The principal wife, Donna Maria Segunda, excused herself for her neglect of her husband by saying: "Dem man, he be fool man; he no sab treat him wife proper." Fortunately for his majesty the wives felt some shame at their domestic differences being exposed to a stranger, and soon after Neamlau got his meals regularly.

After cooking food a woman goes to the fields, taking with her water and provisions for the day; her children she may leave with a friend, but if they are small she generally takes them with her. After a walk of two or three miles she comes to the clearing, already prepared by her husband, and sets to work to hoe it or plant it with maize, bananas, manioc, ground nuts, etc., according to the number of years it has been under cultivation.

If she does not work fast the Mucilongo other men join him, for husband and wife never eat together. About six she takes her evening meal with her children, having taken from her husband's booty what she required; this over, she sets to work to clean earthen cooking vessels and wooden platters.

By the courtesy of Mr. J. W. McCann.

AN *AL FRESCO* TOILETTE ON THE GOLD COAST (*see* p. 343).

As a rule women dress each other's hair.

woman is a stayer; her baby on her back, she bends over her hoe hour after hour, stopping but once to take a little refreshment, perhaps at 11 o'clock. Towards four or five her field work is ended, and she piles on her back a quantity of wood—as much as a hundred-weight sometimes—and brings it home, baby and all. When she reaches her hut she finds her husband has been hunting and has brought home an antelope, some palm nuts, fish or fowl, according to his luck. This she sets to work to cook in her own hut, and takes it over to the two-roomed hut, which is her husband's private property, for his evening meal, to be taken alone, unless

Then, if a feast or a dance is in progress, she goes forth on pleasure bent.

At a woman's dance she, with two or three others, will stand in the centre of a circle, and wriggle, for no other word will adequately describe this performance. At a men's dance, on the other hand, her show is confined to joining in the chorus; but men's and women's dances are performed on the same occasion. A native ball of this description may finish at daylight, but is equally likely to go on for two or three days.

Between supper and bed time, which is about eight o'clock, the usual pastime is gossip, which is carried on, not in confidential whispers, but at the top of the voice from hut to hut.

The usual time for ablution is the early morning. The richer class send female slaves to fetch water for them, the poorer fetch their water themselves and bathe in the river at the same time; the children are bathed in the river or at home.

In the dry season the women make mats while their husbands are hunting or cutting the bush; they use the leaves of the *fuba* tree (screw-pine) and plait them. The mats are used as seats, shrouds to wrap cloth in, etc. When a visitor arrives a mat is put down for him under a tree or in the house.

Mucilongo Dyes.

A great industry is that of dyeing. The Mucilongo women dye all their clothes a kind of dull red, which contrasts very well with their silver ornaments. The dye is made of *tucula*, camwood, ground up with water on a stone, and made up into balls, which are used as they are needed; the dye powder is more like mud than anything else. A black dye is used for mats, so too is a yellow dye, the former extracted from gall nuts and iron, the latter from a yellow wood.

Mucilongo Costumes.

The dress of a Mucilongo woman is comparatively simple; first she has a white loin cloth of Congo cotton, over this comes a red cloth, some fifteen yards long and fifty inches broad, which she wraps round her waist and throws over her shoulder. The ornaments are usually of silver; leg-rings made of English shillings by the native blacksmith are given by men to their favourite wives and daughters; these are called *kwini bota* (queenly good) from the head of the late queen stamped upon the first that came into their hands. These rings are generally plain, but a crocodile's head may be cast on the side, where it will be cut through in order to allow of its being put over the foot. Armlets and bracelets of silver, gun-metal, pewter, or even galvanised iron, are worn, cast in the same way, usually plain, though bracelets are sometimes decorated with a fret pattern. There are also thin neck-rings, open and joined by a loop at the back, and various magical bracelets. The hair is worn *au naturel*.

Birth Customs.

Birth is an easy matter on the Congo—sometimes the mother has a friend with her, sometimes she manages alone. A woman will exhibit a baby in the morning of whose arrival no one has been aware, or bring it back from the field, walking two or three miles with one or two rests on the way. The first thing to do to the new arrival is to wash it, and this is usually done in warm water. Children are as white as white babies for a couple of days, and then they begin to darken, until in a week or ten days they are like their brothers and sisters. In the first twenty-four hours the child gets nothing but cold water to drink; then it receives its natural nourishment. When the mother is at

Photograph by Sir H. H. Johnston, G.C.M.G., K.C.B.

A WOMAN OF OLD CALABAR.

The full clothing is due to contact with Europeans. The next picture shows the unsophisticated native woman.

work the child may be suckled hanging on to the mother's back.

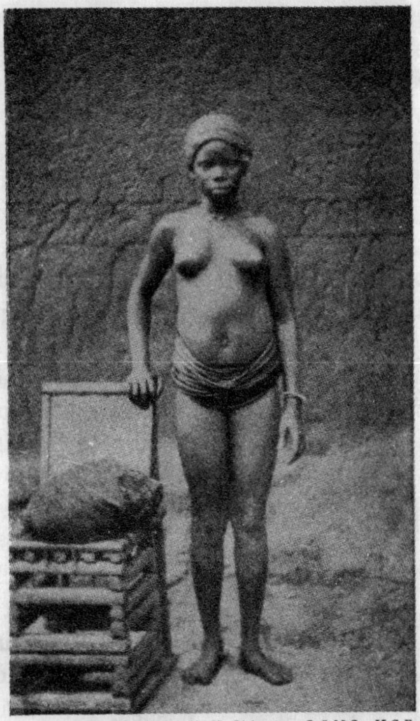

Photograph by Sir H. H. Johnston, G.C.M.G., K.C.B.

A WOMAN FROM THE INTERIOR OF OLD CALABAR.

(Cross river, W. Africa.)

How Children are Trained.

Shaping the child's head is an important process. The mother warms her hands and applies them to the sides and front. Probably no real shaping of the baby's head is attempted or accomplished; the idea is to close the sutures. Children are also massaged; the mother warms her hands and rubs the child to straighten its legs; sometimes she picks it up by the hands, so as to stretch the arms and straighten the body.

Children begin to crawl and walk much at the same age as European children, but some never go on their hands and knees, but go with straight legs; attempts at walking begin at ten to fourteen months. They are weaned at eighteen months or two years, though they receive solid food earlier.

Until a child is four or five it stays with its mother; it will play at "being mother," and go for water with its own little pot. A girl learns to cook at a very early age; at the age of seven she is serving her apprenticeship, playing with her mother's pots and helping to prepare the family meals.

A girl goes naked till ten or eleven, and then takes a loin-cloth. She assumes ordinary dress when she has been through the "paint house" (*i.e.* initiation).

When the mother is in the fields the girls play with little hoes; they learn to paddle the canoe, to make mats and so on, till at thirteen or fourteen their education may be regarded as finished, and they are received into the society of their elders. Bits of wood dressed in a scrap of cloth do duty as dolls, but they do not figure largely in their lives. The existence of the white child is one continual holiday compared with the life of the black child. There is not much play about a native, but we find knucklebones played with palm kernels, and the ubiquitous *warri*, something like backgammon; but make-believe, which passes into real work, is the chief amusement of the Congo child.

Child Marriages and Conjugal Fidelity.

Parents agree to betroth their children, even before birth, and the boy, from the age of seven or eight onwards, will take presents to his wife; the marriage proper takes place at the age of thirteen or fourteen.

Conjugal morality is severely enforced among the Mucilongo; an offender pays a heavy fine to the aggrieved husband, but by a singular provision if any one but the husband detects the offender and publishes the fact, he, and not the real culprit, is responsible to the husband.

Women as Doctors.

All women know the use of herbs in medicine, and occasionally a woman is found acting as doctor in more serious cases, such as bites of scorpion, etc. The surgeons on the other hand are always men.

Funeral Customs.

At death a woman is buried simply; she is wrapped up and smoked like a man. When she has been a kind of head of the family, there may be a big funeral, but as a rule there is very little fuss made over the death of a woman.

After the funeral ceremonies of her husband a widow—who was formerly buried with her husband—paints her face black with oil and ashes. Widows are not allowed to marry until after the real burial, which may be postponed three or four years. A woman goes back to her own district if she can when her husband dies.

There are many curious customs which space forbids us to describe, but mention may be made of an institution which should rejoice the heart of the suffragette. The Mucilongo woman, if she is not strictly the keeper of her husband's purse, is certainly the guardian of his property. In the face of this it is disappointing to have to record that when she returns from the fields or brings anything to her husband, she is required to salute him by kneeling down and thrice clapping her hands.

By the courtesy of Mr. R. E. Dennett.

TWO KABINDA WOMEN.

Position of Mucilongo Women.

The lot of the husband of a Congo princess is a curious one. She may marry anyone she chooses, and he becomes her slave; but though she may put him to death or divorce him when she wants a change, he is nevertheless a very big man; should he survive her he inherits her property. According to Andrew Battell this practice led in the old days to a curious result, for it appears that the husband only became the heir if there were a child by the marriage. This desirable result attained, the husband was, of course, still at his wife's mercy, for she might divorce him or have him killed; so, the old traveller tells us, the happy father cut the Gordian knot by putting his wife out of the way before she had time to play him a similar trick.

Loango people are to the Mucilongo as the Bini and Yoruba are to the Jekri and Ijo; they are land people. Mr. Dennett's first introduction to the woman question in Africa was seeing an old woman walk into a huge bonfire in Kabinda Bay; she had been accused of causing the death of her husband by witchcraft. As she loved her husband very much, and her accusers were really anxious to get her out of the way owing to the idea that she had hidden a great deal of his wealth, she, knowing her innocence, full of faith in it, walked into the fire, and was burnt to death. Properly speaking the fire is the punishment for witches, not an ordeal, but this woman walked in of her own accord.

By the courtesy of Mr. R. E. Dennett.

A GABOON WOMAN.

The Kabinda and Kakongo Women.

By the courtesy of Mr. R. E. Dennett.

A LOANGO WOMAN.

Mr. Dennett's next experience was hearing of the fact that a large number of a great man's wives had been buried with him in a vil-

By the courtesy of Mr. R. E. Dennett.

LOANGO HALF-CASTE GIRL AND HER MOTHER.

lage close to Kabinda. In this ceremony a huge hole was dug, then the funeral car proceeded to the grave, and the coffin was taken out and placed in it. Food and ornaments were thrown in, then some of the slaves, the number varying according to the rank and wealth of the deceased, and other slaves presented by neighbouring chiefs, with their arms and legs broken, were thrown into the grave. Finally a certain number of wives volunteered to be buried with him; their arms and legs were broken, the grave was filled up, and the car placed over it.

Wife Burial.

Mothers are often being called upon to take *casca* (poison), owing to constant miscarriages or frequent deaths of their offspring; it is considered that they are possessed by *ndongo*, or witch power.

The Kabinda women have a greater reputation for beauty than their Mucilongo sisters, but it is a matter of taste whether the Kakongo are more beautiful than the Bavili. The Kakongo are far truer to their husbands, and have a greater sense of the sanctity of marriage than either of the other tribes. Mr. Dennett knew one old couple, about eighty years of age, who had lived together for over fifty years in monogamous union.

Kakongo Conjugal Fidelity.

As far as occupations go, the people of Loango are chiefly noted for mat- and basket-making; the Kakongo for their pottery. In mat-making they dye the leaves red, yellow, and black, and work the different colours into patterns. Sitting on the ground they have two pegs before them, fixed the width of the mat apart; a string runs from one to the other, they fold the leaves over it, and then begin plaiting. They make baskets, some of *fubu* leaves, and some of *piassava* (bamboo ribs); the latter have a wooden bottom; the first row is plaited of *piassava* alone, and they go on plaiting *piassava* and *zimbamba* (outer skin of the cane) together. Bottles are also covered in a similar manner.

Women's Work.

Pottery is made without a wheel; if a water-pot is to be fashioned the potter

By the courtesy of Mr. R. E. Dennett.

A GABOON WOMAN AND A LOANGO MAID.

Note the difference in type between the lady and the lower class woman.

generally has the broken bottom of an old pot to start with, and with the prepared clay moulds on it the bottom of the new one; then as the sides grow she keeps one hand on each side, adding clay, and turning the pot continually. Next it is allowed to dry in the shade, and afterwards in the sun, and finally baked in a sort of bonfire. Open vessels for cooking are also made.

By the courtesy of Mr. R. E. Dennett.

A LOANGO LADY RECEIVING A VISIT FROM INFERIORS, WHO KNEEL BEFORE HER AND CLAP THEIR HANDS.

The women play with a doll shaped like a bullet when they have lost a child or are childless. They buy fish from fishermen, carry it thence four hours inland to a market and exchange it for rubber, palm oil, or kernels. On one day the women are not allowed to work in the fields.

Kabinda Dress and Ornaments.

The Kabinda woman wears an underskirt of ordinary cloth; a piece fifty inches broad, fifteen yards long, is pleated on a waist string, and which forms a voluminous skirt; over her shoulders, and covering a quarter of her skirt, is a white short-sleeved chemise. Then comes a shawl—a piece of fifty-inch cloth, nine or ten yards long.

If she is married she has a *lembe* bracelet, and ornaments of the Mucilongo type, or of copper and brass, are also worn, but not zinc or pewter.

Kabinda women are very fond of a little gold wire earring, coral beads round the neck, or the tail of an elephant. Anklets are generally of brass, but are not always worn.

A bushwoman will only wear a little piece of grass cloth. The waistband consists of a number of longitudinal strings made of very fine grass, plaited and ending in a single string, worn in front. When one woman has told another a lie, the latter can put it to the test by saying "*Siba lixete*. Hitch up your waist-band," and if it is not true, she will not touch it.

The first thing that is noticeable with regard to the women of Angola is that they are nearly all *lavadeiras* (washerwomen). The laundry is the river bank, and those who have not got a washing board beat the linen on a stone, the instrument of percussion being in either case the hand.

Angola Women.

Besides being washerwomen they do most of the business of the markets; they receive cloth in payment for their service, and go to market to trade this, unless perchance they think a new dress for themselves is a pressing necessity. Singularly enough the favourite colour for the dress of the "Upper Ten" is black.

The washerwoman is proverbially talkative, the negress no less so, and the voice of the Loanda woman is singularly high.

Loanda Market and its Women Traders.

Loanda market is not a mere open space like the ordinary native market, and when there is a crowd of a thousand women in it the general effect, heard all over the town, is much the same as that of a flock of starlings, all shrieking at once.

The Angola women are great wanderers, and when they leave their native land they retain their commercial instincts; in fact they form the petty traders of all the districts where they are found. Loanda being the capital, they look down on the people among whom they go, and the fact that they are baptised, and have some white blood in them, adds to their prestige.

The Loanda women are famous for their skill in making farîna.

How Farîna is made.

They take the root of the manioc, and shred it into a large tub, in which it is soaked; the mush is put into a cloth, squeezed, dried, and then roasted in brass pans. The next operation is to sift it, after which it is ready for use, and eaten raw or boiled.

The water that is squeezed out into the tub is allowed to clarify, the very fine powder accumulates at the bottom, the water is poured off and the residue is used as starch.

Livingstone says, in his "Missionary Travels in South Africa," that the chief recreations of the natives of Angola are marriages and funerals.

Angola Marriages.

When a young woman is about to be married she is placed in a hut alone, and anointed with various unguents, and many incantations are employed in order to secure good fortune and fruitfulness.

Here, as almost everywhere in the south, the height of good fortune is to bear sons—wives often leave their husbands altogether if they have daughters only. In their dances, when a woman may wish to deride another, in the accompanying song a line is introduced "So-and-So has no children, and never will get any." The insult is felt so keenly that it is not uncommon for the victim to rush away and commit suicide.

After some days the bride-elect is taken to another hut, and adorned with all the richest clothing and ornaments that the relatives can either lend or borrow. She is then placed in a public situation, saluted as a lady, and presents made by all her acquaintances are placed around her. After this she is taken to the residence of her husband, where she has a hut for herself, and becomes one of several wives, for polygamy is general. Dancing, feasting, and drinking on such occasions are prolonged for several days.

In case of separation the woman returns to her father's family, and the husband receives back what he gave for her. In nearly all cases a man gives a price for the wife, and in the case of a mulatto as much as £60 is often given to the parents of the bride.

SOUTH AMERICA

By THEODOR KOCH GRÜNBERG

Misconceptions of Indian Character—Position of Indian Women—Probationary Rites for Girls Betrothal and Marriage—Tests for Bridegrooms—Temporary Marriages—How Brides are Obtained—Marriage by Capture—Plurality of Wives—Conjugal Fidelity—Penalties for Infidelity—Divorce—The General Position of Woman in South America—Influence of Indian Women—Birth Customs—A Birth "Fast"—Diet of Parents—The "Couvade"—Indian Childhood—Where Charms Fade Early—Curious Pets—Indians as Parents—Ornamentation of Children—Girl's Duties—Death and Burial Customs—The Economic Importance of the Indian Woman—An Indian Woman's Work—Preparation of Manioc—The Indian Woman's Burden—Woman as Potter—Women as Weavers—Women Artists—Indian Dress—The Question of Adornment—Fashions in Distortion—Division of Labour—Women Eat when the Men have Finished—Curious Ceremonies—The Intelligence of the Indian Woman—Her Kindliness

Misconceptions of Indian Character.

BY many travellers—especially those of early days, the Indian woman was represented as an inferior being, the slave of her husband, degraded to the position of a soulless beast of burden. Such descriptions are based on superficial observations made, perhaps, on Indians living in contact with the white man. In his native wilds the Indian meets the European with distrust, for only too many of our fellow whites are adventurers, not to say out-and-out rascals. But treat the Indian well, and he soon realises that his visitor means well with him, and lays aside his mistrust. He is a harmless child of nature, who repays the traveller's good deeds with the most complete confidence.

By courtesy of the South American Missionary Society.

LITTLE MAPUCHE GIRL.

Thus the traveller who looks on the Indian as a fellow-man rather than as a subject for experiment soon gets glimpses into the family life of the native, and learns how great is the part played in it by woman; she enjoys respect both as wife and mother; she is the equal of her husband, and in diligence and artistic skill perhaps even his superior.

Position of Indian Women.

During my travels in South America in 1903-5 I lived nearly two years with the wild Indians, and took a delight in watching their pure family life. Perhaps it is not too much to hope that the following pages will help the Indian woman of South America to her rights.

Probationary Rites for Girls.

When the time comes for the girl to put off childish things and take her position as a member of the community with full rights, she has sometimes to undergo a severe probation. On the Içana and Caiary-Uaupes, tributaries of the Rio Negro, I observed that the puberty rites opened with hair-cutting and painting the girl's back with dark-blue genipa; this is done by the mother, or an old woman, in the house, her friends sitting round, and at the conclusion each takes a lock of hair for use as head decoration, etc. For four weeks the girl may eat only manioc, pepper, *maniuara* ants, and, in some tribes, small fish; her drink is manioc water; on no account may she eat large fish or warm-blooded animals.

When the month of fasting is over, her father sings before sunrise a long monotonous chant, reciting the fruits and animals which are now again permitted to her; the opening words of each verse and the refrain are invariable. Then the maiden bathes, and a great pot, full of all manner of fish, flesh, and fowl, is set before her, and her fast is at an end. In celebration of the occasion she is painted with *carayuru* (*Bignonia Chica*), and of course there is the inevitable drinking party afterwards. Among the Warrau of British Guiana the girl's hair is cut, and a dance follows, in which she appears decorated with beads and bird-down gummed on her clean-shaven head, legs and arms.

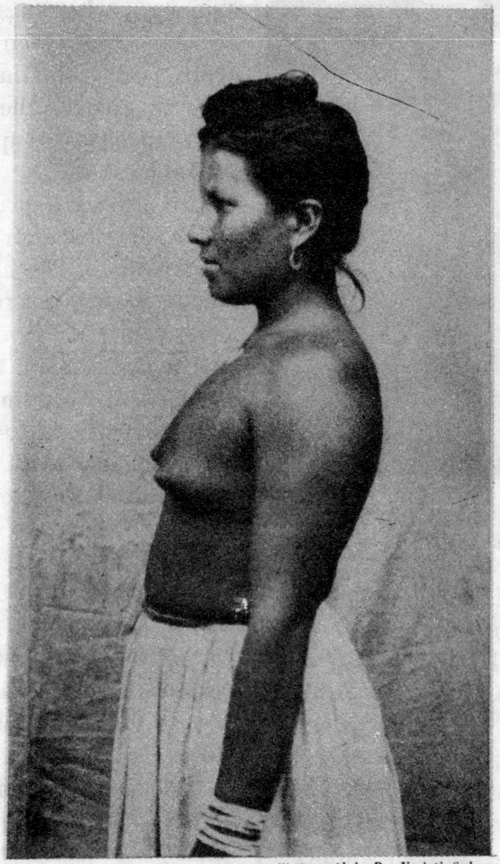

Photograph by Dr. Koch Grünberg.

UAIANA WOMAN, RIO CAIARY—UAUPES, NORTH-WEST BRAZIL.

Some of the Uaupes tribes, as A. R. Wallace tells us, made the initiation more painful. After fasting on bread and water for a month, the girl was brought out perfectly naked into the midst of a group of friends armed with *sipo* strips (a creeper), with which they inflicted five or six severe blows apiece, repeated four times in the twenty-four hours, as a result of which the girl fell senseless or even dead. In this case, too, numerous pots of all kinds of meat have been prepared; but the initiate is only allowed to lick the *sipo* rod, which is dipped into the pot.

Among the Macusi Indians the girl is cut off from all intercourse even with relatives, for she is considered impure; her hammock is hung right in the top of the hut, the smokiest part, and for the first few days she may not leave it, except at night; then she lights a fire and sits at it till it is time for her to climb into her hammock again. After some days she is allowed to occupy a screened-off corner of the hut, where she still lives on her cassava bread. Ten days later the magician appears, murmurs spells over the girl and all she has touched, and thus frees them from the magical power she has imparted to them; pots and other breakables are shattered, and the fragments buried. But this is not the end of her troubles. After bathing, she is beaten by her mother at night, and must sustain her ordeal without uttering a sound, for if she woke the other occupants of the hut she would suffer for it in the future.

The beating is repeated on another occasion, and then the maiden is free; if she has been betrothed, her future husband appears and carries her off without more ado.

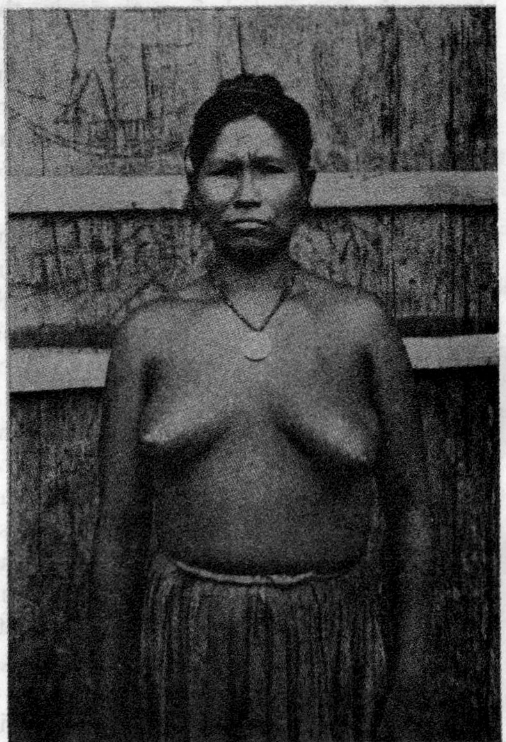

Photograph by Dr. Koch Grünberg.

KAUA WOMAN, RIO AIARY, NORTH-WEST BRAZIL.

Among the Caribs of British Guiana, the ordeal was even more severe. The girl's hair was burnt off, and the magician made two deep cuts with *dasyprocta* teeth down and across her back, and rubbed pepper into them; and here, too, the operation had to be endured without a sound. Then the girl was laid in her hammock, her arms tied to her body, and an amulet of teeth round her. In this condition she had to lie for three days without food and drink, absolutely silent. She was then taken back to the stone which served as a seat during the first operation—and on the way her feet might not touch the ground —and her fetters were taken off; but she had to lie up in the hammock for a full month, and eat only uncooked roots and cassava bread. At the end of the month the whole performance was repeated, and not till the third month was the girl at the end of her trials.

Spix and Martius tell us that most of the Amazon tribes compelled their girls to undergo this operation. Elsewhere the rites were less trying. The Caraya of the Araguaya River tattoo the girls as a sign that they are full-fledged members of the tribe.

But the girl who has "come out" does not enjoy her liberty long; children are betrothed quite in infancy, and, as we have seen, the maiden becomes a wife in some cases as soon as her ordeal is at an end. But sometimes the future husband has to give to the girl's parents proofs of his capacity to support a family.

Betrothal and Marriage.

In most of the tribes of British Guiana marriage takes place at a very early age. Girls of eleven or twelve are mothers of experience. The choice of a bridegroom is made years before the bride is handed over, and the favoured male has to serve his parents-in-law till he enters the married state, and, as a matter of course, to show little attentions to his future wife, such as adorning her with beads. Where a youth has not been betrothed, the matter is simpler; he pays one or two calls on the lady of his heart, makes her a few gifts, and agrees with the parents whether she is to be his in return for a few gifts, or whether he must serve the customary year or more for her. This over, he clears a patch of ground, which the girl henceforth cultivates.

Breach of promise cases are unknown in British Guiana, for Im Thurn tells us that the *fiancé* may marry anyone he pleases, and if he casts off the old love he demands the return of all the beads and other ornaments he has given her.

Tests for Bridegrooms.

The test of the bridegroom takes various forms: the Uacarras of the Uaupes require the man to submit to a trial of skill with the bow, and if he does not show himself to be a good marksman, the girl refuses him on the ground that he will not be able to shoot fish and game enough for the family. Among the more primitive Mura, all the girl's lovers assemble, and the one who comes out "top dog" in a game of fisticuffs carries off the girl. Among the

Yahgans of Tierra del Fuego the man lives with his wife's parents, and serves them till he has made a boat and earned the right to run a separate establishment.

Temporary Marriages.

Among the Arawaks of British Guiana infant betrothal is practised, but unbetrothed young men set out to find wives for themselves. A man gains the support of the relatives of his lady love, and assures the father of the girl that without a wife he is miserably poor, to which the father assents. If the damsel then sets food before the man, it means that he is a successful wooer; he eats the food and the wedding is over. If the girl is too young for marriage, the prospective father-in-law hands over to the wooer as a temporary wife a widow, or an old maid from among his relatives, who acts as a substitute till the girl can take her place, when she retires from the married state and becomes the servant of the bride.

How Brides are obtained.

As a rule, a girl is not asked which suitor she prefers; the Yahgan father chooses the strongest candidate, and on the Rio Içana I found the same practice among the Siusi. The chief's daughter fell in love with one of my men, a young Kaua, but an unbending father married her to a chief of the Huhuteni. Among the Tehuelche of Patagonia, however, the girl of sixteen is of age to be courted, and it is for her to say whether she will have a wooer or not; though she often marries early, she may remain unwedded for some years. Caraya parents, too, ask their daughter's views as to the merits of her suitors before they accept a young man's proposals.

In many cases the bride is simply bought. The Goajiro father fixes a price, usually in cattle, and, this paid, the girl is a wife and must supply her husband with food and clothing. Among the tribes of British Guiana the payment consists of axes, knives, cloth, etc., or the father may hand over the girl in return for services rendered, and the husband removes to his father-in-law's hut with all his possessions.

Among the Toba of the Gran Chaco a price is paid for the bride, but the suitor has also to undergo a test. He must dance before the hut of his love to the sound of the drum, beating out his tune on a skin-covered mortar half-filled with water. If he is invited to come in and sit down, it is a sign that his proposal has been accepted. Among the Tehuelche, on the other hand, the bride-price is practically non-existent, for bridegroom and father-in-law exchange presents of equal value.

Marriage by Capture.

Some of the Uaupes Indians practise a kind of marriage by capture. The bridegroom's father sends a message that he is going to call at the bride's father's house with a party of friends; if the marriage is looked upon with favour, there are then preparations for a feast, which may last for two or three days, when the visitors will carry off the bride in their canoes. My own observations on the Uaupes and

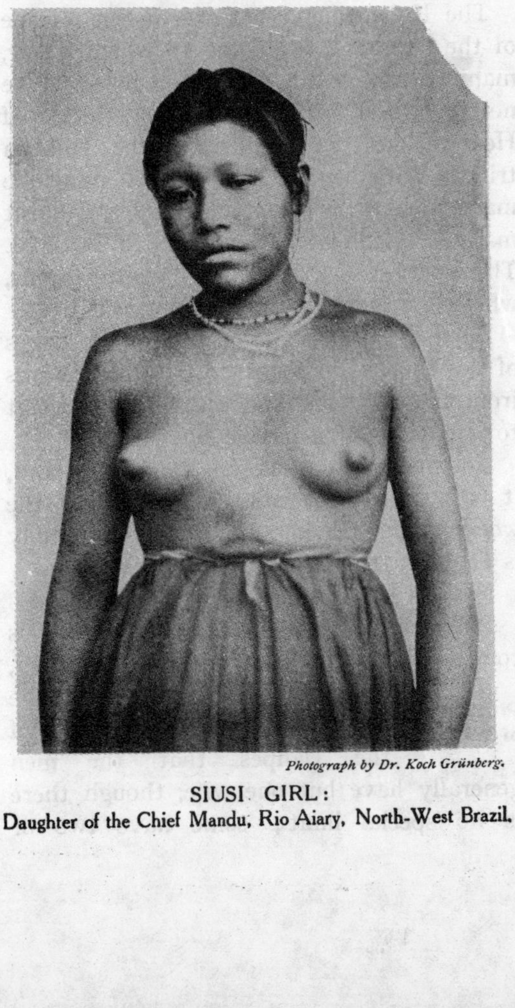

Photograph by Dr. Koch Grünberg.

SIUSI GIRL:
Daughter of the Chief Mandu, Rio Aiary, North-West Brazil.

Içana agree in the main with this. If a Kobeua youth wishes to marry he first obtains the consent of the girl's father, and then remains for five days, during which there is a great dance, accompanied by much drinking. For the entertainment of the guests the young man supplies smoked fish and game. The wedding proper consists in the handing over of the girl by her father, who makes a long ceremonial speech, and recommends her to her husband's care. Then the youth takes her by the hand and hurries down to the river; behind them comes the girl's father, lamenting and lightly striking his weeping daughter on the back with his hand. He is followed by the tearful mother, bearing her daughter's trousseau — hammocks, baskets, pots, etc.—which she lays in the canoe, and the newly-married couple go off at top speed. In this tribe the wife always goes to live with her husband, who, as a rule, lives with his parents. The bride-price consists of hammocks, baskets, sieves, and valuable dance decorations.

The Kobeua have a story of the "Rape of the Sabines," according to which many, many years ago the Uanana, who still live near, carried off the two daughters of Hemanehike, the founder of the Kobeua tribe. With his two brothers, Hemanehike made war on the offending tribe, and burnt many of them in a house which he fired. The survivors fled to the Caruru rapids, where the chief of the Uanana still lives.

To this day it is the custom of the tribes of the Upper Rio Negro to take their wives from another tribe, and this seems to point to a custom of marriage by capture.

Among the Ipurina, on the other hand, it is the girl who runs away, and, if the wooer can catch her, no further ceremony is required to make her his wife.

Plurality of Wives.

Polygamy — the plurality of wives — is comparatively infrequent in South America, and often the privilege of the chief alone. Wallace says of the Uaupes that the men generally have but one wife, though there is no special limit; some have two or three, while the chief may have more. The oldest wife is—and remains—the mistress of the house.

Personally, I only saw two chiefs on the Uaupes who had more than one wife. In both cases the wives lived at peace with one another, and shared the household duties—I never saw any favouritism. The custom of the Kobeua requires that a second wife may be taken only if the first gives her assent.

The Macusi permit polygamy, but it is rarely found. Schomburgk found one case in which a man married three sisters. Among the Chaco tribes it is the chief alone who takes more than one wife, and he may have as many as he can support. The Caraya have, as a rule, only one wife, but sometimes a man is compelled to take a second when the first gets old. This is due to the peculiar custom according to which young men marry old women, and *vice versâ;* this is, perhaps, the cause of their small fecundity. Von den Steinen observed this unnatural custom among the Bakairi, and Hyades among the Yahgan, but in the latter case it is the exception. Polygamy is also rare, but powerful men possess two, three, or even four wives. A Tehuelche may have as many wives as he can keep, but does not often have more than two, one being the rule. Among the Araucanians Musters saw a chief with three wives, who lived in the greatest harmony, and impartially looked after each other's children. The Ipurina may take one or two wives over and above the first.

The Warrau and other British Guiana tribes permit polygamy, and every man takes as many wives as he can get—or, rather, as many as he thinks necessary to take care of him. Chiefs have regular harems, and when one wife gets old he hands over to her for education a child of seven or eight, and she enters upon her wifely duties as soon as her training is over. However many wives there are, the first one is undisputed mistress, but there are one or two favourites who accompany the husband on all his journeys.

The magicians especially indulge in a

Photograph by P. Neville Edwards, Littlehampton.

A DUTCH GUIANA GIRL.

very large number of wives, for the immense influence which they exercise over the other Indians enables them to acquire any number they please. An Indian, when asked for his daughter, or even sometimes for his wife, by his *peaiman*, dare not refuse. In this way it happens that the house of the *peaiman* is generally full of women.

Polygamy is said to be universal among the primitive Botocudo of Brazil. A man has as many wives as he can support, sometimes even ten or twelve; but Prince Maximilian of Wied never saw instances of more than three or four wives to one man.

Conjugal Fidelity.

In most tribes a girl enjoys the greatest freedom before marriage, but though her innocence is far from being unquestionable, the standard of married life is high, and it is but seldom that either spouse proves unfaithful. When I asked the chief of the Siusi what the punishment for adultery was, he replied proudly: "It never happens." During the many months that I lived in familiar intercourse with the Indians in their "long houses," inhabited by large numbers, I never saw any signs of marital infidelity, nor even, under normal circumstances, of quarrels between husband and wife, though in our civilised Europe scenes of this kind are unfortunately by no means uncommon in many circles. It is true that at a drinking festival, when the *kashiri*, their light alcoholic beverage, gets into their heads, they literally fly at one another's throats, but even these cases are infrequent.

At a great Siusi wedding celebration a young married couple came to blows in my presence; the wife was the ultimate victor, and broke on her spouse's head her whole store of pottery. But this is the only case of marital unhappiness that came under my notice on my travels, and even this does not really count, for the man had been in the service of more than one European, and had acquired white vices. Moreover, he was famous in the whole neighbourhood for his quarrelsomeness, and very unpopular even among his fellow-tribesmen.

Im Thurn bears testimony to the morals of the natives of British Guiana: "Indian husbands and wives," says he, "are, as a rule, very faithful to each other; even on the comparatively rare occasions on which there has been some looseness before marriage, there is none after. Husband and wife, without being demonstrative, are decidedly affectionate towards each other."

The Fuegians are very jealous, and stand up for conjugal fidelity. A man will never at any price yield his wife, and travellers who assert the contrary have apparently mistaken the unmarried girls for married women. The latter must remain chaste, while the former have full liberty. Adultery is severely punished by the husband, but there is no recognised penalty. In revenge, jealous wives make their husband's lives a burden; but, strange to say, jealousy among the unmarried is unknown in either sex.

Among the Toba a man's wives are often desperately jealous of each other, and sanguinary conflicts are the order of the day, ending often in the death of one of the rivals. If a wife has committed adultery she may be put away either by divorce, or by the hand of her husband.

Penalties for Infidelity.

If a Goajiro woman, by exception, proves untrue, her father must repay the bride-price; if he is not solvent, the seducer is responsible. The Caraya punishes his erring wife with blows, or burns her flesh with glowing pieces of wood; sometimes he even goes so far as to burn her to death. The husband's misdeeds are punished by his relatives-in-law. Everywhere, says Ehrenreich, is seen the endeavour to repress all that tends to a breach of the family peace; hence young married people are kept strictly in hand.

Among the Paravilhana the seducer enjoys a bath of Spanish pepper; the woman is exposed to the bites of large ants.

Rude in all his customs, the Botocudo is not least so when he is jealous. If a husband surprises his wife in the society of another man, he takes his revenge with blows, snatching up the first thing he can lay hands on as a weapon; this may be a burning brand, and women often bear marks of such wounds on their bodies. Many men use the knife in such cases, says the Prince of Wied, and cut open arm

In Tierra del Fuego, on the other hand, where marriage is early—a girl may be a wife at thirteen—it is not regarded as irrevocable till three children are born. Not infrequently a woman changes husbands either because she is fickle, or because she has been ill-used.

Photograph by Dr. Koch Grünberg.

ARAUCANIAN (CHILI) WOMEN HAIR-DRESSING.

or leg, so that the unhappy wife has, years after, great scars, often one beside the other. He even saw one case in which an Indian from Belmonte shot his wife, who was famous for her qualities of mind and body.

Though marriage is thus inviolate, divorce is relatively easy, but only if there are no children. A Macusi may leave his wife or even sell her; but one can hardly say that her lot is thereby rendered hard, for she has often found another husband before the sun goes down. But should children have been born a separation of husband and wife is a rarity, and justifiable only by a charge of adultery.

Divorce.

If a Caraya married couple do not hit it off, the husband may agree to exchange with another man. A divorce entails celibacy on the man in name only, for he may take a housekeeper. Among the Tehuelche, if a married couple part company, the wife receives the presents given at marriage by her parents to the husband; but divorce is rare with them.

The Prince of Wied relates that there were no marriage ceremonies among the Botocudo, consent of the parties and of their parents sufficing, and that divorce was equally easy. It is related that a woman left her husband, in his absence, for another whose bag of game was larger, without inconvenient results to herself. If a man repudiates his wife young children remain with the mother, but go back to the father as soon as they are old enough.

Photograph by Eric Graf Rosen.

CHOROTE GIRLS, BOLIVIAN CHACO.

Once I was among the Bara, at the sources of the Tiquie, the largest tributary on the right bank of the Uaupes; a young wife left her dying husband and sick daughter, taking with her a healthy boy, and went back to her first home. Though there was a noisy scene with the sick man's father, my impression was that it was simply a matter of form, and this was made probable by the indifference of the bystanders.

However barbarous it may appear to us to leave a dying man, all travellers agree that it is practised, and for primitive man there is nothing unnatural in the idea, for a patient means more household work for one whose value to the community is nil.

In all the tribes that I visited the position of woman and her relation to man is a worthy one. It can readily be seen that she even exercises no inconsiderable influence upon him—a fact to which all travellers who have had much intercourse with Indians testify.

Macusi women have indeed hard work to do, but their husbands treat them with kindness. Robert Schomburgk never saw a quarrel between man and wife in all the years he lived in the interior; but the coast Indian, a victim to European vices, may treat his wife tyrannically.

The General Position of Woman in South America.

The same traveller expresses his surprise at the high position of women among the Caribs. Hard her work may be; the man clears the ground, and the wife tills it and harvests the produce; but she is by no means the degraded slave that some have made her out to be.

If a Carib should be so well to do as to possess a shirt, he removes it as soon as rain begins to fall, and brings it under shelter; but if his wife is shivering beside him, he protects her by putting it over her head and shoulders. So, too, among the Caraya the wife has heavy duties, but she is no beast of burden. The husband takes counsel of his wife in all important matters; the chief shares his position with his wife, and ill-treatment of a woman is unknown.

Photograph by Dr. Koch Grünberg.

KAUA WOMAN, RIO AIARY, NORTH-WEST BRAZIL.

Returning from work in the fields. She is carrying a large basket full of manioc roots, suspended by a band from her forehead. The child sits astride her hip.

Im Thurn tells much the same story of the Guiana Indians. Woman's work may seem to us heavy, but it is, for the Indian, part of the natural order of things. The man's work of hunting and clearing is no less heavy, though more irregular. Moreover, the physical strength of the two sexes is about equal, and it is by no means certain that the average man would be the master of an average woman in a fight. Musters, who lived long in the midst of the Tehuelche, and tells us much of their continual feuds, praises, as one of the finest traits in their character, their love of wife and children; husband and wife never quarrelled, wives were never struck, and the real sorrow with which the loss of one was mourned had nothing civilised about it, for the widower destroyed all his property and burnt everything he possessed. We learn from Karl von den Steinen how charming is the relation of husband and wife on the Lower Xingu among the Yuruna, or at any rate of the husband and his favourite wife. The chief had three wives, and the youngest was really pretty, of uncommonly graceful figure, and her face told how much she loved him. She was inseparable from him, followed him like a dog—they were a real pair of love-birds. Of the Macusi, Schomburgk says: "The husband loves his wife as deeply as a civilised man can, but he regards it as improper to show his feelings in the presence of others, and so regards with contempt the white man who cannot repress his feelings." To the truth of this I can testify as regards all the tribes with whom I came in contact. If soon after my arrival the men were favoured with the sight of some of my curiosities —my watch, my camera, a picture-book, etc.—they went to fetch their wives, and I had to go through the performance a second time. A husband never sold me the most insignificant object belonging to his wife without her express permission.

Photograph by Dr. Koch Grünberg.

KOBEUA WOMAN AND CHILD, RIO CUDUIARY, NORTH-WEST BRAZIL.

Infants ride in a broad bark band at the mother's breast.

Their self-control was really wonderful, even when the men returned from a long journey. A young married couple were sometimes an exception. I often saw a young Kaua as he sported harmlessly with his charming wife in their rather gloomy apartment. A young couple among the Kobeua were inseparable; if the husband went fishing, the wife steered the canoe; if the wife had work in the plantation, the husband went along with his bow and arrow, so as to hunt near her. After the heat and burden of the day, they sat, as a rule, on the "village green," and combed each other's hair (in the literal sense), or caught gnats on each other's backs. Never, during my two years' stay among the Indians, did I see a shadow of indecency in the relations of married couples.

Much weight is given to the views of women, and this is true also when the question is of tribal relations with strangers. An old woman was the speaker in several villages, though men were also present, when a speech of greeting had to be made.

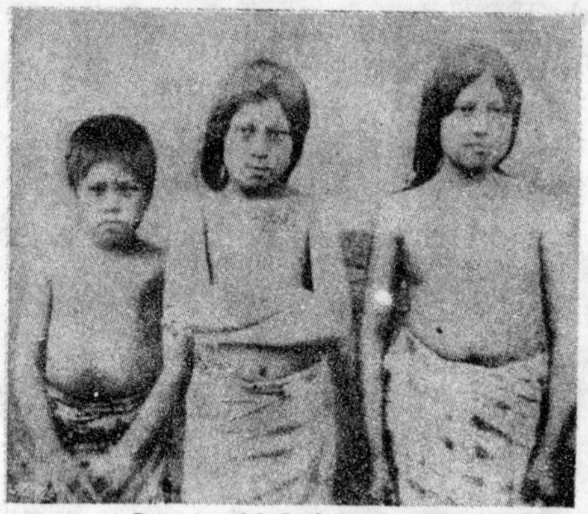

By courtesy of the South American Missionary Society.

CHACO SCHOOL GIRLS.

A Siusi was quite disposed to sell me his elegant canoe, but his wife said "No," and there was an end of the matter. On the other hand, a Kaua was persuaded by his wife to sell me his treasured blow-gun with quiver and poison pot, because her vanity called for several yards of coloured calico with which to decorate her person.

Influence of Indian Women.

Other travellers agree as to this influential position of the wife. Martius won the hearts of the women with beads and handkerchiefs, and got from the men all he wanted. Von den Steinen was likewise struck by the prominence of women among the Kustenau; they joined in the discussions without being asked, and were always against giving anything. Among the Arhuaco a bargain is invalid if the woman's consent is not given. Wives accompany their husbands on their journeys, and always lead the way.

Though he draws a dark picture of the character of the Miranha on the Yapura, Martius cannot but confess that among this rude people a woman, notwithstanding her servile position, has great power over her husband as mistress of his house. Among the Tehuelche, women and girls play an important part in the horse races. Among the Toba, woman plays an active part in the life of the tribe. If a fight takes place, women exhort the men to stand fast, though in other tribes they are prominent as peacemakers. It is rare for a woman to get drunk at one of their festivals; on the contrary, in common with a few warriors, temporarily teetotal, it is their duty to prevent quarrels and excesses, though they are not always successful.

Goajiro women, too, put an end to strife, and in general it may be said that a traveller accompanied by women is safe, for they are never attacked.

In some tribes woman's equality has made way for woman's superiority. Among the Siusi I saw a woman doctor, though it is true she did not make use of all the trickery and mystery inseparable from the leech-craft of the magician. Among the Caraya the chief arbitrates in quarrels between men, his wife between women. Among the Macusi an old widow once ruled a whole village, and the singular thing was that even the Caribs, a tribe often hostile to the Macusi, submitted to her commands

Photograph by Eric Graf Rosen.

CHOROTE WOMAN AND CHILD, BOLIVIAN CHACO.

To this predominance of woman is due, perhaps, the fact that in marriages between

different tribes in Guiana the children follow the tribe of the mother; if a Warrau woman marries an Arawak, the children are Warrau.

Thus there are many competent witnesses to the worthy position of the South American Indian woman in family life and in the life of the community. The few writers who bear contrary testimony are of small importance, for their evidence is drawn in some cases from tribes on a very low level of civilisation, or rather of savagery; in others the peoples whom they describe have been in contact with Europeans and have thus suffered corruption of their original manners and customs; or, finally, they are tribes whose kindliness has vanished as a result of interminable forays and other sanguinary expeditions. Some of the evidence, however, may perhaps be cited.

By courtesy of the South American Missionary Society.

YAHGAN GIRL.

The Mura, a nomadic people of the valley of the Amazon, keep their women, according to the distinguished traveller, von Martius, in a state of humiliating servitude.

Maximilian, Prince of Neuwied, says that laziness is the principal trait in the character of the Botocudo. He left to his wife and children the task of accomplishing the greater proportion of the work. A wife had to show servile obedience to her lord and master; and, only too often, numerous scars on the body of the woman bore witness to the hasty and ungovernable temper of her husband.

Richard Schomburgk, in contrast to his brother Robert, gives to the Caribs of

WOMEN AND CHILDREN OF AN ARAUCANIAN (CHILI) CACIGULO FAMILY.

British Guiana an exceedingly bad character. He writes of them as follows: "The Carib is arrogant and tyrannical in his dealings with other Indians, and his behaviour to his wives is on all fours with this; it would probably be difficult to find a single woman whose body did not bear a multitude of scars and even of wounds as the result of her husband's cruelty and tyrannical behaviour. At nearly every drinking festival the male population lowers itself below the level of the beasts; when he is in a state of drunkenness the Carib selects his wife, as a rule, as the most suitable victim of his ill temper, and the reason for this is not far to seek."

Photograph by Eric Graf Rosen.

CHOROTE WOMAN AND CHILD, BOLIVIAN CHACO.
Showing the method of carrying the baby.

With regard to this, however, it should be observed that the traveller in question visited this tribe precisely at the period of their great drinking festival, and that hardly a single individual of them would then be found in a moderately sober condition. Moreover these Caribs had been for some time closely associated with white men; they had adopted several civilised vices; and, last but not least, the continual slave raids which they undertook against their more peaceful neighbours had degraded them into a state of real savagery; they were not only savages but savage.

Their near relatives, the aboriginal inhabitants of the Caribbee islands, who have now vanished from the face of the earth before the progress of civilisation, are also reported to have had an equal want of appreciation of the value of the female sex; but they were living at the period in question under very abnormal conditions, and it would hardly be fair to quote them as evidence. Their incessant warlike expeditions, their restless desire for a wandering mode of life, their cruelty towards their enemies, and their extensive cannibalistic practices must all have helped to stifle every tender feeling in their breasts; they captured their wives, their weapons in their hands;

and under the circumstances it is, perhaps, hardly surprising that they looked upon them as slaves.

Birth Customs.

Important as is the *rôle* of woman as spouse and counsellor of her husband, she is even more important as mother of his children, for that is her natural province, and she alone has the care and education of the children. Even before the little stranger puts in an appearance, its parents are concerned for its health. Spix and Martius found the diet of parents before the birth of a child strictly regulated in some Brazilian tribes. Both abstain from the meat of certain animals for a time, and live chiefly on fruits and fish. Among the Mauhe pregnancy involves a considerable amount of fasting for both husband and wife, who live only on fungi, ants, and *guarana*. The purpose of this abstinence is to prevent the bad qualities of the various animals from being imparted to the child through their persons. A month before birth a Kobeua woman eats all kinds of birds and fish save the *silurus pirarara*, enjoyment of which would entail many ill consequences. All four-footed animals are forbidden to her.

Birth takes place either in the hut itself or in a hut a little removed from the ordinary one, or else in the forest ; it is accompanied by usages which seem peculiar to the European.

Wallace says of the Uaupes: "The women are generally delivered in the house, though sometimes in the forest. When a birth takes place in the house, everything

A FAMILY OF ARAUCANIANS (CHILI).

Showing a baby strapped in a native cradle.

is taken out of it, even the pots and pans and bows and arrows, till the next day; the mother takes the child to the river

Photograph by Dr. Koch Grünberg.

KOBEUA WOMAN AND CHILD, RIO CUDUIARY, NORTH-WEST BRAZIL.

and washes herself and it, and she generally remains in the house, not doing any work, for four or five days."

I witnessed the same customs on the Uaupes and Isana of to-day, with but small variations. Birth usually takes place in the "long house," and all the married women stand by to give advice or help. The apartments of the family in question are shut off by mats, and the young mother keeps her room five days, cheered by the company of her spouse. They may do no work, and only eat light food like manioc and roasted ants. Any infraction of this rule would be considered injurious to the child. The five days over, all three take a bath, but not till the next day does a near relative—usually the husband's brother—bring them fish to eat, as a sign that the fast is over.

Before the young couple go for their bath, all their furniture, weapons, etc., are carried out of doors, and the other dwellers in it leave the house by the back entrance, so that the place is empty till the parents return from their bath; then their possessions are gradually brought back, and three days later a drinking festival is given in honour of the child, and all the relatives are invited. The paternal grandfather names the child, choosing the name of some animal in most cases. A boy has two names, a girl only one.

The Siusi mark the close of the fast by a monotonous chant, in which the husband's father grants permission to the parents to eat food as usual, exactly as the father does to the girl at puberty.

Photograph by Dr. Koch Grünberg.

LITTLE KOBEUA GIRL.

Children are placed in these swinging chairs so that they may learn to walk—and be out of their mothers' way.

When I was among the Tuyuka on the Rio Tiquie in 1904, I saw the close of one of these five-day fasts. About five in the morning, not long before daybreak, the

Photograph supplied by Miss J. Ackermann

ARAUCANIAN INDIANS.

The woman in the foreground is wearing the characteristic large silver ear-ornaments.

Indians carried most of their goods—and especially the weapons—into the open air, and asked me to do the same—or at any rate to take the guns out. This I did readily; then all the others left the house, and a singular procession wended its way to the river. In front marched the mother of the husband, smoking red-hot coals on a potsherd before her, which she fanned to spread the smoke about her. Behind her came the young mother with the child, and she was followed by the happy father. The grandmother censed the whole strand, then embarked in a canoe, and treated the water likewise. Then parents and child bathed, and returned home, and the grandmother brought them a potful of fish, their first solid food for five days. I saw a similar performance among the Kobeua later. This seems to show that the parents and child are regarded as unclean—hence the bath. The abstinence from food, the censing of the path and the water, and the removal of the goods, and especially of the weapons, are meant to save the new arrival from harmful influences.

By courtesy of the South American Missionary Society.

MAPUCHE (SOUTH CHILI) MEDICINE WOMEN

With the symbols of their profession.

A Birth "Fast."

Among the Maxuruna the young mother may not eat monkeys; her chief article of diet is the Hocco fowl. The Culino, too, restrict the mother's diet, but compel the father to practise complete abstinence for the first five days. Paca and tapir meat is forbidden to the mother, who may, however, take pork. When the child is a week old, the magician fumigates it for a whole day with cigar smoke, and it then receives a name.

Diet of Parents.

Among the Marauha the child is bathed

in warm water, and then the mother lies up in her hammock for three weeks, and with her husband partakes only of manioc flour, together with certain birds and fish. When the mother leaves her hammock the oldest relative names the child in a dark room, choosing a title hereditary in the family. The Omagua woman may eat only the tracaja turtle and fish, but no mammals, and the father must practise the same restrictions till the child can sit up. The Passe compel the mother to remain in the dark for a month, and eat only manioc; her husband does the same, and in addition blacks himself and remains in his hammock. Bororo parents

By courtesy of the South American Missionary Society.

MAPUCHE MEDICINE WOMEN TREATING A PATIENT.

eat nothing for two days, and then take a little warm water.

One of the most singular usages, reported by the earliest authors, is the so-called *couvade*. This custom demands that the mother shall resume her household duties as soon as the child is born, whereas the husband must lie up and allow himself to be coddled.

The "Couvade."

Im Thurn found this remarkable custom among the Indians of Guiana. The woman works till the hour of birth is near at hand; then she retires to the forest with one or more women, hangs up her hammock, and awaits the progress of events. A few hours after, she gets up, washes the child and herself in a neighbouring stream, and returns to the village to take up her ordinary work, while her husband lies for days, and perhaps weeks, in his hammock. He may eat only a decoction of manioc meal; he may not smoke, and may not wash; he may touch no weapons, and enjoys the services of all the women in the village as nurses. Schomburgk says that he may not even touch his body or his head with his nails; but must scratch himself with a palm leaf nerve hung near his hammock. Any infringement of these rules is held to cause the death, or lifelong illness, of the child. If, for example, the father eats *capivara* meat, the child's teeth will grow like those of the animal, and be prominent. If he eats the meat of a spotted animal, the child's skin will be spotted.

More or less similar customs are recorded of the Mundurucu, among whom the husband is visited by his neighbours as he lies in his hammock; by the Bakairi, and by the Paressi. The Ipurina mother does not return from the forest till four or five days after the birth of the child, and for a whole year her husband may not eat pork or tapir. The custom of the *couvade* is to be explained by the Indian belief that the child—boy or girl—is, as it were, a part of its father, just as if it formed a portion of his body. All injurious substances which the father ingests into his body are thus considered to be transferred to the child.

Indian Childhood.

From its birth onwards, until the child can go on its own legs, the mother is seldom parted from it. A few days after birth she begins to take it with her to the plantation, protecting the little head against the heat of the sun with a banana leaf or a sieve. I have often met canoes in which whole families were off to a dance at a relative's some days' voyage distant. They take with them all their worldly goods, and with the powerful strokes of his broad paddle, the father drives the boat along, aided by his youthful progeny, who ply their tiny paddles no less manfully: while at the helm sits the mother, her newborn child at her breast.

While the babe is very small, it is carried in a broad bark band, hung over the mother's right shoulder. Later, when it can sit alone, it rides on the mother's hip, supported by an encircling arm; and the pair often take part in the men's dances.

Quite tiny girls take charge of still smaller children, and it is amusing to see the intense seriousness with which the little mothers, imitating their elders, fulfil their office. If the child interferes with the performance of household duties, it is hung up in a swinging chair, a clever contrivance of supple pieces of wood and strips of bark, in which the child can sit or stand (*see* p. 374). This arrangement satisfies both parties, for the mother is relieved of the care of it—it can neither fall nor crawl on the ground and eat earth and get into all sorts of mischief; but, on the other hand, if the chair is hung low enough, its feet touch the ground, and it can learn to walk.

To coddle children is the last thing it would enter an Indian's head to do; on the contrary, they are hardened from youth up, and bathed by the careful mother every day in cold water in some shady forest stream. Children are suckled long, and I have often seen youngsters of three and four years old run away from their games for a draught of their mothers' milk. In a Tukano village on the Lower Uaupes I was received by a very energetic lady, no longer in her first youth, who, in the absence of her husband, received us with full honours. While she was chatting with us a three-year-old boy ran up, took the cigarette out of her hand, puffed at it a few times, gave it back to her, and then settled down in her lap to enjoy his natural nourishment. During the whole performance the mother's flow of conversation was unbroken.

According to Schomburgk, Warrau children are weaned at the age of three or four, and two children of different ages may be seen, one on the mother's arm, the other standing at her side, taking their quantum of refreshment. The most absurd thing of all is to see a lusty boy descend from the top of a high tree, laden with fruit, and run to his mother for a little liquid nourishment. More curious still, in some of the Guiana tribes the grandmother supplies the needs of the elder children, while the mother devotes herself to the wants of the last born. It is said that the women, however old they may be, have a method of prolonging the activity of the milk glands.

Where Charms Fade Early.

There are, it is true, very youthful grandmothers among the Indians; many marry at ten or twelve, and are grandmothers at an age when the European girl is thinking of marrying! I once saw a Tukano girl of thirteen who was already the mother of two children. To the early puberty and marriage of Indian girls is perhaps due their early loss of charms.

Though girls are strong and healthy enough in North-West Brazil, where I have travelled, good looks can hardly be reckoned among their advantages. But in other parts of South America the graces of the maidens are sung by many travellers. The women of British Guiana are noted for their beauty, the symmetry of their figures, the sturdy swell of their limbs and their charms of face; but those who sing their praises lament that they grow old too soon. At the age of twenty their bloom has disappeared, symmetry of body and limb is gone, elasticity of step has been replaced by a suggestion of effort; finally, the rounded beauty of the body is replaced by horrible and unsightly accumulations of fat, which are not hidden from the gaze by a shred of clothing.

By courtesy of the South American Missionary Society.

CHACO WOMEN DRESSED FOR A FEAST

Other women get thin as their families grow large, their bones stand out, and some of the old women are regular witches with bleary eyes.

Curious Pets.

The Indian woman does not confine her love and care to her own children; she has a whole menagerie of pets, which it is her pride to tame and bring up. Any young animal she can catch takes turn and turn about with her own child at her breast, and the creatures—especially the apes—become so attached to her that they follow her everywhere.

In 1904 I lived among the Kobeua for several weeks, and hardly a day passed without my receiving visitors from the neighbouring villages. People came for miles to see the white stranger and his wonderful possessions, perhaps also to do a little profitable business with him. Among the pets which I saw were several young sloths, and these dull-witted dwellers in Brazilian forests hung round the necks of their foster-mothers like so many children, and shared the nourishment which nature meant for the two-legged nurslings.

One day a hunter shot a monkey and saved her young one alive. His wife tried to get it to take the breast, but the little brute scratched and bit; finally the woman took it by the throat and trickled her milk into its mouth.

The Guiana Indians allow four-legged and two-legged nurslings to share their mother's love and tenderness, and their pets are mainly monkeys, rats, and the like.

Indians as Parents.

Parents are usually loving towards their children, though they hide their feelings before strangers. In some villages where I resided for some time, and came to be regarded as one of the family, I observed that the parents displayed just the same tenderness towards their children—especially the small ones—as Europeans do. I saw mothers play with their children by the hour, and if a tiny baby demands all the mother's care, or she has to attend to her household duties, she readily entrusts to the grandmother the care of an older child and she, to amuse her small descendant, plays just the same games and makes just the same inarticulate sounds as a European would do.

By courtesy of the South American Missionary Society.

AN ONA FAMILY (TIERRA DEL FUEGO).

A mother's tenderness is also displayed by the lavish adornment of the child with necklaces of teeth, seeds, and laboriously pierced stone beads, which no small child ever lacks. Nothing wins a mother's friendship sooner than gifts of beads to a child; they are strung at once and hung round its neck, and the whole family breaks out into ejaculations of admiration. I seldom omitted a present to the smallest child at the breast of a mother who helped to carry my goods.

The mother loses no opportunity of painting her child red, sometimes with *urucu* as a decoration, sometimes with *carayuru* as a prophylactic against catarrh and other diseases. Mothers often brought sick children to me, and begged me to heal them; their care for them is touching, and their grief at the death of their darlings quite moving. In the early days of a friendship a woman would in piteous tones tell over the names of children torn by death from her arms, and point sadly to the ground to show their fate. Child mortality is heavy, and to this is due the fact that the fecundity of the women does not, in the area of which I have a knowledge, lead to an increase of population; in some tribes there is even a steady decrease.

Children give signs of great intelligence at an early age. Of course, there are naughty children among the Indians, as there are elsewhere, especially among the smaller ones, who have not acquired the calm and self-control of their parents. Then they are reproved, but I never saw a parent led by anger to act unjustly or to ill-use a child.

On the Tiquie I saw how an Indian woman can give a lesson to a European; the two-year-old son of a Tukano chief was a special favourite of mine. One day my servant brought me a splendid *morpho* butterfly, quite perfect. I laid it aside, intending to put it away later, but my small friend who was playing at my feet made a grab and broke the wings. I am sorry to say that I lost my temper and scolded him; the youngster looked at me first with surprise in his big round eyes, and then ran to his mother crying. She was elderly and energetic, and treated me like a son, so she read me a long lecture, saying how wrong it was to scold a small child which had done wrong in ignorance. I felt ashamed of my hasty temper, and became a reformed character.

Other travellers give similar accounts: the Warrau mother loves her child fondly—almost foolishly, though the father takes but little notice of it; but it is never punished by either. Caraya children are incessantly cared for in their tender years by their mothers, and often painted and hung with ornaments.

Among the Macusi and other tribes a mother's first care is to paint her child. Yuri women spend hours in this occupation; then the elder children perform the toilette of mother and grandmother, and who had a still more impatient customer to deal with—an ape which was even more unwilling to allow the elaborate pattern to be painted on his face. Every reproof which the mother addressed to her son was repeated ten times by the daughter before the task was complete, and a few rows of beads could be hung round the creature's neck.

Girls' Duties.

Girls soon begin to help their mothers; the smallest can peel cassava roots, watch a pot on the fire, or collect firewood. Among the Yuri the men go off fishing or hunting, and this is the mother's opportunity for educating the children. Then the girls learn how to net hammocks, spin cotton, make pottery, and so on. Cultivation of the fields and cooking the children can learn of themselves.

By courtesy of the South American Missionary Society.

ALACALUF WOMEN IN EUROPEAN COSTUME.
This tribe dwells on the Coast of the Straits of Magellan.

not till then do they think of breakfast. The Passe mother pierces her daughter's ear, and begins the painful operation of tattooing for her, as the father does for a boy.

Ornamentation of Children.

Schomburgk once saw a charming scene before a Warrau festival. A mother was painting an impatient youngster, who could not stand still for a moment. Beside her sat a pretty child

Death and Burial Customs.

In death, as in life, the wife has equal rights; baskets and sieves are burnt on her grave, pots are broken and cast into the forest; and thus nothing remains to provoke the dead to return and punish the living for neglect or meanness. Neither widower nor widow may marry till a year is past; but lamentation for the dead is mainly the business of the women.

The Macusi widower must mourn some ten or eleven months—that is, till the manioc field of his first wife provides the raw material for the drinking festival which welcomes the new spouse. The hair of the Arawak wife is cut short, and she must put off her clothes till it is grown again.

Among the Goajiro a wife is simply bought, and if she dies in childbed the bride-price must be paid a second time, as compensation to her family.

The Economic Importance of the Indian Woman.

We have shown how high woman stands in most tribes as wife and mother; we have now to show her economic importance, for she has upon her shoulders the whole care of the household, and—especially in the tropics—tends the manioc, which forms the chief article of food.

Before marriage the husband has cleared a considerable piece of ground, cut down the trees and let them lie to dry in the sun. When they are burnt, the fruitful soil is still more enriched by the ashes. This done, the man's share of the work is at an end; all else is the task of his wife. The planting season is determined by certain constellations. Manioc cuttings, usually short stems with two or three nodes, are stuck slanting into the earth and left to themselves, for in these fortunate climes nature's operations are subject to no irregularities. Harvest and preparation of the roots make greater claims on the endurance of the woman.

An Indian Woman's Work.

The diligent housewife rises before daybreak, bathes in the nearest stream, and fanning into a flame the fire, which the low temperature of the nights renders necessary, she prepares breakfast. Soon her husband emerges from his hammock and takes his morning tub. The meal over, they go about their respective businesses; in the fields the wife has new plants to put in, weeding to do in the young plantations, and ripe roots to dig for daily use. Towards mid-day, when the heat makes work impossible, she returns home, bending beneath her well-filled basket, which hangs from a forehead band. Small children take her hand or ride on her hip; the older ones with their little baskets help with all the seriousness in the world.

Preparation of Manioc.

No time is lost in preparing the supplies, for they do not keep; manioc roots are peeled and ground on concave boards set with pointed splinters of stone in elegant patterns. Holding the board in her lap, the woman sits, and exhales her breath with a hissing sound through her teeth in time to her work. The white mass of manioc, resembling mashed potatoes, is then freed of its poisonous sap by kneading on a sieve that stands on a triangular frame, or in a basketwork funnel of cane strips, which hangs from a projecting beam; sometimes it is weighted at the bottom, sometimes a beam, on which half the family sits, effects the work of removing the sap, which runs into a clay dish below.

This done, the meal is freed of lumps and spread on the baking hearth, used in common by all the inhabitants of the "long house," and situated in it or in a shed where the women spend most of their day; here the meal is completely dried and baked into flat cakes, which are turned from time to time.

The meal keeps better when the root is slightly fermented by being kept in water for some days, so that the rough outer skin can be peeled off with the fingers; in this case the meal is roasted as before, without being made into cakes, but the process is carried further. It will keep for months, and is put up in baskets of 50 lb. for trade purposes. When the sap has stood for a time, a fine meal settles, which is also roasted; this is tapioca, and is used in many dishes.

Many kinds of drinks are prepared from manioc meal; prepared with cold water, it furnishes a refreshing drink in the heat of the day; for breakfast it is made into warm soup, or the manioc cakes, warm

Rubbing the peeled manioc roots on a board set with splinters of stone on its slightly concave upper surface.

Manioc meal being pressed through a sieve hung on a triangle. The juice, which contains a quantity of prussic acid, runs into the pot below.

from the fire, are crumbled into the water. The drink tastes best when it is made from tapioca, which is also cooked in a gelatinous mass with small fish and pepper, and the manioc cakes dipped into it; or an attractive drink may be prepared from it by mixing it with pine-apple juice. Even the sap serves a purpose; freed from prussic acid, it gives a sauce as good as the best Worcester.

But the favourite drink, always to the fore at festivals or even friendly visits, is a kind of light beer, known in the west as *chicha*, in the east as *kashiri*. On the Uaupes and Isana it is thus prepared: the women crumble burnt manioc cakes into a trough and add water; to hasten the fermentation they chew cakes and add the paste; the leaves of a certain tree, and sometimes sugar cane sap, also furnish intoxicating ingredients. After careful kneading the trough is covered with fresh banana leaves or mats and set by the fire; on the next day it is the harmless *payauru*. *Kashiri* is formed after two days' fermentation, and is intoxicating. It is made by pressing the brown pap through a sieve; the juice runs into a pot, from which hostess or host fills the calabash. The moist meal in the early stages may be stowed away in pots, covered with a net to prevent bursting, or in banana leaves, till wanted for use.

Woman's culinary powers are by no means exhausted by the preparation of manioc; bananas, wild fruits, etc., are made into tasty dishes, and the Indian's bill of fare is by no means so monotonous as people think.

Photographs by Dr. Koch Grünberg.

Pressing manioc in the strainer. A tube, plaited out of elastic reeds, is filled with manioc meal, and the lower end weighted to press out the poisonous juices.

KOBEUA WOMEN PREPARING MANIOC.

Manioc is the staple food of this race.

The Indian Woman's Burden.

The household work in North-West Brazil, which I have described from personal experience, is typical of the work of woman elsewhere, though ways and means may differ. Everywhere the burden is on the woman's shoulders; she must fetch wood for the fire, and water; at night she must keep in the small fires lighted beneath the hammocks to keep off mosquitos; she has to clean the house, a frequent performance resulting in clouds of dust; and on journeys she carries the children and all the household goods, while her lord and master stalks along with bow and arrows only. Hunting, fishing, canoe-building, and care of his weapons occupy him; all else is beneath his dignity, and when he comes back to his house he throws himself into his hammock, and as he swings watches with an indifferent air the toil of his wife, or calls upon her to give him refreshment. He is the head of the family, yet we cannot say with truth that woman is his slave.

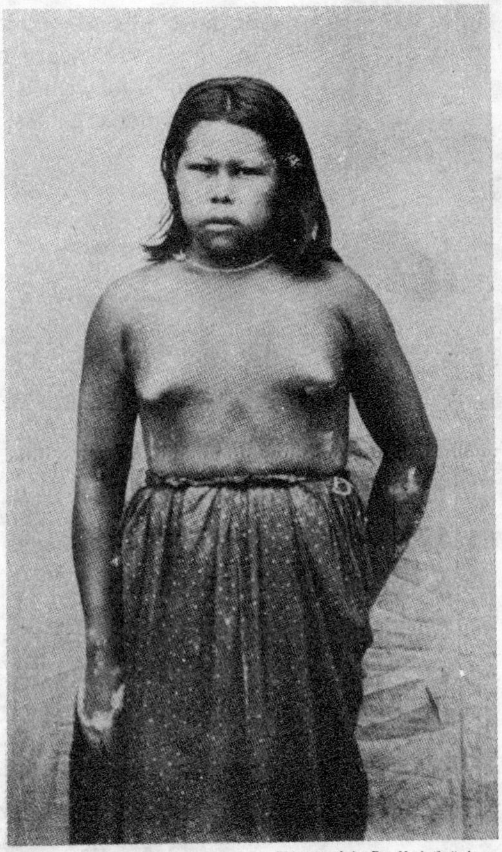

Photograph by Dr. Koch Grünberg.

YOUNG KOBEUA WOMAN, RIO CUDUIARY, NORTH-WEST BRAZIL.

The marks on the body are from manioc meal.

Woman as Potter.

As the wife presides over the house, it is natural that she should be skilled in making household goods. All over South America pottery is made by women, and, save among the nomadic Maku, the artistic standard is high, though the means are simple. The material is a fine blue clay found in small deposits on river banks, to obtain which some tribes make long journeys. It is not washed, but carefully kneaded and freed from hard lumps, and ash from the *caraipe* tree is added to give it firmness. The worker squats, and with open hands upon a mat makes long rolls of clay, and with them builds up the vessel in spirals. With the left hand she then presses the rolls together, and with her nails, or a small piece of wood, she effaces the hollows, and finally smooths the vessel with a shiny pebble.

Sometimes she adds two handles, moistening them with saliva to make them adhere. The pot is dried on a platform in the house for three or four days, then for three days more in the sun, the mouth being supported by small pieces of wood. The pot is burnt in a small hollow, mouth downwards, on three clay supports or a few stones. Wood is piled over it, and then bark, and when all is reduced to ashes the pot is red-hot; it gradually cools, but sometimes an unexpected shower will reduce it to fragments.

On the Isana the technique is specially good, and meander patterns are drawn on the sun-dried vessels and covered with powdered resin, or the sap of the *cuma* tree, which forms a varnish in the burning.

Such painted pottery is commonly used only for fetching water, for *kashiri* in the long run spoils the varnish and the design;

but at ceremonial visits and dance festivals they serve as bowls for manioc drinks.

The greatest variety of form, size, and style is found in Indian pots; manioc vessels vary from giants of thirty inches diameter to tiny children's plates; there are dwarf pots for *curare*, and *kashiri* pots three feet high and nine feet round; there are pots quite classical in style, and others in the shape of animals. Woman is everywhere the potter, and, when she has married into an alien tribe, has sometimes brought her art with her.

Photographs by Dr. Koch Grünberg.

KOBEUA WOMAN POTTER.

In the first illustration the woman is seen rolling the clay, and in the second placing the rolls spirally to form a bowl, squeezing them into position with the left hand.

Women as Weavers.

As a rule, woman does the weaving, spinning, and the like, but to this there are some exceptions. In British Guiana women prepare hammocks for sale, do the beadwork which forms their only dress, spin cotton, or make little hammocks for their children. It is not surprising that they have few leisure moments. But among the Uaupes tribes hammocks are made from palm fibre by both sexes; and the male sex undertakes the preparation of all baskets, with their regular red and black patterns, and even the sieves and tubes for the preparation of manioc are their work. Both sexes wear knee bands of *curaua* fibre, and these are woven by the women, who produce the same patterns in them as in the bead aprons and on their pots. It may be said, on the whole, that woman is in no way inferior to man in artistic gifts.

KOBEUA WOMAN POTTER.

Finishing off a pot before it is dried and baked.

Women Artists.

One opportunity of displaying this is seen when they are called upon to paint the men for a dance festival with dark blue *genipa*, which they do with great skill and speed. My servant and I could give the women no greater pleasure than to beg them to do us the same service. Among the Yuri the women paint the whole family every morning, and Martius once for a joke added a few grotesque scrolls to the work of an old woman on her granddaughter's face. She was so charmed that she begged him to set to work on her, and the next morning he found a whole row of girls and women in front of his hut waiting to be operated on.

Among the Macusi and other Guiana tribes the women seem to take to painting of other objects too; if a man has finished a weapon he hands it over to his wife for her to add an intricate pattern, which she does without any design before her. The Taruma told Schomburgk that some sculptures on the rocks near had been done long, long ago by women, a testimony to mere man's mistrust of his own powers.

Indian Dress.

This brings us to the question of woman's dress and ornaments. Dress is usually reduced to a minimum; in most of the primitive tribes, woman is quite unclothed, and the further you go up the Uaupes the less she has on. Among the Apiaka on the Upper Tapajoz, where the men have European dress, like the whites whom they serve, woman is in the state of Eve when she lived in Paradise. When a small covering is worn, as among the Bakairi and other Xingu tribes, it is intended as a protection against insects, not as a covering demanded by modesty. Yet, in spite of the lack of clothing, I never saw a woman behave in any way improperly, and even completely unclothed women are so decent in their behaviour that one forgets their nakedness.

The Question of Adornment.

Woman in South America is anything but indifferent to adornment, and seeks to enhance her charms to the utmost by artificial means. Long, glossy, black hair, combed and oiled every day, is in many tribes an envied possession. Tehuelche girls wear their hair in two plaits; it is coarse, and hardly so long as that of the men; but on festive occasions they supplement it artificially, probably with horsehair decorated with blue beads; the ends are adorned with silver ornaments.

As we have seen, face-painting is a favourite occupation; on ordinary days the colour is red, and no patterns are used, but for a festival the whole body is covered with patterns in *genipa* juice. A European comb for putting up the hair is an acquisition, and a woman loves to wear silver coins and beads strung as a necklace, or bead bracelets. For a dance her adornment is far simpler than a man's, and is limited in the tribes I know to a tasteful bead apron.

Fashions in Distortion.

Vanity takes singular forms here, as it does in the rest of the world. The lobe of the ear is usually bored, and oval pieces of wood, cane, or even European earrings are worn. In the underlip is a disc, or, as among the Caribs of British Guiana, a needle, point outwards, is passed through it. Sometimes this adornment grew to a huge size, and the Botocudo woman wore in her lip and ear a disc which was but little smaller than that of her husband, and attained a size of nearly three inches in diameter and a thickness of nearly an inch. Some tribes pierce the septum of the nose and pass through it a piece of cane, bird's bone, or, on festive occasions, a coloured feather.

More disfiguring is the Miranha custom of piercing the side of the nose and wearing in it a cylinder of wood or a shell. The women outbid each other to such an extent that some have to hang the ring of flesh thus produced over the ear to prevent it from hanging down too far.

The tattooing of the face is often an important process; in North-West Brazil I only saw it in one tribe, the Desana on the Uaupes, in which both sexes wear on the lower lip two lines parallel to the chin, produced, as is everywhere the case in tropical America, with a palm prickle and *genipa* juice.

In British Guiana the Warrau and Acawoio pull out their eyebrows and tattoo the places as well as the corner of the mouth with curved lines, which gives them a characteristic and not uninteresting appearance. Among the Caraya both sexes receive the tribal mark at puberty—a circle on each cheek. Some of the Guaikuru stock of the Gran Chaco—the Toba, Takshik, and others—have a very complicated pattern, which covers the whole face, and is usually confined to females.

Some tribes—like those of the Calchaqui Valley, in the west of Argentina, and some in ancient Peru—deformed the heads of the children; and this was also done till recently by the Omaguas on the Upper Amazon. Bands round the children's heads produced a horn which tapered towards the back. Another singular eccentricity, noted in the Caribbee Islands by some of the earliest voyagers, reappears, according to Schomburgk, among the Caribs of the mainland. To give the calf an unnatural thickness, which is looked upon as one of the chief beauties of woman, girls have from youth upwards cotton bands, three fingers broad, beneath the knee and above the ankle; these she wears till she is full grown, and the result is to atrophy the muscle beneath the bands, while in between it forms an unshapely mass.

ARAUCANIAN WOMEN (CHILI) SPINNING.

Division of Labour.

I have often mentioned the strict division of labour between the sexes, important especially in the preparation of household goods and in the ordinary work of the household. Woman has to cultivate and prepare the manioc from start to finish; men do a little roasting on their own account, but never any cooking. This is true of the Xingu sources, of Guiana, in North-West Brazil, and probably all over South America. Im Thurn tells a story of how he was once forced by famine to take cassava roots from an Indian field; but as all his companions were men, no one would undertake the preparation; at last one was persuaded, but he was ever afterwards scornfully pointed at as "old woman." There is in South America a widespread custom which enacts that men and women shall not eat together; this is perhaps due to the division of labour in other matters.

Women Eat when the Men have Finished.

As regards meals, the first is at daybreak in the long houses on the Isana and Uaupes, immediately after the morning bath. All the married women bring flat baskets, with flat manioc cakes and a pot with a very peppery dish of fish, and put them in the middle of the house. The men squat round it in a circle and fall to on the warmed-up fragments of yesterday. The meal over, the women hand round big bowls of manioc drink, and last of all calabashes for washing of hands and mouth. Not till the men have gone do the women sit down. A second important meal is taken shortly before sunset; and between times a man, when he comes in from hunting, may eat a mouthful or two with his family in his own apartments. Lafitau remarked the singular custom of eating apart among the Caribs of the islands, and put it down to their servile position, which it probably is not.

Among the Guiana tribes, too, men and women eat apart, and the latter get only the crumbs of the feast; but they know how to look after "number one," and keep a heap of little pots filled with dainties stowed away in every corner of the hut; and these provide them with a hearty meal when the males have withdrawn.

Curious Ceremonies.

There are a certain number of religious ceremonies from which women are excluded among some of the tribes. These are the secret societies of the men whose festivals are often closely connected with the puberty rites of the young men and their initiation into full tribal rights. It will be well to give some account of these, for, as will be seen, women were more concerned in these matters than might appear at first sight.

The Orinoco tribes hold a festival, which is described by Humboldt, in honour of the good spirit, Cachimana, who presides over the seasons and brings to maturity the fruits of the earth. In the rites the initiated breathed out their souls and spent their breath in playing upon long trumpets of burnt clay; and as a variation submitted to flagellation, fasting, and other interesting and exhausting religious exercises. Not only were women strictly excluded from celebrations of this kind, but they might not even so much as cast eyes upon one of the trumpets. If one had the mischance to do so she paid the penalty, and her silence as to what she had seen was ensured by sending her to the bourne whence no traveller returns.

Dr. Ehrenreich found a similar festival among the Ipurina, which was named Kamutshi, after the evil spirits which then make their appearance. These spirits choose as their place of abode the musical instruments used in the festival—large flutes and horns made of bark twisted in a spiral to the proper shape. When the dancers and other performers approach, the women hastily disappear into their huts, and there put out all fires. If any of them were so unfortunate as to catch a glimpse of the bark trumpets, the Kamutshi issued from their lair, penetrated into the body of the woman, according to the native account, and never failed to bring about her death.

When some kinds of palm fruits are ripe, tribes on the Isana, Uaupes, and southwards as far as the Yapura, celebrate a festival to the honour of a hero, in which are used instruments in every way similar to those described. Participation in the festival is the privilege of the adult males, and they submit to severe mortifications and castigations. Even the initiation into this secret society is preceded, as I noticed on the Uaupes, by painful flagellations and privations. No female of any age may be present at the festival, nor even small boys; if they so much as see the instrument, the spirit kills them, or, in other words, they are put to death.

ARAUCANIAN WOMEN (CHILI) SPINNING AND WEAVING AT THEIR PRIMITIVE FORM OF LOOM.

The Tariana tribe on the Uaupes has the same festival, and the men wear a kind of mask woven of human and monkey hair, which is likewise strictly kept from the gaze of women. A quarter of a century ago a Franciscan monk in Ipanore, a large village of the Tariana, was nearly killed by the enraged men because he had profaned these ceremonies by speaking of them before the women in the course of a sermon.

Among the Caraya, women and children may look on while the masked dances are in progress, but they may not see the masks without their wearers, for the men persuade them that what is behind the mask is the veritable spirit of the animal whose mask it is; at most, the oldest women are now and then initiated into the secret. If a woman, out of curiosity, penetrates into the secret hut in which the dance costumes are kept, or if she utilises any other opportunity to catch sight of them, she is condemned to death or, at the least, to a very heavy penalty.

By courtesy of the South American Missionary Society.

YAHGAN (TIERRA DEL FUEGO) FAMILY IN CANOE.

In the basin of the Xingu, women are likewise strictly prohibited from seeing the masked dances; the house in which the masks and musical instruments are kept serves also as a house for the entertainment of guests, but women may nevertheless not pass over the threshold on pain of death.

In South America, as everywhere else where such secret societies and festivals are known, the air of mystery which is thrown round the whole business arises from the desire of the men to maintain their authority over the women, and to add to it. Of course, it is also possible that the precautions are actually intended to protect the weaker sex against the spirits in whose existence the men no less than the women believe, and whose might they dread at the bottom of their hearts just as much. Once I was asking my friend, the Siusi chief, about the name and importance of certain spirits, and before he answered me he sent away his two grown-up daughters, who were standing close by. "Women," said he, "may not hear about the spirits."

If we take a final survey of the Indian woman's life, we must admit that it is full of toil; but this very fact permits her to unfold to their full extent her qualities of head and heart. She is anything but a dull-witted beast of burden; but whereas the man's powers are devoted in the main to the service of the community, the woman plays her *rôle* in the smaller circle of the family. If, however, the heaviest duties are hers in this sphere of labour, hers also are the chief privileges in the household.

The Intelligence of the Indian Woman.

In her care for her child, both before and after it is born, we may see one of the chief expressions of her mental life. Her great intelligence is united to a spirit of pure good nature, which finds utterance not only towards members of her family and tribe, but also towards strangers, as I can prove from my own experience.

In every village where I resided for any length of time, I was treated by the women as one of their own community. Food and drink were never lacking for me, and my welfare was a matter which concerned them all. As a rule, it was an elderly woman who played the part of mother to me. In the Kobeua village of Namokoliba on the Cuduiary, where I passed several peaceful and interesting weeks, it was the wife of the chief whose protection I enjoyed. It really was no difficult matter for me to address the good old woman, who had three grown-up sons, as "mother," especially when I saw how much pleasure it gave her

Her Kindliness.

Photograph by P. Neville Edwards, Littlehampton.

TEHUELCHE WOMAN AND CHILDREN (TIERRA DEL FUEGO).

and her family; and I am free to confess that it gave me no less pleasure when she called me her son. Every morning when I woke she sent her little girl to my hammock with fresh water for minor ablutions, and many a titbit and refreshing drink I owed to her kindness. When the time came for me to take my leave, all the good folks came to the bank to see me off—only my "mother" and my "little sister" were not there; they had gone to the plantation before daybreak, so as to miss the final parting.

Wherever I went sympathetic and tactful inquiries were made by the women about my family relationships. Pictures of my *fiancée*—or, as they called her, my "wife"—aroused the greatest interest. They gave her the honourable name of "elder sister," and I enjoyed the title of "husband of our elder sister."

As I travelled along the Tiquie in February and March, 1905, making for the Amazon along untrodden paths, I was greeted as an old friend in all the villages. In one place the Tukano women celebrated the eve of my departure by a party, and, with faces painted in red patterns in my honour, they squatted round my hammock. Of course, I had to sing, and I gave them a performance of every song I could think of, cheerful and sad, soldiers' songs and sentimental ditties, anything that came into my head. And still they said: "Sing us one more song, doctor." Who could refuse them? I sang till I was hoarse, and then they sang to me; and though the range of tone is small, their efforts were not lacking in melody. Finally, they turned to improvisation of songs on my relatives; songs on my travels, my return and my meeting with my "wife." Next morning they all stood on the high bank of the river, and as long as they could follow the boat with their eyes they called after me, "Give our love to your wife, Elsa."

Photograph by Dr. Koch Grünberg.

A SIUSI VILLAGE.